SOCCER EMPIRE

The publisher gratefully acknowledges the generous support of the Ahmanson Foundation Humanities Endowment Fund of the University of California Press Foundation.

SOCCER EMPIRE

THE WORLD CUP AND THE FUTURE OF FRANCE

LAURENT DUBOIS

UNIVERSITY OF CALIFORNIA PRESS

BERKELEY   LOS ANGELES   LONDON

University of California Press, one of the most distinguished
university presses in the United States, enriches lives around the
world by advancing scholarship in the humanities, social sciences,
and natural sciences. Its activities are supported by the UC Press
Foundation and by philanthropic contributions from individuals
and institutions. For more information, visit www.ucpress.edu.

University of California Press
Berkeley and Los Angeles, California

University of California Press, Ltd.
London, England

Library of Congress Cataloging-in-Publication Data

Dubois, Laurent.
    Soccer empire : the World cup and the future of France /
Laurent Dubois.
        p.   cm.
    Includes bibliographical references and index.
    ISBN 978-0-520-25928-7 (cloth : alk. paper)
    1. Soccer—France—History—20th century.   2. Soccer—
Social aspects—France.   3. Zidane, Zinédine, 1972–   4. Soccer
players—France.   5. World Cup (Soccer) (2006)   6. France—
History—20th century.   7. France—Social conditions—20th
century.   I. Title.

    GV944.F8D85   2010
    796.334'6680944—dc22   2009042962

Manufactured in the United States of America

19 18 17 16 15 14 13 12 11 10
10 9 8 7 6 5 4 3 2 1

This book is printed on Cascades Enviro 100, a 100% post
consumer waste, recycled, de-inked fiber. FSC recycled certified
and processed chlorine free. It is acid free, Ecologo certified,
and manufactured by BioGas energy.

For Anton

We should score spirits as we score goals.

ZINEDINE ZIDANE, 9 JULY 2006

CONTENTS

ILLUSTRATIONS

PREFACE

Scoring Spirits

WHEN THE REFEREE BLEW HIS WHISTLE much of the globe fell silent. An estimated three billion people watched as the final game of the 2006 World Cup tournament began. The bar in Paris where I was sitting had been loud with conversation moments before. Now we turned as one toward the giant screen set up in the back, hypnotized, suspended in time.

I had followed the first part of the World Cup tournament in Michigan, where the faithful gathered in a university cafeteria to watch the games. Hundreds of Korean students, decked out in red and playing drums, showed up for one game. A handful of Ghanaians draped in flags braved nasty looks from U.S. fans as they cheered their team to victory. Many, though, arrived to watch without a deep commitment to any team. Part of the beauty of the World Cup is the freedom it gives us to choose sides. Especially as the tournament goes on and teams get eliminated, fewer and fewer people can actually root for a home team; most fans have to adopt one. They might opt for a powerhouse like Italy, Argentina, Germany, or Brazil, or lean toward a lesser-known team on an unexpected run, like Senegal or South Korea.

Sometimes the choice is infused with deep meaning and makes a statement about who we are. Sometimes it is just the expression of a fleeting affinity. In the film *The Great Match* a Touareg in the middle of the Sahara insists that those who surround him to watch the 2002 Brazil-Germany final on his television must root for Germany rather than Brazil. His reason? The good working relationship he once had with a German visitor. The West African migrants in the group are dismayed and refuse to follow the command; they see Brazil as their team. They're not alone: for decades, in a world of soccer (or, football, as it is called in most of the world and as I will call it here) that is still largely dominated by European professional and national teams, Brazil has carried the hopes of Latin America, Africa, and the Caribbean.

I've long rooted for another team: France. Though my name is as French as it gets, I was born in Belgium and have lived in the United States since I was three weeks old. So when I root for the French football team, it's not really about rooting for the French nation. I am rooting for something bigger than that. In contrast to nearly all European teams—the Dutch team has at times been the notable exception—the French team is and has long been a remarkably diverse group. It is a global team, a kind of transcultural republic on the field, whose players have roots in West, Central, and North Africa, the Caribbean, the far-flung Pacific territories, Armenia, and France's edges in the Basque country and Marseille. Like many other fans of the French team, I see in it the promise of solidarity, tolerance, community, and cooperation. Of course that wouldn't be enough if we didn't also like how they played. Luckily the French team often produces "matches that leave us breathless, that intoxicate us." At their best, the players offer "a triumph of beauty, technique, daring, surprise and elegance."[2]

The French team, however, can also be alarmingly inconsistent. The team that won the World Cup in 1998 and the European Cup in 2000 fizzled at the 2002 World Cup, where it was eliminated from competition without scoring a single goal. In 2004 two of its most important players, Zinedine Zidane and Lilian Thuram, retired from international competition. In 2006 the French coach convinced the two of them to come back and play for France one last time. But France's early World Cup games were disappointing. They tied against both South Korea and Switzerland and ended up in a situation where they had to beat Togo by several points to move on to the next round. Thankfully they won the decisive game. I rode my bicycle home that afternoon, belting out the "Marseillaise," France's strident and bloody national anthem, to the empty streets of East Lansing, Michigan. A few days later France defeated Spain. And then, in the quarterfinals, they defeated Brazil. Crossing my fingers that they would win in the semifinal against Portugal, I bought a plane ticket. I would watch the final in Paris.

During the World Cup the globe turns into a giant stadium, but Paris was particularly vibrant the day of the 2006 final. The city hummed with the anticipation that comes from equal parts hope and dread as people prepared to watch their team play. French fans prayed for a national victory, of course, but they hoped just as much that they would watch Zidane—according to one poll the most beloved French citizen—end his remarkable career in the best way possible: holding up the World Cup in triumph. Waiting for the game to start, I wandered through the streets in my France jersey and bought a large, overpriced French flag from a merchant doing brisk business. Among the milling blue-, white-, and red-painted fans I watched the cars roll by flying flags and carrying signs saying, "Merci Zizou," Zidane's oft-chanted nickname. In front of me, along the Seine, a beat-up Citroën came to a stop, and I saw a lanky young man sitting in the backseat, holding a homemade flagpole with two small flags fluttering together: the red-white-and-blue French flag and next to it the Algerian flag, green and white, with its crescent and star. Zidane's parents had migrated from Algeria to France when Algeria was still a French colony. In 1962, after a brutal war, Algeria won its independence, but Zidane's parents remained in France. Zinedine Zidane spent his life at the haunted crossroads between the two countries. Flying on the same pole, fluttering against one another, the two flags became a single banner—for Zidane, for the French team, for Algerian France: a dream of reconciliation.

Settled in a bar with friends that night, I watched the opening ceremony, which featured a duet by the Colombian singer Shakira and the Haitian-born Wyclef Jean, who sported the Haitian flag on his shirt and his head. Many Haitians are passionate football fans, but the country has been in the World Cup tournament only once, in 1974. Through his music Wyclef Jean had found another way to give the Haitian flag a prominent spot in the tournament. On the field, meanwhile, gathered the largest group of Caribbean players ever to compete in a World Cup final. Standing at attention for the French national anthem were Thuram, born in the French department of Guadeloupe; Florent Malouda, born in French Guiana; and Eric Abidal, William Gallas, and the star striker Thierry Henry, all born in metropolitan France to parents from either Martinique or Guadeloupe. Several more players of Caribbean background, including Sylvain Wiltord, looked on from the sidelines.

Fans in the French Caribbean have long leaned toward Brazil rather than France, rooting for a team of players they felt best represented them rather than the team of their nation. By the 1990s, however, French Caribbean players were increasingly prominent on the French team, and younger fans from the region began supporting France, sometimes harshly criticizing their parents for continuing to support Brazil. Some pointed out that, especially in 2006, the French team had significantly more black players than the Brazilian team. As France faced Italy in the final the difference in the makeup of the teams was even more striking. It was as if two totally different visions of Europe were represented on the field. Almost all of the players for France had roots in the Caribbean or Africa and shared a history of empire and global exchange. Unlike France, of course, Italy never had an expansive empire in Africa, Asia, and the Americas; still, there are increasing numbers of immigrants, notably from its one-time colony in Ethiopia and North and

West Africa, in Italy today. Nearly all players on the Italian team, however, have family roots in Italy, although—as has long been the case—a few have links to Italian communities outside Europe, notably in Argentina.

Just after France and Italy faced off, the French forward Thierry Henry was knocked to the ground in a rough collision with an Italian player. The next minutes were confused, physical, a little ugly. Then the referee called a foul against the Italian team after Florent Malouda either was tripped (according to French fans) or dove dramatically after having lightly touched the foot of a defender (according to Italian fans) in front of the Italian goal. Zidane stepped up to take the penalty kick. Through years of play he has scored countless such kicks, usually by sending the ball streaking into the net. This time, however, he sent the ball flying up toward the goal's upper post. It spun off and downward, right behind the Italian goalie, Gianluigi Buffon. Amazingly, in the most important football competition in the world, he had scored a penalty kick in the most risky and theatrical way possible, with what is called a *panenka,* after Antonín Panenka, a Czech footballer who in 1976 scored a vital penalty kick by chipping the ball over the goalkeeper into the center of the net. It was as if Zidane was playing around, showing off in an afternoon pickup game with friends, teasing the goalie for fun. "He's mad!" the elated French goalkeeper Fabien Barthez shouted to the sky as he watched Zidane score.

France held the lead with one point, but not for long. Soon after Zidane's goal, Marco Materazzi headed the ball past the French goaltender off a corner kick. And then, to those of us watching, hypnotized, all around the world, the game went on. And on. Seemingly endlessly. France shone, playing the smooth and fluid football they're capable of at their best. But they didn't score. And still they didn't score. And neither did the Italian team. By the end of regulation time all the players were clearly exhausted. Just watching them was exhausting. Thuram held together the French defense, as he had done in the semifinal game against Portugal. Zidane fought, sweating, his shoulder aching from a tangle earlier in the game, his captain's band hanging limply on his arm, where he kept fidgeting with it. Then he sent a header toward the Italian goal. It looked for a breathtaking second like it might be a replay of 1998, when Zidane scored a header against Brazil that put his team in the lead, followed by another later in the game. But Buffon made an amazing, reaching save and tapped the ball over the top of the goal. We screamed, looking up to the sky in desperation, and so did Zidane. Again, no goal.

A few minutes later Marco Materazzi tugged lightly at Zidane's shirt. Zidane spoke briefly to the Italian defender and started to walk away. But Materazzi called out a string of insults.

FIGURE 1. Zidane during the latter phases of the France-Italy World Cup final, 9 July 2006. Bob Thomas/Bob Thomas Sports Photography/Getty Images.

Later, looking back on the event, the next moment seemed to happen out of time. But as it occurred, those of us watching on television and even fans in the stadium saw none of it. The ball was elsewhere on the field. When the game stopped, we didn't know why. Then they showed the replay.

As Materazzi continued to bait the Frenchman, Zidane turned around, took a few quick, careful paces, and head-butted the Italian in the chest full force. Materazzi went flying to the ground.

Silence, disbelief, then groans filled the bar where I sat stunned. A few young men cheered, impressed. Zidane's action seemed to strike them as "a moment of real and instant justice, a rarity in the world."[3] On the field, after a few confused minutes, the referee held up a red card, banishing Zidane from the game. For his final exit, he walked briskly past the World Cup trophy, looking down. As he sat alone in the locker room, Italy defeated France in penalty kicks. While the Italian team celebrated, Lilian Thuram waved to French fans, tears in his eyes, the last French player on the field.

Paris was as if in a daze. On the metro two teenage boys hugged, one of them crying. I walked for a long time that night, so visibly stricken that several people stopped to give me pep talks, saying that it was okay, that there would be another World Cup, that France had played well, gone further than anyone expected. Everywhere in the city strangers consoled each other. One even uttered that seemingly reasonable but truly nonsensical attempt at consolation often heard by football fans, telling me that it was just a game. I walked past the Hôtel de Ville, where a crowd of triumphant Italy fans gathered, huddled or leaping for joy. Some passersby looked on good-naturedly; others shouted "Fuck you!"—in Italian, to make sure they were understood.

I barely slept and then woke up in a depressing place indeed: Paris the day after France lost the World Cup. But, really, I was lucky. At least I wasn't alone, back home, being teased by friends who rooted for Italy. I had plenty of company for my misery. As the day went on, though, I noticed something. Though many people were mourning—I spoke with one woman who had tears in her eyes—most people were talking about Zidane. And his head. And the amazing way he sent Materazzi to the ground. And why he did it. And what Materazzi must have said to make him do it. And whether he was right to have done it. People were talking, even laughing in amazement, pondering right and wrong, insult and dignity, violence and responsibility. And all around me people—not everyone, of course, but still a lot of people— were gradually realizing, as I was, that they were captivated, even thrilled by Zidane's head-butt.

Many saw Zidane's action as a disappointing, even tragic ending to his career, lamenting that in allowing himself to be provoked by Materazzi he stupidly fell for the oldest trick in the book. Others condemned it as an inexcusable offense against the core ethics of the sport. But such interpretations didn't sit well with everyone. Indeed many rushed to defend Zidane, and even to celebrate him for what he did, usually assuming that he was the victim of a racist insult that required a dramatic response. In Paris and throughout the world, as people heatedly debated what had happened they projected their own fears, phantasms, and hopes on the head-butt. Indeed the French term for head-butt, *coup de boule*—literally "strike with a ball," the ball in this case being a human head—suddenly became a shorthand and a symbol.

Zidane left us with an offering. He exited the global theater of the World Cup by giving us his own, striking, answer to a universal question: What does it mean to face an insult? In doing so, he spurred millions of conversations, agreements, and disagreements, governed by endless returns to the game and to his final act on the field. A good number of the three billion people who had seen the *coup de boule* had an opinion about it—often a strong one—and felt compelled to analyze it, talk about it, moralize or joke or celebrate it. In France the discussion of the head-butt—impassioned, diverse, at turns comical and dead serious—powerfully illustrated how football can both condense and propel larger political debates. Less than a year earlier a massive, month-long insurrection had broken out in poor *banlieue* neighborhoods throughout the country. Young protesters, many of them the children and grandchildren of immigrants, were enraged by the police brutality and demanded that French society respect their rights as citizens. Zidane had grown up the child of Algerian immigrants in such a neighborhood. In a France still reeling from the riots, many interpreted his *coup de boule* in relation to the ongoing struggle over the legacies of empire and the place of immigrants born of that empire in French society.

Drawn into the national and global conversation Zidane started, I read everything I could about the history of football in France. As a historian, I've spent the past fifteen years studying the history of the French Empire in the Caribbean and beyond, and I had seen only passing references to the place of football within that history. But once I started looking I discovered that football—a bit like Woody Allen's Zelig—was everywhere. It shaped and was shaped by all of the major transformations of the twentieth century, from World War I and World War II to the brutal conflicts over decolonization. A Frenchman, Jules Rimet, established the World Cup in 1930, when the French Empire was at its height, and administrators and teachers in the colonies did what they could to spread the sport seeing it as a perfect way to diffuse Western ideals among the colonized. But they could never control football. It spread with startling speed in the colonies, notably in Algeria and the French Caribbean, and often became a vehicle for anticolonial protest. As early as the 1930s France's professional teams were recruiting players from the colonies, especially North and West Africa. Zidane and Thuram, I realized, were part of a long athletic tradition in which empire shaped generations of French football. The history of football illuminates the complexities of colonial rule and anticolonial resistance in the French Empire, as well as all that came in between. And returning to that history helps us understand how and why this sport has created its own empire, which shapes the experiences and perspectives of vast numbers of people.

This book focuses on the history of France and its empire, especially Algeria and the Caribbean, in order to tell a larger story about the link between football and politics. Throughout the world football teams become symbols for towns, regions, or countries to rally around, and games become opportunities for people to celebrate and perform their allegiance to a particular place. But precisely because people identify so intensely with teams and make links between teams and something bigger—a town, a nation, a history—football also serves to crystallize and condense questions, debates, and conflicts about the collectives that teams represent. When a team takes to the field, fans say, "They are us, and we are them." But sometimes that can also force a question: "Who are they? And who are we?"

Football makes icons, and many fans develop a tight, even mystical connection with their sporting heroes. I focus on two of the most important French football icons, Zidane and Thuram, following their exploits both on and off the field. Both were born in 1972 and grew up on the edges of French society, subject to marginalization and racism, and despite their dizzying rise to stardom and wealth, they have never been totally free from those forces. Through their victories and defeats on and off the field, they have both exposed and challenged the forms of exclusion that shape French society. Starting in 1996 and through the World Cup of 2006, their presence on the field generated perhaps the most widespread and sustained public conversations about the topic of race in France in decades. With their teammates—including the Ghana-born Marcel Desailly; Christian Karembeu, born in the French Pacific territory of New Caledonia; and Thierry Henry, whose parents are from the French Caribbean—they have performed miracles on the football field, inspiring the French to dream of political miracles that could transform society and truly fulfill the promises of equality that form the bedrock of France's Republican political culture. Perhaps most important, they have also pushed people to do the work necessary for such promises to be fulfilled, to grapple with the past of empire and its many effects on the present. On the turf, Zidane and Thuram have been bearers of an uncomfortable history, both soothing and reviving the wounds left by that history.

In early versions of football, players kept track of goals by scoring lines into the goalposts with something sharp, such as a rock picked up on the field, leaving a permanent mark of what they had achieved. Because of the practice, people began referring to making a goal as "scoring." As he prepared to play in the World Cup Final against Italy in 2006, Zidane described to his teammates what they should do on the field that night: "Il faut marquer des buts en marquant les esprits." The beauty of the phrase revolves around the double meaning of the word *marquer*, meaning "to score" but also "to mark" or "to leave an impression." Likewise, the word *esprit* means more than "spirit," combining mind, spirit, heart, and even soul in one. The goal of the players, Zidane declared, should be to pursue victory by playing beautifully, scoring the spirits of those who watched. They should strive to leave an imprint deeper than a victory, so deep that it cannot be erased.[4]

Introduction

The Language of Happiness

In 1953, at the age of seventeen, Smaïl Zidane left his village in the French colony of Algeria, heading north. He traveled to Paris, where he found a job at a construction site in Saint-Denis, a suburb famous for an abbey church that houses the tombs of generations of French kings. Unable to find lodging, he spent the winter nights on the ground near where he worked. He remembers the day he received his first paycheck: "I experienced the first real happiness I had since arriving in France. That day, I didn't feel the cold anymore." He sent most of his earnings back home to his parents. Soon he met other men from his village, and together they rented a small room in Saint-Denis. They were among hundreds of thousands of colonial workers who helped rebuild France in the wake of World War II.[1]

A year after Smaïl left home, a bloody anticolonial uprising began in Algeria. A political organization called the Front de Libération Nationale (F.L.N.) launched a series of attacks in Algiers. In 1955 the French declared martial law, rounding up thousands of men and using torture to crush the insurrection. Many Algerian laborers in metropolitan France supported the F.L.N., which soon instituted a "revolutionary tax," collected by its operatives in the shantytowns where the workers lived. In 1958 a group of well-known professional football players from Algeria sneaked out of France and gathered in Tunisia to create an F.L.N. football team. Traveling to Eastern Europe and Asia, they used the sport as a weapon of war, a tool of diplomacy, and an act of political imagination. When the team played, the flag of the revolutionary movement was raised and its anthem sung, and imagining that Algeria would one day be independent became a little bit easier.

Three years later the F.L.N. carried out a series of deadly attacks against police in France. The government declared a state of emergency in early October, banning Algerians from meeting and circulating at night and allowing police to search their homes at any time and without a warrant. On 17 October 1961 twenty thousand to thirty thousand Algerian men, women, and children marched into Paris from the shantytowns outside the city to protest the curfew. The demonstration was peaceful, but the Paris police chief organized a fierce response. As columns of protestors approached the center of the city, the police brutally attacked the crowd. They threw into the Seine the bodies of demonstrators they had beaten unconscious or to death. In some parts of Paris bodies were piled up in the streets. The police detained fourteen thousand demonstrators, holding them in stadiums on the edge of the city. Some were also kept in an athletic facility, the Palais des Sports, though they were moved elsewhere after a few days so that French fans of soul music could enjoy a concert by Ray Charles. Many were beaten, and more were killed, while in custody. For days afterward bodies of demonstrators washed up along the banks of the Seine. Seared into the memory of witnesses, the truth of the massacres of October 1961 was nevertheless carefully suppressed by French officials, unacknowledged and uninvestigated for decades. The killings remained a kind of subterranean haunting that many remembered privately but few spoke about publicly. Only relatively recently, through books, trials, and the popular film *Caché,* has the memory of these killings been publicly excavated.[2]

Smaïl Zidane lived in Saint-Denis at the time, and the French police's brutality could have been on his mind when, after Algeria gained its independence in 1962, he decided to go home. But he never made it back to Algeria. On the way he stopped in Marseille, where he visited relatives and met a young woman from his village named Malika. The two quickly fell in love. They married and settled in Marseille, eventually living in the neighborhood of Castellane, to the north of the city. With Algeria's independence in 1962 they were transformed from French colonial subjects into Algerian citizens, and they remained in France as foreigners. They had five children in France. The youngest of them, born in 1972, they named Zinedine.

Six months earlier, in Guadeloupe, Mariana Thuram had a child she named Lilian. The island of Guadeloupe is largely populated by the descendants of slaves brought there from Africa by the French to work on sugar plantations. Mariana Thuram, like many others in the Caribbean, still worked the cane, even as she carried Lilian, and when she wasn't in the fields she worked as a domestic servant to make ends meet. When Lilian was eight, Mariana decided to join a stream of migrants leaving the islands for metropolitan France. So Lilian Thuram grew up in a *banlieue* (suburb) to the south of Paris. Both Zinedine and Lilian were avid and talented football players, and as teenagers were recruited to football academies. When they met for the first time, it was at tryouts for the French national team.

Since the 1950s, when Zidane's father worked there, the town of Saint-Denis has mushroomed into one of Paris's many large *banlieues*. Pocked with concrete projects, it is home to immigrants from North and West Africa and to their children and grandchildren. Looming over the town, not far from its ancient abbey church, is another, newer temple: a football stadium called the Stade de France, built to host the 1998 World Cup. Though the tournament began with worry about rowdy crowds and disinterest in the tournament on the part of much of the population, as victory followed victory, people began to rally around their team. In a riveting semifinal game against Croatia, Thuram scored two miraculous goals to secure France a place in the final. A few days later, on 13 July 1998, Zidane scored two goals against the widely favored Brazilian team to win for France its first World Cup.

Paris erupted in a massive celebration. The city projected Zidane's face on Napoleon's Arc de Triomphe, and chants of "Zidane Président!" echoed through the streets. Older residents remembered only one event that compared: the liberation of Paris from the Germans in 1944. For a few days it felt as if France was a unified, joyful, hopeful nation—a nation capable of anything, even overcoming the racism rooted in its colonial past. Politicians, journalists, and intellectuals rushed to celebrate the victory, often proclaiming that it signaled the dawn of a new era in French political and social life. The team, they declared enthusiastically, represented the possibilities of the collaboration of white and black, immigrant and native born. It signaled the birth of a new French identity that, like the French flag, brought together three colors: black, white, and *beur*—the last a term describing children of North African immigrants. It showed France what it could be: a nation free from racial divisions and conflict, a nation that gained strength from its diversity.

In the next eight years such hopes came to seem utopian. The far-right Front National party led by Jean-Marie Le Pen, whose platform claimed that immigration was destroying France, attracted many voters. The *banlieue* neighborhoods, where the majority of immigrants and their children and grandchildren live, festered in continued poverty and isolation, frequently exploding into insurrection, most powerfully in November 2005. In the wake of those riots Thuram spoke up on behalf of young *banlieue* residents, attacking the government and reminding people about the ways the history of empire and ongoing racism had created France's contemporary problems. When the football team took to the field in the summer of 2006, France couldn't help but be reminded of its complicated past or its conflicted present. Seventeen of twenty-three players on the team that year came from families with roots in West or North Africa, the Indian Ocean, or the French Caribbean. And nearly all of the players had grown up in the *banlieue* areas of France, still smoldering from the previous year's uprising.

Le Pen attacked the team—as he had once before, in 1996—for having "too many players of color." For Le Pen the diversity of the French team was a distressing symbol of how immigration was changing the face of France. It also, of course, put him in an interesting bind. Whom should he root for: his country, represented by a team that challenged everything he believed, or, in an act of shocking disloyalty, the other team? Like the runners John Carlos and Tommie Smith, who famously raised their fists in a salute to black power as they received their medals for the United States in the 1968 Olympics, the French team simultaneously represented and challenged the nation.

When Zidane and Thuram stepped onto the field for the 2006 World Cup final, they entered the largest theater that has ever existed in human history. This has been true for every World Cup for several decades, and it will be true again in 2010, when teams and fans from throughout the world pour into South Africa, assured that they will witness a dramatic new chapter in history unfolding. The competition is now the largest sporting event in the world, surpassing even the Olympics in the size of its audience, crystallizing political conflicts and hopes, and creating a seemingly endless and inexhaustible site into which people have pumped their hatreds and phantasms, not to mention their money.

Today there is no sport more popular and powerful in its global reach, or more tightly linked to international politics, than football. Indeed football may well be the most universal language that currently exists, its empire more extensive than that of any political or religious ideology. "The only denominator common to all people, the only universal Esperanto," one enthusiast wrote in 1954, "is football. . . . What? A game has done what the cardinal virtues, laws, and modern science have not? Yes!" Football was a "world language, whose grammar is unchanging from the North Pole to the Equator," its worldwide influence predicated on the fact that it is "spoken in each corner of the globe with a particular accent." If that was already largely true in 1954, it is even more so today, as boosters of the sport, notably the powerful international football organization F.I.F.A. (Fédération Internationale de Football Association), constantly remind us. Our planet is now saturated with professional and international football: from individual games, to proliferating tournaments and regional and continental competitions, to, increasingly, international competitions for youth and women's teams.[3]

The World Cup, however, remains the defining competition for the sport. Its games focus national hopes on a vivid drama. Novelists and filmmakers often struggle to transform individual characters into symbols of a larger collective. But for its fervent fans, a national football team really *is* the nation, at least for a time. An athlete can instantly become a national icon after even one play on the field. When this happens, the accident of his biography, of the story that brought him to the crucial moment when he changed the course of a game, and therefore history, become charged with larger meaning. At such moments football produces a crossroads between personal history and national history that illuminates and shapes the language and practice of politics.[4]

Indeed in the midst of a World Cup the choices made by football players can seem much more significant than the actions of elected politicians. Writing about the 1966 World Cup in England, which unfolded in the shadow of a government crisis linked to the state of the economy, Alastair Reid recalls, "Breaking open the morning papers and reading banner headlines like 'England in trouble' our hearts would sink for a while until, after a closer glance, we found that they applied merely to the state of the economy" and "not, as we first feared, to the football team."[5]

What is it about football that generates such passions, transforming what detractors identify as an artificially constructed and futile game, dominated by and infused with capital and accused of corruption and corporate influence, into a terrain of political passion, utopian longing, and philosophical reflection? To answer this question, we need to think about the form of football itself. On the one hand, the stage of football (and other sports) seems the ultimate embodiment of the promises of egalitarian meritocracy, a place where the mythological promise that any individual, of any background, can succeed if he or she is talented and disciplined enough, can actually come true. As such, the field of play condenses the broader, often diffuse promise of a certain kind of liberal democratic society into a spectacular physical drama. At the same time, however, it also foregrounds a potentially conflicting necessity for collective action, in which players often need to efface themselves, passing the ball to someone in a better position rather than seeking to score themselves. Just as important, the game also constantly highlights the basic and disturbing truth that life is, with stunning consistency, completely unfair. Football is, after all, notoriously unpredictable, a realm of constant surprise. The ball, as anyone who has played knows, fully obeys no one, even those who would seem to be its absolute masters. And because games are often won or lost on the basis of a few points, mistakes matter dramatically.[6]

So does the role of the referee, whose instant and irreversible decisions often determine a game's outcome. Referees make split-second decisions without the benefit of video replay. They interpret the flow of the game, since they are allowed to ignore a foul if they determine that to call one would disadvantage the attacking team. But players well know that the referees often are unable to fully see what has happened, and that they inhabit a "flawed system of justice." Trickery and playacting are therefore a crucial and time-honored part of the game, and many fans deeply appreciate the ability of a player to get an advantageous call, whether or not it is deserved. It often seems as if nearly every call and decision by the referee is the subject of some kind of protest at the time, from fans or players. Many calls become the subject of intense debate after the game, and some particularly pivotal decisions are lamented for decades. Each football match, then, produces an unending field of interpretation, not only about talent and success, but also about justice and injustice, fate and luck, fakery and virtue. It is a "drama of fortune in the world," and as such it opens up enormously diverse possibilities for narrative and symbolism.[7]

No matter how lopsided the matchup, you can never be sure what will happen in a game. French football fans of an earlier generation, as one scholar notes, vividly recall how this truth came home in 1957, when a small football club from the town of El Baïr, a suburb of Algiers, defeated the Stade de Reims, then one of France's greatest teams, in a knockout game of the French Cup competition. It is also a "particularly unstable" game, in which the score is often tied through large portions of a match, which heightens the stress and intensity of the experience of watching.[8]

All of this makes for a particularly riveting form of theater. Indeed one French theater director wrote in 2006 that she couldn't help feeling jealous upon realizing that football was "a new theatre that makes entire crowds hum with emotion and passion." The sport had replaced her profession, brilliantly evoking the drama of the larger society as theater once had done among the ancient Romans and Greeks. Lilian Thuram also thinks of a football match as a theatrical performance that begins with a "magical ritual." It is "unforgettable," he writes, to walk out of the locker room, down the hallway, and out onto the field to be greeted "with shouts and applause.... It's the unchanging prologue to a play that lasts ninety minutes, performed with the greatest improvisation imaginable."[9]

Over the years the theater of football has been invested with great hopes.

Jules Rimet, a French veteran of World War I and the founder of the World Cup, envisioned an international tournament that would create communication and collaboration between nations, who could meet on the field of play rather than the field of battle. Others shared this vision. In 1938 a journalist in France wrote that the competition could "civilize" conflicts and even help to solve "the great problem of our times, peace." Another suggested that it was possible to see the tournament as "a kind of active, living United Nations, inspired by a common idea and subjected to universal, formal rules accepted and respected by all." Football certainly didn't bring peace in the bloody decades that followed. But it has become a deeply powerful force in politics, a place where nations take shape in the form of eleven players on the field, and where the hopes of these nations are worked out on a green rectangle surrounded by white lines.[10]

"Soccer is never just soccer: it helps make wars and revolutions, and it fascinates mafias and dictators," writes Simon Kuper as he embarks on a journey that highlights the fusion of football and politics from Cameroon to Scotland. For Franklin Foer, meanwhile, football literally explains the world, helping us to understand the formation of identities and the complexities of globalization.[11] Football has many, often contradictory and even ambiguous effects, just as globalization does. As some walls come down, others go up. If some people move around the world more easily than ever, others are stopped at the border or forced into increasingly deadly attempts to cross it. In today's world football crosses and even seems to erase some barriers. At the same time it also helps to deepen and sometimes even create differences and barriers. What makes the sport particularly powerful, though, is its unpredictability, the space for maneuver and improvisation it allows fans and players, many of whom, notably Zidane and Thuram, are many things at once, occupying shifting positions, taking on multiple affiliations, in the fields of both football and politics.

In his classic book on cricket in the West Indies, C. L. R. James famously described how sport is always much more than a game. The "social and political passions" of the islands in the early twentieth century, he wrote, were "fiercely" expressed through cricket. Indeed the sport was a kind of apprenticeship for the political activism to which James devoted much of his life: "Cricket had plunged me into politics long before I was aware of it. When I did turn to politics I did not have too much to learn." "Apolitical sport does not exist," the scholar Youssef Fatès has argued more recently. Athletes who compete internationally are told, with justification, that they are "ambassadors for their country," and often that they represent a certain "economic or social system" as well. "The ceremony of sport, with its raising of colors, the resounding of national anthems," is "a condensation of politics," in which "athletes become true living flags." Writing about the 2008 Olympics in the *New Yorker,* Anthony Lane put the point more succinctly, describing the "attempt to keep politics out of sport" as being "as futile as trying to keep the sweat out of sex."[12]

In fact in many places, notably France, the nation exists as a widely shared and performed symbolic form only thanks to international football games. As in neighboring Germany, nationalist symbols in France are relatively rare and even regarded with justifiable suspicion by many citizens. But football unleashes an effusion of body painting, flag waving and draping, anthem singing, and general celebration. Football has produced the most significant moments of national unity and public celebration in France during the past decades. Precisely for this reason the commentary and celebration that surround football have delved deep into the question of what France is, what it has been, and what it can become.[13]

France's national football teams have, since at least the 1920s, consistently been diverse. All of the national teams' great leaders have been the children or grandchildren of immigrants. Three legendary players led the team through its best periods: Raymond Kopa, the son of Polish immigrants, in the 1950s; Michel Platini, grandson of an Italian immigrant, in the 1980s; and Zinedine Zidane, the son of Algerian colonial migrants, in the 1990s and in 2006. These three men embody the history of immigration into France, recalling the vast migration of Polish workers to the mines of northern France before World War II, the arrival of Italian workers throughout the twentieth century, and the large-scale migration of North Africans that began with individual male laborers in the 1920s and then accelerated, and increasingly involved entire families, from the 1950s through the 1970s. The national football team has served as a reminder of an aspect of French history that has sometimes been conveniently forgotten: France is a nation deeply marked by immigration, a nation in which, according to the historian Gérard Noiriel, fully one-third of those living there in the 1980s had at least one parent or grandparent born abroad.[14]

But if French football has been shaped by migration, it also has its roots firmly planted in the history of empire. In Guadeloupe and Martinique, Algeria and Tunisia, Senegal and the Pacific islands of New Caledonia, politics infused football throughout the twentieth century. Kopa's generation included several players from French colonies in North Africa, including the Algerian Rachid Mekloufi, and Platini played with the Guadeloupean defender Marius Trésor and the Mali-born Jean Tigana. One of the earliest French football stars, who played on the French team in the late 1930s and 1940s, was the Moroccan-born Larbi Ben Barek. And at the 1938 World Cup a man named Raoul Diagne, the son of the well-known Senegalese politician Blaise Diagne, played for France.

The presence of players of immigrant or colonial background sometimes spurred discussion. Were these players truly French? Could they truly represent the nation? Until 1998, however, no French team ever won the World Cup. With victory in that year, the stories of individual players, and their families and communities, became the story of a nation redeemed and reawakened. And because of who Thuram and Zidane were, that national story was inescapably shot through with the story of empire.

The team powerfully announced an often overlooked truth about the French republic: that its history and institutions have been, from the beginning, deeply shaped not just by the project of empire but by how the subjects of empire responded to, confronted, and remade that republic. Republican France has always been what one scholar dubbed an "imperial nation-state." Territory, population, and state have never lined up neatly. Instead overlapping legalities and political formations defined by a series of contradictions, as well as by movement within and across borders, have shaped and continue to shape French politics and culture.[15]

The far-right Front National led by Jean-Marie Le Pen, and many of its sympathizers, claims that the uncomfortable legacies of empire can be expunged from France. Immigrants from former colonies can be either deported or made to carry the full burden of integrating themselves into French society. The past can be massaged, colonialism presented as something that might have involved blood and conquest but that also had a "positive role," in the words of the legislators who passed a 2005 law regarding the teaching of colonial history in schools. Though such revisionist attempts represent an extreme and do not go uncontested—the 2005 law was widely criticized and ultimately abrogated by President Chirac—they are aided and abetted by the fact that in school and university curricula the history of empire is usually presented as a relatively minor sideshow in the broader history of France rather than as one of its constitutive elements.

But it is too late to imagine a French republic free from empire. It has been too late for a long time. It was already too late by the early twentieth century, when the French Empire stretched from the Caribbean and Africa to India and Vietnam. It was too late in the 1830s, when a French invasion of Algeria laid the foundation for tight economic and political links between the two regions. It was too late by the 1700s, when France's economy boomed thanks to the sugar and coffee produced by over a million African slaves brought to their Caribbean colonies on French ships. For four hundred years France has been an empire, and this history made France what it is today. In London in the 1980s some migrants from former British colonies in the Caribbean responded to racist attacks with a powerful slogan: "We are here because you were there." Immigrants and their descendants in France can say the same thing.

Through nearly four hundred years of interaction the colonies and their populations left a durable imprint on France. You can see it in the background of some of France's most cherished figures: Alexandre Dumas was the grandson of a Caribbean slave, Edith Piaf was the granddaughter of an Algerian woman, and Albert Camus was born into a settler family in Algeria. You can see its traces on the history of France's economy, expanded thanks to slavery and the slave trade in the eighteenth century, and in the course of its wars, which for nearly three centuries have involved disputes over colonial territories and have been shaped by the contributions and sacrifice of troops recruited in the colonies. And you can see it play itself out every day on the streets in the racial stereotypes and suspicions that permeate French society.

This colonial history also shaped the very values and ideas that most French people believe make up the core of their identity, and that many accuse immigrants of threatening. From the eighteenth century on, the radical universalism and egalitarianism that most French people rightly take pride in were shaped in important ways by the actions and ideas of colonial subjects. The colonized consistently fought against the exclusion and oppression they experienced by wielding and sharpening the most powerful tools available to them: the republican political ideas touted by the French state. In the eighteenth century intellectuals and revolutionaries in Paris spoke and wrote about the natural rights shared by all human beings; African slaves in the French Caribbean (most notably in Haiti) put those ideas to their most radical use when they insisted that they had rights too and successfully fought for and won their freedom. In the process they transformed the abstract universalism debated in Paris salons into a robust and dangerous political weapon. Throughout the nineteenth and twentieth centuries colonial subjects, often in collaboration with radical French activists and intellectuals, broadened and concretized republican ideas.[16]

Sport, and particularly football, played a crucial role in shaping this larger political reality. While many colonial administrators saw football as a vehicle for inculcating the colonized with the values of European civilization, in many colonies, particularly in the Caribbean and Algeria, it rapidly became a powerful vehicle for individual and community expression, as well as for demands for equality and justice. This contrasts intriguingly with the parallel history of race, racism, and sport in the United States, where athletes like Jackie Robinson challenged the segregation of sport. By overcoming segregation such athletes also challenged the broader social order, opening the way for other challenges to the system. In France sport was never officially segregated, though in practice in many colonies there was de facto segregation in that most teams drew only from one particular social group. But in many colonies there were some teams in which people of different backgrounds mixed together, and since the 1930s France's national football teams have consistently included black and North African players, which for several decades distinguished them from other European teams. These athletes, often beloved and celebrated, have performed in the midst of a larger situation defined by exclusion, violence, and repression, limited opportunities for political representation, and the constant struggle to think and act against the brutality of colonialism. The story of the empire of French football condenses and illuminates the complexities and ironies of French colonialism. But it is also the story of how athletes used the equality and freedom of playing, and winning, on the football field to confront the inequalities and injustices of the system in which they lived.

To tell this story, I begin by exploring the history of football in the French Empire before turning to the intertwined stories of Thuram and Zidane and of their road to victory in 1998. We first follow the story of Thuram, on his way to a remarkable moment on the football field during the semifinal game of the 1998 World Cup, and then the story of Zidane, who sealed the victory that year. The second half of the book is the story of what happened after 1998: of the disappointed hopes, conflicts on the football field, of Zidane's last gesture on the field in 2006 and what it came to mean in France and beyond.

The biographies of Zidane and Thuram are woven through the book. Teammates on the field, the two have played very different social and political roles off it. They have both been in the media spotlight constantly and been tapped for endorsement deals, and they have both navigated the complexities of a professional football world in which players are often pawns and careers can be made and unmade with striking rapidity. But they have also

FIGURE 2. Thuram, right, and Claude Makelele, center, congratulate a pensive Zidane after he scored a penalty kick against Portugal during the semifinal of the 2006 World Cup. Pascal Pavani/AFP/Getty Images.

been highly politicized figures. Especially since 2005 Thuram has embraced this role and become a prominent public intellectual in France, speaking out against racism within football and in the broader society, supporting and participating in cultural efforts aimed at increasing knowledge and understanding of the history of slavery and colonialism in France, and taking on powerful government figures, such as Nicolas Sarkozy, who was elected president in 2007. Zidane has cultivated and profited from many celebrity endorsement deals, but has been more laconic in his political statements and has worked hard to avoid certain kinds of personal exposure. Some have criticized him for not being more openly political. But, perhaps in spite of himself, Zidane's actions on the field, and his occasional statements off it, have been a catalyst for political debate, especially during and after the 2006 World Cup. "Zidane *is* political," notes one scholar, "because his persona

FIGURE 3. Thuram, far left, and Zidane, center, accompanied by teammates, take flight in celebration after defeating Spain in the 2006 World Cup. A. Bibard © Maxppp, Panoramic, Action Press/ZUMA.

represents so many conflicting identities. His image is politicized, whether he does anything about it or not. His every action takes place on a minefield of identity and memory." "If Zidane fascinates us so," writes another, it is because throughout his career, simply through his presence in the games he played, "he made sport into something other than sport."[17]

Though much of the difference between the two players is certainly a difference in personality, how they have been perceived and how they have responded to these perceptions have been shaped by their family histories. These histories link them to two very different colonial experiences. Thuram comes from the Antilles, which have been French colonies since 1635 and whose residents are French citizens. He is part of a long tradition of political activism in the French Antilles, which has insisted that the promises of French universalism be fulfilled by ending discrimination and creating a truly egalitarian society.

Zidane's inheritance is quite different. The wounds left by the Algerian war run deep in French society, and the children and grandchildren of Algerian (as well as Tunisian and Moroccan) immigrants are the most stigmatized of all French citizens. Few have ever lived in North Africa, yet they are still seen as a group apart. For many among them Zidane's stardom was a vindication. Some dared hope it would convince the white majority that, rather than being dangerous outsiders, they are an indispensable part of French society. Zidane has been made to carry the uncomfortable burden of challenging deep-seated, ongoing racism in French society. Reasonably enough, this never seemed to be a burden he really wished to carry, and while in the spotlight he worked hard to maintain his privacy, even silence. In contrast to Thuram, he rarely spoke out publicly about politics. What he did want to do—and what he did consistently do—was to awe and entertain his fans by a kind of playing that was smooth, at times euphoric, and often surprising. He played by the rules, most of the time, but like most great football players also learned how to bend the rules, to dribble around and through them. Throughout his storied career he also repeatedly broke the rules, striking out against other players as he did on his final day on the field.

"Who came up with these rules?" Many an offside forward, yellow-carded defender, or infuriated fan has asked the question. The answer—those English public school boys!—isn't much of a consolation. People all over the world have kicked or knocked balls around for millennia, with varying degrees of organization involved. The oldest written rules for a ball game come from China, where they played a game "with two teams on a market pitch with goals at the two ends." Across the Pacific in ancient Mesoamerica, civic and religious events often centered on elaborate ball games, in which players couldn't touch the rubber ball with their hands, using their hips, shoulders, feet, and head instead. In Renaissance Italy a rough and physical ball game called *calcio* was played in the plazas of Florence.[18]

The immediate ancestors of today's football are the muddy and sometimes brutal ball games played in English towns starting in the Middle Ages, and perhaps before. Players in these games tackled and kicked each other, aiming the ball at a goal placed anywhere from across the plaza to the other side of town. Authorities regularly outlawed the games, seeing them as "an ill-defined contest between indeterminate crowds of youths, often played in a riotous fashion," that "produced uproar and damage to property" while "attracting to the fray anyone with an inclination to violence." Many people still feel the same way about football. But then, as now, it was futile to try to stop the games. The orders to stop playing kept coming over the centuries, but it doesn't appear that people ever paid much attention. In the eighteenth century the game was sometimes considered not just a public nuisance but a threat to the social order. Football provided a gathering place for unruly apprentices who enjoyed spending the time away from their masters' control. In 1764 the game was put to direct political use when locals in Northamptonshire, angry at the government's enclosure and privatization of previously commonly owned land, organized a game on the land. "The message was clear and the outcome predictable. Within moments of kick-off, the football match degenerated into an overtly political mob which tore up and burned the enclosure fences."[19]

These games had about as many different rules as there were towns in which they were played. But in the nineteenth century ball games increasingly found a new home in the public schools of England (the equivalent of prestigious private schools in the United States), where teachers and administrators considered them an ideal way of channeling the energy and hostility of their students into something organized and contained, even educational. The rules initially varied from school to school, but by the mid-nineteenth century a common set of regulations began to emerge. In 1863 a group of men hailing from different public schools met at Cambridge and produced what became known as the "Cambridge Rules." A few days later, at Freemason's Tavern in London, representatives of several football clubs met and formed the Football Association. In meetings over the next months these representatives hashed out a set of common rules for the game. Although these rules still allowed limited handling of the ball, they privileged a dribbling game and also banned "hacking," or kicking opponents. This chagrined one representative, who complained that eliminating hacking would "do away with the courage and the pluck of the game." Worse, he threatened, "Frenchmen ... would beat you in a week's practice."[20]

Conflicts over the rules led to the withdrawal of one representative and ultimately the creation of the rival Rugby code, which thrived throughout England and also took root in North America, where it was the foundation for the development of American football. But the Cambridge Rules created in 1863 became the core of "Association football." The rules continued to evolve over time. But the basic structure of this remarkably resilient form of play was firmly in place in England by the last decades of the nineteenth century, to spread from there along the sinews of British formal and informal empire, as well as through war, migration, and the seemingly unstoppable volition of football itself. The inexhaustible human appetite for playing with bouncing and flying balls had found a specific form that would spread throughout the globe with startling rapidity.[21]

The fact that football has become humanity's most popular sport might be seen as further proof—if any such proof is needed—of our basic perversity as a species. A major triumph of human evolution, after all, is the ability to grab things with our opposable thumbs as we stand upright. But our most popular game forces us to use our poorly controlled feet to move a ball around a field. Of course, that may be precisely why we like it so much. The sport exposes and perhaps pushes at the limits of our evolutionary abilities. In a June 2006 report on a recent scientific study of football a scientist noted wryly, "For a whole month from June 9 of this year all civilized activity and conversation will be silenced by the quadrennial competition for association football's World Cup," an event in which "32 national teams will try to slot an air-filled plastic sphere through a rectangle measuring 2.4 by 7.2m. . . . This is not as easy as it sounds," the scientist noted, pointing out that frequently teams fail to score at all. One useful technique for actually getting the ball into the net is the "banana kick," by which a player kicks an arcing ball whose trajectory is very difficult for the goalie to read. Stars such as Ronaldinho and David Beckham have used the banana kick to devastating effect, for according to the study, "the natural environment provides no reason for human perception to have developed [the skill of handling] fast-spinning objects with unpredictable trajectories." As a goalie for a club team in Algeria, where he grew up, the writer Albert Camus "learned right away that a ball never arrives from the direction you expected it." Sometimes you can do something about it, sometimes you can't. So it goes, unfortunately, for goalies.[22]

The Englishmen who codified football saw it as a civilizing activity that could channel the energy of youth into a pastime that taught them the virtues of fair play, respect, and acceptance of the rule of law in the form of the referee. Camus insisted that "what [he knew] most surely about morality and the duty of man" he had learned playing football in Algeria, and many others would agree with him.[23]

Despite the intentions of the rule makers, part of the attraction of football was that it was a place where hierarchies could be challenged, even broken, because—at least in principle—it didn't matter who you were or where you came from, as long as you could play. Like other sports, football can be seen as a beautiful condensation of the ideology of meritocratic egalitarianism that is a fundamental part of liberal democracy. "Just as suffrage is based on the formal equality of those who vote, no matter their social condition," writes one historian, "modern sport is founded on the identity between individuals denuded, during the time of the competition, of the characteristics of their social being." Boosters of the sport, and those who represent its durable national and international institutions, often go further, seeing football as not just an embodiment of democratic ideals but as an ideal environment in which young people learn the values that constitute responsible democratic citizenship. The idea that football and other sports can be a socially progressive civic force has been particularly popular in France, where many government officials have sought to rein in the movement to privatize teams, and where the state has traditionally invested more heavily than other European states in public sports infrastructure.[24]

There is, of course, one categorical limit to how well a football team in the World Cup can represent a nation: all the players are men. There are many prominent female athletes in international competition, notably in tennis and track, and women's football—including the women's World Cup competition started in 1991 by F.I.F.A.—is increasingly popular. But when people talk about the World Cup it is generally understood that they are talking about the *men's* World Cup, unless they specify otherwise. The audiences for the men's World Cup do include a large number of women, unlike audiences for professional football, which are overwhelmingly male. But the fact that women are excluded from the teams that are the most popular and fervently supported athletic representatives for their nations reinforces their broader symbolic and political exclusion.[25]

Many contemporary critics, meanwhile, argue that sports mainly celebrate and reify individualism and commodification, and that their major social role today is not to serve any greater good but simply to serve the interests of corporations by encouraging the consumption of sports media and the ever-expanding pile of sports paraphernalia on sale throughout the world. For the French philosopher Robert Redeker, sport represents the death of progressive politics, and football fandom is an abyss into which all hope for community, humanity, and political mobilization vanishes. Wherever there is sport, Redeker declares, "nothing civilized can grow again." The media, multinational corporations peddling sportswear, and owners of teams all conspire in killing our political imagination, so that sport becomes the only metaphor for life and capitalism the only life we can imagine. "Sport erases the past, history, the future, political projects," he declares, and is the "author of a devastation of existence."[26]

Though particularly vehement, Redeker's arguments are just a recent twist on a long and often powerful tradition of criticism. For much of the twentieth century many intellectuals have considered sport a form of leisure and recreation unworthy of serious consideration. Sport has been presented as a form of "bread and circus" to placate and distract the population or as a vehicle for fascistic populism, a tool dangerously useful to dictators and demagogues like Hitler and Mussolini. "Trotsky had said that the workers were deflected from politics by sports," writes C. L. R. James, although based on his experience in the Caribbean he found the claim unconvincing. "With my past I simply could not accept that."[27]

There is no doubt that capital suffuses and in many ways commands today's sports culture and that football has repeatedly been mobilized by fascist and authoritarian populism. But, as I show in the following chapters, it has also been mobilized for very different ends. Today football fans, players, and managers are about as varied in their political perspectives as the population of the world is. They also are quite aware, and often apt critics, of the corruption, ugliness, and cynicism that exists in the athletic world. Given both the tremendous reach of football and the diversity of its fans, those who dismiss the sport or consider it of only marginal political importance risk sounding like what Edouardo Galeano has described as "ideologues who love humanity but can't stand people." James responded similarly, decades earlier, to a "professor of political science [who] publicly bewailed that any man of [James's] known political interests should believe that cricket had ethical and social values." "I had no wish to answer," James writes. "I was just sorry for the guy."[28]

In fact, as Grant Farred shows, football spurs many people's political imagination, anchoring them in a political geography that spans long distances and creating complex affinities and commitments. Describing his attachment to FC Barcelona, for decades a symbol of Catalan national pride and therefore resistance to Franco's centralizing authority in Spain, he defines football fandom as "an absolutist, deeply political commitment." Football, Farred writes, "makes political conflicts accessible" and "animates them for you as a fan and a political animal." The sport is "foundational, if not singular, in its ability to move you to take sides in a long-standing political animosity." This is in part because of its role in political and geographical pedagogy. Sport, particularly football, is perhaps the most effective teacher of world geography, a continual lesson about the existence of far-off lands with unfamiliar names and interesting flags, about the surnames of people who come from there. Farred writes, "[Football] engendered in me the need to know about other places, other histories, other forms of violence and oppression."[29]

Football's political power lies largely in its ability to condense and channel feelings of belonging, loyalty, and commitment. Of course football is not always linked explicitly to politics. Much of the time it is a social activity, and fans' team loyalties don't take on any larger political meaning. Even in such contexts, though, local sporting institutions, which have often been at least formally structured by democratic principles, continue to shape civic life in important ways; at the national level state representatives and policymakers have invested in sports education, often aimed at improving performance in international competitions. The intensity of involvement and feeling that football often evokes exerts a seemingly irresistible pull on political actors, who recognize that the game creates the conditions of possibility for later political mobilization. In times of crisis or change, through the action of fans, managers, or players, teams can be transformed into political symbols.

When football and politics do directly link up, they do so in ways that are nearly as varied as the many contexts in which football is played. Sometimes football can become a proxy in a larger political conflict between neighborhoods, towns, regions, or states, channeling but not altering larger political circumstances. And yet the story is frequently more complicated than that. Political actors instrumentalize football at their peril, since what happens on the football field is dangerously unpredictable. It is not just that teams can lose as often as they win, dragging down the political symbols they are burdened with as easily as they elevate them. What happens on the field has a certain autonomy, as do the players who create beauty or ugliness on the field. The story that follows is about a place and a time in which football has escaped the political certainties that surrounded it. The players who made up the French team, particularly Zidane and Thuram, revealed and illuminated realities of France's history, and its present, that otherwise have remained concealed, forcing a public discussion of and confrontation with the issues that will crucially define the future of France: the question of empire, the meaning of race, and the role of migration. The players didn't—they couldn't—resolve these issues, but they helped to force them into the public sphere, constituting a political discussion and therefore helping to shape political reality. In the past decades European football has often been in the news because of the actions of violent and racist fans. But if football has been turned to ugly and xenophobic ends, it can also be, as I show in the pages that follow, a powerful forum for imagining and enacting political alternatives.

As an eight-year-old I watched the legendary 1980 Olympic hockey game between the U.S. and the U.S.S.R. with my heart pounding. It was thrilling to feel that the entire population of the United States was watching an international sports event, waiting for the seconds to count down to seal an unexpected and signal victory. It was the last time I can remember feeling that way in this country. Cities and college towns might rise up in celebration, and sometimes riot, after a team's victory, but these are local celebrations, not national ones. A vast majority of Americans might tune in to the World Series or the Super Bowl, but they do so divided, with many viewers agnostic about the outcome. The Olympics sometimes galvanize viewers, but in general the competitions are cumulative and dispersed; although the fate of one athlete hangs in the balance of one run, dive, or performance, the fate of the entire nation never does. Soccer is not important enough in the United States to make our appearances in the World Cup the cause for mass mobilization, and the international competitions surrounding the sports that are more popular here are simply nowhere near as global as the World Cup.

In 1998 I was captivated by the victories of the French team, and by the way those victories mobilized and challenged French society. But I long assumed that the kind of spontaneous, national street celebrations that shook France in 1998 and 2006 simply could never happen in the U.S. But just as I was finishing this book, on 4 November 2008 Americans throughout the country poured out into the streets to celebrate the election of Barack Obama, waving flags and posters and singing the national anthem at full voice into the night. Celebrants danced in front of the White House, taunting the current resident, and throughout the country—even in normally sleepy downtown Durham, North Carolina, where I live—they honked horns as they paraded through the streets and hugged and slapped hands with strangers. Certainly not everyone was celebrating. But the scope of the celebrations, which took place throughout the country and in many parts of the world, was startling. The election, like a World Cup competition, was a truly global event, with people from Paris to Kenya keeping vigil throughout the night, waiting for the result, exploding in celebration when it was announced. At the beginning of election night, I thought the evening might turn out to be *almost* as stressful as watching France play in a crucial World Cup game. In the end it turned out to be even more stressful, something I never thought possible. The half hour between 10:30 and 11:00, when the election was finally called, felt like a never-ending game in which your team is ahead but you can't breathe until the referee blows the final whistle.

Sports and politics both thrive on hope, and both consist largely of disappointment. In many democracies, at least those where voting is a well-established ritual, many voters go to the polls with some weariness, casting a ballot for a candidate they know will probably lose, just as fans returning to watch a team on a losing streak still show up and cheer. Fans also often feel helpless in the face of the mistakes, bad luck, and sometimes the outright stupidity of managers, coaches, and players of the teams they love. Still, they keep returning, hoping that their presence and their prayers might make a difference, just as voters aware of the political corruption and the limits of democracy nevertheless keep returning to the polls. Sport and politics have in common a belief among the faithful that even when in practice the game or the government seems hopelessly corrupted, the form itself remains pure, worth preserving, a potential source of redemption. They are both driven by a hope for victory and the knowledge that one victory can stand in for many defeats.

Football has a ritual structure, made up of events that recur with tedious consistency. The games and rivalries seem endless, each confrontation the sequel to a previous one and the prelude to another. Yet within this fixed structure football games open up incredible spaces of mass mobilization, public fervor, and hope. They give spectators the rare feeling of being "exactly at the right place at the right time" and "at the centre of the whole world," writes Nick Hornby. "When else does that happen in life?" Despite all the disappointments created by losses, tedious games, and the corruption and ugliness that often infuse the sport, each game begins with a surge of promise and possibility. "Always, at the start of each match, the excitement, often the only moment of excitement, that this might be the ONE match," writes the novelist B. S. Johnson, the one "where the extraordinary happens," the game "one remembers and talks about for years afterwards, the rest of one's life."[30]

At their best, football matches condense and sometimes seem to stop time. They streak across it, creating connections between past, present, and future. No game is "temporally hermetic," writes Grant Farred. It is always "crowded by the past (previous victories, the memories of excruciating losses)," as well as by the future. Fans know that games are unpredictable and victories fleeting, yet many experience them as though they are irreducibly and eternally significant. Football may be a curious and arbitrary construction, but it is an inescapable one, as real as any government or church.[31]

C. L. R. James described sport as a particularly powerful "mode of apprehending the world, history and society." That is, in part, the foundation of its political power. But if it mobilizes people so dramatically, it is also because of the incredible joy that it can produce. The experience of communion around sport, whether in defeat or celebration, mourning or ecstasy, literally constitutes a community. That community is often evanescent, with little power to produce any effect outside itself. Sometimes it channels and even deepens xenophobia and exclusivist nationalism. But it can also push people to imagine alternatives, to alter their vision of themselves and the communities they are a part of. If sport is politics it also creates a sphere in which a different imagination of community, of the foundation for politics, is possible. And if that is possible, it is ultimately because of the beauty that, amid all the ugliness that also haunts the football field, sometimes shines on this deadly serious site of play, "a beauty that has no desire to destroy us," but only to "bring light to our lives." Asked in 2006 "What is football?," Lilian Thuram answered, "It is the language of happiness."[32]

ONE

A Beautiful Harvest

THREE HUNDRED FIFTY MILLION PEOPLE tuned in on 16 November 2005 to watch "paunchy men pulling pieces of paper out of bowls." At the headquarters of F.I.F.A. (the Fédération Internationale de Football Association), lots were being drawn to determine which group each nation that had qualified for the 2006 World Cup would be in. The fate of teams, and of their fans, lay in the balance, for if a team ends up in a particularly competitive group—commentators always dub one group of teams the "group of death"—their chances of making it out of the first round of play are seriously diminished. Those "paunchy men" in Switzerland, in other words, determine the fate of nations.[1]

Through its many competitions and its lucrative licensing and broadcasting deals, F.I.F.A. controls the world of international football. Founded in 1904 by two men, one from France and one from Holland, F.I.F.A.'s original mandate was to "police" the growth of European football clubs and assure the consistent application of the rules of football across international borders. It was originally composed entirely of European countries, but by 1914 Argentina, Chile, the United States, and South Africa had joined. Today F.I.F.A. boasts more member nations than the U.N. and is one of the most important and wealthiest international organizations on the globe. Its fame and fortune rest primarily on a competition, invented by an unassuming man and mediocre football player, from a small French town: Jules Rimet.[2]

In a photograph taken during World War I Rimet poses with seven soldiers in a trench. All of them stare at the camera, one puffing wearily on a cigarette, while another soldier stands on the ground above them. After arriving at the front in 1914, Rimet rose rapidly to the rank of lieutenant, making his mark by inventing an instrument called the Télémire, which measures distance across open space, information vital for the effective firing of artillery at enemy trenches. Like other French soldiers, Rimet would have found that in the hell of the trenches was a startlingly diverse community of soldiers, gathered from throughout the nation and the empire.[3]

Watching their troops decimated during the early months of the war, French officials turned to what one officer described as "an inexhaustible reservoir of men": France's African colonies. The 380,000 soldiers recruited in North, West, and Central Africa were often used as shock troops in trench warfare. One officer described West African soldiers as "cannon fodder" whose role was to die "in place of good Frenchmen." At least thirty thousand West African soldiers were killed, and many others returned home permanently disabled. A few years before the war, the French minister of war demanded that Africa pay back "the men and the blood" France had expended bringing civilization to the continent, "with interest." Many African veterans who survived the trenches, though, believed France owed them. In one town in Mali after the war, a veteran who had left both legs and a forearm in the trenches of France sat in front of the local colonial commander's officers day after day, demanding compensation for what he had lost.[4]

Some Caribbean and African elites saw the war as an opportunity for the colonized to simultaneously demonstrate their loyalty and demand political equality. In 1916 two black politicians—Blaise Diagne, a representative from Senegal, and Gratien Candace, from Guadeloupe—described the recruitment of colonial soldiers as the "most beautiful harvest of devotion to France that history has ever known.... Muslim Algeria, Morocco, black Africa, Madagascar, and Indochina," all sent soldiers, and France "affirmed its complete unity above any question of origin or race."[5]

Although France thought of the colonial soldiers as volunteers, one French colonial governor admitted that very few were volunteers "in the real sense of the word." Recruits and their families had few illusions. One Algerian described how his three brothers were "forcibly recruited by the state." In West Africa colonial officials ordered local indigenous leaders to provide them with soldiers, and they often offered men the community considered "dispensable"—"the poor, slaves, orphans, outcasts, or even younger sons"— who had little choice in the matter.[6]

What about the soldiers in the photograph with Rimet? They are difficult to identify with any certainty. They might have been recruited in the Antilles, where all residents were considered French citizens and therefore

FIGURE 4. Jules Rimet in the trenches of World War I. From the private collection of Yves Rimet.

served directly in French infantry units, rather than in colonial regiments, alongside Rimet and other soldiers recruited in metropolitan France. But their uniforms look more like American or British uniforms than French ones. These soldiers were probably among the African Americans who fought in the war starting in 1917, most of whom were incorporated directly into French units and put under the command of French officers like Rimet. Because American officers were concerned that French officers would treat the African American soldiers as equals, the French army issued a secret document—later denounced in the National Assembly by representatives from Guadeloupe—insisting that officers follow American standards of racial segregation and avoid eating or shaking hands with these troops or spending time talking to them about anything but military matters. Rimet, it seems, ignored the directive at least long enough to have a photograph taken as a keepsake, something to bring home from the war. Perhaps encounters with these soldiers, or with others who came from other continents to fight for France, helped shape the dream Rimet pursued when he returned from the front: to use a ball instead of bullets to resolve international conflict.[7]

Born in 1873 in the tiny French village of Theuley-les-Lavoncourt, in a region close to the German border, Rimet moved with his family to Paris when he was eleven. It was probably there that he first encountered football. The game crossed the channel from England in the late nineteenth century, and in 1872 France's first football club was formed in the Atlantic port of Le Havre. During the 1870s it was already being played in parks in Paris, where English expatriates founded a club in 1887 and where a French club was founded in 1892. Rimet's family lived close to Napoleon's tomb at the Hôtel des Invalides, where, on the grass esplanade in front, he played football with friends. He was never much of a player, but he came to believe deeply in the game as a tool for education and social progress, an embodiment of fair play that inculcated virtue in those who played it. In this Rimet was part of a larger movement, for in England many boosters of the sport saw it as an ideal way to train young men for lives of service both at home and throughout the British Empire. He also believed it could help create bonds within a French population divided by class, politics, and religion. In 1897 he created a sporting association called the Red Star Club and coached its football team to a few victories in French tournaments before the war.[8]

In the decades before World War I football also spread informally through the French Empire with sailors, settlers, and soldiers. It was immediately popular in the French Caribbean and in Algeria. An Algerian soldier named Ali Hamrouchi, for instance, who died at the front in 1914, had been a goalie on a local club since 1906, and there were many others like him. Football also spread (though more slowly) into the colonies of West and Central Africa, where teachers and missionaries considered it an ideal vehicle for spreading the values of European civilization.[9] Pierre de Coubertin, the French founder of the modern Olympics, wrote in 1912 that sports could help make the colonized "more malleable." Of course, he admitted, there was always a danger that the colonized would get too good at them. A victory of "the dominated race over the dominant race," Coubertin wrote, could have "dangerous implications" and might "encourage rebellion." Some sports, he conceded, might even provide training for such a rebellion. But Coubertin believed officials could avoid such dangers as long as they didn't turn sports matches into "official spectacles" at which "an indigenous victory" could serve to "diminish the authority of the governors."[10]

Soldiers from the colonies who hadn't played football at home before World War I were likely to encounter it on the battlefield. All soldiers needed to play was a ball and some open space, which they found easily in the fields at the rear of the front. English soldiers organized games from the moment the war began, and France, Britain, and Germany sent "thousands of balls" to the front. Footballs were sometimes used in charges by British troops, with officers kicking a ball out of the trenches and soldiers running out after it. The technique worked in part because the style of "kick and run" was still prevalent in England: a team ran alongside the player with the ball, blocking other players, the way players still do in American football and rugby. In one German prison camp British prisoners created "leagues and elimination competitions, disciplinary boards, and appeals committees" and organized matches that drew as many as a thousand spectators, including guards. Austrian prisoners of war in Russian camps also organized football matches. The game famously offered a brief reprieve from the hell of conflict during one Christmas truce when German and Allied soldiers played football with each other. Although the war disrupted leagues and tournaments, it gained new converts for the sport. "French rural conscripts" who often had "never seen the game" learned to play, and kept doing so when they went home. Many colonial soldiers also had their first introduction to the sport during the war, and some went home carrying footballs.[11]

When he came home at the end of World War I, Rimet continued his work as a booster for football. In 1919 he was elected president of the newly formed Fédération Française de Football Association (F.F.F.A., today the F.F.F.), which oversaw football clubs throughout metropolitan France as well as its colonial territories and ran France's major football competition, the French Cup. He remained president until 1945, during decades that saw a massive expansion of the sport in France. By the late 1930s there were four thousand official matches taking place every week, drawing as many as two million spectators. A "veritable sports intelligentsia" arose in France, with writers commenting on football matches in newspapers, expanding their readership and the number of football fans at the same time. Political parties and movements in France understood the power of the sport and played an important part in its diffusion. The French Communist Party, for instance, while criticizing the development of sport as a consumer spectacle, used football matches as opportunities for agitation and recruitment. At times communist groups also formed their own amateur clubs and encouraged the enjoyment of sport in what they considered its "pure" form, as a celebration of solidarity and collective values.[12]

In 1920 Rimet was selected as the new president of the Fédération International de Football Association, founded in 1904. He announced his hopes that a "renaissance" of sporting culture would redirect the passions and conflicts of the contemporary world "towards peaceful contests in the stadium, where foundational violence is submitted to discipline and the rules of the game, loyal and wise, and where the benefits of victory are limited to the wild joy of winning." He remained president for twenty-three years and created the event that F.I.F.A. is now most famous for: the World Cup. Having survived the trenches of World War I, Rimet helped invent a new field of international conflict, one that had the major virtue of being much less deadly than the killing fields he had survived.[13]

At the 1924 Olympics a remarkable team from Uruguay took the football competition by storm, winning the gold medal in front of sixty thousand spectators, trouncing many teams (including the U.S. and France) along the way. The Uruguayans repeated this victory in 1928. These victories seared themselves into the Uruguayan national consciousness. "The sky-blue shirt," writes Edouardo Galeano, "was proof of the existence of the nation: Uruguay was not a mistake. Soccer pulled this tiny country out of the shadows of universal anonymity." The team, and particularly its star black player, José Leandro Andrade, were welcomed as celebrities and feted in Paris. Uruguay's triumph inspired Jules Rimet and his colleagues at F.I.F.A. to create a new international football competition, which, unlike the Olympics, would not be limited to amateur players.[14]

The sport took root in Latin America starting in the 1860s, brought by sailors, merchants, and government representatives as Britain asserted itself as the main commercial power in the region. In 1916 Argentina, Uruguay, Brazil, and Chile held an international football tournament, which gave birth to a regional football organization called the Confederación Sudamericana de Fútbol. From the beginning, the symbolic stakes involved in these competitions were high, and there were controversies about the composition of certain teams. In 1916 a Chilean journalist accused the Uruguayans of fielding two professional players from Africa, unfairly breaking regulations that allowed only Uruguayan nationals to play on the team. In fact, however, these two players were Uruguayans whose ancestors had been slaves.[15]

After the 1928 Olympic games F.I.F.A. accepted a motion put forth by its French delegate, Henry Delaunay, to create a "competition called the 'World Cup,'" to take place every four years. The first competition was scheduled for 1930, and F.I.F.A. selected Uruguay, which was celebrating the centennial of its independence in 1830, as the host. Only four European teams made the crossing to Uruguay. France was one of them, and on 13 July 1930 the French team defeated Mexico in the first game of the first World Cup tournament. Uruguay and Argentina faced off in the final, and thirty thousand Argentine fans left Buenos Aires to cross the river to Montevideo to watch. In what some Uruguayans probably took as a welcome sign that God (or at least nature) was on their side, a thick fog descended over the river, preventing the boats from carrying many Argentine fans to the game. Uruguay won and took home the gold-plated Jules Rimet trophy depicting Nike, the Greek goddess of victory.[16]

The second World Cup was organized in 1934 in Rome, under the watchful gaze of Mussolini, who used the tournament to showcase the glories of Italy and his regime, as Hitler would do for Germany during the Olympics two years later. Mussolini trumpeted Italy's victory as a public demonstration of Italian superiority. The team was strengthened by the inclusion of several Argentine players of Italian ancestry who were granted dual-nationality so they could play. But one of the stars of the Italian national team, Angelo Schiavio, refused to join Mussolini's party. The Italian coach convinced the government to keep Schiavio on the team anyway, and he scored a crucial goal. In 1938, as the third World Cup began in Paris, some hoped that the tournament might be a force for peace. But that optimism was difficult to sustain. The Italian team, which won its second tournament that year, wore black shirts—like the Fascist paramilitaries then operating in Italy—in their game against France. During the tournament the German team at one point sang the National Socialist anthem and raised their arms in a Nazi salute. The Austrian team never got to participate in the competition because the nation of Austria, just annexed by Germany, had ceased to exist.[17]

Germany fielded several Austrian players in the competition. The French team also had an Austrian, Gusti Jordan, though they used a simpler technique to get him than the Germans had: they made him a French citizen. Jordan announced that he was "very moved, happy and proud" to have been welcomed into the "family of French footballers" and was honored to wear the tricolor jersey. One French journalist complained, "It's indecent to include

Jordan, who has been Austrian for three decades, who has barely abandoned his country for ours. Since he doesn't know what it is to be French, he can't proudly carry our national colors." But a former captain of the French team, Gabriel Hanot, defended Jordan, declaring that he was "French in every way, French for football, not in three months or six months, but immediately, without discussion or quibbling."[18]

The French team as a whole was remarkably diverse in its origins. Along with Jordan there were two other recently naturalized players on the team, one Uruguayan and the other Swiss. The goalkeeper, Laurent Di Lorto, was a Marseillais of Italian background, and the star player Ignace Kowalcyzk had been born in Poland. Another important player, Mario Zatelli, was born in Algeria to Italian parents. He was one of several players from the European settler communities in French North Africa, but there were also native Algerians on the team with him. Abdelkader Ben Bouali played in the 1938 World Cup; a few years earlier the former dockworker Ali Benouna had appeared on the team as well. Also on the team with Jordan, Zatelli, and Ben Bouali in 1938 was a player named Raoul Diagne, born in French Guiana of a father from Senegal and a mother from France.[19]

Raoul Diagne's father, Blaise Diagne, was born in 1872 on Gorée island, a former slave-trading port near Dakar, Senegal. The son of a cook and a domestic servant, Blaise was adopted by a wealthy local family and studied in the town of Saint-Louis. He entered the French customs service, embarking on a career as a bureaucrat that took him to Benin, then Madagascar (where he married a French woman, Odette Vilain), and ultimately French Guiana, where his son Raoul was born. He got into trouble everywhere, earning "the distinction of receiving similar notations on his personnel dossier after leaving each post: 'Never to be sent to this colony again.'" But in 1913 Blaise decided he wanted to represent Senegal in the French National Assembly, and he began a political campaign.[20]

In the four cities in Senegal known as the *quatre communes,* as well as in the colonies of the French Caribbean, male residents had the right to vote for representatives in the French National Assembly since the mid-nineteenth century. This was a unique privilege, for at the time the vast majority of the subjects of the French Empire had few political rights. In Algeria, for instance, Muslims had to disavow Islam, seen as an alternative juridical system incompatible with French republicanism, in order to gain citizenship rights. There was staunch resistance in colonial circles to extending political rights broadly within the empire. If all colonial subjects had been given proportional representation according to the laws in place in the metropole, they would have been a majority in the National Assembly. But Blaise Diagne took advantage of the privilege he had as a resident of the *quatre communes* to launch a campaign in which he offered himself as the candidate of black Africans. He spoke out against recent policies that, in the context of the expansion of the French Empire in West Africa, had sought to strip local residents of some of their rights. "They say that you aren't French," he told one crowd, "and that I'm not French! I tell you that we are and that we have the same rights!" Diagne claimed he could represent all parts of the population: "I am black, my wife is white, my children are mixed—what better guarantee of my interest in representing all our population?" He emphasized his knowledge of different French colonial settings by describing himself as a "citizen of the empire."[21]

He shocked both local elites and colonists and the French government by winning the election, and he set off for Paris on the eve of World War I. Diagne strongly supported the recruitment of African troops, sensing that wartime service "could be exchanged for concessions" from the French government. In 1916 he pushed through a military recruitment law that declared that the residents of the *quatre communes* "are and remain French citizens." Through such victories he earned a reputation "as a spokesman for the rights of all Africans" and was known as the "Voice of Africa" in the National Assembly. In 1918 he personally led a recruitment drive in French West Africa and was "astoundingly successful," even in areas where French efforts to draft soldiers had previously incited rebellion. His loyal service to the empire surprised the African American scholar W. E. B. DuBois, who, though he had earlier celebrated Diagne's achievements, criticized him in 1921 as "a Frenchman who is accidentally black." French colonialism, DuBois concluded, had simply opened up the "ranks of the exploiters" to black men. Indeed Diagne served France so well that in 1931 he was nominated to the high-ranking ministerial post of undersecretary of the colonies.[22]

Blaise's son Raoul was raised in Paris, where he attended a prestigious lycée and played football as a student. He was recruited to the Racing Club de Paris, one of the city's most important teams, and became a professional footballer on the team, earning several championships with them before World War II. His father was not pleased with his choice of career—he would have preferred that Raoul enter the civil service—and wrote several pieces for the magazine *L'Auto* declaring that he didn't consider football a decent profession. Raoul, however, defended his choice as a legitimate one due as much respect as work in the government or one of the liberal professions. And, like his father, he ended up serving the French nation: in 1931 he was recruited to play on the French national team and appeared on the team eighteen times during the next decade, including during the 1938 World Cup. After his retirement from professional football in the wake of World War II he coached teams in the French colonies in West Africa and in Algeria, and in the 1960s he coached the newly formed national team of Senegal, where he is considered one of the founders of professional football in the country.[23]

Fans and journalists celebrated Raoul Diagne, but they also frequently called attention to his color and background. He was given the nickname "the Black Spider" and portrayed according to dominant racial stereotypes as a naïve, happy-go-lucky, and childish player and individual. Still, his appearance on the French national team was remarkable in the European context. It was only starting in the 1950s that Portugal began incorporating black players from its colonies onto its national teams, and only in the 1970s that the Netherlands began famously fielding players of Surinamese background. The first black player on the English national team, Viv Anderson, appeared in 1979. But the pioneering presence of Raoul Diagne and the Algerian Ben Bouali on the team was consistent with a French colonial system in which Blaise Diagne had been a deputy and later the undersecretary of the colonies, and where in 1938 the governor of the colony of Guadeloupe was a black man named Félix Eboué. While committing horrendous violence against those who resisted colonization, instituting forced labor in the colonies, recruiting massively among the colonized for its wars, and refusing the most basic rights to most of its colonized subjects, France allowed for small numbers of elites to gain access to education, professions, and even political careers that reached the highest levels of government. Indeed "the limited possibilities for access and success offered to people of color" in the French Empire, writes one historian, "were well in advance of any other predominantly white Western nation."[24]

The fact that there was always a small opening for African and Caribbean elites to participate in the political life of France made it much less problematic for an athlete like Raoul Diagne to join the French national football team and be celebrated for his participation. Though many in France probably didn't see him as their equal, Raoul was not considered a foreigner. He was what his father had called himself: a "citizen of the empire." In their public lives both Blaise and Raoul Diagne sought out and secured positions as representatives for France, even as they operated in the midst of an empire that denied most of its subjects the right to represent themselves.

In 1938 a man was secreted from the hold of a ship docked in the port of Marseille. He was a Moroccan named Larbi Ben Barek, born in Casablanca in 1914 into a family that originated in Senegal. At the age of seven he started playing football in the streets near his house with a balled-up piece of cloth and made a reputation early on as the "terror" of games played between neighborhoods in Casablanca. In a pinch he could represent his neighborhood with a team of two, himself and a goalkeeper, and win. In the 1930s he was selected to play on the team representing the French protectorate of Morocco and gained notice during a 1937 game between Morocco and France. Olympique de Marseille, one of France's greatest professional teams, bought him a first-class boat ticket to come meet with them. On the trip he was treated like a "head of state" by the crew. But he had to sneak off the ship because word of his arrival had spread through football circles, and two other clubs had sent envoys to Marseille to try to recruit him. Ben Barek signed with Olympique de Marseille and played with them for the next four years. Before that, he had worked for a gas company in Morocco. His new contract multiplied his income "fifty times over." He became an "instant star" in France and, after his selection on the French national team four months later, a "French icon."[25]

Football had spread quickly in the colonies after World War I. During wartime recruitment drives, colonial officials were dismayed at the number of men who were deemed too unhealthy for service. Thinking ahead to the next war, they believed sports education would improve the health of potential recruits, who, as one official wrote in 1927, would therefore be prepared to answer to "the needs for national defense." With that goal in mind they encouraged participation in sports. Soon, just as the colonies had once provided soldiers, they began providing recruits for the weekly battles that took place on French football fields. Ben Barek was part of a large migration that brought football players from the colonies to metropolitan France's professional leagues.[26]

Like Coubertin, colonial administrators also saw sport as a useful tool for social control. Anxious about the increasing number of migrants from rural areas who were coming into the expanding African cities, they saw sports education as useful for containing the activities of youth and increasing the productivity of African workers. Over the next decades colonial schools increasingly emphasized physical education, including gymnastics and football. In metropolitan France one journalist who supported this policy wrote, "Along with school education, sporting education of our black brothers must give marvelous results. . . . Initiation to football is less arid, I think, than initiation to literature or rhetoric, but sporting education is highly civilizing, without a doubt."[27]

In 1937 a French sergeant who had served in Togo wrote similarly that sports were a useful "social discipline" that increased "the productivity and the quality of the available human capital," turning Africans into 'tomorrow's agricultural laborers and artisans." Sports would also, he believed, make Africans more loyal to France. A 1951 magazine article argued that sports provided a way to gently encourage Africans to shed their traditional beliefs and escape their "primitive mentality." The experience of playing sports would change their way of seeing the world and instill new values. "The athletes will learn that, through patient and methodical training, they will get better results than by using a fetish." They would learn that "solidarity between men" could be developed outside of "the generally suffocating constraints of clan or tribe. . . . Forced to respect the rules of the game, [the athlete] might guess that injustice and chance are not the powerful masters he once assumed, and that in the end it is the best who wins."[28]

Administrators pushing sports sometimes encountered resistance. In West Africa in 1931 one French official noted that many colonial subjects shied away from participating in physical education, worried—and rightfully so—that it was the first step toward long-term recruitment into the army. They were particularly unenthusiastic about the gymnastics exercises popular during this period, which had been encouraged in France starting in the late nineteenth century as a way to prepare youth for soldiering. Football, however, was more popular. In 1921 in Timbuktu a football association created by the local French military initially confronted the "hidden hostility" of many inhabitants, but soon 130 recruits joined, attracted by the increasingly popular game.[29] Football quickly escaped the walls of schools and garrisons, taking off as a popular pastime in many parts of Africa. By the 1930s several African cities in the French colonies had football clubs, often organized around ethnic affiliations. In 1930 a club called Le Canon was founded in Yaoundé, Cameroon, by players from the Ewando ethnic group, and in 1935 the Oryx club was founded in Douala. By 1943 there were 184 sports clubs in French West Africa, 55 of them in Senegal. After World War II French officials actively encouraged and subsidized such clubs in the hopes that they would draw people away from organizations with a "purely political" purpose, though some French colonists were unhappy with this policy, rightly realizing that sports associations were in fact powerful vehicles for political mobilization. Football was by far the most popular sport in the colonies, with more than five thousand licensed players in French West Africa in 1952 and more than ten thousand in 1957.[30]

Football also rapidly conquered the French North African territories of Tunisia, Morocco, and Algeria. A football club was founded by a group of European settlers in Algeria in 1897, and others soon followed there and in Morocco and Tunisia. The European settlers in these regions included not only French but Italian, Spanish, and Maltese immigrants, and early football clubs were often organized along ethnic lines. Jewish communities in Algeria, some of which had been established in the colony hundreds of years before the French conquest, formed teams as well. One of the most prominent early clubs in Algiers, the Racing Universitaire Algérois, was populated by the sons of the local colonial gentry, though its goalie for a time was a student from a poor family, the writer Albert Camus. In 1913 the first Muslim football club formed and fielded native Algerian players. Over time such clubs multiplied, becoming one of the most important vehicles for the expression of anticolonial and nationalist sentiments in Algeria. By the 1930s "there were more registered players in Algeria than in the Paris region," nearly 13,500, even though there were only twenty stadiums in the country, as compared to 110 in and around Paris. By the time of independence in 1962 Algeria had 254 clubs in three leagues, with 27,000 licensed players, while Tunisia had 4,200 licensed players and Morocco 8,000.[31]

As they did in West and Central Africa, colonial officials in North Africa saw sports as a way of elevating and civilizing colonial subjects. They also hoped that sport would overcome hostility between different groups in the colonies. One French general declared in 1936 that "sport should be the link that unites French and Muslims" and that it could "eliminate all rivalries between religions and races." One of the largest and most successful Muslim clubs, the Union sportive musulmane d'Oran, had a board of directors that brought together Europeans and Muslims and a European president, a veteran of World War I. In 1935 the board wrote to colonial officials that their "noble" goal was to educate "strong and healthy" young people who would "show themselves worthy of their older brothers" who had "defended the sacred soil" of France during World War I. Through sports, they continued, "we learn to know each other better, to love one another, to be brothers," unified by the "joy" of playing.[32]

North African clubs were tightly integrated into the French football world. After World War I Algerian clubs joined the French Football Federation, were organized into three leagues, and participated in championships pitting them against teams from Morocco, Tunisia, and France. Beginning in the 1930s the French champion team toured Algeria each year, and there was also a yearly match between the "B" selection of the French national team and a selection of players representing Algeria. By 1954 the five regional leagues in North Africa—Morocco, Algiers, Oran, Constantine, and Tunisia—each had its own championship, as well as participating in two regional championships. In the 1954–55 season, the F.F.F. began allowing North African clubs to participate in the French Cup, something the federation had resisted for decades. North African teams playing in these competitions already suffered from a problem that would long haunt football in Africa: the best players kept moving to metropolitan France to play on teams there. It was particularly difficult to hold onto strikers, who left in the largest numbers to try their luck across the Mediterranean.[33]

The first athletes who were actively recruited in the colonies by French coaches were not footballers but runners. In 1914 the French sports magazine *L'Auto* organized races in Algeria to find runners for the French Olympic team, and during an elimination race in Paris the winner and three of the other top five finishers were all from Algeria. During the 1928 Olympics the Algerian El Ouafi won the gold medal in the marathon for France, and in 1936 the French runner who placed highest in the marathon was another Algerian. The Guiana-born colonial administrator Félix Eboué wrote a magazine article in 1931 urging readers to search for potential athletes in Central Africa. He described the athleticism involved in various practices he observed in the Oubangui-Chari in the French Congo, where he had long served as a colonial administrator. Initiation rites involved physical challenges as well as ritual dance, he noted, and played a role similar to that of sports associations in Europe. Impressed by the athletic abilities he had seen, he declared that the region was "a nursery of athletes." With the installation of sports facilities and training, the French could produce "surprising results," especially in the "socially important" practice of team sports.[34]

At the 1936 Olympics in Berlin the African American track star Jesse Owens famously won four gold medals, to the dismay of Adolf Hitler. The French teams meanwhile totally flopped. French athletics, wrote J. Godet, the editor of *L'Auto*, desperately needed help, and they should look to the French Empire to find it: "What are we waiting for? We should go search the brush of our colonies for subjects who could represent the French race with dignity, while we wait for the French nation to decide to take care of its own health." Godet's writings were infused with a deeply racist vision of the world; at one point he claimed that if you ignored the Berlin stadium as you watched Jesse Owens run, you could believe you were "in Africa." But his call suggested that African athletes could represent the "French race" maybe even better than failing white athletes. The prospecting tours organized by the magazine were not successful, and they stirred up some ire in France: "We're going prospecting among the blacks," complained one writer, when the focus should be on training athletes in France itself.[35]

But on the terrain of football, the fastest growing and most lucrative sport, recruitment from the colonies took off. Between 1932 and 1962 at least eighty-six players from Algeria played professional football in France, most of them during the 1950s, when several of France's most prominent stars came from the colony. During the same period there were at least thirty-five professional players from Morocco and six from Tunisia. There were also many players from West and Central Africa on French professional teams, especially during the 1940s and 1950s: seven from Senegal, two from Mali, five from Togo, six from the Congo, thirteen from the Ivory Coast, and nineteen from Cameroon. In 1959 the magazine *France Football* counted seventeen West Africans playing on major French professional teams, and in 1960 there were forty-three. In the next two decades another generation of players from these regions would find positions throughout France, now as immigrants from new nations rather than as colonial subjects.[35]

Then as now, such players confronted racism on and off the field. In 1937, when a Tunisian player in Nice requested a raise, an outraged French journalist wrote that the "football world" had enough problems already and couldn't "afford to accept ridiculous requests from primitives." The player, he went on, should "consider himself happy enough to earn good money with his feet, given that the other extremity, his brain, is of little help to him." At the same time the Moroccan Ben Barek became one of the most celebrated—and highly paid—French football stars of his generation. He was a "veritable celebrity," one of the first in the history of French football. He played seventeen games with the French team between 1938 and 1954, making his the longest running career in the team's history. When he played his first game in Rome, Italian fans focused their ire on him, chanting racist slogans as he ran onto the field. His response was to sing the "Marseillaise" with particular vigor, a performance that earned him affection among French fans. They gave him the nickname "the Black Pearl," which communicated their admiration but also the fact that he remained a kind of aberration whose skin color would always be remarked. Still, some considered him one of France's most important monuments. In 1948 he became "the first French player to be transferred to a major foreign club" when Spain's Atletico de Madrid recruited him, paying the highest transfer fee paid until then within the Spanish leagues. One French journalist cried, "Sell the Eiffel Tower! Sell the Arc de Triomphe! But don't sell 'the Black Pearl.'" Forty years old in 1954, he participated in a final game with France in the run-up to the World Cup, assisting his Moroccan compatriot Just Fontaine in a crucial goal against West Germany. He retired that year and spent the rest of his life as a coach in Morocco and Algeria.[37]

When athletes like Ben Barek represented France in international competitions they stood for France itself, at least for a time. Coaches didn't worry too much about the political implications of their choices, of course; they wanted to win and were looking for the best athletes. Because colonial subjects were not foreigners, they could be incorporated into French professional teams as well as the French national team with no difficulty. But once they were on the team, and especially once they shone on the field, the symbolism of their presence was difficult to contain.

World War II stopped the progress of the World Cup—the 1942 tournament was scheduled to take place in Germany, which wasn't particularly convenient—but in 1950 crowds thronged to Brazil to watch the world teams compete once again. There, with 200,000 mostly Brazilian fans watching in the Maracanã stadium, then and now the largest in the world, Uruguay defeated Brazil in the final game. Worried about the reaction of the devastated Brazilian fans, officials canceled the formal ceremony handing over the trophy; Rimet wandered around in the crowd by himself, pushed from all directions, until he found the Uruguayan captain and shoved the Cup into his hands, rapidly shaking his hand before being swallowed up by the churning crowd. In Brazil the defeat is still considered one of the country's major traumas of the twentieth century. Rimet's World Cup had created an event in which the fate of nations seemed to hang on something as unpredictable as a goal.[38]

By 1954 Rimet could look back with satisfaction at the first few decades of the World Cup. He published two books, one of them optimistically titled *Le Football et le rapprochement des peuples* (Football and the Bringing Together of Peoples). He argued that, even more than the Olympic games—which, because of their "dogma of amateurism," remained "too refined" and focused on "perfection"—the World Cup was a force for progress that could spread "comprehension and reconciliation between the races." The competition was destined, he believed, to play a pivotal role "in the generous work of eliminating suspicions and conflicts that, still today, set people against one another."[39]

With its Diagnes and Ben Bareks, France's World Cup teams themselves seemed to embody Rimet's utopian hopes for football. Writing in the 1940s, the former football player Gabriel Hanot, who had defended Gusti Jordan in 1938, celebrated the diversity of the French team, which he felt was, as one historian writes, a "model for rebuilding national strength." The team showed that the "new blood" that came from immigration could strengthen the nation, which in the wake of the war needed to replenish "the quality and quantity of its citizens."[40]

Through the 1940s and 1950s French football continued to be sustained and indeed led by the children of European immigrants and players from the French Empire. Between 1945 and 1962 eight Algerians and four Moroccans played on the national team. In France few seem to have complained publicly about this, though in 1953 a journalist in Ireland warned his compatriots about the team they were about to face: "Watch out! The French team you will see is not the real French team, but a group of naturalized citizens and foreigners. Our team will not be charging against France's real footballers. Boo them!" Four decades later Jean-Marie Le Pen of the French far right would make a similar accusation.[41]

The most prominent player of immigrant background on the French team in the 1940s and 1950s was Raymond Kopa. Born in 1931 in the north of France into a family of Polish miners, he became a symbol "not only of the possibilities of social mobility but the successful and full integration of the immigrant." His parents had moved to France in 1919 as teenagers, part of a larger Polish migration to the north of France, and when he was growing up they still spoke Polish at home. The Poles were subject to discrimination in employment, and Kopa couldn't get an apprenticeship as an electrician, so he worked in the mines with his father and brother. He attributed his success in football to his intense desire to escape that life. "If I had been born into a wealthy family, there would probably never have been a Raymond Kopa. Without the mine, I'd have been a good player. Nothing more. But there was the mine. My name was Kopaszweksi and to get out I had nothing but football."[42]

Kopa played alongside Just Fontaine, born to a Spanish mother in Marrakech, Morocco. A stunning player, Fontaine was part of Morocco's

FIGURE 5. Raymond Kopa (left) and Just Fontaine in their national team uniforms in 1959, showing off their brand-name footballs. © Universal/TempSport/ Corbis.

regional team, and after he played in a game against France in Marseille he was recruited to play professionally in Nice. He was soon invited to join the French national team, where he was a key player from 1953 to 1960. During the 1958 World Cup he scored a remarkable thirteen goals, setting a record that still stands. Fontaine and Kopa played alongside the Algerian-born goalie Georges Lamia, who played on local club teams in Algeria before moving to France in 1956. But Fontaine's teammates also included several other North Africans of Arab background: the Moroccan-born Abderrahmane Majhoub, who played for the Moroccan national team in the 1960s, Larbi Ben Barek, and the Algerian-born players Mustapha Zitouni and Rachid Mekloufi.[43]

The French national football team has consistently been a diverse and multiethnic assembly. Although this has meant very different things in different periods, only in the 1990s was this long tradition transformed into a widely shared and celebrated political metaphor. But it has always been part of the ongoing conversation in which French fans have argued over and wondered about what their team's successes and failures in the World Cup said about them and their country. Fans in France have participated in a larger global tradition of seemingly endless commentary about the way the particular style of play of a national team reflects aspects of their nation's character. Such discussions are, of course, full of dangerous intellectual pitfalls and often tend toward absurd stereotyping. After all, the stylistic and tactical choices of a football team can never truly represent a nation. And yet many fans and commentators have felt that they do. Football can never really truly answer the questions it raises: "What is a nation? Who are we?" But it has taken on a crucial role in raising those questions by creating a space for impassioned and intense discussion. The World Cup has turned the game into a churning terrain of self-representation and self-criticism, of vindication and rage, of aspiration and despair. Invented out of utopian hopes that saw football as a tool for pursuing a kind of universal peace, it now represents something in its power and reach that Rimet himself could scarcely have imagined.[44]

While games promise a certain kind of escape, and in France have sometimes represented hopes of political equality, they take place in a world shaped by the inequalities rooted in old (and new) empire. This fact has shaped the way the French team has been viewed, both in France and throughout the world, in the past decades. When Rimet wrote in 1954 of football as a route to "universal peace," he probably sounded strangely utopian to many in France and its colonies. In that year a decade of violent warfare in French Indochina culminated in the stunning French defeat at Dien Bien Phu, which secured a tenuous independence for divided Vietnam. In Algeria the Front de Libération Nationale was beginning its armed struggle, using football as a weapon of war.

Football played a significant role in anticolonial struggles throughout Africa. The colonial authorities who encouraged the spread of football throughout the continent in the 1920s and 1930s thought football would help them hold on to their colonies, not lose them. But Coubertin had warned that once football mixed with the spectacle and symbols of politics it would be very difficult to control the results. He turned out to be right. As early as the 1920s football games became a "forum for protest and resistance against European rule." Some football clubs were directly linked to nationalist movements; whenever a team of Africans played against a team of Europeans and won, crowds celebrated not only that victory, but the promise of a more significant reversal in the social order. Football matches were the perfect place to fly nationalist symbols and sing protest songs. The leaders of anticolonial movements rapidly "recognized the potential of football as an instrument for generating resistance to colonialism and promoting nationalist aspirations."[45]

When the French colonies won their independence, one of the first things the new rulers did was to join F.I.F.A. Joining the association was a way of "completing and confirming the international recognition gained by joining the United Nations." For the leaders of newly independent nations, athletics served to mobilize popular support and patriotism and to announce their presence on the international scene. Though there were many other pressing needs, many African states invested heavily in sports programs, focusing particularly on football.[46]

But new nations in Africa quickly discovered that F.I.F.A. itself needed to be decolonized. The leadership of F.I.F.A. was made up of Europeans; its presidents in the 1950s and 1960s, Jules Rimet and Stanley Rous, hailed from the two great crumbling empires of the day, France and Britain. Both Rimet and Rous, writes one scholar, were imbued with a "patronizing, Eurocentric and neo-imperialist" attitude toward football in Africa, which lay "the foundations for the inequality and power imbalances which have underpinned relations between FIFA and the Confédération Africaine de Football (CAF) in the second half of the twentieth century." Another scholar has argued that Rimet's vision of football was "deeply rooted in an entrenched colonialism." Indeed in its first decades "F.I.F.A. was so Eurocentric that no need was seen for any separate European organization." Rous complained in 1965 about the fact that African states were so heavily involved in football programs, and in several cases F.I.F.A. suspended a few African federations they considered too closely linked to their states. At times, of course, state involvement in sports in Africa—as in many other places—was a vehicle for corruption and nepotism. But it is difficult to see how new African states could develop strong and competitive athletic programs without strong state support, which in any case was also forthcoming in European countries.[47]

The World Cup meanwhile remained a rigidly exclusive tournament. In the mid-1960s the only way an African team could make it into the competition was via "a play-off between the winner of the African Cup of Nations and the Asian equivalent," which meant that at best there could be only one team from *either* Africa or Asia present, while European and Latin American teams had many more slots. In 1966 Kwame Nkrumah, president of Ghana, persuaded the African Football Confederation to boycott the World Cup in protest, demanding that at least one slot be reserved for an African team.

Jolted by the boycott, F.I.F.A. quickly voted to open up the competition to African teams. The configuration of power within F.I.F.A. itself began to shift, particularly after 1974, when the Brazilian João Havelange began campaigning for the presidency. By then African and Asian countries comprised seventy-two of F.I.F.A.'s 141 members. Havelange understood that, since each member nation of F.I.F.A. had a vote, if he could gain the support of African and Asian countries along with those of Latin America, he would secure himself the presidency. He traveled throughout the world, meeting with representatives of national football associations in Africa and Asia, promising to transform F.I.F.A. and make it more inclusive, as well as find ways to help support the growth of sports infrastructure in certain nations. He won the election, marking the start of a significant transformation in F.I.F.A. and in the World Cup itself. Havelange's rule, as promised, opened up more opportunities for African and Asian teams to compete, which helped spur football programs in many parts of the globe, and under his watch the first World Cup tournaments held outside of Europe and Latin America were planned. To finance the ambitious programs he had promised, Havelange turned F.I.F.A. into a global brand and a marketing giant. He successfully marketed the broadcasting rights to World Cup games, raising huge sums of money for F.I.F.A. in the process. Under his presidency F.I.F.A. was transformed into an international organization, global corporation, and media conglomerate all rolled into one.[48]

Today Europe remains the center of the world football economy. Its clubs are the wealthiest and best known, their merchandise is sold internationally, and they attract the best players from throughout the world. Unsurprisingly the lead players on many national football teams play professionally in Europe, returning to their home countries only to train for the World Cup and regional competitions. Among the 110 players on five African teams who played in the 2002 World Cup, more than three-quarters played outside of Africa, mostly in Europe. The Senegalese team that defeated France during that tournament included nineteen players who played professionally in France. And in 2006, 80 percent of African players in the World Cup played on professional teams outside of their countries, compared to 50 percent of European players. African players played primarily outside their continent as well, while European players abroad largely played in Europe itself. The coaching and experience African players gain playing professionally in Europe make them stronger competitors when, during World Cups, they face off against teams often staffed with athletes they have played with and against all year.[49]

By the 1980s African leaders facing serious economic crises frequently took advantage of the global football economy rather than using state funding to sustain their national football programs. The president of the football federation of the Ivory Coast declared in 2002 that he would "track" all those players from his nation playing in European and Asian professional leagues in order to find "hidden talents" and convince them to wear the jersey of their country in international competitions. Starting in 2003, when the football federation of the Democratic Republic of Congo (formerly Zaire) established a national youth team, they set it up in Belgium, where many of the young players were in football academies or playing professionally. Such strategies can be very effective, but they do put African countries in the position of depending largely on European coaches to prepare players for their national selections. And because many players born in Africa either have or acquire European nationality, they often choose to play for more prominent European national teams. As a result, African nations don't have access to some of the most talented players. If players are sometimes torn between more than one national team, they also often find themselves torn between their professional and national teams. Before 1981 professional clubs weren't required to release their players to play on national teams, but that year F.I.F.A. passed a regulation requiring all football clubs to allow their players to leave to play in international competitions. Still, given the steady increase in the number of professional and international games and the long distances players sometimes have to travel to participate in both, meeting that requirement can be difficult. Sometimes players resolve this difficulty by turning their professional success into a kind of national victory. In May 2008, for instance, the striker Sulley Muntari wrapped himself in a Ghanaian flag when he won the English F.A. Cup with Portsmouth. Having helped to secure the victory for his team, he also claimed it for Ghana.[50]

Today streams of young African players seek passage to Europe as the ticket to a lucrative career in sports. The possibility of success through migration is broadcast far and wide, during each match of English and French premier teams, nearly all of which feature African players. But there are also powerful and exploitive economic forces at work shaping this migration. European teams spend less to recruit African and Latin American players than players from other parts of Europe. Teams can sometimes make a great deal of money off such recruits if they are successful and can be transferred to another team, but the players themselves often don't reap much of the benefit from such transactions. "Most of the income coming from players transfers," notes one scholar, "ends up in European bank accounts." Some contemporary commentators and scholars compare the steady flow of African footballers into European leagues to a new "slave trade" or "scramble for Africa."[51]

If football seems to be, and in a few cases is, a golden opportunity, the door that leads to even the lowest paid of professional salaried positions is hard to squeeze through. Many of those recruited by European teams end up in dead-end careers, and many young players brought into training academies end up without a professional contract. Because they usually arrive in Europe with short-term tourist visas, they quickly find themselves without immigration papers and slip into a clandestine life, one they share with many other immigrants. One Cameroonian player recalls how he found himself in a "spiral," without a residence permit and unable to get even a tryout with clubs because he didn't have papers. Such cases are common enough that in 2000 a former footballer who played on the Cameroonian national team, Jean-Claude Mbvoumin, founded an organization in France called Foot Solidaire, one of whose goals is to "defend the rights of young African footballers." It has worked with about six hundred players in precarious situations in France.[52]

Several films have captured the complexities of African football migration. In Abderrahmane Sissako's 2006 film *Bamako,* an African courtyard hosts a trial against the International Monetary Fund for its devastation of Africa; one of the observers is a dusty young boy with a battered football, who peers over the wall. In the 2006 film *The Great Match,* a lighthearted story about three isolated groups of people trying to get to a television so they can watch the 2002 World Cup final, a bus crossing the Sahara carries a young West African man who explains that he is on his way to Europe to become a professional football player. In a 2008 Finnish documentary about African immigrant voyages, scenes of the life of agricultural laborers in Spain are framed by shots of a dusty football field back home in Africa, where at sunset players practice with intensity.[53]

The Guinean filmmaker Cheik Doukouré explores the ambiguities of African footballer migration in *Le Ballon d'or,* the story of a young player named Bandian. The boy lives in a small village with his sick mother; his father's second wife mistreats him, and after accidentally starting a fire in his village he leaves with the help of a friend, a sympathetic doctor from Médecins sans Frontières. Before Bandian leaves the doctor gives him a football. Arriving in a larger town clutching the ball, he is accosted by a desperate referee, who tells him that he needs the ball for a game being played on the central plaza because the one they were using has burst. Bandian, a clever negotiator, agrees to let them use his ball if he can play. Despite being much smaller than the other players, he scores goals and catches the eye of a merchant with a video camera. The merchant later catches up with Bandian in Conakry and promises to help him get into professional football. The merchant is unscrupulous—he sells "fish, videos and football players"—but he gets Bandian a place on a team being trained by a stern but respected coach. The coach is played by Salif Keita, a star Malian footballer who played for A.S. Saint-Etienne in France in the late 1960s, when the team was the champion of France three times and where his teammate was the Algerian star Rachid Mekloufi. Keita then left France to play in Spain and Portugal. In 1970 he won the first African Ballon d'Or, the prize for the best African footballer, and in 1994, the same year the film *Le Ballon d'or* was made, set up a training center for footballers in Mali.[54]

In the film Keita hopes that, rather than leaving for Europe, African footballers will stay in their homelands and play for their teams. He describes the departure of young footballers like Bandian as a "new slave trade" and works hard to resist it. But Bandian is ultimately convinced by his merchant patron to take advantage of an offer to go to a youth football training academy in France, which has offered him a scholarship. He leaves with fake papers that have transformed him from thirteen to sixteen, and the film ends as he enters a taxi at a French airport, far from home and entering an uncertain new life. Though often funny, the film is also unsettling. Keita's dream of supporting African football is compelling, but it is the merchant in the film who shapes Bandian's choices. He arrives in France, another young man leaving to do battle in Europe, a little bit like those who left to fight in World War I generations earlier, though with much less to fear and much more to gain.

TWO

Caribbean France

"LIFE TASTES LIKE HONEY," the football star Marius Trésor announced
in a 1978 song. "A child of the islands," he was "born under the sun" in Sainte-
Anne, Guadeloupe. In 1935, fifteen years before his birth, football players in
his town founded a team called Juventus de Sainte-Anne (after the legendary Italian team), bringing together students and workers from a local sugar
refinery. Trésor played on the youth squad of the club. In 1964 Juventus de
Sainte-Anne won a tournament among teams from Guadeloupe, Martinique,
and French Guiana, then traveled to metropolitan France to represent the
Antilles in the French Cup competition. A few players from Juventus de
Sainte-Anne went on to professional careers in France. By the late 1960s
Trésor played on the main squad of the club, which won the island's championship in 1967 and 1969, and his exploits on the turf were frequently cel-
ebrated in the local newspaper, *France-Antilles*.[1]

In Paris an Antillean working in the administration of the French professional league had a subscription to *France-Antilles*. He started clipping
reports about Trésor and sent them to coaches he knew. The clippings were
convincing: a team in Corsica got in touch with Trésor and offered him a
contract. He left Guadeloupe at the age of nineteen, heading for another
French island. The decision, he explained in his 1978 song, was easy: Corsica
was a "hot country," just like Guadeloupe. A few years later Trésor left to play
at the Olympique de Marseille, where he stayed for eight years before moving to the Girondins de Bordeaux, where he remained on the coaching staff
after his retirement. The pinnacle of his professional football career came in
1976, when he was captain of an Olympique de Marseille team that won the
French Cup. He received the trophy from President Giscard d'Estaing, who
in an interview spoke of a recent trip to Sainte-Anne, Guadeloupe—which
he described as the "homeland" (*patrie*) of Trésor—and declared, "Today all
French people are very proud [that it was Trésor who] led the Marseille team

to victory." As a group of French humorists later pointed out, the statement was a strange and evasive way of evoking Trésor's status as a black French citizen, a sort of uncomfortable dribble with the question of precisely how French Trésor was. The humorists wondered why the president believed that French people should be especially proud of Trésor's leadership rather than that of another Frenchman. Was it, they joked, because he was the only French person on the Marseille team, which indeed often featured many star foreign players? Or maybe because he was the most French of the foreigners on the team? Or the most foreign of the French people on the team? Or just because the French president wanted to pat himself on the back for his recent trip to Guadeloupe? They also suggested that fans of the Lyon team defeated by Marseille might not feel particularly proud that Trésor had caused their defeat. Trésor himself seems to have been little affected by the political nit-picking about his status. He had secured himself a place in the pantheon of French footballers, and his 1978 song, punctuated by shouts of "Good old Marius!," celebrated his success and his cosmopolitan life. "I'm comfortable in my skin," Trésor sings out, "like a fish in water."[2]

During the 1970s and 1980s Trésor gained admirers in metropolitan France and became an idol in the French Caribbean. In 1971 he began his long career on the French national team. He played in sixty-five international games before his retirement in 1983, appearing more times than any other French player had before. In 1976 he became the first black player to be team captain. A pillar of the French defense for more than a decade, he played alongside the future coach of the French team, Raymond Domenech, and the Senegal-born player Jean-Pierre Adams. He also scored legendary goals, against Brazil during a 1977 friendly match played in Rio's Maracanã stadium and against Germany during the 1982 World Cup.[3]

One of Trésor's unconditional fans was a Guadeloupean from the small island of Désirade, the father of a young boy named Thierry Henry, who would became one of the greatest strikers of his generation. Henry recalls how his father "venerated" Trésor, calling him "the Monument" and treasuring an autograph from the player. Henry and his family lived outside Paris, visiting Désirade in the summers. He remembers that, when he was five, he watched the 1982 World Cup there: "I'll always remember the people jumping up and down all around me when Marius Trésor scored his goal against Germany." Lilian Thuram also idolized Trésor. When he met him for the first time as he was beginning his own professional career, Thuram trembled.[4]

Before the 1960s few French professional teams looked to the Caribbean to recruit players, but when they did they found remarkable talent. Trésor was only the first in a long series of Antillean players to leave their mark on French international football. Playing alongside Trésor on the French national team were several other Caribbean players, including the Martinican Gérard Janvion and the Guadeloupeans Luc Sonor and Jocelyn Angloma. By 1998 the French team included three Antillean players (Thuram, Henry, and Bernard Diomède), along with goalie Bernard Lama from French Guiana. The number of Antillean players would increase in the next decade. In 2006 nine of the twenty-three players on the team were born in either the French Caribbean (including Guiana) or the French metropole of Caribbean parents. Of those, six—Thuram, Henry, Eric Abidal, William Gallas, Florent Malouda, and Sylvain Wiltord—played in all or most of the major games. Guadeloupe alone claimed four major players. Since then, several other Antillean players, including Nicholas Anelka, Gael Clichy, and Jimmy Briand, have played on the French team as well.[5]

The combined population of Guadeloupe, Martinique, and French Guiana is about one million, with at least another 300,000 living in metropolitan France. They make up a tiny portion of the French population of sixty million, but in 2006 they made up almost half of the French national football team and a majority of its most prominent players. What explains the prominence of Antilleans in French international football? One Antillean market seller interviewed in 2006 thought she had the answer; pointing to the fruit piled on her stand, she suggested it was the quality of the local food the players ate that made them so successful. The fruit might have helped, though probably not as much as talent, hard work, and luck. But their pursuit of success through sports is also the reflection of a larger social reality that shaped and constrained opportunities for Antilleans, making sport an attractive avenue for advancement. These players are part of a long tradition of football in the French Caribbean. For most of the twentieth century, football has been considered by many in the region to be not only a vehicle for individual success, but also an ideal tool for collective recognition. Football has facilitated, animated, and at times generated local pride in a town or island, as well as in the Antilles more broadly. C. L. R. James wrote in 1963 of the way that West Indian fans of cricket brought "the whole past history and future hopes of the islands" to important matches. "The islands are small—during big cricket people talk fanatically about nothing else. Every street corner is a seething cauldron of cricket experiences, cricket memories, fears, suspicions, hopes, aspirations." The same has been true of football in Guadeloupe and Martinique.[6]

The sport has been important in the region in part because it enables athletes and fans to navigate the complex affiliations that come from being part of France and the Caribbean at the same time. Antilleans are Americans, their history rooted in the plantation slavery that profoundly shaped politics and culture throughout much of the Americas. They are Martinican and Guadeloupean, anchored in local geography and experience circumscribed by water and amplified both by the distance from metropolitan France and by the relative disconnection from other parts of the Caribbean. And they are tightly linked economically, politically, and culturally to France, which most are very comfortable seeing as their nation. Some activists and intellectuals, as well as outside observers, perceive these multiple affiliations as fundamentally contradictory. But for most Antilleans, the fact of being both French and Caribbean is not a contradiction. It represents a shifting field of challenges and problems but also possibilities and options. For decades the football field reflected, condensed, and embodied this larger field. Football has been a way for players and teams to show that the Antilles, both French and Caribbean, existed. Football players have become symbols and ciphers for the larger negotiations, feints, runs, and dribbles Antilleans practice out of necessity in their daily lives.

Throughout the twentieth century and into the twenty-first, athletes and coaches in the French Caribbean navigated between and often combined two goals: they sought to conform to French metropolitan models of sport and find recognition within the French sports world, and at the same time they used sports as a way of seeking full emancipation and a recognition of their difference. When French Caribbean fans cheer for players with roots in the Caribbean who play for the French team, they are both supporting France and asserting their participation in, indeed their essential contribution to the nation and bathing in the pleasure of seeing members of their community excelling and extolled.

In the film *Entre les murs* (The Class), which won the Palme d'Or in 2008, a student of Antillean background who is one of the best footballers in the group is teased by some of his classmates, fans of the national football teams of Mali and Morocco. "Where is your national team?" they ask to provoke him. "France!" he responds, and rattles off the names of several Caribbean players.[7] During one 2006 World Cup game, two young women in the stadium did something similar; they held up a French flag, but across the white stripe of the flag they had written *Gwada*. The term is a *kréyol* shorthand for *Gwadloup* (Guadeloupe), and it refers not only to the place but to the behaviors, styles, and attitudes connected to it. "That's really Gwada," you might say of an outfit, a song, maybe even a move on the football field. Cheering on a French team with a solid Gwada defense held together by Lilian Thuram and William Gallas, with Thierry Henry in front, the women waved a flag that spoke for France and Guadeloupe at the same time.

When sailors disembarked in the ports of the Caribbean in the late nineteenth century, it felt good to move around in a space that wasn't locked in by the sea. They often stretched their legs playing football, happy to compete with the locals who showed up to challenge them. In port cities, seaside parks became football fields as sailors played against local workers and students, the constitutive "us and them" an effect of a ship's arrival. When the ships were gone, those who stayed behind kept playing, though since the sailors took their footballs with them this at first meant playing with fruit or balled-up cloth. In a 1986 newspaper obituary one early player recalled how he and his deceased friend had played together in the courtyard of their high school using "young breadfruit, firm and hard," for a ball. The deceased man's sister was happy he had published that detail. "Thanks to you, historians of football writing in the year 2000," she predicted, "will add the un-ripened bread-fruit to the list of the ancestors of the football."[8]

Local students and professionals who went off to metropolitan France in the late nineteenth century and early twentieth often returned as football aficionados. By the 1890s some of them, along with local priests and teachers, founded football clubs like those proliferating in Europe. As it did elsewhere, football flowed into these societies remarkably quickly, helped along by the French state and its schools, which after the defeat in the Franco-Prussian War of 1870 pushed sports education as a way of preparing the next generation of soldiers. But sports rapidly spilled out of the military academies and schools and became a major leisure activity, drawing players and crowds throughout the islands.[9]

What did football mean in the French Caribbean? According to the historian Jacques Dumont, it epitomized the republican values cherished in this postslavery society: liberty, since control of one's own body promised the "pursuit of perfection" and indeed "emancipation"; equality, since "any individual, whatever their origin or place of birth," was fully equal to all other members in a sports association; and the fraternity produced by playing together. Many of those who first played football and founded clubs in the French Antilles were wealthy elites, though colonialism still limited their opportunities. Over time, however, the sport also attracted players who labored in towns or on rural plantations. For such players, the sport represented something more: the freedom to use one's body for something other than work. Sugar plantations still dominated the colony, and most of the population did low-wage agricultural labor. In a hierarchical colonial society "all cultural expression," notably forms of dance and fighting arts originating in Africa, were "judged dangerous and outlawed" and could resurface only in "a euphemistic form." Football and other sports "suddenly made possible the exhibition of physical qualities, and the pleasure of free movement." Sports "emancipated" the body from production, channeling it into the pleasure of play. Such physical freedom was, of course, inviting in all societies. But it took on a powerful meaning in places where slavery had dominated for so long and where, even after it was abolished, it haunted social relations and cultural memory. Organized sports were a way to pursue the "promise of equality and dignity" that could come from full French citizenship long denied colonial subjects in the Caribbean. Early players of the game in Guadeloupe and Martinique might well have agreed with the famous declaration of the Caribbean musician and prophet Bob Marley: "Football is freedom."[10]

In Martinique privately founded clubs began to proliferate in the late nineteenth century, and in 1912 players created an islandwide association to bring them under one umbrella. Football games drew big crowds, particularly when they were played against visiting British sailors or, occasionally, traveling professional teams. Antillean football players and journalists learned the English terminology that went with the game and often used English names for their clubs. Two young students, Aimé Césaire and Léon Gontron Damas—who would remain lifelong friends and, with Leopold Senghor, become the founders of the literary and political movement known as Negritude in the 1930s—formed a team called Good Hope. The team of the prestigious Lycée Schoelcher where Césaire was a student and later a teacher was called Good Luck.[11]

At the center of Fort-de-France, Martinique's capital, is the Savane, a large grassy expanse lined with palm trees: the perfect place for a football game. In the 1920s and 1930s it was overrun with players. The "vast lawns" of the park, wrote one priest, were "abandoned to football associations" who "battled" there each evening. The games provided competition for the church, since many students skipped their religious education classes to watch them. Church officials did the only thing possible: they gave in, organizing their own athletic activities and teams to hold on to their students, helping to spread a new gospel in the process. "If you go just to the Savane on a Sunday morning or a Thursday morning or any afternoon," one man observed in

1935, "you'll see that there is not an inch of ground that isn't occupied by football players, big and small."[12]

Football clubs appeared more slowly in Guadeloupe. Starting in 1914 a priest organized popular football matches on the Champ d'Arbaud. The town soon boasted a few teams, one of which, the Diabolo club, sometimes marched through the town to a cadence set by the whistle of their team captain. In Pointe-à-Pitre matches at the seaside Place de la Victoire were important social events. Representatives from the island's leading teams, on the lookout for recruits, lined the field. Local officials and wealthy families gathered at one end, called "the alley of the aristocrats," while prominent Syrian and Lebanese merchants sat at the other. As football got more and more popular it outgrew the plazas, and teams found additional fields in town and around sugar factories on which to practice and play matches. By the end of the 1920s both Basse-Terre and Pointe-à-Pitre had several sports clubs, and by the early 1930s smaller towns had founded clubs, with names like Arsenal de Petit-Bourg. In 1929 Edouard Chartol founded an islandwide sports association that brought together these clubs and organized increasingly regular tournaments. Born in Guadeloupe, Chartol had left after World War I to study medicine in Paris. There, he later recalled, he "met many Antilleans who wanted to play football," and they decided to form a league for Antillean players, which he directed for several years. When he returned to Guadeloupe his "Antillean comrades" urged him to do something similar. The association he founded evolved and expanded steadily during the following decades, laying the foundation for the creation of the Ligue guadeloupéenne de football in 1952.[13]

Individuals and private associations drove the early institutionalization of the sport in the Antilles. That changed, however, thanks to a man named Félix Eboué, who was governor of Martinique and Guadeloupe in the 1930s and who used his power to fulfill his vision of sport as salvation. Eboué's story, a crucial part of the history of football in the French Caribbean, is also a remarkable illustration of the complexities and intricacies of French colonialism.

In the late eighteenth century a man named Eboué arrived in French Guiana on a slave ship from West Africa. His name was probably a form of the term "Ibo," which names an important group in the region. Family tradition held that he "came from a royal African lineage," and African cowrie shells said to have belonged to him were passed down from generation to generation. He died in 1848, the year slavery was abolished, and his children took his name as their family name. They left the plantations and eventually moved to the capital city of Cayenne. Eboué's great-grandson Félix was born there in 1884. A descendant of slaves born into a stratified colonial society, the boy would nevertheless make his way to the heights of the French colonial administration and one day govern a vast territory on the African continent.[14]

Eboué succeeded in school and won a scholarship to study in Bordeaux, where a small number of promising Antillean students were sent each year. He joined his high school rugby team, leaving a lasting impression on a classmate who sixty years later remembered him as a "handsome deep black athlete" playing with "finesse." Eboué read avidly about Africa and became fascinated with the fighting of the Boers against the British in South Africa. He grew a long beard in homage to the Afrikaner leader Paul Kruger, earning the nickname "Kru-Kru." He shared his interest in Africa with a student who had come to Bordeaux from Martinique, René Maran, who became a close friend.[15]

Like many Antillean students, Eboué decided to pursue a career in colonial administration. He attended the Ecole coloniale in Paris, where he studied the history of empire and sat through lectures propounding the inferiority of African languages and society. He took up two new habits, smoking and football, becoming a successful forward at Sporting Club Universitaire de France. After finishing his training at the Ecole coloniale in 1909, Eboué was sent to the French Congo, in the tropics of Central Africa. He served there with a few interruptions until 1931. He oversaw the extraction of rubber and later the cultivation of cotton, the ever unpopular taxation of residents, and the forced labor the French used to build roads. Eboué imprisoned those who resisted and cultivated relationships with cooperative local leaders to suppress local rebellions. On one military mission he was nearly killed by an assassin who had orders to kill the "black whiteman" who was hated by many in the region.[16]

Eboué was a lover of good food and kept a stock of pâté de foie gras. At one point during a district tour he "savored a bottle of champagne kept cold in a small stream." Newly married and returning to Oubangui-Chari in 1923, he and his wife made the eighteen-day journey to his station in two large canoes, one of them carrying his wife's piano. In 1925 the French writer André Gide, on a tour through the area, stopped by the Eboués' house, and Félix killed a pig in order to make *boudin noir,* a blood sausage beloved in the Caribbean. "Endless meal at the house of Mr. Eboué," Gide wrote about the evening, though he described his host as a "remarkable and friendly man." During his time in the colony Eboué was also likely able to maintain his passion for football. By the 1920s the sport was being played in the roads in and around the colonial capital of Brazzaville. Just before visiting Eboué, Gide stopped in the tiny outpost of Foroumbala. There they watched the children in the school doing gymnastics exercises. After that, in a shaded plaza nearby, Gide and his companions joined in a "very joyous" football match the children played, using an orange as a ball.[17]

Eboué's friend René Maran also served in the colonial administration in Africa, and what he saw prompted him to harshly criticize the injustices of colonial rule in a 1921 novel, *Batouala*. "Civilization, civilization, pride of the Europeans and charnel-house of the innocents," he famously wrote. "You have built your kingdom on corpses. . . . You are not a torch, you are a conflagration." But Eboué always remained publicly loyal to the French state he served, intently pursuing advancement within the system. He believed French colonialism could help Africa's economic progress, and along with several other colonial administrators of the time he argued for an approach that respected and protected culture and forms of authority within Africa and worked cooperatively with local elites. He produced ethnographic studies, examining African languages and music.[18]

Eboué confronted the hostility of some whites in the colonial administration, but he had a powerful ally, Blaise Diagne. In 1931, when Diagne became undersecretary of the colonies, he used his authority to secure Eboué a plum position in Martinique. When, a few months after his arrival, the governor of the island was called away, Diagne and others lobbied successfully to have Eboué named interim governor. A pleased René Maran wrote to Eboué that the promotion represented "a new victory for our race." The appointment made news in the United States, where Howard University professor Mercer Cook wrote an article about Eboué for *Opportunity* magazine. Many Martinicans were also delighted to have a black man in such a prominent position; almost all administrators and many teachers and other civil servants in the colony were white. Eboué's time as interim governor was short, but he left his mark on the sporting culture of the island. He secured state funding for the construction of a stadium, the first in Martinique, and an athletics center in Fort-de-France. At the opening of the building Eboué was celebrated as a "protector" and "counselor" who had helped develop sports in Martinique, as well as a "comrade" who, himself an "old champion," faithfully attended football games on the island.[19]

Eboué was passed over for the position of permanent governor in Martinique and was instead sent to be acting governor in the French colony of Soudan. After the 1936 election of the left-leaning Popular Front government, he was appointed interim governor of Guadeloupe. There, as a representative of the new government, he inaugurated a minor social revolution. A decades-old French law reducing the workday to eight hours had never been applied in the Caribbean, where cane workers continued to work from sunup to sundown. Eboué decreased the length of the workday and instituted paid vacations for all workers. One commentator worried about the disorder this would cause, fearing that the workers would escape one form of master for another, flocking to bars, "where alcohol and debauchery are sovereign masters."[20]

Eboué had a solution: sports. Leisure time was a right, he believed, but it had to be channeled into activities that sustained individual and social progress. Popular Front policies sought to expand access to sports and leisure activities for the entire French population, and Eboué saw sports as a way to develop "a spirit of cooperation, fair play and teamwork among Antilleans" within a divided and hierarchical society. To Eboué sports were a model for life. In a speech called "Play the Game" at a prize ceremony for high school students at the Lycée Carnot in 1937, Eboué enjoined, "Playing the game means respecting our national values, loving them, serving them with passion, with intelligence, living and dying for them." Playing the game also was a way to "repudiate prejudice": "In the end playing the game means deserving your liberation, and demonstrating the purity, the sanctity, of your spirit."[21]

During his time as interim governor he worked hard to improve the infrastructure for sports on the island. Living in Basse-Terre he came to know the leaders of a local team, Le Cygne Noir (Black Swan), named by its founders after a popular brand of shoe polish, and granted them land in the town to build a headquarters with a small stadium; he even found free building materials for them. He created a special agency in the local government focused on physical education. He oversaw the construction of a series of new sports facilities, including two large stadiums, the first to be built in Guadeloupe, and signed a lease granting the use of the stadium to a local federation of four teams known as the Union sportive de la Basse-Terre.[22]

Not surprisingly, athletes and managers of local clubs adulated Eboué. They liked his supportive policies, and they liked the fact that he exercised in the gardens of the governor's palace in full view of passersby. When he was replaced with a white governor in 1938 they organized a farewell ceremony at the partially finished stadium in Basse-Terre. "It is with deepest consternation that all true athletes of Guadeloupe heard the news of your sudden departure," a speaker declared. The "athletic youth" of the island "owed everything" to Eboué, who had taught them to "commune in a common spirit: that of the good, of the beautiful, of the truth that we gain from practicing sport." The speaker promised that the memory of what Eboué had achieved would be kept alive because those he had helped would make sure that the stadium would henceforth be called the Stade Félix Eboué.[23]

Eboué's regretted departure from Guadeloupe enabled him to carry out the action for which he would become legendary in France. He was serving as the governor of the isolated colony of Chad in 1939 when Germany began its stunningly rapid and successful invasion of France. According to the historian Marc Bloch, an eyewitness to what he called the "strange defeat," the onslaught made the French feel like Africans. The "ruling idea" of the Germans was "speed," and the French were completely outmaneuvered, having failed to understand "the quickened rhythm of the time." It was as though the "two opposed forces" were from two different periods of "human history," as if the advanced Germans had colonized a backward French nation: "We interpreted war in terms of the assagai [spear] *versus* rifle made familiar to us by long years of colonial expansion. But this time it was we who were cast for the role of the savage!"[24]

The French surrendered, negotiating a deal by which they retained autonomy in some parts of the country while ceding other parts to the direct control of the Germans. The new French government established itself at Vichy, the town that gave its name to the collaborationist regime. In June 1940 a young officer named Charles de Gaulle, who had escaped to England, issued a radio call denouncing the Vichy regime and declaring that the true government of France was in exile. France had been defeated, he declared, but was "not alone." In addition to her British allies, she had "a vast empire behind her."[25]

But for all his powerful rhetoric, de Gaulle was the commander of an office in London and little more. He sent envoys to French colonies, hoping they would rally to his Free French movement. Though the Vichy regime claimed to govern all the territories of the French Empire, it had no direct control over them. Counting on support from nearby British colonies, colonial administrators could easily rally to de Gaulle. In fact, however, a large majority of colonial administrators and French settlers either tacitly or openly welcomed the Vichy regime, which they correctly realized would strengthen their position and turn back some of the colonial reforms of the previous decade.[26]

The major exception was Félix Eboué, who in Chad greeted de Gaulle's envoys warmly, arguing publicly that the colony should rally to Free France. His support for de Gaulle was decisive, and soon the colonial administrations in all of French Equatorial Africa, as well as Cameroon, rallied to the Free French movement. Eboué's actions transformed the movement from "a dispirited group of people gathered in London" to a project with a home in a "vast, strategically located territory" in Africa that included a population of more than seven million people. Eboué, announced de Gaulle, had "shown the path of duty" and "given the signal of recovery to the whole French empire." In thanks, he promoted Eboué to the powerful position of governor-general of French Equatorial Africa.[27]

In 1943 Eboué presided over the Brazzaville Conference, which was meant to determine the postwar direction of French colonial policy. He proposed a series of reforms, arguing that elite Africans be granted more political rights and local control, as well as being encouraged to form "literary, discussion and sporting societies." The Brazzaville Conference helped lay the foundation for colonial reforms put in place at the end of World War II, which granted more freedom to colonial subjects to organize locally. Writing in 1950, Jean-Hilaire Aubume, a protégé of Eboué, argued that the Brazzaville Conference could be "considered a real Declaration of the Rights of African Man," which, though "timid and incomplete," was "rich in possibilities." Though the reforms were in fact quite limited and have been judged harshly by historians, they created an important opening. Some of the new organizations created in the wake of the reforms morphed into early political parties, which along with trade unions drove the West and Central African anticolonial movements of the 1950s and 1960s. As he had in the Caribbean, Eboué also left his mark on the sporting world in Africa. The night before the conference began de Gaulle and the other representatives watched football matches played by both African and European teams in a new stadium named after Eboué. Throughout the coming decades that saw rising anticolonial activism and, in 1960, the independence of Cameroon, the stadium remained a focal point for sporting and social life in Brazzaville, hosting football matches between local teams. To this day the stadium carries Eboué's name.[28]

In the French Caribbean the Vichy regime embodied not only cooperation with Nazi Germany but also a reversal of decades of hard-won political advancement on the part of the black population. Many prominent local leaders on the island argued in favor of joining de Gaulle, but the French colonial officials instead carried out the application of Maréchal Pétain's National Revolution with remarkable fervor. They deported, imprisoned, or tortured leaders who supported de Gaulle. They censored the press, eliminated democratic institutions, and replaced many black mayors with white ones drawn from the island's wealthy elite. They refused a plan to ship Jews from metropolitan France to the Caribbean, shutting down one of the few routes out of Europe for French Jews. They also carefully regulated everyday life: meetings of more than five people were outlawed, cafés and bars carefully watched. And, even though the Vichy regime was deeply invested in promulgating physical education and provided funding for football clubs in both Guadeloupe and Martinique, they were suspicious of the opportunities for discussion and gathering represented by sports events. In February 1941 the governor of Guadeloupe ordered a greater police presence at all sports events on the island, and in December the governor of Martinique banned sports clubs from using the Savane in Fort-de-France for training and games, eliminating what had become a cherished and popular pastime in the town.[29]

Many Antilleans were inspired by Eboué's rallying to Free France. About four thousand young men, among them the future anticolonial activist and philosopher Frantz Fanon, left Martinique and Guadeloupe by boat to escape to British Dominica, where they joined the Free French forces, going on to fight in campaigns in Africa and Europe. They joined the resistance "in much greater numbers, proportionally, than [those] in the metropole," though after the war they were not admitted into veterans' organizations, which feared that they would put their war-time service to "anti-French" political uses. Within Martinique and Guadeloupe the power of the Vichy regime was such that resistance mostly took very subtle forms, at least at first. Aimé Césaire, his wife, Suzanne, and other Martinican writers famously contested Vichy authority by publishing subversive poems in a surrealist language that befuddled censors. In Guadeloupe the government had to explicitly ban drivers from beeping out "Victory" in Morse code while driving through the streets. Some crafty activists organized a public auction; among the objects for sale were a portrait of Maréchal Pétain, the leader of the Vichy regime, and a puffer fish. "Bidders haggled frantically over the fish, raising the price disproportionally, while the marshal's picture fetched a pittance," broadcasting a "deliberate denigration of the icon" of the Vichy regime.[30]

In March 1943 the Vichy governor in French Guiana was overthrown and expelled from the colony by supporters of the Free French movement. Several of Eboué's relatives who had been imprisoned by the Vichy government—

one of them at the infamous island prison of Devil's Island—were released. The uprising there also inspired activists in Guadeloupe and Martinique. On 30 April 1943 a group of men in the town of Port-Louis, a sugar-growing region in the north of Grande-Terre island, cut the local telephone lines and then stormed an isolated police station with machetes and sticks. It was the first act of open rebellion against the regime, and news of it spread across the island.[31]

A few days later a football match took place in Basse-Terre between two prominent clubs, Racing Club and Le Cygne Noir. After the game supporters of the Cygne Noir team marched into the center of town to celebrate their victory. The column of football supporters was chanting "Vive le goal! Vive le goal!" as they marched, using the English word common in Antillean football. Then, with a tiny change in pronunciation, they transformed their celebration into a protest. "Vive de Gaulle! Vive de Gaulle!" the crowd began chanting, as they joined a group already gathered in front of the governor's mansion. Police fired into the crowd, killing a seventeen-year-old Cygne Noir fan named Serge Balguy and severely wounding several others, including the head of the Racing Club, whose leg was hit by a bullet and had to be amputated. The incident enraged residents, who gathered in protest and mourning on 5 May in the Basse-Terre stadium and later constructed a monument to Balguy at the site where he was killed, declaring that he "died for Liberty." A few weeks later an uprising took place in Martinique, and after police and sailors refused to suppress it U.S. envoys stepped in, arranging a deal in which the Vichy governors of both Martinique and Guadeloupe were able to leave the islands safely. Both islands rallied to de Gaulle in July 1943.[32]

In Africa Eboué was relieved at the news of the uprisings in Guadeloupe and Martinique. Soon afterward, however, he fell ill and died during an official journey to Egypt. In July 1944 a group of Antilleans in Morocco formed the Club Félix Eboué, whose goal was to celebrate the man's achievements and to push for the political assimilation and equality of the overseas territories. Free France, they and other activists recalled, had found its first significant home in Africa, and the Antilles had demonstrated their patriotism by supporting de Gaulle. In return they deserved full inclusion and citizenship rights. Antilleans also pushed for official recognition of Eboué's place in the liberation of France, requesting that his bones be transferred from his grave in Egypt to the Panthéon, the temple of French heroes in Paris. In 1949 Eboué became the first black man entombed in the monument. His name was given to roads, plazas, and buildings in many left-leaning towns and cities in metropolitan France, as well as throughout the French Caribbean. A statue of him watches over the main plaza in Cayenne. But the most visited monuments to Eboué have surely been the football stadiums named in his honor. One of these was in Asnières in the *banlieue* of Paris, where he owned a house. Another was the Basse-Terre stadium he started building during his time in Guadeloupe, where crowds packed in to watch the increasingly popular sport of football. Indeed it was in the Stade Félix Eboué that, in 1945, the local sports federation organized a large celebration commemorating both Bastille Day, France's national holiday, and the liberation of Guadeloupe from Vichy two years earlier. The two-day event involved a series of parades and sports competitions, culminating in a match of local football players divided into two teams: married men and bachelors. The event had another goal: to honor Eboué's vision of a thriving and well-supported sports culture on the island. The money raised at the event was used for necessary repairs at the Eboué stadium, including repairing the degraded turf on the football field.[33]

The end of World War II marked a turning point in the history of the French Caribbean. In 1946 Guadeloupe, Martinique, and French Guiana became full departments of France, and their populations gained all the juridical and political rights of other French citizens, full representation in the national assembly, and a greater say in local governance. Most Antilleans supported the change and hoped that the French state would invest in the islands, addressing health problems, improving education, and expanding the economy. When, in 1948, Antillean leaders commemorated the hundredth anniversary of the abolition of slavery, they pointed to departmentalization as the fulfillment of the deferred promise of emancipation.

Even as they celebrated their link with France, however, Antillean leaders also asserted their connection to the Caribbean. Part of the 1548 commemoration was a football competition called the Trophée Caraïbe, which brought together teams from throughout the Caribbean, including Haiti and Trinidad. Although Eboué had organized sports competitions between Guadeloupe and Martinique when he was governor, this was the first international sports competition to take place on the islands. Propelled by their home-team advantage, Martinique and Guadeloupe made it to the final, which they played in Guadeloupe in front of five thousand spectators, among them high-ranking officials. Journalists and trainers welcomed the event as an opportunity to showcase Antillean athletes. Guadeloupe won, and one journalist hoped that the island's success would make it renowned for football, just as Senegal was thanks to Raoul Diagne and as Morocco was thanks to Larbi Ben Barek.[34]

Antilleans lobbied for the creation of larger competitions in which they could showcase local talent. In 1945 a group calling themselves the Comité Félix Eboué proposed a biannual sports competition during which "the best athletes of our overseas territories" would compete in Paris against one another and "their comrades from the metropole." In 1947 another group proposed a national event modeled on the Olympics that would bring together all the territories of the newly formed French Union, which after the war had brought together the colonies in Africa and Asia within an altered system of imperial governance. The first such games, named in honor of Eboué, were planned for 1947. Excitement brewed over the selection of athletes from Guadeloupe and Martinique for the tournament. When his selection was announced, one athlete got a visit from his father, whom he had never known. The man offered his son a new suit to wear on his journey to France.[35]

As the athletes prepared to leave the islands, they received stunning news: the games had been canceled. It was one of a series of disappointments. Antilleans hoped that, with departmentalization, they would receive state support to upgrade the stadiums that Félix Eboué had built, which were falling apart. But although one new stadium was built, the old ones remained nearly unusable. The paucity of state funding, combined with the cancellation of the Eboué games, was taken by many as a lack of recognition and respect. Then in 1952 the French government agreed to fund the journey of a team of football players from Guadeloupe across the Atlantic to play a series of professional teams. An "all-star" team was formed with the best athletes drawn from Guadeloupean clubs, and when they arrived in France they were welcomed enthusiastically by Antillean students and professionals. A special train ran from Paris to Le Havre, where the Guadeloupe team played their first game, so that Antilleans from the capital could attend. In their final game at the Parc des Princes in Paris, a crowd of five thousand Antillean fans cheered on the team. "All of Guadeloupe was there," recalls one man.[36]

French journalists responded to the visit with supercilious, and at times openly racist commentary. They complimented the players for their "natural" abilities and their improvisation—they were, one wrote, "nimble, spontaneous, naturally fast and individualist"—but declared that they lacked discipline and cohesion. "Our good blacks lose their head," one journalist wrote, "when, having arrived at a good distance from the opponent's goal, they keep dribbling flashily instead of taking advantage of an opportunity when it presents itself." Writing in *France Football*, one journalist wrote nastily, "The Guadeloupeans, according to all predictions, won't be lynched. . . . But in order to get back to Pointe-à-Pitre, they'll probably have to get jobs as coal-men or cooks on a boat. That will teach them to stop believing in Santa Claus." Guadeloupean newspapers fumed at the racist insult.[37]

Such commentary was part of a well-established tradition of belittling the achievements of black athletes. In the 1950s and 1960s African and Caribbean football players were often praised and criticized in the same breath for being shaped simultaneously by "gift and immaturity." European commentators considered them skillful and talented as individual players but weak tactically, suggesting that their strength lay in their physical skills rather than in their intellect. Because broader racial stereotypes often depended on the idea that Africans and people of African descent were closer to nature, less in control of their bodies, sexually promiscuous, and often animalistic, the idea that their success in sports was a result of "natural" or "innate" qualities rather than intelligence, discipline, or hard work helped to limit the meaning of that success. African players "were considered, almost unfailingly, as instinctive players. They played the game but easily gave up. They were nice to watch but not really efficient. Workers with little skill, they were unsuited to tactical schemes." Such stereotypes have been remarkably resilient. In 2008 Gennaro Gattuso, a well-known Italian defender who played on the country's national team, claimed that although the French national team was very strong, France's professional teams were surprisingly weak compared to their Italian counterparts: "It's very strange. All you have is these big blacks, physical beasts. Seriously: real beasts. But tactically, it's so bad, it's unbelievable!"[38]

Such racialized representations of black football players never stopped coaches from recruiting them. In 1952, for instance, three of the Guadeloupeans who toured in France were offered contracts on French professional teams. Though two of these players soon returned home, one stayed on, playing for Bordeaux. They were among the first Antilleans who found their way onto French professional teams, but others soon followed, such as the Martinican Camille Ninel, who played for Olympique Lyonnais from 1950 to 1960. Such examples inspired others to try their luck; in 1961 one young player from Guadeloupe took advantage of his club team's journey to metropolitan France to stay there and try to make it onto a professional team. In 1964, after a hurricane devastated Guadeloupe, Raoul-Georges Nicolo, a prominent engineer from the island working in metropolitan France, wrote to the president of the French Football Federation proposing that a fund-raising match be held to help the island. Guadeloupe, he noted, was "one of the ancient regions of FRANCE," having been "French since 1635." He proposed that a French team—he suggested the "B" team of the French army—play an "Equipe Antillaise" comprised of seventeen players from French clubs, though it seems that the proposal was not accepted. In the 1970s, when Marius Trésor was playing in France, he and other Antillean footballers formed a team and traveled to Guadeloupe and Martinique to play some games, where they received a "fabulous welcome."[39]

By the 1950s Guadeloupe had thirty-four football clubs and Martinique had twenty-eight organized into autonomous island federations. As part of the ongoing project of institutional assimilation of the Caribbean departments, the local football federations joined the French Football Federation in the early 1950s. While Antillean clubs adapted to F.F.F. guidelines, though, they felt they gained little in return. Indeed the F.F.F. excluded them from the national football championship, the French Cup. They were far from metropolitan France, and the F.F.F. decided that incorporating them into the competition would be too expensive and complicated.[40]

By the early 1960s, however, as decolonization swept Africa and pro-independence activism expanded in the Antilles, the French government started to pay closer attention to sports in the Antilles. Maurice Herzog, appointed to oversee the new Ministry of Youth and Sports in 1958, responded to long-standing requests from Antillean leaders to incorporate their teams into the French Cup. Though the F.F.F. opposed the project, the French government, well aware of the symbolic importance of sports in the Antilles, successfully pressured the organization, and teams from the region were finally included in the 1961–62 French Cup competition season. There was one slot reserved for a team from the Antilles, and a well-attended yearly tournament pitted clubs from Guadeloupe and Martinique (and, starting in 1963, French Guiana) against each other to decide who would have the honor of representing the region. Within a few years the department of Réunion (in the Indian Ocean) and the French territories in the Pacific (New Caledonia and Polynesia) were also included.[41]

Writing in 1970 in *France Football*, one journalist celebrated this inclusion for making it clear that the "nation's sovereignty" spread far beyond the European continent. He described the "beautiful adventure" of the French Cup: "French people from all horizons cross the oceans, sometimes in one direction, sometimes in another, in order to meet with other French people.... [This allows] our brothers from these far-off shores ... [to] affirm and concretize their belonging to the great family of French football." Although the participation of overseas football clubs was "constantly put in question," it would be a mistake to exclude them. Without their participation, the competition "would not truly be a French Cup."[42]

A few years earlier, in 1967, the F.F.F. had canceled the participation of the Caribbean teams for a season. They claimed, as they had for decades, that the expense and logistical difficulties involved in including teams from the Antilles in the French Cup competition were simply too great. The assembly of Martinique's football league "expressed its stupor and its profound emotion" at the decision. The incorporation of Antillean teams into the French Cup, it declared, had "strengthened the links of fraternity that united the French of the Departments of the Americas with those of the metropole." Their sudden "eviction" in 1967—after sixteen teams in Martinique had agreed to participate in the tournament—had spread "consternation" throughout the "sports community" of the department. More important, the teams' exclusion risked "being seen as an act of bullying by the young people of the Department." The worried police chief of Guadeloupe, questioned by many on the island about the decision, wrote to the minister of youth and sports to draw his attention to "the serious consequences provoked by the refusal to pay for the travel of the local team selected for the French Cup to the metropole." The decision was "considered by the youth" of Guadeloupe to be "unjustly discriminatory."[43]

The police chief had good reason to worry about how Guadeloupeans would respond. Just a few months earlier, in May 1967, several days of rioting broke out in Basse-Terre after a dog owned by a white merchant attacked a black artisan. Soon afterward, in Pointe-à-Pitre, police fired into a demonstration of striking workers. (It is still not known precisely how many were killed; a common estimate is eighty-seven, though officials admitted only seven deaths. Recently the event became the subject of public commemoration and intense debate.) In such an atmosphere the exclusion of the football teams was a dangerous provocation. Though the Antillean teams were not part of the 1967–68 competition, the F.F.F. assured the participation of teams the next year.[44]

Throughout the 1960s football matches in the Antilles were intense events, sometimes charged with racial tension. The old stadiums were almost always overcrowded; although they were built to hold two thousand to three thousand spectators, as many as twelve thousand fans often squeezed in and were difficult to control. Pitch invasions were common; they were, "if not a ritual, certainly a solidly anchored habit." The Stade Félix Eboué in Basse-Terre was notoriously chaotic. One police report described the fans of the town as "particularly anarchic and chauvinistic," and another complained that the stadium desperately needed fences to prevent spectators from going onto the pitch. Increasing numbers of police were assigned to patrol games, and officials called on help from the C.R.S. (*Compagnies républicaine de sécurite,* France's elite riot-control unit). But the presence of such forces only made things worse. Unlike the local police, which included many Antilleans, the C.R.S. and the Gendarmerie (the national police force) were made up almost entirely of whites from the metropole; their interventions during games inevitably took on a racial cast at a time when nationalist sentiments and activism were a powerful force on the islands. "The presence of these police forces turned the stadium into a site of symbolic confrontation," writes one historian. "Sport became a space of liberty invaded by the exercise of repression."[45]

By the late 1960s activist groups in Guadeloupe and Martinique were advocating for independence, arguing that departmentalization had just led to further subjugation and economic decline and that Antilleans had a unique culture that powerfully differentiated them from the population of the French metropole. Although pro-independence political groups were never able to gain an electoral majority in the Antilles, they contributed to an important shift in the region's cultural life and in the way Antilleans viewed themselves as both part of France and distinct within it. Athletics became a major vehicle for the performance and assertion of that distinctiveness. Activists in the French Caribbean were inspired by the Black Panthers, and more broadly by the ideas of Black Power emanating from the United States in the late 1960s. In 1968, a year after riots shook Guadeloupe, many were moved by what would become the iconic image of that year's Olympic competition in Mexico: the fists raised in protest by the victorious African American runners John Carlos and Tommie Smith as they received their medals. The gesture helped confirm the sense that sports was a vehicle for the "affirmation of a culture" and a way to confront metropolitan France while asserting a connection with other colonized and oppressed peoples.[46]

In 1969 local sports teams organized a youth football tournament in Guadeloupe, calling it the Coupe Delgrès. It was named after a military officer, Louis Delgrès, a contemporary of the legendary Haitian general Toussaint

Louverture. In 1802 Delgrès led an uprising against French troops sent to the island to reestablish slavery there. Unable to defeat the French, Delgrès refused to surrender, and he and his followers blew themselves up on a plantation, putting into practice their promise to "Live Free or Die!" The naming of a football competition after Delgrès was part of a larger movement in which his memory was increasingly mobilized as a symbol of the violence of French rule and of the need for independence. The football team that represented Guadeloupe in regional competitions, meanwhile, also became a focus for nationalist hopes. In 1971 the team's coaches and managers talked forcefully of the need to succeed in order to showcase the power of the "Guadeloupean personality." They referred to the team itself as a "national team." In one strident speech the coach of the Guadeloupean youth team told his players that they bore great responsibility, as they represented "their country." "It is inadmissible for the reputation of a country," he admonished, "to be tarnished by the poor showing of its national team."[47]

The rise of nationalism in the French Caribbean was both a part of and a reaction to the decolonization of much of the rest of the French Empire in the 1960s. But it was precisely that process that finally opened the doors for a fuller inclusion of Antilleans into French athletics. Many African athletes worked professionally in France during the late 1950s and early 1960s, but most of those represented their newly independent home country in international competition. Antillean athletes, however, were French citizens, and if they wanted to play for a nation they had only one choice: France. Recruiters for France's national teams increasingly began to look to the Antilles, where they found a series of talented runners and football players.[48]

Some athletes sought to simultaneously represent their island and France. Roger Bambuck from Guadeloupe, a star runner who electrified the French Caribbean with his successes in the 1960s, ran in a race in Paris with the word *Guadeloupe* written on his jersey. At the 1972 Olympics another track-and-field athlete from Guadeloupe—who had been in Mexico in 1968 and watched Smith and Carlos raise their fists and was influenced by pro-independence ideas—pinned onto his French uniform a piece of green cloth taken from the uniform of Guadeloupe that he wore in regional competitions. These athletes condensed the broader complexities and contradictions of being French and Caribbean at the same time. As they competed *for* France, they powerfully asserted that Antilleans were a part of the French nation. But when they won, particularly against other French athletes, they also inspired pride among Antilleans, who felt vindicated by their victory *over* other parts of France. The success of this generation of Antillean athletes laid the foundation for a massive expansion in track and field in the region, which gave France a series of remarkable runners during the 1980s and 1990s. The French women's relay team at the 1986 Los Angeles Olympics was made up of two Guadeloupeans and two Martinicans, and in 1992 the Guadeloupean Marie-José Pérec won the 400-meter gold medal, the first French woman to do so since 1968. For Guadeloupeans and Martinicans these victories represented a kind of "revenge" and a "much delayed recognition" of their place within the French nation. At the same time, the victories were celebrated as those of Antillean individuals and of the Antillean community as much as of France. The political importance of athletic success was confirmed when, in 1988, the former track star Roger Bambuck was named minister of youth and sports, becoming the first Antillean to hold such a high-ranking position in the French government since World War II.[49]

Even as Antilleans reached the pinnacle of athletic success as representatives of France, many in the region argued that it was more important for Guadeloupe and Martinique to use athletics to make connections with their Caribbean neighbors. Already in the 1950s some in Martinique had tried to resist the incorporation of their leagues into the F.F.F., advocating instead the creation of a Caribbean-based football organization. Throughout the 1960s and 1970s athletes from Guadeloupe and Martinique participated in regional Caribbean sporting events and tournaments, and many continued to argue that this was a better course than seeking inclusion in French athletics. In 1980 a writer in Guadeloupe declared that the French Cup was an "Assimilation Cup." Just as Antilleans had aspired to full assimilation with France, he complained, Antillean football teams had aspired to inclusion in this national competition. In both cases their aspirations led only to frustration. "The French Cup," he argued, "is really nothing but a mystification." After decades of seeking inclusion in French sports, some leaders in the Antilles felt that they would never be fully accepted, and that seeking acceptance itself was a sign of deep cultural alienation. In the 1980s Alfred Marie-Jeanne, a teacher, mayor, and director of a sports club in Martinique—who would become the most prominent nationalist leader in Martinique and today is a deputy in the French National Assembly—declared that his team would no longer participate in the French Cup. The decision was part of a series of public actions he took as he established himself as a political voice on the island.[50]

In the decades that followed the 1948 Trophée Caraïbe, Guadeloupe and Martinique occasionally took part in regional competitions, and Guadeloupe was involved in the 1951 formation of the Caribbean Football Association.

Though teams representing the islands played in some regional competitions over the years, they did not establish a long-term pattern of participation in such competitions. In 1983, however, leaders of the leagues in Guadeloupe and Martinique began attending meetings of CONCACAF, the regional football federation for the nations of the Caribbean, Central America, and North America, and by the early 1990s they were members of the federation. Their status in CONCACAF is complex; unlike the other teams in the confederation they are not members of F.I.F.A. and therefore do not compete in the World Cup qualifying games, which are the major activity of CONCACAF. To request membership in F.I.F.A., Guadeloupe and Martinique would not necessarily have to be independent nations; among F.I.F.A.'s members are not only Scotland and Wales, but also Palestine and the French territory of New Caledonia. But they would have to establish their *athletic* independence by separating their island leagues from the French Football Federation. Doing this, of course, would have major implications for both the Antilles and France itself, for it would mean that Antillean players would have to make the choice between playing for their island team and playing for France. And in a world in which Europe remains the core of the football industry, the separation of Antillean leagues from the F.F.F. could represent a professional disadvantage for Antillean players. In crafting a relationship with CONCACAF, however, Martinique and Guadeloupe have found an elegant solution: they can participate in the major regional competition, the Gold Cup, without giving up their connection to the F.F.F. Antillean teams have sometimes shone in the Gold Cup, becoming a source of pride for island residents. Teams from Martinique had some success in the 1990s, making it into the Gold Cup in 1993, 2002 (when they made it to the quarterfinals), and 2003. Guadeloupe also competed, though before 2006 it never made it into the Gold Cup tournament.[51]

In November 2005 journalists from the newspaper *France-Antilles* asked several Antillean footballers who had played on the French national team what they thought of the idea of forming a team to represent the entire French Antilles: Guadeloupe, Martinique, and French Guiana. Marius Trésor responded, "I never considered the possibility. . . . Representing France is a great honor and a real joy." Still, he admitted, if the Antilles did create their own team, "it would be pretty incredible! . . . It would strike hard." Trésor's former teammates Luc Sonor and Gérard Janvion were both pessimistic about the prospects for a successful Antillean team, though like Trésor they grew excited thinking about how good it could be. "We can dream about it but we'll never do it," lamented Sonor. "If you ask the guys to choose between a selection with Les Bleus and one with the Antilles, their choice will quickly be made." Choosing the Antilles, he suggested, would be particularly difficult because the players had all gotten their training and their opportunities in the metropole. "It's hard to imagine betraying those who believed in us. . . . It's true that it would be a great team, a thunderous team even." Janvion was similarly divided. "We'll never be able to because we're not independent," he declared. "But we have the players to do it," he added, at least if players who were of Antillean background but born in the metropole were included. "Otherwise we wouldn't have enough high-level players. . . . We'd definitely be better than teams like Jamaica or the U.S.," Janvion boasted, "and not far from the French team." "We've thought about it, but nothing more," said Jocelyn Angloma. "In our mind, it's France before everything else!" The player who was most enthusiastic about the idea was the youngest, Steve Marlet, born in 1974 in a *banlieue* outside Paris. "I would have no problem wearing the Antillean jersey," he announced, though he wondered if he could be part of the team given that he had been born in the metropole. "It's a project for the future," he added.[52]

Soon afterward Angloma decided to join the Guadeloupean team that would play in the Gold Cup in 2007. He helped recruit several players of Guadeloupean background, including one born in the metropole, who were on professional teams in France to come and play for the team. They made it into the Gold Cup competition and then surprised everyone by taking the competition by storm. They advanced to the semifinals, defeating Canada and Honduras in the process, before being eliminated by Mexico. The uniform for the Guadeloupean team is green and red, two colors Antilleans recognize as a reference to the green, red, and black flag of the nationalist movements in Martinique and Guadeloupe.

The French Caribbean teams probably have a bright future if some of the star players on the French team follow Angloma's path and one day play for their island. In 2006 Thierry Henry (who has scored more goals for the French team than any other player in its history) told a journalist in Martinique that he remained deeply connected to the Antilles. Although he had grown up in a *banlieue* of Paris, he had always "lived in the Antilles in [his] mind." His grandfather Teka died in 2000, and Henry dedicated his goals during that year's European Cup competition to him. "I played for the nation. But also for him," he said. "If there had been an Antillean national team, I would have been on that team. Just like someone of Senegalese background wants to play for his colors." Perhaps Henry will one day put on the green and red of the Guadeloupean team. If his former teammates join him, he could play up front, confident that Lilian Thuram and William Gallas had his back. Maybe they could convince Marius Trésor to quit his job in Bordeaux and coach the team of an island that, for a fleeting moment on the football field, sometimes becomes a nation.[53]

THREE

Crossings

"You ARE, GREAT TRÉSOR, our ebony and our gold," the French writer Patrick Demerin wrote in a tongue-in-cheek 1986 prayer for Marius Trésor. Demerin was seemingly unaware that for many Antilleans these words would call up powerful memories. Illegal slave traders sometimes referred to their human traffic as "ebony" and sometimes exchanged gold for people. For Demerin, though, Trésor was a literal treasure on the football field. "What do we have to worry about? / When our adversary attacks / Your foot always drags where it should." The prayer ended, like those written for other players, with a new form of "Hallelujah" based on the football chant "Allez les Bleus!" (Go Blues!): "Allélébleu."[1]

Demerin's prayer was heartfelt, for a few years earlier Trésor and his teammates seemed to finally bring France back from two decades of failure in international sports. After the generation of Kopa and Fontaine retired in the early 1960s, the French team became "a seriously sick patient, with little hope of recovery." France qualified for the 1966 World Cup in England but didn't do well in the competition and didn't manage to qualify for either the 1970 or 1974 World Cup. The losses in sports condensed and confirmed a broader malaise in the wake of decolonization and in the context of the economic difficulties of the 1970s. But in 1976 the French team hired a new trainer, Michel Hidalgo, and he got the French team into the World Cup in Argentina in 1978. They didn't make it into the second round, but Hidalgo qualified his team again in 1982 for the World Cup in Spain. Hidalgo was a relaxed and sympathetic coach. "It's not a war you are going into," he told his players before one game in 1980, speaking with a sense of proportion that was probably rare then, and is even rarer today. "It's just a football game.... As victors, you won't be heroes, and as losers you won't be pariahs."[2]

In 1976 Hidalgo brought a young player named Michel Platini onto the team. He was to become the best-known and most beloved French player of

FIGURE 6. Marius Trésor during the France-Austra game of the 1982 World Cup. Bob Thomas/Bob Thomas Sports Photography/Getty Images.

his generation, and he gained the admiration of Italians when he played at Juventus in the 1980s. Platini's career on the French national team stretched until 1987, during which he scored forty-one goals. He was famous, as Zidane would later be, for making goals from free kicks with brilliantly curving balls that confused and terrorized goalies. For much of his time on the team Platini was the captain, and he became its moral center as well. The grandson of an Italian immigrant, he led a team populated with players of Caribbean, Spanish, and North African backgrounds, including William Ayala, who was born in 1961 in Algiers and was from the Jewish community in the colony. There were also two star players born in Mali, José Touré and Jean Tigana.[3]

Tigana arrived in Marseille with his parents when he was three years old, in 1959, the same year Mali gained independence from France. He grew up with his nine siblings in a large housing project outside of Marseille. He was often insulted by his classmates, he recalls, who called him a "dirty little negro" or a "rotten Arab." He responded at first with his "little fists," but soon he found a way to take revenge: football. In the fields surrounding the project where he

FIGURE 7. Michel Platini (left) celebrates a goal alongside William Ayala during the 1984 European Cup. © Jean-Yves Ruszniewski/TempSport/Corbis.

lived, later covered over by "sinister buildings" that expanded like "enzymes that eat everything in their way," he and his friends played "unending games with no half-time." Victories were "priceless," giving him the feeling that he had "taken revenge on life." Like his father, Tigana worked at the post office. He joined the post office football team, getting his first taste of uniforms and regulation fields. His family couldn't afford tickets to watch the Olympique de Marseille play, but Tigana figured out a strategy for sneaking in: temporary adoption. He stood at the entrance, then grabbed "the hand of a man who could be [his] father" and walked in without a ticket.[4]

The coach of a local youth team noticed Tigana on the post office team and recruited him. Soon afterward the managers of the nearby Cannes professional team invited Tigana to play on their youth squad during a tournament in Portugal. He was offered his first professional contract by the team of Toulon, near Marseille, before being recruited to play at the Olympique Lyonnais with a young coach named Aimé Jacquet, who would coach the French national team in the 1990s. Though small and thin, he could accelerate and spin across the field beautifully. He could leap "like a goat" to escape a "violent charge," one journalist wrote, but he could tackle hard too. Like other black footballers of his generation, Tigana attracted his share of patronizing and racist comments. The noted sportswriter Jean-Philippe Rethacker wrote, "It is lucky for French football that a little bit of the Brazilian blood that comes from Africa courses through his veins." One journalist suggested that he was "born with a ball at his feet, like the majority of Africans." According to the celebrated sportscaster Thierry Roland, Tigana exuded the "nonchalance of people of his race, happy and surprised by everything that happens to him." After he retired Tigana challenged such stereotypes by becoming one of the first black professional coaches in France.[5]

With Platini, Trésor, Tigana, and other talented players on the team, Hidalgo managed to qualify France for the 1982 World Cup in Seville. The team made it into a semifinal match with Germany. Half the population of France watched, "entranced by the interminable drama," and "a parliamentary debate was suspended to allow the *députés* to watch." The game also drew a larger audience of women than had previous tournaments. "All my female friends who hated football watched," one journalist later remembered, because the game went "beyond football" to become "something stronger."[6]

The game was tied at one at the end of ninety minutes. Then, minutes into overtime, Marius Trésor scored a goal off a free kick with a beautiful volley. Six minutes later Alain Giresse scored a second goal for France. Fans were ecstatic, and the team was too. With a two-goal lead, seeming for the moment to dominate the German team, the French were confident they would win. Too confident. The Germans, amazingly, came back, scoring two goals in quick succession and then holding on until the end of overtime.

As the French players lined up to take their penalty kicks, some Antilleans watching the game prayed that Trésor wouldn't be chosen to take one. They worried that if he missed and lost the game for France, the adulation he had earned could quickly turn ugly. To their relief, Trésor wasn't among those picked to shoot against Germany. What would have happened if he had been? Perhaps their fears would have been realized, or perhaps he would have made his kick and won for France. Instead, with one penalty missed by both the Germans and the French, it fell to Maxime Bossis to take the final kick. He missed, handing the game to the Germans. The nation was "plunged in a state of shock, drained by the injustice of it all." The French prime minister predicted that the match would live in France's collective memory for a long time.[7]

One moment in particular seared itself into French memory and, like so many moments in football, came retroactively to seem both decisive and utterly unfair. The French forward Patrick Battiston was charging toward the German goal. Harald Schumacker, the German goalie, ran toward him.

Battiston sent off a shot past Schumacker before the German could reach him. But instead of slowing down, Schumacker kept running, jumped in the air, and both kicked and elbowed Battiston in the head at full force. The French player collapsed on the ground, unconscious, his head twisted sideways, his left arm twitching. A horrified Gérard Janvion covered his face. Platini ran to Battiston, thinking his friend was dead. All eyes were on the referee, expecting an immediate red card and the expulsion of the German goalie. But he did nothing; no foul was called. Schumacker walked away, standing by the goal and bouncing the ball in his hand as the unconscious Battiston was taken off the field, accompanied by Platini. The game went on with Schumacker in goal and one of France's best players lying unconscious in the locker room. Had the brilliant German goalie been expelled or a penalty kick granted to the French team, fans imagined, the outcome of the game would almost certainly have been different. Schumacker is still vilified among French fans for his action on the field that day, to the point that his name is sometimes used as an insult. But the French fans ultimately got some relief. Having watched their hero, the grandson of an Italian immigrant, defeated by the Germans, they took solace a few days later when Italy defeated Germany in the final game. There was an "explosion of joy" in Paris, recalls Platini. "They descended by the thousands on the Champs-Elysées, shouting with a sympathetic and spontaneous fervor: 'I-ta-lia! I-ta-lia! I-ta-lia!' . . . And you won't get me to believe that all these one-night *tifosi* [Italian fans] were the sons of immigrants or waiters in pizzerias."[8]

A year before the World Cup the socialist François Mitterand won the presidency, inciting massive celebrations in the streets of Paris and hope for new, more tolerant policies regarding immigration as well as better housing and schooling for France's poor. One of his first actions was to declare that he would end the policy of expelling immigrants that had been put in place by the preceding administration. The decision outraged conservatives. France, one newspaper declared, was threatened by "young Arab" immigrants who had escaped expulsion from France: "[They will] steal our cars and rape our daughters." Such fears of immigration were being stoked by the increasingly popular far-right National Front party. But Mitterand's policy reversal was initially a relief for many immigrants, who had high hopes that the election heralded a decisive shift in policy. Such hopes ultimately would be disappointed, for Mitterand never fulfilled a campaign promise to extend the right to vote in local elections to certain immigrants, and in time his government resumed the expulsion of immigrants. The summer after the election, meanwhile, saw serious riots in *banlieue* regions outside Lyon, Marseille, and Paris, triggered in one case by the deportation of a young woman to Algeria and in others by violent incidents between youth and police. Young men, angered at their lack of opportunities and mistreatment by the police, developed a particularly theatrical and ultimately long-lived form of protest: burning cars. Most were stolen from wealthier, center-city areas and then driven to the *banlieue,* where they were set on fire. The alarm at these events propelled the creation of a set of far-reaching government programs aimed at addressing poverty and social marginalization in the *banlieues.*[9]

In this context some saw the football team as the symbol of a new kind of France, one that could embrace its diversity and profit from it. Patrick Demerin recalled joyfully a few years later how the "technicolor" French played against the completely "black and white" Germans in 1982 The team "brought with it a France" that stretched "from Dunkirk to Tamanrasset" (an oasis town in the Sahara desert in southern Algeria). The use of this phrase was striking, for it was a common way of describing the reach of the French Empire during the early twentieth century and was famously used in a speech by Charles de Gaulle in which he invited Algerians to consider remaining part of that empire. France's team, Demerin went on, looked like one of those all-star teams from "the rest of the world" put together for gala matches against a champion, with the bonus that they actually had the "cohesion" of a team and "friendship." It was "the anti–Front National team," he wrote, "like all French teams," which had been full of Kopas, Ben Bareks, and Mekloufis. "It raises the colors of France high, all the colors of France, it lights them up," he effused, listing the different colors of the players: the "copper" of Janvion, the "bistre" of Jean Tigana, and the "ebony" of Trésor." Like some of the enthusiastic writing about the French team in 1998, Demerin's text celebrated the racial egalitarianism and diversity of the players in a way that was both thrillingly evocative and curiously redolent of an older, imperial vision of France.[10]

Trésor and Janvion retired from the team after the 1982 World Cup, just a little too soon. In 1984 Platini led the French team to victory in the European Cup of Nations, securing the country's first major international title. The team returned to the World Cup in Mexico in 1986 with high hopes, defeating Italy and then Brazil in a grueling penalty-kick session. But in a semifinal game against Germany they lost once again. "Football is a simple game; 22 men chase a ball for 90 minutes and at the end, the Germans win," the English footballer Gary Lineker quipped after his team suffered a similar defeat in the 1990 World Cup. The year 1986 marked the beginning of another dark period for French football: the national team didn't qualify for the 1990 or 1994 World Cup. The team seemed to be waiting for a new generation of players, and a new leader.

In 1986 a journalist writing in *L'Equipe* predicted that, as the earlier generations of French football stars had emerged from the waves of Polish and Italian immigrants, the next generation would come from among the North Africans, who had become the largest immigrant group in France. "Tomorrow, the Beurs?" he wondered. The footballer Nourredine Kourichi, who was born in France to Algerian parents and played on the Algerian team in the early 1980s, prophesied the arrival of a great North African player, "born in France, who would be recognized by everyone. An Algerian Kopa or Platini." Within a decade such a player had arrived: Zinedine Zidane, who, like Tigana, grew up in the *banlieue* of Marseille and, like Kopa and Platini, would become the star and the cement of the French team of the 1990s. But if Zidane succeeded it was also because, like Platini, he worked with a solid defense; the new star of the French team would have his goal protected by a defense held together by a brilliant Guadeloupean player named Lilian Thuram, who, when one game demanded it of him, also scored goals.[11]

Lilian Thuram was born on 1 January 1972 in Anse-Bertrand, Guadeloupe. The timing of his arrival earned him his first appearance in the newspaper. He was the first baby born in 1972 in Guadeloupe, and he and his mother, Mariana, earned a front-page photograph in *France-Antilles*. He was a small and sickly baby. "You could have fit Lilian in a shoebox," his mother liked to tease her son when he was older. His size, Thuram later wrote, was the result of his mother's "difficult life." During the last few months of her pregnancy, she continued to work every day, gathering and tying together stalks of sugar cane on the plantations several kilometers from Anse-Bertrand (sometimes accompanied by her eldest son), and then traveling to Pointe-à-Pitre to make a bit more money by cleaning houses. It was an old story: for centuries, going back to the days of slavery, women in the Antilles spent their pregnancies working in cane fields.[12]

Anse-Bertrand is a small town on the ocean at the northern tip of Grande-Terre, one of Guadeloupe's two connected islands. It is a dry region, but to the south rich and productive sugar plantations have existed since the seventeenth century. Throughout the twentieth century workers and small farmers struggled over prices for sugar cane against the company that owned the large cane-processing plant in the region. But by the 1970s, when Thuram was growing up, the sugar economy was in steep decline. Anse-Bertrand is also known for its powerful tradition of *gwo-ka* music, a style of drumming and dance in which the dancer often drives and commands the music, challenging the drummers to keep up. As Thuram writes, the people of Anse-Bertrand consider themselves "ardent defenders of tradition."[13]

"There was a feeling of freedom," he recalls of his childhood in Anse-Bertrand. "It was paradise. . . . It was a little village where everyone respected each other." Unlike most of his friends, he didn't swim well and avoided the water. His mother feared that her children might drown and forbade them to go into the ocean alone. She had been raised by her father, a fisherman named Apollo. Such fishermen navigated the unruly Atlantic in small boats, chasing after schools of fish, and they often disappeared into the ocean; Apollo had lost several of his companions over the years. If Thuram inherited a respect for the dangers of the ocean from his grandfather, he didn't inherit any of his skills; while his friends caught fish with improvised poles, Thuram's hook got caught in the rocks.[14]

Thuram's "domain," he recalls, was football. With his friends he played in empty lots or on the paved street in front of his house. "We took the ceremony of the sport quite seriously. We built goals out of pieces of wood we gathered in the forest, planted in a vacant lot. We invented jerseys." They played without shoes. Once in a while nature interrupted their games with one of the small earthquakes that occasionally shakes the island. They would wait it out and start playing again. "The games between neighborhoods stretched long into the night. It took all the authority of our mothers to get us to stop."[15]

Though he was constantly thinking about and playing football, Thuram, unlike many kids, didn't pretend he was a particular star player: with no T.V. in the house, he didn't know any of their names or anything about the world of professional sports: "I didn't even know that they paid people to play football, that it was a profession." Moved by the way the priest in the local church transformed bread and wine into body and blood during the Eucharist, Thuram instead dreamed of becoming a priest. The priest struck Thuram as the ultimate example of "generosity" for sharing the host with all those present.[16]

Thuram projects modesty and surprise about his accomplishments. In 2006, asked if he considered himself part of the history of football, he recounted how he once showed a young cousin a video that named the biggest stars in the game. After watching, the boy asked innocently, "Who's Maradona?" "Maradona!" recalled Thuram, surprised the boy had never heard of the Argentinian footballing legend. "I was doubled over laughing, and at the same time I was attracted by the purity of the commentary. History?" Luckily, he thought, there will always be a kid to ask "Who's Thuram?"[17]

Thuram had four brothers and sisters born of a series of fathers, and Mariana raised the five children by herself. Thuram's father was a baker in nearby Port-Louis, where he had another family. Making his rounds by truck to deliver his bread, he dropped some off as a form of child support. This was the only contact Thuram had with his father. The situation, Thuram writes, was "neither shocking nor troubling" to him. It was a family structure common among what he called "women of my mother's generation," though he imagines it generated a "stifled pain" that may have encouraged his mother in her eventual decision to leave the island.[18]

Mariana struggled to make ends meet, working two jobs and raising chickens and rabbits to eat and to sell. She sometimes opened up her empty wallet and showed it to her children so they would see there simply wasn't any money. In 1977 she managed to purchase a prefabricated wooden house for the family; twelve years later a hurricane carried it away. By then, however, Mariana and her children were far away, across the Atlantic, having joined a massive stream of migrants who left Guadeloupe and Martinique for metropolitan France in the 1960s and 1970s.

When Guadeloupe and Martinique became departments in 1946, political leaders and much of the islands' population hoped that France would develop and expand the local economy. The French bureaucracy provided employment for many people, along with education and health care, making Martinique and Guadeloupe (along with Puerto Rico) the wealthiest islands in the Caribbean today. But the economy stagnated and unemployment soared; today it remains at about 35 percent, roughly the same as in many of the *banlieue* regions of metropolitan France. Rather than seeking to expand the local economy the government offered another solution: mass migration to the French metropole. In 1963 they created the BUMIDOM (Office for the Development of Migration in the Overseas Territories), which for the next decade assisted Antilleans in migrating to France, finding them low-level civil service jobs in the post office or other agencies or in hospitals. Many more migrants left without the assistance of the BUMIDOM, using personal contacts with other Antilleans to find work in the metropole.

The movement was massive; an organization of Guadeloupean students estimated that in 1978 between 120,000 and 150,000 Guadeloupeans were living in the metropole. The group, which was agitating for independence from France, considered the BUMIDOM program a plot to destroy any hope of separation between Guadeloupe and France. "Emigration is a massive hemorrhage that is emptying our country," they complained. It sucked the youth who were capable of resisting "French imperialism" out of the island. Though the intent of the BUMIDOM was less conspiratorial and more prosaic, the students were right about its impact. Today separation between France and the Caribbean islands is nearly unimaginable. Almost a third of French citizens of Antillean ancestry live in metropolitan France, and the links between the Antilles and Paris are much tighter than those between the two islands and their Anglophone Caribbean neighbors. While jet planes full of tourists and Antilleans regularly fly back and forth to Paris, travel to St. Lucia, which you can see across the water from Martinique, is much less common. Almost all Antillean families are, at this point, transatlantic, with members frequently traveling back and forth.[19]

In 1980 Thuram's mother, fed up with her situation in Guadeloupe, decided to join the exodus for metropolitan France. Wanting to find a job and a place to live before she brought her children over with her, she left them behind in her house, with her oldest son in charge under the supervision of a nearby aunt. She sent packages home, including one containing a pair of athletic shorts and a shirt, both marked with the word *France*, which Thuram treasured. A year later she returned with enough money to move her family. In 1981 they left Anse-Bertrand to settle in the Parisian *banlieue* of Bois-Colombes. Thuram recalls the move as a joyous occasion. The family was dressed as though "for a wedding": "I still remember my blue suit, my striped shirt, and my beautiful bow-tie." The airport in Paris seemed "immense," and on the way into the city he was confused by the sight of many Eiffel towers, one after another, along the highway: "I had learned that there was only one of them." He was surprised when he learned that they were electrical towers. Their apartment was tiny, even compared to their small home in Guadeloupe, but a welcoming neighbor prepared them a dinner of couscous. He remembers, "Everything was beautiful. Guadeloupe was fading already. I discovered an unknown season, autumn."[20]

The Thuram family, like many other Antillean migrants, arrived in the *banlieue* just at the time when life there was getting worse and worse. They found that the situation in metropolitan France was more difficult than they had been led to expect. Antilleans, Thuram recalled in 1998, had an image of "an idyllic France" and thought that by migrating they would secure better jobs and better education for their children. Although many found jobs through the BUMIDOM in post offices and hospitals, the salaries were low, and it was difficult to live anywhere but in the poorer *banlieues* of Paris or other cities. The hip-hop group the Nèg' Marrons sings of the disappointment of migrants from the French Caribbean: "They made my mother believe that in France she would have a good place to live / And there would be no problem finding work / That she would have no problem taking care of her kids." Once she arrived, though, the song continues, she discovered that she had been "bluffed" and found herself alone in the "concrete jungle, . . . left to herself and condemned to struggle." When she went to the A.N.P.E. (Agence nationale pour l'emploi, the state employment agency) she got little help. What A.N.P.E. really stands for, the Nèg' Marrons declare, is "Aucun nègre pour l'emploi": "No Jobs for Blacks." And the children have inherited the situation, they complain, as finding employment is nearly impossible. Indeed by the 1980s unemployment in the *banlieue* was about as high as it was in the French Caribbean that migrants had left behind.[21]

Many of the *banlieues* outside Paris and other cities are populated by middle-class residents who live in single-family homes, which they frequently own. But especially in recent years the term *banlieue* has been used to refer to areas with large housing projects populated by poorer residents, many of them of immigrant background. These projects, also referred to as *cités,* are not always in the *banlieue;* in Marseille, for instance, many projects are within the city itself, especially in its northern districts.

The earliest *banlieue* projects were built outside Paris in the 1950s and multiplied during the 1960s. Urban planners aimed to assuage urban poverty by offering access to better housing and green spaces in the suburbs to members of the lower middle class, as well as the poor living in the shantytowns populated by North African workers that then ringed parts of Paris. For many early residents the housing represented an improvement over where they had lived before, and when the projects were opened they were often greeted with great fanfare and hope. The housing blocks, which usually included at least five hundred units in a combination of low-rise and high-rise buildings, were meant to centralize "housing, commerce, education, and recreation" close to automobile factories, where many of the *banlieue* residents worked. Some companies purchased apartments to rent to their workers and organized transportation to the factories. But the recession and de-industrialization of the 1970s hit the *banlieue* regions hard, and unemployment soared. During the 1980s, furthermore, government policies encouraging home ownership enabled residents with more stable employment to move out. By the 1990s the average unemployment rate in *banlieue* areas was 20 percent (twice the national average), and in some *cités* the proportion was much higher, often reaching above 30 percent for young residents.[22]

Under such economic pressure, the "utopian experiments" of the *banlieue*, often flawed in their conception from the beginning, unraveled, leaving behind grim, sterile, and depressing stretches of high-rise buildings. Shopping centers closed from lack of investment and problems with vandalism and theft. For residents, Thuram notes, this was a major problem, as the absence of shops "provokes the feeling of living in a ghetto." The buildings, often constructed quickly and with relatively cheap materials, started to fall apart, and by the 1990s "an estimated 80 percent of buildings" suffered from "water damage, insulation problems, broken elevators, or worse." The spatial isolation of the *cités* was another problem, as many residents had to travel long hours on transportation systems that poorly served them. Since the transportation plan of Paris (and indeed of most of France) is axial, with all rail and subway lines going into the central city, moving between different *banlieues* with public transportation takes a long time. The result is "physical and symbolic separation" of each *banlieue* from others nearby and from Paris itself. In 1986 the writer François Maspero published an account of a trip to the *banlieue,* presenting it as a journey from Paris into another world. The low quality of schooling, continuing racial discrimination in the workplace, and stigmatization of the styles of dress and speech of *banlieue* youth all deepen the sense of distance, isolation, and entrapment for those who live there.[23]

Of course not all *banlieues* are alike; many are relatively decent places to live. Mariana Thuram was able to settle her family in a comparatively good place, moving them after a year at Bois-Colombes to a different *cité* a little bit farther from Paris. It was called the Cité des Fougères, and it was located in Avon, just outside of Fontainebleau, a town famous for its forest, once the hunting grounds of aristocrats and, later, Napoleon Bonaparte. The *cité* is a relatively small complex of buildings on the edge of Avon and close to shops and the train station that takes commuters into Paris. On Thuram's first day in his new home, his mother sent him down the street on an errand to one such shop. On his way back, bewildered by the puzzle of identical-looking towers, he got lost in the *cité,* wandering until he saw one of his sisters waving from a window. It quickly became clear that his mother had once again proven her "powerful intuition." Their apartment faced the bucolic

Fontainebleau forest: "Up on the eighth floor, we were not far from paradise. You went out the building by door E11, walked ten meters, climbed over a fence, and you were in the forest."[24]

The presence of the forest, where Thuram took long walks, shaped and softened the relationships between the young residents of his *cité*. There was room to play football games and to learn the mysterious rules of cricket from a Pakistani friend. The open space helped maintain the "harmony" between groups of residents with different backgrounds, which he admits could easily have been broken, provoking "each group to turn in on itself." Although some commentators argue that the difficulties of *banlieue* life are the result of "the diversity of communities or the multiplicity of cultures," Thuram argues that the real problem is that in many *banlieues* there is an "absence" of opportunities for "encounters with others" that can sustain "mutual comprehension." But thanks to the forest, he and his friends experienced diversity as an opportunity. "Our cultural differences imbued our exchanges with intensity and freedom," he writes. "There was magic in our relationships."[25]

Although politicians and journalists in both France and the U.S. increasingly broadcast worries that the *banlieue* is rapidly becoming, or already is, an "American-style ghetto," there are in fact profound differences between the two, as the sociologist Loïc Wacquant has recently argued. Many cities in the U.S. remain among the most racially segregated sites on the planet, with startlingly high concentrations of poor African American residents in certain areas. The difference in quality of life between the ghetto and other areas in the U.S. is extreme, with much higher rates of infant mortality as well as homicide and incarceration in the ghettos. In France, however, this is much less true. With universal access to health care, *banlieue* residents have the same infant mortality rate as other French citizens, and although petty crime (especially vandalism of buildings and cars, as well as theft from and of cars) is often a real problem in some *banlieues,* there are more burglaries in Paris proper. "The favorite delinquent activities of teenagers," writes Wacquant, include "riding the train to Paris without paying, sneaking into cinemas for free, stealing from stores . . . street larceny (motorcycles are a favorite target), or acts of minor vandalism such as 'tagging' or destroying post boxes or other building equipment."[26]

Journalists, politicians, and social workers in France increasingly worry about the presence in the *banlieue* of what they call *bandes.* The term translates as "gangs," calling up images of Crips and Bloods, drive-by shootings, and heavy weaponry. But *West Side Story* is a better point of reference when it comes to the "gangs" of the *banlieue*. The homicide rate in the late 1990s was about four times lower in France than in the U.S., and homicides do not seem to be particularly concentrated in the *banlieue*. Many *banlieue* neighborhoods do have bands of young men quick to confront outsiders, whether groups from other neighborhoods, the police, or the media. Although some of these bands are involved in small-scale drug dealing (largely of marijuana), they serve as low-level distributors and mostly seem to have little control over the larger structures of the drug trade, which are in the hands of European-wide cartels. And though such bands also fight over turf, and such fights are occasionally deadly, these are generally carried out with sticks and knives; guns, especially handguns, are relatively difficult to purchase in France and are much less common than in the United States. In the Cité de la Courneuve, often cited as one of the problem housing projects north of Paris, years often pass without a single homicide, and in the 1990s residents still talked about the death of a nine-year-old boy that had taken place in July 1983 as a shocking and memorable tragedy. Indeed the killing made national news, and the president visited the neighborhood in its wake. In many U.S. cities, meanwhile, the killing of young school-age children, even within schools, is a horrifyingly regular event.[27]

Banlieue neighborhoods in France have long been "preeminently multiracial sites," home to many working- and even middle-class French families, immigrants from Europe, notably Portugal and Italy, as well as West, Central, and North Africa, Asia, and the French Caribbean. Over the past decades the proportion of what some scholars call "visible minorities"—people of North African and African descent specifically—has increased steadily in many *banlieue* neighborhoods, though in fact they still comprise the minority of the population in many neighborhoods. Their increasing presence is the result not so much of long-standing structural forces that create intense and ongoing residential segregation, as in the U.S., but of their concentration at lower economic levels. This situation is sustained and worsened by racial discrimination in employment. But the effects of concentrations of poverty and unemployment in France are quite different from the effects of a deeply rooted history of racial segregation sustained by a concatenation of legal and economic forces that have shaped life in many U.S. urban areas. Whereas state services have increasingly been withdrawn from many poor neighborhoods in the U.S. in the past decades, in the French *banlieue* services have actually become *more* available in many cases, though with uneven and often unintended consequences. Health care is readily available, and the public housing administrations continue to oversee large numbers of residences and to build new housing and renovate old. The public housing administrations have also worked purposefully to *avoid* concentrations of particular ethnic groups within the *cités*.[28]

In the *banlieue* French citizens of different backgrounds live alongside immigrants of dozens of nationalities. It is a patchwork of cultures, but also of legal status; although most are French-born citizens or permanent residents, others are in the precarious situation of being undocumented immigrants. On Thuram's arrival in Bois-Colombes, his first friends were a Chinese boy and a boy from Martinique, and he had North African neighbors. For him, this diversity was a great joy. Asked in a 2006 interview about his memories of the *banlieue,* Thuram responded, "Mixing: Moroccans, Algerians, Zaïrois, Spaniards. A Pakistani friend who went to play cricket in the Fontainebleau forest, with his mother wearing turbans, a red dot on her forehead, dresses of all colors. . . . I discovered Zaïrois parties, too, with dancing, beer, grilled chicken. Then I played football with the 'Portuguese of Fontainebleau,' with grilled sardines after the match, and hanging out. They are good memories."[29] Thuram's depiction of his youth in the *banlieue* runs counter to the prevalent portrayal of life in such communities in contemporary France, which often highlights unemployment, the drug trade, violence, and riots. "We have to shatter this image of the *banlieue,*" Thuram declares. "I was happy in my *cité.*"[30]

"I was lucky to live in this multicultural environment for nine years," Thuram writes. "Neighbors spoke about their homelands and in the end their stories seemed familiar to me. . . . I discovered the way they lived, which was an enriching experience, normal and therefore joyous. None of us felt like we were locked in." He spent evenings with the family of his friend from Zaire. "They took me for a Zaïrois. . . . I dove into the African world." The family had fled Mobutu, and Thuram listened to them discuss politics. His friend's father had graduated from university in Zaire but had difficulty finding work in France, and he was obsessed with the problem of renewing his residency papers, something Thuram's family did not have to worry about. Unlike some friends who had recently arrived in France, Thuram also had the advantage of speaking French. In Guadeloupe, though he spoke the local *kréyol* language with friends, he writes, his mother did "the right thing in imposing French . . . at home."[31]

"Inhabitants of the *banlieue,*" writes Thuram, "live in their environment as if it is delimited by the existence of an invisible border." On the other side of that border, because of the color of their skin, their accent, or their style of dress, they are often looked on with suspicion. Indeed the "territorial stigma" attached to the *banlieue* is one of the most demoralizing and frustrating forces shaping the lives of those who live there, who often find that a mention of their address is enough to assure that they will be turned down for a job. "My friends who lived outside Fougères," Thuram remembers, "affirmed with certainty that we were poor, and therefore didn't pay rent or for electricity." They were also convinced that the *cité* was a dangerous place. Hearing his home described this way, he had a powerful feeling of "injustice, rejection, and discrimination." Some of his friends responded with aggression. One got involved in a *bande* and starting speaking a *verlan,* or slang, that Thuram didn't understand. Suddenly Thuram felt as though he was caught up in "a bad movie: a group of guys dressed in paramilitary clothes from head to toe." They spent time practicing martial arts and at one point urged him to join them in fighting against another band. "Are you crazy?" Thuram replied. "[The incident] marked me," he recalls. He never joined a *bande,* which made him an outcast among some of his friends. In retrospect, he believes that he escaped a situation that could easily have overtaken him. It is crucial, he insists, to be able to say no, to "go against the majority."[32]

Thuram does remember being singled out after his arrival because of the color of his skin, something he was spared in Guadeloupe. He was tagged with the nickname "La Noiraude." This was the name of a T.V. cartoon character, a black cow who, in contrast to his white companion, always did stupid things. Sometimes on the football field he heard players or fans shout, "Dirty black, go home!" "I didn't respond. I've never learned to respond. Someone calls you Black: What do you do? Call them White? . . . When someone says 'dirty Black,' what do you say? 'Dirty White'? It disarms you. When you are little it hurts, though you don't really know why." In France, he writes, a "young black person" will grow up "knowing that his color is linked to something negative." He advises, "It is up to him to be careful to educate himself" in order to understand and therefore resist the forms of racism that continue to exist in "the collective culture."[33]

Thuram also remembers one neighbor who was openly racist, refusing to say hello to him and his friends or ride the elevator with them. The man once fired a gun at some neighborhood kids who were sitting on the hood of his car. In one particularly strange incident, Thuram was speaking in the hall to a Spanish friend, repeating a history lesson from school—"The Moors invaded Spain in 711"—when the neighbor exploded out of his door, yelling, "Go talk about Arabs somewhere else!"[34]

"When we got together for football games," Thuram remembers, "all differences vanished." Visiting his former *cité* in 1998 he recalled, "We played the World Cup here." He pointed to a tattered bench, explaining to the kids following him around how they scored by sending the ball through a broken slat on the back of the bench. Though it had been ten years since Thuram had left, the bench was still broken. Such improvised games were like those he had played as a boy in Guadeloupe, but a Spanish friend encouraged him to join the local football team, Les Portugais de Fontainebleau. Portuguese immigrants had arrived "first and in greatest numbers" to Les Fougères and created a community sports club. It had a youth team, which Thuram joined. "We wore a pretty jersey, black with white stripes!" he remembers. There was no fee to join but also "no training," and they played in sneakers, which, one rainy day, meant that they lost 17 to 1 against a team wearing cleats. Thuram was fast, and the coaches played him forward. Their "tactic" was "simple": "I was supposed to get the ball and run as fast as I could towards the other team's goal." Never much of a goal scorer in his professional career, he jokingly recalls, "I'm not sure why, but it never worked!" Thuram loved the Sunday games, surrounded by "an extraordinarily festive" atmosphere created by the local Portuguese community. "The smell of grilled sardines and *merguez* [sausages] filled the air; Portuguese flags were flying; songs were taken up until everyone was exhausted. We were in Portugal, and I was Portuguese for a few hours."[35]

After two seasons playing with the Portugais, Thuram tried to get into a better club in the town of Fontainebleau. The club had the reputation of being bourgeois, and the managers, hinting that his residence in the *cité* was a problem, told him that he would be uncomfortably outside of his world on their team. But a determined Thuram went to the club's open tryouts soon afterward, and he impressed the coaches enough to be selected for the team. Having proven himself, he was welcomed "with the same conviviality" he had received from the Portugais, and he worked to prove that their "pre-conceived" ideas about him were wrong. He became friends with a player from a wealthy family in the town: "He lived in a house with a garden, each kid had their own room, his father and his mother worked, there was a ping-pong table, and they also played tennis." Their different "ways of life," Thuram writes, could have created an "intractable barrier," but they "became inseparable thanks to football." The new club required him to pay for a sporting license and buy football cleats, an "exorbitant sum" for his mother. But he paid for them both by working part time in the market at Fontainebleau. He did well on the new team, scoring four goals during his first game, one of them from the middle of the field. "It was incredible. Everyone was looking at me with big eyes, as if I had done it on purpose." It was a fluke; Thuram was just trying to pass the ball forward. Soon he played regularly, receiving a small salary.[36]

He transferred to a middle school in nearby Melun that offered a special sports track, which gave him more opportunities to play and train. Joining the team in the town, a step up from Fontainebleau, he spent two years playing there. One of his teammates was a young player named Claude Makelele, who was born in Zaire and had come to France as a boy. (Years later the two played on the French national team together.)[37] Two years later, when he was sixteen, Thuram signed a contract as a professional football player with the Racing Club de Fontainebleau. It was a low-level Division 4 team, but they paid Thuram a decent salary. He didn't envision a career in professional football, and his mother insisted that he stay in school so that he would have his *baccalauréat* degree to fall back on. Thuram explained, "When she arrived in France, her objective had been for us to receive that precious piece of paper. It was a question of honor for her." Still, she was supportive of her son's playing, and the money he made helped the family get by. Thuram, however, banned her from attending his games after one during which she had loudly cheered him on, using a diminutive nickname for him, "Allez Lico! Allez Lico!," something he experienced, as many children of overenthusiastic parents surely do, as "a nightmare." It was four years before he allowed her to watch him play again. By then he was playing in places where it would have been difficult for him to hear his mother's shouts anyway.[38]

"I hate this cliché that football somehow 'saved' Thuram," he declared in 1998. His journey into football, he insists, doesn't represent the story of opportunity but rather of its limits. If many prominent athletes in France have come from the *banlieue,* that is because sports are one of the few avenues open to them. In 2006 Thuram wrote the foreword to a novel by Thomté Ryam called *Banlieue noire,* which tells the story of a young man with a promising future as a football player who gets caught up in the violence of the *banlieue.* "This could have been my own story," Thuram notes, suggesting that his own success is an aberration rather than a model. The number of people who find sports to be a route to social advancement, after all, is tiny. "One can love football," he wrote, "and still think that there will only truly be a 'Republic' when the greatest dribbler on the street can someday become an engineer, a C.E.O., or a labor leader—and that this will be normal for everyone."[39]

If Thuram's story shouldn't be taken as an example, it can be seen as part of the larger history of institutions in France, whose government over the past decades has invested in sports as a way of simultaneously addressing athletic woes and social problems. The prominent sports journalist Jean-Philippe Rethacker, who wrote for the newspaper *L'Equipe* for nearly fifty years, wrote in 1954 that football is "an ideal method for education," one that develops children's "social qualities." But sports education is good not only for children, insisted Rethacker. It is also good for France, for it is through such education that the nation will find and train the athletes to represent it on the international stage.[40]

For most of the twentieth century the French state invested heavily in sports education in schools as well as in public athletic facilities. A 1920 law required all municipalities to provide sports facilities for their residents, and today the centralized French state invests more heavily in sports infrastructure than do other nations in Western Europe. Nearly 40 percent of the financing for sports facilities in the 1990s, for instance, came from state funding, as compared to 15 percent in the United Kingdom.[41] Successive French governments have treated sports as a common good that needs not only support from the state but also careful regulation. They have worked hard to retain their control over sports in order to "keep it in the public domain" and "protect it from the laws of the free market." Sports teams in France were long governed by a 1901 law regulating the functioning of non-profit organizations, which required them to be run according to democratic principles, with officers and members elected by the members. Only in 1974 did the government allow sports clubs to begin functioning as companies instead, and then only as mixed public and private companies. In recent years France has moved increasingly toward privatizing its professional football teams, as team owners and managers have argued that state intervention has stunted French professional teams, who have not been able to compete with the huge financial outlays made by teams in the United Kingdom, Italy, and Spain. As they have pointed out, nearly all of the players in the French national squads in the past decade have spent most of their career playing outside of France, drawn by the much better pay. But there has been resistance to this trend as well. Marie-Georges Buffet, the minister of youth and sports from 1997 to 2002 under Jospin's socialist government and a member of the French Communist Party, strongly resisted the full privatization of sports, emphasizing "the public service mission of sport" and its contribution to "social cohesion" and "the struggle against social inequality" in France.[42]

Both the centralized state and local governments in France have seen the funding of sports programs and facilities as a way of addressing the social problems facing youth in the *banlieue*. Indeed the construction of the massive Stade de France in Saint-Denis was partly motivated by a desire to bring employment and economic development to an area dogged by unemployment and poverty. Organized sports activities play a central role in the daily life of many residents in the *banlieue,* as do the informal games played in the plazas and (often limited) green spaces found in the *cités*. Local groups have established recreational leagues and teams that are among the most active civic institutions in many neighborhoods, and local state-funded organizations, and sometimes the police, have organized sports events as a way to provide recreation and education and make connections with local youth. Sometimes the state's involvement turns into a liability, however; *banlieue* insurrections often target sports facilities, which are seen as state institutions like schools and police stations, as dramatized in the classic *banlieue* film *La Haine.* At the beginning of the film we meet one of the main characters, Hubert, furiously hitting a punching bag in a sports facility that has been trashed and looted. The ransacking of the facility seems almost miraculous: in the middle of the boxing gym is a smashed car, but none of the facility's doors is big enough to fit a car. Later a policeman commiserates with Hubert, promising funding to build a new facility. A disillusioned Hubert answers that kids want to hit more than punching bags.[43]

The French state also established institutions aimed at identifying and extracting talented athletes in order to train them for both professional and international competition. Already in the 1950s the F.F.F. was overseeing the work of Centres d'initiation for young footballers as well as a variety of youth competitions in the country. Over the next decades the state invested heavily in football academies for young players. Concerned about extremely poor performances in international sports competitions, the government began investing heavily in sports education during the 1960s. In 1973 the government funded the creation of the Centres de formation—what one historian has aptly described as "a mini boarding school for elite youth football players"—requiring each professional team in France to create and run a center. In 1988 the government opened up its own national football training academy, the Institut National du Football, on a beautiful site at Clairefontaine, fifty miles from Paris. In the 1990s a system of national and regional youth training centers was set up for thirteen- to fifteen-year-olds.[44]

Although they are governed by French policy, the academies are run by professional teams. When they recruit students, they agree to provide an "athletic formation" that is to be "accompanied by" schooling or training in a profession. Most academies offer scholarships to cover food and lodging expenses. In return, they gain the exclusive right to recruit successful students onto the professional teams they are linked to. Students who turn down such an offer and within three years sign with another team owe the academy the cost of their education. (This cost can be borne by a professional football club wishing to recruit a player.) Students who are not offered a contract by the academy are free to look elsewhere, and if they do not secure a professional contract the academy is supposed to help them with their "reconversion" to another school or into a profession.[45]

A minority of students in these academies actually do make it into professional sports. At the Nantes academy, for instance, "an average of three out of ten youths sign professional contracts," though in many cases these do not lead to long or successful careers. The odds are always against players, as is eloquently depicted in the documentary *Une équipe de rêve,* which follows the fates of the young players close to Zinedine Zidane during his years at a Cannes academy, none of whom pursued successful careers in sports, in contrast to the remarkable one their friend has had. But for those who are completely devoted to the sport and whose families consider it the best option for their child, the academies represent an opportunity.[46]

The academies have also created an opportunity for France, fulfilling the hopes of the politicians who saw the formation of such academies as a way to create successful generations of athletes who would compete for France in international competitions. Writing in the wake of the World Cup victory of 1998, Jean-Philippe Rethaker, author of the 1954 comments about the importance of youth training, could look back with pride at what had been achieved by the academies. Every member of the 1998 World Cup winning squad, he noted, had come up through a football academy somewhere in France.[47]

Today scouting for these academies is intense, with selections beginning as early as the age of twelve. Academies primarily draw from their local regions, although there are exceptions for older candidates. Some also have agreements with clubs in West and North Africa to bring young players into France. Many scouts, probably inspired by the prominence of players like Lilian Thuram, focus particularly on *banlieue* areas, seen as a rich source of players. The scouts for one academy, writes Rethacker, "scour France ceaselessly, especially the Ile de France region where the African and West Indian immigrant communities have proved such an abundant source of talent for French football."[48]

✪

In the spring of 1989 Arsène Wenger, the coach of the prominent Monaco football team, recruited Thuram to the academy run by his team. There the young player began a new life. Wenger was a well-established figure in French football and would go on to great prominence as the coach for London's Arsenal team starting in 1997. His Monaco team had several major stars on its roster, including the Guadeloupean Luc Sonor, who had played alongside Marius Trésor on the French national team. Thuram recalls, "[Sonor] took me under his protection, encouraged me, reassured me." Also at Monaco was Sonor's former teammate on the French national team, Patrick Battiston, who recovered from his collision with Schumacker in 1982 and continued to play professionally throughout the 1980s. Battiston told Thuram, "Don't change the way you play," warning him that the football training centers sometimes created "stereotypical" players.[49]

When he played during a few friendly matches with the Monaco team in 1991, Thuram found the feeling "incredible": "I was living between the conscious and the unconscious, a physical and psychological state in which it's hard to really understand what is happening." It was in just such an altered state that he would seem to be playing when he became a legend during the 1998 World Cup. Growing up Thuram had idolized Jean Tigana, and as he started playing at Monaco he was thrilled when a newspaper in Fontainebleau announced, "There is a bit of Tigana in Lilian Thuram." Soon after, Monaco played against Tigana's professional team, and Thuram was able to meet him during the game.[50]

Now in the spotlight at Monaco, Thuram was invited to Clairefontaine, the training camp for the French national team, for a tryout. There he noticed a "lone player" dribbling the ball in the air with an "incredible facility": "I was stunned by such mastery. It was art. I'd never seen a player with that level of technical skill. Who was it? I learned that he was of Algerian background, that he played for AS Cannes, and that his name was Zidane!" Thuram wasn't selected for the team on his first visit, and neither was Zidane. It would be a few years before the two would meet up again.[51]

Thuram usually played midfield, but after he suffered a serious knee injury his coaches at Monaco put him on defense. He was angry at the time, feeling that he was being relegated to a less important position. Later, though, he realized that the coaches had been right to make the change. His inability to score goals—at least against the other team—became a long-running joke. In 1991, he later remembered, he scored against his own side by sending a fast and misplaced pass back to his goalie as he was being pressed by a striker. "It was a good thing," because after that as long as he did better than that—which wasn't *too* hard—his teammates would say, "He's not that bad!" Fabien Barthez, who would later play with Thuram on the French national team, was with Thuram at Monaco. He remembered that even if Thuram was right in front of the goal, he waited for someone else to arrive to shoot. But on the other end of the field, things went much better. The Monaco coaches soon had all the proof they needed that they had a treasure on their hands. Whenever Thuram played defense, the number of goals scored against them dropped. Accepting his strengths and weaknesses, Thuram contented himself with a defensive role, though he also surged forward and set up offensive plays in many games. Showcased by Monaco, he soon began a vertiginous ascent through the world of professional football, emerging as one of the greatest and most sought-after defensive players of his generation.[52]

Like other young footballers trained in the French academies during the late 1980s and early 1990s, Thuram began his professional career at precisely the right time. Before 1995 European professional teams were allowed only a small number of foreign players. But in that year a footballer named Jean-Marc Bosman, whose team in Belgium had refused him a transfer to a French team, brought his case to a European court, attacking the system governing transfers of players between European countries. The court decided that national restrictions on the number of foreign players represented an illegal restriction on the free movement of workers within the European Community. The results of the case were far-reaching: the transfer market within Europe opened up enormously; teams started paying much more money to get players from other teams, and players' salaries also increased exponentially as the competition between teams heated up. In the 1990s salaries and transfer fees skyrocketed, with new records set again and again. The football training academies in France became a route into what, for a small number of players, was now a stunningly lucrative career. Marcel Desailly remembers being teased as a student at the Nantes academy by an older player beginning his professional career. "I'm going to make lots, lots, lots of money. It's too bad for you guys, because in two to three years, there won't be any more money in football! The bubble will burst and you will arrive too late." But, as Desailly notes, he was off the mark: "If he'd only known."[53]

To fight for players football teams needed money. Luckily for them, the changes in the transfer market were accompanied by changes in the media. In France television and football had expanded in tandem. In 1958 there were a million television sets in French homes. When France made it into the semifinal of the World Cup that summer, fans who wanted to watch their team bought two hundred thousand television sets over the course of a few days. Once the televisions were in the house, they stayed, and one of the things many people wanted to watch was more football, which was increasingly shown on television during the 1960s and 1970s. But in France, as in most other European countries, all stations were state-run. During the 1980s, however, television was increasingly privatized. The private subscription channel Canal + was created in 1984, and TF1 was privatized in 1987. Those who owned these channels knew that one sure way to make a profit was to acquire the right to show football matches, lots of them, all the time. Canal + owed much of its expansion to the profits from broadcasting matches, and the number of games shown on television multiplied exponentially during the 1990s. As TF1 and Canal + bid for the rights to show games, prices went up. And as profits from football increased, the payments made to football clubs to gain the rights to air the games went up as well. Corporate pioneers—Canal + in France, which in the early 1990s bought a stake in Paris Saint-Germain, and Silvio Berlusconi in Italy—brought together investments in media and football and helped propel a huge expansion in the money available for football teams.[54]

Those who profited most were the owners of teams and of television stations, but so did players. Thanks to the Bosman ruling, those who were citizens of a European country could now pursue opportunities throughout the European Community. French players were among those who gained the most. While French training academies were turning out many strong young players, the salaries in French leagues lagged behind those of England, Spain, and Italy. In the 1990s the best French players left to play elsewhere in Europe. The manager of the Italian team Juventus, Marcelo Lippi (who was also the coach of the Italian team during the 2006 World Cup), noted that the advantage of "buying a French player is a good education, a good attitude, very professional, very focused and tactically fully aware." Although many in France lamented the departure of so many players, dubbed "the exodus," the process strengthened the French national team, whose players come back to play for France in its international competitions often much stronger thanks to their time on foreign professional teams.[55]

In 1996, the year the Bosman ruling went into effect, the Italian team Parma recruited Thuram from Monaco. He stayed with Parma until 2001, when Juventus recruited him for a transfer fee of thirty million euros, then the largest amount ever paid for a defender. Although he never gained the attention lavished on goal scorers, he became one of the most highly prized players in Europe. Thuram gained essential training and experience in Italy and earned the admiration of tough-to-impress Italian fans. The historian John Foot, disgusted by the "innumerable chat shows, post-match interviews, clichés, violence, racism, hysterical protests, dives and fake injuries, biased referees and corrupt Presidents" in Italian football, found solace in watching Thuram. When the player, "for the thousandth time in his career, trapped the ball, looked up, and passed it elegantly to a midfielder," it was clear that something beautiful remained.

Thuram is an imposing and rigorous defender, tireless and fast, often bursting forward to help set up plays farther up the field. At his best he exudes a remarkable combination of serenity and intensity. To get himself in the mood to play, he often listens to Bob Marley. In 1999 he announced that his goal was "to play football like Miles Davis [plays jazz]": "We're not there yet. But I haven't given up hope."[56]

FOUR

Roots

"SHITTY COUNTRY, SHITTY BLACKS, SHITTY SKIN," the Bulgarian star striker Hristo Stoïchkov muttered to the French player Marcel Desailly during a 1996 game. The two teams, and the two players, were facing off in the group stages of the European Cup of Nations in a tense match. In 1993 Bulgaria humiliated France with a 2–1 defeat that ended the country's bid to qualify for the 1994 World Cup. If they won again, they could stop France from moving on in the European Cup. Stoïchkov hoped to provoke Desailly, who had been shadowing him throughout the game. An effective defender, Desailly had been insulted plenty of times by his opponents. Off the field he was an easygoing joker. He had two cell phones that rang constantly, something his French teammates teased him about relentlessly—unlike Italy, France hadn't been invaded by the gadgets yet—and Desailly joined in good-naturedly. But watching him with Stoïchkov, Lilian Thuram was worried. He had never seen Desailly so irritated. Thuram also took Stoïchkov's words personally: "Once again, the color of my skin was insulted."[1]

Thuram and Desailly were part of a new generation of players that the French coach Aimé Jacquet had recruited in the previous years. They were there to win the tournament. But Jacquet was also looking forward to the World Cup of 1998, which would take place in France, hoping that the young stars he'd brought in would coalesce into a solid and coherent team. While fans hoped with him, some took note of something other than the players' skills. The promising young star Zinedine Zidane was of Algerian background, and many of the other prominent players on the team— Marcel Desailly, Christian Karembeu, Lilian Thuram, Patrice Loko, Jocelyn Angloma, Bernard Diomède, and Bernard Lama—were black. Stoïchkov thought he could gain an advantage in making something of this. So did the French far-right politician Jean-Marie Le Pen. During the tournament he attacked the players on the team, calling them "foreigners" and "fake

97

Frenchmen." As he often does, Le Pen was employing slick insinuation. The players on the team were all, of course, French citizens; they have to be to play. What Le Pen was really suggesting was that the black and North African players on the team—and, by extension, the many citizens of France who looked like them—were not and could not be true French citizens. The makeup of the French team in 1996 provided him with a new opportunity to ask a question he had been asking throughout the 1980s, gaining increasing attention and votes as he went: Could the children of the French Empire ever be truly French?

Le Pen, however, miscalculated in 1996. Rather than strengthen his cause, his comments helped turn the French football team into a symbol of a new, multicultural and multiracial France. From then on, when the team won, the symbol won too. And as French fans followed the team's work on the football field, they also came to learn about the players' lives, their complicated and twisted roots in different corners of the globe. In 1996 and especially in 1998 France's unruly past danced onto the turf.

In 1962 Marcel Desailly's mother, Elizabeth Addy—thirty-one years old, divorced, with three young children—lived in Accra, Ghana, and worked in a department store. The French embassy was located in the same downtown building as the store, and one day the French consul, a white man named Marcel Desailly, gave her a ride to work in his car. Desailly was an older man; born in 1899, he joined the army when he was sixteen and fought in World War I and later in the Free French forces during World War II. He also served the French Empire, first in Lebanon during the 1920s and then, in the early 1950s, in French Indochina, before starting a career in diplomacy that led to his service in Ghana. Each morning Desailly drove by the bus stop where Elizabeth waited with her children, and eventually he stopped. He had more in mind than a ride to work, though, and started courting her. Soon the two moved in together. Desailly, however, had a wife in France, and when he left Ghana in 1965 he didn't ask Elizabeth to come with him. He left her money and a piece of land and went home.[2]

In 1968, in the midst of a divorce, Desailly returned to Ghana. Elizabeth was pregnant with a fourth child. The father was a prominent architect, but he already had three wives who were unhappy with the prospect of Elizabeth's joining the family. When Desailly returned Elizabeth again moved in with him. The father of the child wanted to name him Odenkey. Instead he was named after the man who became his adoptive father: Marcel Desailly. Four years later, after another coup had shaken Ghana, the two Marcels and Elizabeth left for France, where they were later joined by her other three children. The young Marcel Desailly grew up in Nantes, he recalls, as the "only little black boy among whites," surrounded by the "sons of engineers and doctors." His older brother, Seth Odonkor, was a talented football player, as was Marcel, and both of them were ultimately recruited to the Nantes team's training academy and eventually to the Nantes professional team. Although he visited Ghana as a teenager, Desailly recalls that initially Africa felt "foreign" to him, that he felt "white" and completely French there. His world was Nantes and the football training academy. It was, like other such academies, a cosmopolitan place. Desailly's friends included a young man born in Mali and another from Martinique, as well as an uprooted French Basque named Didier Deschamps, who became one of his closest friends and who would play alongside him on the French national team in 1996 and 1998.[3]

By the time of the 1996 European Cup, Marcel Desailly was playing for one of Italy's greatest football teams, AC Milan, owned by the media mogul and politician Silvio Berlusconi. Like other black players in Italy, Desailly regularly encountered racism among players and fans. During one early game with Milan, opposing fans made monkey noises every time he touched the ball. (This, along with tossing bananas onto the field, was a common practice among racist fans in Europe.) Desailly looked at the crowd and applauded them sardonically. One of his teammates told him to just ignore them, but Desailly did not: "[It was] my response to their stupidity, my way of saying: 'Ok, good going guys, you really are the king of idiots to be stooping so low.'" Speaking to journalists after the game, Desailly didn't make much of the incident. He was similarly understanding when opposing players spouted "Watch out, shitty black!" after he tackled them. He didn't perceive this "as real racial hatred" or as "premeditated," attributing it simply to "irritation" and the "excitement of playing."[4]

Stoïchkov's insults in 1996 struck Desailly as something else. To be sure, he had given Stoïchkov reason to be frustrated. Desailly defended against him physically; one British journalist accused him of working Stoïchkov "like a New York cop." At one point early in the game the two exchanged words and bumped chests. But it was after the French scored a goal that Stoïchkov approached Desailly. "Hey, Desailly, do you know that little kids are dying of hunger in your country?" he said. "I looked back at him, stunned," recalls Desailly. Then Stoïchkov let fly his string of insults about Desailly's background and his "shitty skin." "He said it very calmly, coldly, without there being an incident in the game that could serve as an excuse," remembers Desailly. Desailly didn't reply, and Stoïchkov, clearly looking to provoke a response, repeated what he had said. "We were face to face," recalls Desailly. "I stared at him. . . . I was burning with the desire to give him a right hook, but I managed to restrain myself."[5]

By the end of the game Desailly could feel satisfied that his team had taken revenge on the field. Though the star Bulgarian striker scored one goal, the French did better, winning with three goals, the last of them scored by Patrice Loko, whose father had migrated to France from Brazzaville in French Equatorial Africa in the 1960s. At the postgame press conference Desailly publicly accused Stoïchkov of having used racist insults. As he left the press conference he told Stoïchkov, "You don't have the right to behave this way, and I've just told the press." Stoïchkov responded, "No problem. In any case, I believe what I said." Asked about the incident, the Bulgarian striker simply declared that what he had done was perfectly normal, his insults of a kind regularly exchanged on the field. In retrospect, Desailly said that he "almost wanted to thank" the Bulgarian. "That day, by insulting Marcel Desailly, he awakened his Ghanaian double." After that, wearing his French jersey, he "felt at once French and African": "[I was] proud of my two countries, black and white. And it felt good."[6]

Marcel Desailly had joined the French team in 1993. A year later Lilian Thuram was recruited. Together they formed the backbone of the defense in 1996 and 1998. One sports commentator saw in the Desailly-Thuram team the return of a famous collaboration between Marius Trésor and Jean-Pierre Adams in the 1970s. The "succession" of these earlier players, he wrote, was "assured" through Desailly and Thuram, whose presence in front of the goal he found deeply reassuring.[7]

The 1996 team included four Caribbean players. In addition to Thuram, there was the veteran Joceyln Angloma, who gently teased Thuram for not speaking enough Guadeloupean *kréyol*. The parents of another player, Bernard Diomède, were also from Guadeloupe, though he was born in metropolitan France. Diomède and Thuram shared a room during the 1998 World Cup. "We're the ideal couple," Thuram joked, since they both loved Antillean zouk music: "Zouk in the morning, at noon a little zouk, and in the evening a little zouk. It was perfect for succeeding in the World Cup." The team's goalie, Bernard Lama, had grown up in French Guiana. Thuram admired the way Lama proudly claimed "his Guyanese roots without ambiguity." Lama, Thuram writes, taught him "to embrace [his] origins." The encounter had important consequences off the field, encouraging Thuram to think about and ultimately speak out about the place of the Caribbean within France.[8]

These Caribbean players, along with Desailly and Loko and a player from New Caledonia named Christian Karembeu, made up the group of blacks on the French team. According to Thuram, they also had an honorary member, Robert Pirès, the son of a Portuguese father and Spanish mother. "He was always with us," Thuram recalls. With Zidane and another North African player, Sabri Lamouchi, nine of the twenty-three players had connections to Africa and the Caribbean. Players from these regions had always been a part of the French national team, but never had they been so numerous and so prominent.[9]

"It's a little bit artificial," the Front National leader Jean-Marie Le Pen complained in the midst of the 1996 European Cup, "to bring in foreign players and to baptize them 'Equipe de France.'" Some of the players, he continued, were "fake Frenchmen who don't sing the Marseillaise or visibly don't know it." A few days later, questioned by journalists about his comments, he extended them: "There's something that shocked me a little bit, and that is to see that players from other countries . . . sing their national anthems . . . and our players don't because they don't want to. Sometimes they even pout in a way that makes it clear that it's a choice on their part. Or else they don't know it. It's understandable since no one teaches it to them."[10]

If Le Pen's comments were insulting, they were also incoherent. By definition none of the players on the French team was foreign: only those with French nationality can play on the French team. Le Pen must have known this. The personal stories of the players, however, were irrelevant to him; his insinuation was that whatever their status as citizens, certain players on the team were, and would always remain, essentially foreign. It was a way of communicating a racist vision without articulating it, spreading doubt about whether immigrants and their descendants, especially those who are black or Arab, truly love France. What Le Pen was actually talking about had little to do with foreigners. It had to do with those, like Zidane, Desailly, and Thuram, who were French citizens of the wrong color, children of its empire, and bearers of the wrong history.

Why did Le Pen choose that moment to express his irritation at the anthem-singing habits of the team? During the previous months the debates about immigration in France, divisive and controversial for decades, had reached a fever pitch. In March 1996 three hundred activists, most of them West Africans calling themselves *sans-papiers* (without papers, meaning that they were undocumented immigrants), occupied the Saint-Ambroise Church in Paris, demanding the right to be regularized citizens and calling for a liberalization of French immigration laws. The movement quickly gained the sympathy of many French activists, intellectuals, and artists, as well as international attention, notably in Africa, where the events were followed closely. It represented a powerful counterpoint to Le Pen's National Front. Le Pen saw the fact that the most prominent public representation of the French nation, its football team, showcased players of such varied, and often immigrant, background as a "powerful opportunity" to target his "principal enemy: multiculturalism," which he considers the cause of "decadence and a loss of identity" in France.[11]

During the 1980s and 1990s several European teams included prominent black players. In the Netherlands, for instance, a series of brilliant players of Surinamese background had been at the core of the Dutch team. The most famous of these was Ruud Gullit. He was beloved of Dutch fans, who took to wearing dreadlock wigs to support their hero. The gesture can seem a little off-putting, a capillary version of blackface, though Dutch fans considered it a sincere gesture of inclusion. Indeed, like French fans in the 1990s, the Dutch often presented their racially mixed team as a sign of their superiority over nations like arch-rival Germany, with its all-white teams and occasionally racist fans.[12]

By 1996 Gullit had retired, but the Dutch team included several players of Surinamese background, including Clarence Seedorf. When they faced France during a quarterfinal game in the European Cup tournament, the decisive moment came during a penalty-kick shootout, when a shot by Seedorf was blocked by the French Guiana–born Lama, who won the game for France with his save. Two players from the same region of the Caribbean basin had faced off to determine which European nation progressed to the semifinal. One African writer wrote in 1998 of his admiration for both the Dutch and the French teams, whose diversity represented a new, multicultural Europe. Indeed, though he traditionally supported Brazil, he found himself disappointed when the Netherlands lost to them in a semifinal game in the World Cup. "I wanted this Dutch team to beat the Brazilians and meet the French in the final," he wrote, "largely to provide a broader racial drama. Both the Dutch team and the French team were so racially mixed that a final between these two sides, irrespective of the quality of the football, would have become a wider commentary about the state of the New Europe."[13]

The English too had incorporated several players of Caribbean background into their national team during the 1930s. "If the best 11 players were black, that would be my England team," announced Bobby Robson, who coached the team throughout the decade. Not everyone accepted black players. When England faced the Netherlands during the 1988 European Cup, England fans booed and made "jungle chants" at the black team captain, Ruud Gullit, and at times singled out for abuse John Barnes, the only black player on their team, when England was not doing well. At one point the players on the national team were actually trapped with abusively racist fans on a long, transatlantic flight back from Brazil. The team was returning from a victorious game in the Maracanã stadium in Rio de Janeiro, where Barnes helped England defeat Brazil by scoring what one scholar called "one of the greatest goals in the history of football": "Barnes beat five defenders—left them sprawling in his wake, mesmerized them, made Brazilians believe that the traditionally stolid English, after all, might have some skill in addition to that famed toughness and endurance." Some of the fans on the plane with Barnes, however, weren't impressed. "You fucking wanker," they yelled at one of the coaches, with Barnes and his black teammates Viv Andersen and Mark Chamberlain sitting nearby. "You prefer sambos to us."[14]

By the time of the 1998 World Cup England had several black players on its team. During one pretournament match played in Morocco, there was a mix-up at the stadium. At the moment when the English national anthem was supposed to boom through the speakers there was a gaping silence; the stadium personnel had misplaced the tape. But two black players, captain Paul Ince and Ian Wright, began singing "God Save the Queen" at the top of their lungs. The England fans in the stadium joined in enthusiastically. The British newspaper the *Sun* celebrated the gesture and featured a photograph of the singing black players on its front page. The moment offered a refutation of racist ideas that associated being English with "compulsory whiteness."[15]

Le Pen's 1996 criticism sought to do the opposite. He infused the most significant and widely diffused theater for the performance of French identity with an insidious doubt about those who were on its stage. His comments generated some sympathetic response in France. Marcel Desailly remembers that several of the players on the French team watched a news program in which people interviewed on the street agreed with Le Pen and "complained that there were too many 'blacks' and 'Arabs' on the team." Such attitudes are shared widely enough that, each year, the president of the French Football Federation receives numerous letters complaining about the makeup of the French team, some of them so "odious" that he refuses to respond.[16]

Le Pen's pronouncement, like the ideology it reflected, was remarkably effective and resilient. People have never stopped worrying over whether or not the French players sing the "Marseillaise" before the games. Even Zidane's sympathetic biographer asked him whether he sang the anthem before games. "Yes," Zidane answered, "inside. I don't need people to see it." Emmanuel Petit, a player from Normandy who was a pillar of the 1998 team, wrote in 2008 that he was "embarrassed" that "certain of the players on the current French team don't sing the Marseillaise." He claimed that it was hypocritical to "take advantage of the aura of the French team and not sing": "Either a player doesn't know the words, in which case I urge him to learn them, or else they don't want to sing because they don't accept the French team and what it represents. In that case, they should refuse to be selected for the team. It's a question of respect." In fact at least one player on the 1996 team *didn't* know all the words to the "Marseillaise." But the player in question was Christophe Dugarry, a white player from a wealthy Bordeaux family. In the fall of 1996 Dugarry started playing with Desailly at Milan, and when they were together Desailly helped him practice the anthem. "There were some gaps in his knowledge," recalls Desailly.[17]

In the end the main effect of Le Pen's comments was to transform a group of sympathetic, popular, and quite successful athletic representatives of France into open enemies of his party and its ideology. He pushed several players, particularly Thuram, to make the first of a series of political interventions in which they used their popularity to lobby for a vision of France radically at odds with Le Pen's. In the next years the French football team became a rallying point for antiracist political commentary.

Desailly remembers being taken by surprise by Le Pen's attack. Maybe some of the players were "shy" when it was time to sing the "Marseillaise," but he describes the team as being deeply respectful of France and saw its makeup as simply a reflection of "the France of the 1990s." "It might seem surprising," he writes, "but before that month of June 1996 I had never questioned my identity. I was, we were, French—it was a truth that was so obvious that there was no need to underline it." Le Pen, however, made it necessary to underline it. The team, along with the coach, decided to respond. Didier Deschamps, the team captain and longtime friend of Desailly, denounced Le Pen's correlation between singing the French anthem and being truly French. Lilian Thuram declared, "When you're intelligent, you don't respond to these kinds of statements; indeed when you're intelligent, you don't make these kinds of statements." Bernard Lama retorted that his ancestors "didn't ask to be deported into slavery." He added, "We're not the ones who have a problem," suggesting that the problem lay with intolerant French people and not with those they victimized. Intellectuals and activists frequently made similar critiques of French racism, of course. But fighting for France on the football field, Lama and his teammates could powerfully contest those who claimed they weren't French enough.[18]

Politicians on the left piled onto Le Pen with glee. The socialist François Hollande proffered a "red card" to Le Pen, Jack Lang called his comments *nullissime* (idiotic), and Bernard Kouchner, founder of Médecins sans Frontières (Doctors without Borders), diagnosed the right-wing politician as having an "attack of extreme racism." Lionel Jospin, leader of the Socialist Party, gave Le Pen a geography lesson: "He's not only clueless about football, he doesn't know anything in History or Geography, since he doesn't know that the Antilles and New Caledonia are part of France." The minister of the Overseas Territories called Le Pen's comments an "insult" to France, an expression of ideas that were in direct contradiction to the core values of the republic.[19]

Members of President Jacques Chirac's conservative R.P.R. Party also rushed to defend the team. The prime minister, Alain Juppé, called Le Pen's comments "disgraceful and intolerable." He added, "Through the manner in which they carry the flag of our country, [the players are spreading a] certain idea of France," suggesting that their diversity showcased the best of French society. Another prominent member of the R.P.R. announced simply, "The members of the French team are French like me and like him. He should leave them alone."[20]

A columnist for *Le Monde,* Pierre Georges, joined the criticism of Le Pen, presenting the French team as "the brilliant antithesis of what he and his party are constantly trying to prove." Georges took gleeful pleasure in parodying Le Pen's view of the world, imagining his outrage at seeing France represented by "a mismatched, cosmopolitan, *métisse* phalange" full of "flashy foreigners . . . blue, white, black." He imagined a disgusted Le Pen thinking, "This thing is like the Foreign Legion," except that "at least in the Foreign Legion" they knew the words to the "Marseillaise." Seeing the "children of France" identify with the diverse group of players, Georges concluded happily, must propel Le Pen into a "state approaching catalepsy."[21]

Le Pen sought to still such criticisms by explaining in a statement that he wasn't talking about any of the players, such as Thuram, who were from overseas departments or territories. He always considered them "fully French," he insisted, trying to prove this by having a Martinican woman from his party deliver a statement for him expressing indignation at the violent criticism he was receiving. He was, he specified, taking aim at those who had received "indulgent naturalizations" to play on the team. There have been cases in various countries, notably in recent years, where players are naturalized precisely so that they can play on a national team, as Gusti Jordan was in 1938. On the French national team of the 1990s, however, there were no such players, and indeed only one player had been born outside the territory of France: Marcel Desailly. Le Pen, a veteran of the Algerian war who was concerned with the North African presence in France, may have been thinking of Sabri Lamouchi or Zidane. But both of them had been born in France and therefore benefited from well-established laws of citizenship that follow the principle of the *droit du sol,* whereby all those born in the territory automatically become French citizens at the age of majority. Because of laws passed at the time of independence, both Lamouchi and Zidane had the right to dual nationality and could have chosen the citizenship of their parents. Indeed Zidane could have opted to play for the Algerian national team rather than for the French team, as several other players born in France of Algerian parents had done in the 1980s. But he had chosen France, explaining in 1993 that his choice was "totally natural": "France is my country. My life is here." Le Pen's claim that there were players on the French team who had *become* French in order to play football for the nation was a phantasm.[22]

Though the French team left the 1996 European Cup without a trophy after losing to the Czech Republic in the semifinal game, the tournament lay the foundation for what would happen, both on the field and off, during the 1998 World Cup. It created an "animosity between the far-right and the French team" that was "official and durable." The players, supported by a "majority of French people and a large number of intellectuals," chose "the anti-racist camp." The press and politicians in France had "unanimously stigmatized" Le Pen's statements, and, for a time at least, he avoided making similar attacks, understanding perhaps that football was a terrain of "lived integration" and therefore a powerfully public refutation of his thesis about the dangers of multiculturalism. In a sense, however, it was too late, for he had helped to prime many in France to rally to the French team precisely as a symbol of an alternative, antiracist nationalism.[23]

The next two years were anxious ones in France. Terrorists placed bombs in trash cans along the Champs-Elysées, killing several people, inaugurating a long period during which public trash cans in Paris were screwed shut and permanently surrounded by trash that people dropped there anyway. There was a second, deadlier bombing on a metro car at the Port Royal station soon afterward. The attacks were the work of a group affiliated with Islamists in open revolt in Algeria. In March 1998 police arrested several members of a terrorist group in Belgium, and in May they launched raids, arresting large numbers of people and putting them in preventive detention with the apparent goal of disrupting a terrorist plot targeting the football match between Tunisia and England scheduled to take place in Marseille early in the World Cup. The plan, according to one account, was to shoot English players and throw grenades into the stands, while simultaneously attacking the U.S. team in their hotel and crashing a plane into a nearby nuclear power station. The plan seems to have been disrupted by the police raids, prompting Al Qaeda to plan other attacks that summer—this time successful—against the U.S. embassies in Kenya and Tanzania.[24]

The Tunisia-England match was spared a terrorist attack, but not the violence of English football fans. French police were braced for the possibility of fan violence during the tournament. Throughout the 1980s and 1990s football fans, particularly English fans, gained a reputation as dangerous "hooligans." Though the number of violent fans was small, this minority was the focus of intense concern and attention, and their behavior supported the perception that fans were perpetually drunk and eager for another brawl. Far-right groups found the football stadium a fertile site for recruitment, and some fan organizations in England, Italy, and France became tightly linked with racist organizations.

In the 1980s a series of stadium disasters only deepened the sense that football was an unpleasant and deadly affair. In 1985, in the Heysel stadium in Belgium, Liverpool fans organized a charge against nearby Juventus fans. It was a common practice, and one that usually resulted only in racing hearts, bruises, bumped heads, and sprained ankles. At Heysel, though, the crush of fans seeking to back away pushed over a retaining wall, crushing thirty-nine people to death. Amazingly, after a pause the game was completed, even as corpses were being carried away. Four years later, at the Hillsborough stadium in England, ninety-four people were killed and hundreds injured during another match involving Liverpool, when a disorganized press of people into the stadium crushed people to death along the fences that surrounded the football pitch.

Such disasters, and the larger problem of football hooliganism, generated a great deal of soul-searching and sociological literature that sought to explain why and how certain football fans, particularly in England, turned conflicts on the field into an opportunity for violence off it. Though violence between fans takes place in most European countries, it was comparatively rarer in France than in England, a fact that drove many British writers and intellectuals, as well as government officials, to worry about football violence as a serious social pathology and drove the production of a series of studies about the problem.[25]

While scholars sought to understand the roots of fan violence, police in Britain and elsewhere in Europe sought to suppress it with harsher policing and penalties against fans and the clubs they supported. British police also tracked fans with records of violence and prohibited them from traveling abroad for international games. But it seemed impossible to completely stop occasional outbreaks of violence at games. Arriving in Marseille to support their team in its first World Cup match, some English fans taunted the French—"If it wasn't for the English you'd be Krauts"—and the North Africans, declaring that Marseille was "just a town full of Arabs." On the day of the game some of them rampaged through a Marseille beach, randomly attacking picnicking families who they assumed were North African. During the game (which Tunisia lost 2–0) English fans threw bottles and ripped-up seats at Tunisian fans. Panic spread through the stadium, packed with families from Marseille who had come to support the Tunisian team. After the game young men from Marseille converged on the center of the city, looking to take revenge on the English fans, but police managed to diffuse the situation. Before another match elsewhere in France, German fans beat up a police officer, who was in a coma through the rest of the tournament and remained seriously impaired as a result of the beating.[26]

As the 1998 World Cup began, many French people, reasonably enough, seemed more focused on the possible disruptions and violence than on any victory it might offer them. "In the beginning," a journalist teased a few weeks later, "the French complained, as usual." A poll taken a few days before the tournament began found that 70 percent of French people were interested either "a little bit" or "not at all" in the event. The history of the French team over the past decades, notably their elimination in World Cup qualifiers in 1994, gave little reason for fans to hope for a victory. The sports press, especially the daily *L'Equipe,* harshly criticized the decisions and tactics of the coach, Aimé Jacquet, who later furiously described the journalists who attacked him as "thugs" who were "dishonest and incompetent." It was not a very promising beginning.[27]

⚽

One of the stadiums in France that hosted World Cup games was the Parc des Princes, home to the Paris Saint-Germain (P.S.G.) football team. Since the 1980s this team has had a notorious group of supporters who call themselves the Boulogne Kop. The word *Kop* was borrowed from Liverpool, where fans named a section of their stadium in memory of the battle of Spion Kop, where a unit of soldiers from Liverpool was decimated during the Boer War in South Africa. The Boulogne Kop, again inspired by British football fans, sported skinhead styles and racist symbols and affiliated themselves with the Front National. Throughout the mid-1990s a "long guerilla war" raged on between some P.S.G. fans and the police. In 1994 one altercation seriously injured two members of the C.R.S., an elite French police unit specializing in crowd control. The owners of the P.S.G. did their best to counter the bad image the team got from its more unruly fans, presenting themselves as a cosmopolitan and multicultural team and running an advertising campaign in 1998 that showcased its diverse players. Indeed there are also multiethnic groups of P.S.G. fans, some of whom sometimes do battle with the members of the Boulogne Kop. The members of the latter group, however, have remained active. One was arrested for planning to assassinate President Chirac in 2002, and in 2006 another was killed by an off-duty policeman who was trying to protect a fan of a visiting Israeli team from being beaten up by P.S.G. fans.[28]

Over the years far-right fans of P.S.G. have literally left their mark on the Parc des Princes stadium. In 1998 fans of the Jamaican team, which was making its first appearance in the World Cup, filled the stadium. Those who went to the bathroom, however, were forced to confront the stadium's history as a gathering place for far-right fans. "Racist graffiti was plastered over virtually every surface of the toilet's areas. Above the sinks where a black man was washing his son's hands, read the inscription 'SKINHEADS' alongside scribbled Celtic crosses and swastikas." Someone had carved an "SS" into the wall of one cubicle, and stickers reading "FN" for the Front National were pasted to the walls. The exit was "daubed in English with the slogan 'White Power.'" English scholars found it fascinatingly dissonant to watch the "multi-cultural footballing reality" of the World Cup confront "the subterranean traces of racist football culture."[29]

On the surface the French government presented a very different message in the opening ceremony for the World Cup, meant to showcase the universality of football. The event was conceived by a theater director who wanted to celebrate "the encounter and the ludic confrontation of peoples and cultures." On 9 June, the day before the first game was to be played, four thirty-ton mechanical giants, each six stories tall, lumbered from four locations in Paris toward its center at the Place de la Concorde. An army of forty-five hundred "dancers, contortionists, musicians, jugglers and acrobats" followed them, along with a heavy burden of bizarre and outdated racial imagery. Each giant represented one of "four families" of the human race: there was a yellow giant named Ho representing Asia; a blue one named Roméo, representing Europe; the orange-colored "Pablo the Amerindian"; and "Moussa, the African," who was dark purple. As they rolled through the streets of Paris, they must have stirred up some questions: Ho? Blue Europeans? Orange Indians named Pablo? Four human "races"? Or else it all seemed perfectly reasonable to the sparse crowds who braved the rain to watch. When Ho, Roméo, Pablo, and Moussa all arrived together in a carefully timed ballet at the Place de la Concorde, they found its famous Egyptian obelisk transformed into a "replica of the World Cup." The actress Juliette Binoche "breathed over the loudspeakers," reciting vague platitudes that sounded like a parody of French philosophy: "The giants confront each other, but do they see a stranger or themselves?" Television commentators, noted Adam Gopnik, "were hard put to find something to say as the big guys inched their way along the boulevards" and "at one point were reduced to noting that the technology that had produced the hydraulic giants had military applications, leaving you with the comforting knowledge that if NATO is ever in need of a crack synchronized team of huge, slow-moving inflatable dolls, the French will be the ones to call." Critics complained about the "insipid ritual" and its "clumsy message." They might also have pointed out that this new ritual was an odd echo of another era, when the French government put the cultures and peoples of its empire on display in Paris.[30]

In 1931 a massive exhibition was mounted in Paris, celebrating the French Empire with dazzling reconstructions of famous sites in the colonies. There were full-size replicas of the Cambodian temple of Angkor Wat (which eclipsed the small Guadeloupe exhibit next to it, despite the fact that its centerpiece was a lighthouse) and of villages in Mali. Included was a "human zoo" in which colonial subjects drafted by officials back home were put on display. From the faraway Pacific territory of New Caledonia came a group of Kanak, who in an effort to titillate visitors were placed in a reconstructed village with a label announcing them as "Cannibal men." Their French keepers ordered them to build canoes out of tree trunks and swim in swampy water. At set times the women danced bare-chested for viewers, something they never did back home. When the exhibit's crocodiles, imported from French Guiana, suddenly died, the exposition's officials traded a part of the Kanak delegation to a German zoo in return for some replacements. Put on display in Germany, the Kanaks requested permission to travel to the battlefields of World War I in order to practice funerary rituals for the Kanak who had died there fighting for the French. The Germans refused.[31]

In 1997 the French novelist Didier Daeninckx traveled to New Caledonia and learned the story of this Kanak delegation. Daeninckx is a well-known writer of *romans noirs,* or police thrillers, whose 1984 novel *Meurtres pour mémoire* deals with the haunting memory of the massacre of Algerians in Paris in 1961. He pursued his interest in the memory and history of colonialism in his novel *Cannibale,* which he was working on steadily in early 1998 in his apartment, not far from the Stade de France in Saint-Denis, as the World Cup approached. But as he wrote, he recalls, "the name of one of the players on the French team, the Kanak Christian Karembeu, kept running through [his] head." One of the men who had been sent to the 1931 Colonial Exhibition was named Willy Karembeu. Wondering if there was a family connection, Daeninckx arranged to meet Christian Karembeu in the months after the World Cup. He brought a photograph of the Kanak delegation and showed it to the footballer. Christian immediately recognized Willy: "That's him, my paternal great-grandfather." Then he recognized two other family members in the photograph, his other great-grandfather and a great-uncle. The three of them had been part of the exhibit in Paris and among those sent to Germany.[32]

Born in 1970, Christian Karembeu grew up in New Caledonia in a large family of nine birth children and six more adopted. He lived on the small island of Kanala until he was ten, then moved to the main island, where he attended high school in the capital, Noumea. Karembeu's athletic training began with the task his parents saddled him with as a boy: running fourteen kilometers to get the family's bread from the closest *boulangerie.* His family lived on the grounds of the school that his father directed, where Karembeu and his brothers and father played football in the evening. Karembeu played barefoot, as he still did several years later when a local trainer first noticed him and tried to talk him into pursuing a career in football.[33]

The residents of New Caledonia are French citizens, though unlike those in the French Caribbean departments they have no representatives in the National Assembly. In the 1960s and 1970s some Kanak campaigned for independence, and when Karembeu was a teenager a group called the Front de libération national kanak et socialiste started an armed uprising against the French state. The group faced off against French forces in the 1980s, and the French government used a law dating from the Algerian war to declare a state of emergency on the island in 1984 and 1985. The context of this war frames the story in the novel *Cannibale,* in which an old man tells the tale of his 1931 journey to Paris to two young armed Kanak with a Bob Marley sticker on their car. The war ended in 1988, and a decade later, just before the beginning of the World Cup, New Caledonia gained increased autonomy from France, though a referendum on independence was put off until after 2014. The region is independent enough, though, that F.I.F.A. has allowed it to be a member and to field a football team that plays in international competition, including World Cup qualifiers.[34]

The first recorded football match in New Caledonia took place in 1910, and the next year European settlers created a club there. Missionaries helped spread the game among the Kanak. By the 1960s there were several local football clubs in the territory, and they participated in the French Cup competition as well as occasionally playing against visiting professional teams from France. These exchanges opened up possibilities for Kanak football players. One of them, Jacques Zimako, was recruited to play at Saint-Etienne, one of France's leading professional teams. In 1981 he was a member of the French national team, helping to secure its qualification in the 1982 World Cup. A decade later Antoine Kombouaré played for Nantes and then Paris Saint-Germain. Kombouaré looked out for other talented Kanak footballers and arranged for Karembeu to come to the Nantes football training academy. In 1989 the young man left New Caledonia for the first time, making the journey to metropolitan France to begin a career as a footballer.[35]

When he arrived in Paris after thirty hours on the plane from New Caledonia, Karembeu was wearing shorts, a T-shirt, and flip-flops in the dreary French November. A border patrol agent from New Caledonia found him wandering in the airport hours after his arrival and helped him make his way to the training academy in Nantes. There Karembeu got used to a different life. He was surprised to learn that whereas he had learned French geography "by heart" in his school back home, the favor hadn't been returned: no one in metropolitan France seemed to know where New Caledonia was. "Is that in the Caribbean?" people asked. "Why is it that a French person doesn't know where I come from?" Karembeu wondered. "It's a French territory. Why don't they know the history of Caledonia, or Guadeloupe, of the colonies? That should be in the textbooks. They have to know that we are French." Confronting the ignorance surrounding his history, he became increasingly interested in the story of French colonialism in New Caledonia, and of his family, who had "lived through difficult times" under the control of the French Empire. At the same time his fame as a player and his presence on the French team helped to put New Caledonia on the map for French people ignorant of their imperial geography but interested in the origins of their star footballers. As Karembeu explained in 2006, the French national team was really "the team of the French colonies. . . . If people accept this French team, it should mean that they accept the colonial history of their country, that they accept to make it real, to put it in its rightful place. To explain how things happened. To not suffocate that."[36]

Karembeu starting playing on the French national team in 1992. As part of the 1996 squad that went to the European Cup, he felt targeted and insulted by Le Pen's comments. "The diversity of the players on the French team is what makes it strong," he responded at the time. "I'm proud to be wearing this jersey." Le Pen's comments about the "Marseillaise" particularly incensed Karembeu. "From that day on, I didn't sing the Marseillaise. To raise people's consciousness, so that everyone will know who we are." It was not, as Le Pen suggested, because he didn't know it: "In the colonies, everyone has to learn the Marseillaise by heart at school. That means that I, from zero to twenty-five years old, knew the Marseillaise perfectly." It was because Karembeu felt that silence was the only appropriate response to Le Pen. When the "Marseillaise" plays, he "thinks about his ancestors" who fought in France's wars, imagining them singing the anthem to 'accompany the cannon fire." "The history of France," Karembeu insists, "is that of its colonies and its wealth. Above all, I am a Kanak. I can't sing the French national anthem because I know the history of my people."[37]

Karembeu's response was also a powerful refusal of the idea of reconciliation that has influenced many responses to the French football team. In a song written a few years after the 1998 World Cup to honor Karembeu, the French singer Francis Lalanne told a story that stretched from colonial violence to contemporary reconciliation and redemption. "Your ancestors lived happily on their own land / That a people who come from other skies wanted as their own / Their property was taken and no one told them why." Lalanne suggested that "today's France" would honor Karembeu by remembering not his first name—Christian, a relic of the impact of Catholic missions among his people—but the Kanak name Karembeu. The chorus of the song asks that colonial France be "pardoned": "Pardonne-la, pardonne-la." When Lalanne played the song to Karembeu at a dinner with the French team, Karembeu sang these lines, but then smiled at the next one: "Today's France is no longer like that." He didn't seem convinced.[38]

FIGURE 8. Before the France-Croatia game of the 1998 World Cup, Lilian Thuram (second from left) passionately sings the "Marseillaise" with Karembeu silent next to him. To Thuram's left are Bixente Lizarazu, Fabien Barthez, and Didier Deschamps. © C. Liewig/Corbis Sygma.

In his novel about the Kanak Daeninckx also seeks a kind of redemption in the colonial past. Several characters in the novel, including an African worker who cleans the subway, help two of the Kanak when they escape to try to find the members of their group sent to Germany. Chased by the police, one of them is ultimately killed, but the narrator, Gocéné, is saved by a French worker who intervenes just as a policeman is about to kill him. The worker is punished with a month in prison for intervening. Years later he moves to New Caledonia and reconnects with Gocéné, and the two become close friends. They are driving together when their car is stopped by Kanak rebels, who ask Gocéné accusingly, "Why were you in the car with a white man?" Gocéné replies, "What do you know about it? . . . [He is] as Kanak as you and me." When, at the end of the book, a French helicopter swoops in to attack the young rebels he has just left behind, Gocéné, remembering the way his white friend took a risk to save his life years ago, turns around to go back and intervene between the police and the rebels.[39]

Reading *Cannibale* Christian Karembeu remembered that, when he was growing up, few people talked about the experience of the family members who had been to France for the Colonial Exhibition in 1931. They did remember, however, that the experience had left them changed, and aggressive. Karembeu explained, "I came to understand [after reading *Cannibale*] that the violent and hateful nature of my great-grandfather, Willy Karembeu, was linked to that journey. He came home traumatized and he never fully recovered. I never dared ask him questions." Karembeu had long known of the suffering inflicted on his family by the French colonial state, the "forced labor, with men chained together to build the railroad lines, the expropriation of land." But the story of his people being exhibited in 1931, and of how they were traded for crocodiles, touched a nerve. It confirmed the decision he made in 1996: to play for France but refuse to sing a national anthem linked to the colonial oppression of his ancestors. Silence became a form of remembrance.[40]

In 1998, in addition to hosting the World Cup, France commemorated the 150th anniversary of the abolition of slavery in the French Caribbean. During the 1980s and 1990s Antillean activists and writers increasingly pushed the French state to incorporate the history of slavery and its abolition into the school curriculum and to publicly acknowledge this history. Among the many commemorative events and ceremonies that took place in 1998, the most memorable was a mass silent march of descendants of slaves through the streets of Paris. The event powerfully emphasized the presence of these descendants in French society, and it inspired the creation of several new organizations dedicated to exploring the impact of slavery on the present.[41]

Senegal's Gorée island has several houses that, in the eighteenth century, served as a depot for slaves being shipped across the Atlantic. One of these is a widely visited monument to the slave trade, a site of pilgrimage and reflection for those seeking to remember the mass deportation from Africa. Images of this house, which artists and activists in the French Caribbean frequently reproduce, were emblazoned on a T-shirt produced as part of the 1998 commemoration of abolition. Bernard Lama used football to transmit the image far and wide. Though he was on the bench for all of France's games during the World Cup, the T.V. camera focused on him just before the beginning of the final game of the tournament. He lifted up his jersey to show the T-shirt, with its image of Gorée, to billions of viewers. Most would not have recognized the symbol, but many Africans and Antilleans would have. When he returned to Guadeloupe after the World Cup, Lilian Thuram wore the same

T-shirt, spreading the image of the slave fort once again in the photographs taken at the time. Both he and Lama also frequently evoked the history of slavery in interviews. Thuram said he thought of the commemoration of abolition not so much as a celebration but as "a moment of mourning" for what had happened under slavery. Asked who his heroes were, he listed Martin Luther King Jr., Malcolm X, and Marcus Garvey. He named his first son, born in 1997, Marcus in homage to the legendary leader.[42]

Marcel Desailly remembers how, during the 1998 World Cup, he watched as Thuram "asked himself all sorts of questions, questions much more serious than a football game. Questions about racism, history, slavery." He seemed to have "gained a consciousness of his *négritude,* thinking more and more often about his roots," moving from a "relative indifference to an intelligent militancy." It was "more than a metamorphosis, it was a revelation!" Thuram frequently talked and debated with Karembeu and with Bernard Lama, whose "strong personality and intelligence" made him an authority for other players. The French football team had created the space for an ongoing, often intense discussion among several of its players about France's colonial history and its meaning in the present.[43]

France played its first game in the World Cup against a postapartheid South African team that brought together white and black players and was led by a French coach. But for Thuram the team mostly represented a nation "that less than ten years earlier couldn't participate in the World Cup because of apartheid; a nation that represents Africa, with all its misery and riches," and the "country of the ferocious struggle of Nelson Mandela." Thuram felt as though he was coming face to face with a part of his past. "Everything was clashing" in his mind before the game, as he thought of his "far-away origins, of slavery, of the slave trade." "I'm with the French team," he thought, "but I could just as well have found myself at that instant in the other locker room."[44]

As they prepared to play, the French team could hear the powerful singing of the South African team resonate through the walls. "It gave me goosebumps," Desailly recalls. "I forgot football, and thought of Mandela." When they exited the locker room to go out onto the pitch, the singing of the South African team grew louder as the players approached from another hallway. The South African players continued singing as they entered the field alongside the French and then passionately sang their national anthem, which since 1994 had included the legendary hymn of Mandela's African National Congress. Then it was time for the "Marseillaise." Thuram sang it out proudly, in a "thunderous" and "generous" voice.[45]

Desailly also sang the anthem that night: "[I sang] maybe not in a full voice, like my friend Lilian Thuram, but with at least as much emotion.... Yes, Mr. Le Pen, EMOTION.... The words came to me by themselves, without calculation." The song called up a face, that of his brother Seth Odonkor, a successful footballer at Nantes who in 1984, when Desailly was a teenager, died in a car accident. At the end of the anthem, ready to start the game against South Africa, Desailly imagined his brother among them on the field. From then on, whenever he sang the "Marseillaise," he felt that his departed Ghanaian half-brother sang it with him [46]

FIVE

Two Goals

"WE'RE NOT GOING TO GIVE AN INCH!" Lilian Thuram told his team-mates as they waited to walk out onto the field. They were about to play a World Cup quarterfinal match against Italy, a reunion match of sorts. Seven of the French players—including Thuram, Zidane, Desailly, and Deschamps—played in the Italian leagues. Being professionals in what is often considered both the greatest and the toughest football leagues in the world had clearly strengthened their game. "We love Italy, and we all had friends on the opposing side," writes Desailly, "who would remain friends no matter the outcome." But the game was a "dream match," and the players exuded "incredible excitement" as they waited to go out on the field. Even Zidane, "the calm one," was "different . . . more motivated, more aggressive, ready to fight, to give a lesson to the Italians."[1]

France had earned its place in the quarterfinal through a series of convincing wins. They had defeated South Africa 3–0, one of the goals scored by Thierry Henry. In the next game they dominated the Saudi Arabian team, winning 4–0 and securing their place in the next stage of the competition. Thuram made the crucial pass in one of the goals, lobbing the ball from the right wing in front of the goal, where David Trezeguet headed it in. They defeated Denmark in the next game, before going on to confront Paraguay, a team anchored by the legendary goalie José Chilavert. He was famous not only for stopping goals but also for scoring them, as he once did from more than halfway down the field on a free kick. Paraguay managed to shut out the French for 113 minutes of play, nearly to the end of the second overtime. At the time F.I.F.A. regulations decreed that, during overtime, whichever team scored first would win the game. With two minutes left, Trezeguet headed a ball to Laurent Blanc, who slammed it into the goal. Chilavert pounded the ground with his fist before standing up to console a sobbing Paraguayan defender. Thierry Henry had hurt his ankle and was sitting on the floor in

FIGURE 9. Fans at the Hôtel de Ville in Paris prepare to watch France play Paraguay during the 1998 World Cup. © Owen Franken/Corbis.

FIGURE 10. The crowd at the Hôtel de Ville in Paris watching the 1998 France-Paraguay World Cup game erupts in celebration as Laurent Blanc scores the winning goal. © Owen Franken/Corbis.

the locker room watching the game on T.V. But the coaches carried him out and he hopped onto the field on one foot, wearing just his socks, to join the celebration. The French were into the quarterfinals.[2]

Against Italy, France found itself completely shut out. Though the Italian goalie had to make several remarkable saves, notably against a shot by Zidane, by the end of ninety minutes the French hadn't scored. But the French defense—held together by its two Italian professionals, Desailly and Thuram—had held up as well. Thuram imposed himself in the penalty box, stopping dangerous Italian advances, moving the ball up the field for French counterattacks. The deadlock continued from one grueling overtime session into another, and the score was still 0–0. The game went to penalty kicks.

Zidane took the first one and slammed it into the left side of the net, but the Italian player Roberto Baggio, who had lost the 1994 World Cup for Italy when he sent the final penalty kick against Brazil sailing over the goal, equalized on the next shot. Then the Italian goalie stopped Bixente Lizarazu's low shot. As Didier Deschamps hugged a despondent Lizarazu, goalkeeper Fabien Barthez came to his rescue by stopping the next Italian shot. The French fans exploded. The next two French players up were the youngsters David Trezeguet and Thierry Henry. They had volunteered to take the shots, and Desailly was impressed at how calm the two were. Both of them shot decisively and made their goals. But the two Italian players who followed did as well. So it came down to the final two penalty kicks. Laurent Blanc walked up to take his kick, smoothing down the grass with his hand before he set the ball down. Henry stood behind Trezeguet and pulled the back of his teammates' shirt in front of his eyes, unable to watch. Blanc sent a powerful shot up into the left corner of the net.

The last Italian player, Luigi Di Biagio, stepped up to shoot. If he made his shot, the two teams would remain tied, and they would have to go on to a sixth penalty kick. On the side of the field, Didier Deschamps and Marcel Desailly haggled over who was to take the sixth kick if it came to that. Desailly was determined not to be the first in line; he didn't want to feel the entire country watch him send a ball over the top of the goal. As Thierry Henry smiled at them in disbelief, the two carried on a "comical scene," almost a television sketch, looking like "a retired couple arguing over who would get to choose what show they are going to watch on TV." "Blanchard," said Desailly, using a nickname for his old friend Deschamps that means something like "whitey," "you're the one who has to shoot. You're the captain, after all." "No, it's your turn." "Me? What, are you crazy? I'll go after you." Deschamps faked a cramp in his leg: "Marcel, I have a cramp!"

"What, a cramp? You're the captain, Blanchard, captain!" "I can't go. Aaaah! I tell you, it's impossible!"[3]

They never had to decide. Di Biagio's powerful shot hit the top bar of the goal and bounced back toward him as he collapsed backward onto the field. The stadium exploded and the entire French team poured out onto the field. For a moment goaltender Barthez wasn't sure what had just happened, and then he realized that the game was finished. France had made it into the semifinals of the World Cup for the first time since 1986. The game had attracted large crowds to giant screens set up in Paris, and when the French team won, people gathered in the streets cheering, while drivers coursed through the town with French flags flying from their car windows and horns honking through much of the night. Similar celebrations took place in Marseille, Lyon, Lille, Nantes, and other cities and towns [4]

The players rode their bus back to the national football training academy in Clairefontaine, where they were staying in relative isolation. They weren't allowed to read newspapers—Aimé Jacquet didn't want them to get irritated by the often harshly critical press coverage—though Bernard Lama managed to sneak in copies of *L'Equipe* and *France Football*. Journalists documented the minute details of the players' lives. They reported on Thuram's love of salads, which he "ate directly from a huge salad bowl." Fans remembered the detail, and during the victory parade on the Champs-Elysées a few days later one fan tossed him a head of lettuce, which he waved joyously. Zidane explained that the players didn't drink alcohol and then added with a smile, "Only wine." As Desailly remembers it, Clairefontaine was an "autonomous Republic" within French territory. There he felt "at once in history and outside of it." The players didn't experience the "popular fervor" they had generated and didn't quite understand the extent to which they had become the "main characters in a national adventure."[5]

France was two games away from winning the World Cup. Standing in their way was the team from the young nation of Croatia, which was shining in its first World Cup appearance. Led by the striker Davor Suker, the team had defeated the Germans to make their way to the semifinal. In Paris a small group of Croatian immigrants gathered to support the team. "Football is the greatest ambassador for a country," one young Croatia fan declared. He wanted his new country to be known for something other than the war that had created it. In Croatia, meanwhile, some fans watching the game singled out Zidane because of his "Muslim name" and booed whenever he handled the ball.[6]

Massive crowds of French fans gathered in Paris to watch in cafés and bars or on giant screens that were set up throughout the city. It had taken a string of victories, but now France was intensely, seemingly unanimously attentive. At the beginning of the second half Suker outran Thuram, who was badly positioned, to score a devastating goal. But Thuram responded immediately and decisively. He streaked up the field on the right side, dribbling all the way, then passed the ball to Djorkaeff, who immediately sent it back to him. Thuram sent the ball flying over the Croatian goalie and into the net. It had been just a minute since Suker's goal, and the game was tied once again.

Thuram turned around, stunned, looking into the distance, as his elated teammates surrounded him. He had always been teased, and had teased himself, about his "awkwardness in front of the goal," and he rarely scored. That night, though, he seemed to have decided it was up to him, and him alone, to get France into the World Cup final. Twenty minutes before the end of the game he once again powered up the field. Closing in on the right end of the field, he gestured to Djorkaeff with his hand: I'll pass it to you, and you pass it back to me. Djorkaeff did, and though the return pass was touched by a Croatian defender, Thuram stretched out, took a few quick steps, and then struck at the ball with his left foot. Though he was far from the goal, it sailed past the goalie and into the net. He turned around and kneeled on the ground, a finger posed lightly over his lips, thinking. It was, wrote one observer, as if "to tell us that Lilian Thuram has risen out of this world. . . . Enlightened, inspired, Lilian Thuram is the messiah."[7]

Thierry Henry ran to him first and took him in his arms, followed by the rest of the team. "What's happening to you?!" Desailly asked him, to which an entranced Thuram replied, "I don't know!" It was as if he had been storing up all of his skills as a striker for years, saving them for when they were needed most, choosing the largest stage a football player can step onto to make one unforgettable intervention.[8]

The goals secured France's victory. At the end of the game players lifted Thuram up onto the shoulders of Bernard Lama as the crowd cheered wildly. Jacques Chirac, sporting a French football jersey, and Prime Minister Lionel Jospin came to the French locker room after the game, as players chanted, "Thuram, Thuram!" An amazed Aimé Jacquet, who had lambasted his team during halftime, warning them that they would lose if they kept playing as badly as they had been, jokingly complimented Thuram: "Luckily we had a black genie who came out of his bottle, and who did something extraor-

FIGURE 11. Lilian Thuram considers his second goal against Croatia on 8 July 1998 in the World Cup semifinal. © Christian Liewig/TempSport/Corbis.

dinary for us.... Every morning I've been telling him: 'You, you'll never score a goal.' Today I look pretty stupid." Jacquet joyfully predicted that the team would win the World Cup in a few days, thanks especially to their "big hearts," because "that is where it happens." "Once, Lilian Thuram wanted to be a priest," a television announcer declared. "Luckily, he became a football player." He had "done miracles" for the French team: "He has offered it the first World Cup final in its history."[9]

Thuram was completely surprised by what had happened. Climbing on the team bus after the game, with the players cheering him, he looked into a filmmaker's camera and announced, "Anything can happen in football! Anyone can score! Even Bebert," he continued, referring to an older assistant to the team, "can score!" Interviewed the next day, he downplayed his achievement. He explained that his "great luck" was that when he was taking his second shot he was off-balance, falling as he kicked. The goal, he suggested, was basically a fluke. Talking privately to his mother after the game, however, he gave himself a little more credit, telling her that, watching his teammates trying to score, sending ball after ball "everywhere but in the goal," he'd been taken by a "rage" to score. He predicted that it would be twenty-five years before he again scored two goals in a match. Although he would remain a pillar of the

French team for years to come, and would occasionally _re in his profes-_
sional games, he would never again score a goal for Franc_

The two goals he did score, however, guaranteed him a per_
in the pantheon of French sports heroes. The next day photos o_ _lace_
decorated the cover of every newspaper in France. And he'd gained _
beyond France: two Albanian couples, "fervent supporters of the Fre_
team," immediately went to the local authorities to change their young boys
names to commemorate Thuram's goals. Ilir and Elvis both lived, from then
on, as Thuram Selimi and Thuram Isai. French journalists rushed to learn
about the nation's new hero. One introduced Thuram a little snidely, outlin-
ing features that would often be evoked in descriptions of the footballer:
"Little glasses, false intellectual airs, the vocation of a countryside priest, a
strong sense of derision—that's Lilian Thuram." In the next decade commentators would frequently comment on his glasses, and many would refer
to him by his nickname, "the Intellectual," expressing surprise at the fact that
a footballer could also be a thinker. With his two goals on the field he had
gained a status and reputation in France that he would maintain—and put
to use—for the next decade.[11]

"Thuram Président!" chanted the crowds pouring into the streets in celebration. Hundreds of thousands of people thronged the Champs-Elysées,
including Thuram's mother and his brothers and sisters, who went there after
watching the game in the stadium. Parades of honking cars with cheering,
flag-waving fans crisscrossed avenues throughout the country. "The wave of
joy carried everything away as it passed, starting with modesty and the most
elementary reason," one commentator sniffed as the T.V. showed scenes of
jumbled crowds grasping French flags and people twisting and dancing with
strangers, jumping and waving their arms with abandon, hugging unrepen-
tantly. Most journalists and commentators effused about the celebrations.
"What is wonderful," the retired football player José Touré declared, "is that
we're seeing joy in people again. And that's wonderful because it's been too
long since we've seen people smile. We should have a World Cup every year!"
Another commentator marveled at the warmth of the street celebrations:
"No incidents in the street, kissing, people talking, all races mixed together,
all religions mixed together, talking to each other, joyfully, in paradise
thanks to the men in blue." He had rarely felt "such communion around the
flag, around the jersey," he added.[12]

A reporter in Poissy, a suburb of Paris, described the enthusiasm of people in the streets, cafés, and shops. "If mixing works for football players," one businesswoman suggested, "maybe it can also work in the streets." A nearby couple concurred: "It means that we can live in harmony rather than in fear. This team, it has a soul, it represents an ideal." A woman admitted that she had voted for the Front National in the previous election, but nevertheless liked the French team for being "sympathetic" and fighting to win. The composition of the team didn't bother her: "As long as you are French, and you respect the customs of this country. . . . It's those who want the advantages of being French but want to keep all their customs that cause the problems." And then she added, perhaps a little shaken in her party loyalty by her loyalty to the football team, "And, really, what Le Pen says is excessive!" Another woman, who also was sympathetic to Le Pen and declared matter-of-factly, "Sometimes, you are forced to be racist," was also supportive of the team: "Well, it's a team that's winning, they picked the best, people of all colors, together, it's true, it makes you dream: We could live like them. And, in the end, why not?"[13]

According to one man, the team should be an example for politicians in France: "The fact that Zidane is the leader transmits hope. It valorizes *beurs* and blacks. If you transposed that from football to the entire nation, imagine the energies it would liberate!" Instead of trying to "recuperate" the victory, he warned, politicians should "imitate it." In football someone could come out of the "street" and win "thanks to his talent." That, he suggested, was how the world should be, rather than being dominated by politicians, who are "white and are all the same."[14]

Bernard Pivot, the prominent host of the T.V. show *Bouillon de culture*, challenged intellectuals who belittled football to reconsider: "It's true that there is a real joy around this team, and also probably around the notion of France, this entity. This time the word 'France' is incarnated in these 22 players and a trainer." Sounding a note that would be constantly repeated during the coming days, Pivot also took joy in seeing people from the *banlieue* celebrating the victory by flying the French flag. "We've seen many people from the *cités* with French flags, and I think football has succeeded in doing what we haven't been able to do through other means, including through political means. Today, those who denigrated football have to render it homage." Others expressed similar pleasure at seeing residents of the *cités*, especially children, waving French flags. As a teacher in a *banlieue* outside Paris put it, "When you're 10 or 12, carrying a flag is a gesture that you remember." It was, according to a priest working in the *banlieue*, "an encouragement to become a citizen, and in that sense it can only do good."[15]

Such comments suggest that what was important about the victory was that, because people from the *cités* could see themselves reflected in the team, they were being pushed to feel more patriotic, to *integrate* themselves into and more fully embrace France. Much of the unbridled and in many ways unreasonable enthusiasm that poured from commentators during the 1998 World Cup about the political implications of the victory depended on this idea. Football obviously couldn't repair the structural problems of unemployment and social marginalization in the *cités* that are the root cause of violence and social alienation there. But if the real problem was the perception that *banlieue* residents had of their place within France, football could create a fundamental transformation.

Journalists intrigued by this possibility rushed to the *cités* to interview people, seeking to capture their vision of the French team. They found that many fans in the *cités* felt they owned the victory, though in ways more complicated than commentators like Pivot suggested. They knew that Thuram, Zidane, and Henry had grown up in *cités* like theirs. In the *banlieue* of Venissieux, outside Lyon, one reporter described the reaction of the young people living there: "[These players are like] big brothers they admire and respect. In their own way, the kids in this neighborhood appropriate their success." It inspired them, one young man told the journalist, to imagine, "We also might do something." Another young man, though he wasn't a fan of football, was a fan of Thierry Henry: "He's Antillean, like my father, he's 21, like me." They were both from the *banlieue:* "He grew up in Ulis, me in Pantin. We could have gone to school together, he could have been my friend." Henry provided this young man someone to identify with: "Here in France, everyone's lost. Me, for example, I'm a *métis,* . . . white and black at the same time." Another Henry fan, Ibrahim, declared, "He's from a *cité,* he runs fast. He's smart."[16]

"If they had found me, I would have become Zidane," claimed a fast-talking young man named Rachid in a *cité* outside Paris. "All of us could have been in his place, in Thuram's place, don't forget it. All the kids, they have a taste for the ball, they have a taste for France. Little Ronaldos, little Zidanes, there are lots of them here! Lots, lots!" In Saint-Denis, in a *cité* close to the stadium, Thuram gained "the status of a hero." A man named Kader, the local "genealogist," jokingly conjured up a connection between the neighborhood and its new idol: "Stanislas, who lives at entry F, he's got an uncle whose name is Lilian and who's from Pointe-à-Pitre. It must be his cousin."[17] Residents in another neighborhood, a journalist reported, were living the World Cup "doubly," "loyal" to the country where their immigrant parents came from, "but at the same time fervent supporters of the country where they were born, France." Many of those with roots in North Africa initially cheered for Morocco and regretted the elimination of the team along with that of all the others from Africa. A few wished it was Morocco instead of Brazil in the final. "Morocco could well have won—they've beaten France before," declared one "defiant" young man.[18]

"Honestly, in the midst of all these victories, it's the first time in my life that I have felt French," a young woman named Tounisia announced, "even though I was born here. . . . It totally cheers me up!" An old man named Mohammed proclaimed—with "his accent," specified the journalist for *Le Monde*—"There! France has given birth to its children." Abdellatif, a shopkeeper, was radiant: "This team, it is *la France moderne!* In the store, everyone is talking about it. The grandmothers come in and say, 'Yes, we won!'" Of Moroccan background, he imagined what he would have done if Morocco and France had faced off: "I would have been happy about a victory for Morocco. But I think I would have been even happier if France won: I was born here." Another man celebrated the French victory by flying a Moroccan flag. Still, he wondered why Zidane had chosen to play for France: "If he had played with the Algerian team, they might have been able to make it to the World Cup." Others turned the celebration of the multicultural team into a joke. "We need a Chinese striker to complete the collection," a man named Samir teased. His friend Yassine added, "It's funny, the sons of foreigners, when they make France win, people say they're French. When they're going to prison, people add that they're of foreign origin."[19]

Holding a Zidane doll, a young woman name Frédérique argued that if people were so enthralled it was actually because the team was "precisely the opposite of what French people live": "There are gulfs between them, ghettos, castes. Solidarity, tolerance, the collective—I don't see people really taking that path." The team, "unfortunately," was "just sport," and also "showbiz," and only "cretins" could believe it was really going to bring about political change. A sixteen-year-old named Lamia believed the World Cup was fixed so France would win it. In any case, she wouldn't really call it a French team: "I call it the team of the rest of the world." But a few older women nearby immediately responded, "The team is France, and everyone recognizes themselves in it. Really, it brings tears to our eyes."[20]

The players, meanwhile, were back in isolation at Clairefontaine. Hearing of the fervor of fans throughout the country, they spoke out about something that had been bothering them. The people in the stadium itself were overwhelmingly wealthy and privileged and had no idea how to support a football team. So many seats had been reserved for politicians, corporate leaders, and other VIPs, they complained, that the real fans were stuck outside. Team captain Didier Deschamps declared, "When we walked onto the turf, on Wednesday, there was almost an entire section full of black suits. You would have thought we were at a funeral. Those people are tight-asses, they come to the stadium as if they are going to the theatre. There is massive fervor, but it is outside. Those who really love football, who are thrilled for us don't have access to the stadium. The farmer and the worker wearing red, white and blue, they don't have the money to buy a seat." Aimé Jacquet concurred that the people in the stadium were not "pushing" the team, just "following" it. While "the entire country" was behind the players, noted one fan, they were surrounded by people who acted as if they were just watching a "spectacle."[21]

What the players needed, said Marcel Desailly, were "flags, outstretched hands holding up scarves, real chants, chants that give you goose-bumps, like the ones [he] had known in Milan or Marseille." The stadium spectators were foreigners to the world of football, lacking "a common culture, a familiarity with the stands, and even, in a few cases, a basic knowledge of the game." During the France-Croatia game one player on the bench actually gestured to the French fans to try to get them to join in a bit more. "It's a bit much that we have to heat up the crowd ourselves," complained Fabien Barthez, the goalie. "A football game isn't a classical music concert with flutes." He recommended that those coming to watch the final wear the appropriate clothes, "jeans and sneakers": "Leave your ties at home!" Those lucky enough to be in the stadium, the players suggested, didn't understand what the people stuck outside did: that football is much more than a spectacle; it is the promise of a different reality, one that the politicians in their suits seem ill-equipped to perceive, let alone create. The VIPs in the stadium, said Thuram, needed to "wake up." These complaints by the team didn't lead to any concrete changes at the time, though a few years later Thuram would buy tickets for a large group of *sans-papiers* to watch a game in the Stade de France. In fact, though, the victories of the team had thrilled so many people that, in a sense, all of France had been turned into a giant stadium, where many who supported and celebrated the team did so as a way of imagining a different place for themselves in French society.[22]

"The Africans saved France!" a Malian man named Maxime shouted the day after the France-Croatia game, running down the Boulevard de Strasbourg, a street in Paris packed with Afro-Antillean barbershops and stores. He described his reaction to the game: "When Thuram scored the second goal, I opened my window and I shouted: 'Now people will have to respect us in France!'" His wife, though, wished a white player had scored; she reasoned that because French people didn't respect them, they should have to "manage on their own," without any favors. But another man, Moussa, who was from the Ivory Coast, agreed with Maxime about the political significance of the match. What he took from the match was "Thuram, Thuram, Thuram": "Because he's black, like me. Because it's a way of saying to Le Pen that we blacks are not what he thinks. It shows that we are French, and that we'll fight for France." Evoking the memory of his father, who "died French"—perhaps as a soldier fighting for France—Moussa declared, "France's battle is my battle. This game was an act of vengeance against the Front National."[23]

For Binsika, a thirty-year-old Zairian man who had spent a decade in France as a *sans-papiers,* fearing deportation and working to get residency papers, the celebration was a vindication. He had recently gotten his papers and a settled job and had young children born in France. After the victory he paraded on the Champs-Elysées and started singing the "Marseillaise." "I did it without realizing it," he remembered. "I wanted to share my joy. I was drinking, dancing, with the French flag in my hand." Seeing Thuram score his goals was "a dream," he said, linked in his mind to his success at getting his residency and to the fact that in recent years he saw "French people, whites," support the *sans-papiers* in their struggles. "It's not the same thing," he added, "but, still, everything is aiming for the same goal." What had to happen now, though, was for people to go beyond the "symbol" of Thuram, to transform his goals into "a political act." That, Binsika declared, would be up to the politicians to do.[24]

But Binsika, Maxime, and many other celebrants had already experienced Thuram's goals as a fundamentally political act, one that extended to them a kind of citizenship previously denied them. During the game, in Paris, in the midst of French fans painted red, white, and blue and singing the "Marseillaise," a young man named Amid explained that he had initially supported Morocco. "Now, I'm completely behind *les Bleus*.... After all, where am I?" he joked, looking down at the ground beneath him, enacting in one simple gesture the meaning of the French *droit du sol,* the idea that birth in France confers citizenship: "In France, of course!" It helped that Zidane was on the team: "He's a *beur,* he's from a *cité,* he's like us, you know?" "We *beurs* have our asses hanging between two chairs," thirty-six-year-old Nasser explained. "The World Cup is our chance to express what links us to this country. We want to show that we were born here." As the journalist was gathering these comments, the crowd exploded: Thuram had just scored his second goal. "Hands in the air, Chinese, Pakistanis, French, *beurs,* everyone jumped for joy," he reported. Amid "exulted," "You're French, I'm French, she's French—we're all French!"[25]

In the Cité des Fougères, where Thuram had grown up, residents took pride in their connection to France's savior. The two thousand apartments in the complex echoed with the shouts and cheers of fans as they watched the game. "Thuram, Thuram! Everyone was shouting his name," explained Ghislain Ifwanga, a young resident from Zaire. After the game ended he led a group of hundreds of young celebrants through the streets of Avon and into the center of nearby Fontainebleau. In his hands was a "relic": the jersey Thuram had worn during the France–Saudi Arabia game a few weeks earlier, signed by Zidane. Thuram had given the jersey to an old friend from the neighborhood during a recent visit, and he had passed it on to Ifwanga, an aspiring football player. Soon a thousand people surrounded Ifwanga, singing a "frenzied Marseillaise" and waving French flags. One young man climbed up the façade of the Hôtel Napoleon, one of Fontainebleau's monuments, ripped down the French flags that were waving there, and threw them to his friends below.[26]

It was a common gesture. "There must not be a single flag on a police station or a town hall—they are all there [on the street]!" a television announcer exclaimed at one point. "Right now the French flag belongs to everyone." On the Champs-Elysées a few days later a young man named Laurent, his chest painted red, white, and blue, flew a French flag taken from the town hall in the small town were he lived in rural France before coming to Paris to celebrate.[27] It was a gesture that combined patriotism with transgression. The flags, after all, were stolen from state buildings, ripped from their poles to become living symbols of something different in the hands of the crowd. Once they had a flag, celebrants didn't salute it or stand underneath it. They took it, running, jumping, crumpling it in their sweaty hands, draping it around themselves, around friends or strangers they had just met, turning a powerful martial symbol of the nation and its history into something tangible, intimate, alive.[28]

"Thuram—Our Hero!" announced *France-Antilles* in Guadeloupe. An "explosion of joy" rocked the island when he scored his goals, and thousands paraded in celebration there as well as in Martinique and French Guiana. In the next issue the newspaper ran a long article about Thuram, congratulating themselves jokingly for the fact that they had started reporting on his life from the day he was born, reprinting their picture of the infant Thuram. Family members described his years as a boy in Guadeloupe as an idyll involving football with friends and romps through the fields seeking mangoes. Twenty-five years after he was born on the island, they reported, "he has made France happy, and his exploits are known throughout the world."[29]

By securing France a place in the final of the World Cup against Brazil, Thuram put many football fans in the Antilles in a complicated position. For decades Brazil, the most successful team outside Europe, a largely black team playing against predominantly white teams, was the favorite of many in the French Caribbean, their proxy and representative. "When I was younger," Thuram himself recalled, "I was Brazilian." Even in the 1980s, when the star Marius Trésor was on the French team and many Antilleans celebrated his exploits, they often continued to support Brazil as their team. It was, among other things, a better bet.[30]

But with Thuram as the star of the semifinal game, and Thierry Henry beside him, the French team was also a Caribbean team. People debated which one to support. Many from the French Caribbean still rooted for Brazil, on principle or just because they were convinced France would lose. But others were ready to root for the French Caribbean, and therefore for France. In some ways the teams were very similar to each other, for the Brazilian team had long been celebrated for its multiracial character both in Brazil and elsewhere. Brazilian commentators suggested that in its composition and its style of play, the Brazilian team represented all that was good about the nation, its "racial democracy" and its culture of playfulness and openness. The 1998 French team was similarly celebrated as a sign that France was open to its own diversity, incorporating its disparate identities into a fluid and joyful presence on the football field. For fans in the French Caribbean it was a luxury to be faced with divided loyalties, to have the option of cheering for a French team that had such strong roots in the Caribbean. There were some, of course, who weren't ready to switch their allegiance. In Paris the night of the final game, one Antillean man taunted a group of French supporters, waving a Brazilian flag, saying that France still played "small football." But many fans in the French Caribbean, and particularly in Guadeloupe, claimed a double victory, for their nation and for their island.[31]

One man, meanwhile, tried to lay a personal claim on the two goals scored in Paris. Joseph Lother appeared out of nowhere to announce that he was

Thuram's father. "I cheered on Lilian," he said, "who is a very talented boy." The man enumerated the football teams in Guadeloupe *he* had played for when he was younger: "He got that from me. . . . He's a disciplined boy, with a lot of *sang-froid*." Lilian Thuram proved the latter to be true when, during an interview the day after the game, a journalist shocked Thuram by showing him footage of Lother's statement. "As usual," the newspaper reported, Thuram "kept his *sang-froid*." He said nothing at the time, but later he told a journalist, "I'm surprised by the behavior of M. Joseph Lother, who is my genitor but can't declare himself my father. My conception of fatherhood is different from his. A father has to raise his son. A father has to give him advice. A father clears a path for him. My mother did all that for me." *France-Antilles* concurred that Thuram had in fact had little contact with his father. But if Lother couldn't claim Thuram, Guadeloupe could. "With Thuram, Guadeloupe saved France." He had gotten the nation, for the first time, into the World Cup final.[32]

SIX

Two Flags

"THERE'S A MURDERER!" Zinedine Zidane shouted in the middle of the night. His father, Smaïl, worked as a night guard at a local supermarket. "From midnight to eight in the morning," Zidane remembers, "I didn't sleep. I had horrible nightmares. Sometimes I woke up shouting, and everyone in the house could hear me." But Smaïl never had any problems at the store, where he got along well with his coworkers. "He's Maghrebin," explains Zidane. "He could have had problems with others. But it never happened. He respected everyone, and everyone respected him." For Zinedine, Smaïl remains a model. "He's a strong man. Real. He's as magnificent as life.... Everything he told me when I was a kid is true. He put me on the right path.... God's path." He always told his son, "Whenever there is a ray of sunlight, you have to capture it."[1]

Looking back on his life in Algeria and France, Smaïl remarked of his new country, "Here, son, we don't have the right to complain." Still, his life in France took its toll. As Zidane was starting his career as a professional football player, his father careened into depression. "He had taken in all the difficulties of life for so long without complaining," Zidane says. "He was suffering, but no one had seen it." Suddenly, he stopped talking and started acting out. Zidane recalled, "When the kids were playing football under his window, he went down and punctured their ball.... He'd spent forty years of his life in the project and he was exploding. There was noise, so much noise.... He needed quiet. His head had taken in too much." To Zidane's relief, his father finally retired. Two years later Zidane bought his parents a house in a quiet suburb of Marseille. "He looks at the sun," says Zidane. "He takes care of his garden. He doesn't suffer from the noise anymore. He has room to live."[2]

Throughout his son's football career Smaïl could never bring himself to watch Zinedine play. While other family members watched the game, he would retreat into another room. Once he knew how the game had turned out, he would watch a recording of it. Thierry Henry's grandmother, living in Désirade island, had the same problem; it was impossible for her to watch her grandson playing, for she always feared he would be hurt.[3]

As Zinedine Zidane has become an icon in France, both Smaïl and his mother, Malika, have become famous as well. In interviews Zidane has emphasized his parents' modesty, their dignity, the strict and righteous way they raised him in the midst of difficult circumstances. Their story can take on the tone of a national fairy tale: two migrants from rural Algeria arrive in France in the midst of a war, fall in love, and settle in a new country. They keep to themselves, work hard, and raise five children, one of whom becomes a wealthy and beloved icon, one of the most popular French citizens of his generation. At the same time, of course, the story of Malika and Smaïl also necessarily brings up uncomfortable history: the brutal Algerian war of independence, the colonial exploitation that created poverty in Algeria and sent the two to France, the only place they believed they could find decent work; the political repression, poverty, and racism experienced by Algerian workers in France; the ongoing discrimination they and their children experience; and the bloody and unresolved conflicts within postcolonial Algeria itself. Smaïl and Malika have never spoken out publicly about their political positions or attitudes toward the Front de Libération Nationale or the Algerian war. They share this silence with others of their generation, many of whom keep memories of these years alive within their families but rarely speak about them in public.[4]

Malika and Smaïl are Zidane's link to Algeria and to its history. Zidane himself has spent little time there. He visited as a boy and has made donations to Algerian charities in the past decade, but it was only in 2006 that he traveled again to the country. Nevertheless Zidane has become perhaps the most powerful and prevalent medium through which French people of many different backgrounds confront and experience the legacies of Algerian history.[5]

Zidane's parents come from the Kabyle region of Algeria, and he expresses pride in this heritage. He grew up hearing the Kabyle, or Berber, language at home and still understands it. "My father is Kabyle," he declares. "The blood of Boukhèlifa, the village where he was born, will always course through his veins. . . . It's the blood of the ancestors, of the blue men who came out of the desert, whose look is proud and direct." In evoking the "blue men," Zidane was using a term usually used to refer to the Touaregs of the Sahara, who are sometimes described as blue men because of the color of their headdresses, suggesting that the ancestors of the Kabyles were also desert nomads.[6]

Contemporary Kabyles, or Berbers, link their history to that of the people who lived in North Africa before the invasion of Arabs and of Islam. They usually see themselves as the original inhabitants of Algeria and often as the victims of a series of invasions, first Muslim, then French, and of continuing oppression as a marginalized minority. The French colonial state cultivated the idea that Kabyles were quite different from, and in some sense superior to, Arab Algerians, and it helped to institutionalize the differences between the groups. Since Algerian independence in 1962, there have been ongoing conflicts within the nation over the status of the Kabyles and their language. The Algerian state has emphasized national unity, seeking to suppress "expressions of regional or ethnic identity" and has "pursued a policy of Arabisation, making Arabic the sole official and national language of the country," to the detriment of the Berber language. Kabyles in Algeria have long protested this policy, as have many among the large number of Kabyles who, like Zidane's parents, migrated to France. They have created cultural and political organizations in France, often protesting Algerian state policies. In the 1990s one such group created its own football team, FC Berbère. In Algeria, meanwhile, activists have long rallied around a football team founded in 1946, Jeunesse sportive de Kabylie, or J.S.K. (*Kabylie* is the word used to describe the region in Algeria where the Kabyles live.) In 1972 the Algerian government forced the club to remove "Kabyle" from its name, but the initials stayed the same. And those initials were readily celebrated in the phrase "Je suis Kabyle!"—"I am Kabyle!" The J.S.K. has been extremely successful on the field, and activists have often used its matches as occasions for political protest, raising banners written in Berber script and criticizing the Algerian state. In 2001 many of the Kabyle protesters who took to the streets in both France and Algeria wore J.S.K. shirts as a sign of their conjoined allegiance to the team and to Berber culture.[7]

The struggles over the status of the Kabyle minority in Algeria have frequently been violent. On 25 June 1998, in the midst of the World Cup, the singer Lounès Matoub, one of the most prominent voices of the Kabyle movement, was assassinated in Algeria. Although Zidane has not been active in Kabyle organizations or spoken out against the Algerian state—to the disappointment of some activists—he opened his 1998 book by announcing how deeply he and his family regretted the killing of Matoub, "whose voice carried the flag of Kabylie high." Kabyle identity, Zidane declared, would "never disappear."[8]

Though within Algeria, and in France itself, some Kabyles distinguish themselves from the Arab population, Zidane has accepted and indeed embraced being identified as an Arab. In a stadium in Casablanca in May 1998 he scored a goal against Belgium during a friendly international match and the mostly Moroccan crowd roared with ecstatic approval. Though not necessarily fans of the French team, they were fans of Zidane. The "incredible welcome" he felt in Morocco gave Zidane "chills for a long time." He recalls, "Even the other players couldn't believe it. They said: 'Are you Moroccan?!'" Zidane responded, "I'm Arab. I have Arab blood in me. . . . I was really proud." In France Zidane has been embraced broadly by North African fans as one of their own. Indeed many fans celebrated the victories of the French team by flying Algerian (and sometimes Moroccan and Tunisian) flags. It is a remarkable gesture. The Algerian flag, after all, was created in the midst of a war with France. But by raising the flag to celebrate France, fans announced the hope that, despite everything—the history, the racism, the far right's portrayals of North Africans as a menace to French society—it was possible, even joyful to be Algerian and French at the same time. But if the gesture represents hope, it also represents doubt. It suggests that the French flag by itself cannot fully represent or incorporate Zidane. Since 1998 the question "Who is Zidane?" has been a crucial way of asking "What is France?" Zidane is a symbol and a cipher for the larger debates about the place of Algerians and their descendants in the future of the nation.[9]

Zidane was born in June 1972 in Marseille and grew up in the *cité* of Castellane, to the north of the city. As far back as he can remember football was his obsession, as it is for many in the city. Marseille is, after all, a "city of football." Every night in front of his building he played the game while thinking about the "exploits of [his] favorite heroes." His childhood was punctuated by some of the most memorable moments in the history of football. During the 1982 World Cup he and his brothers excitedly followed the progress of the Algerian team and watched the devastating match in which France lost to Germany in penalty kicks during the semifinals. Two years later, on his twelfth birthday, he watched France play Portugal in a semifinal game of the European Cup at the Stade du Vélodrome, Marseille's stadium. The winning play was a pass by the Marseillais Jean Tigana to Michel Platini, whose jersey sported the number 10 that would one day become Zidane's. A few days later he and his brothers watched on T.V. as France won the European Cup; the boys celebrated wildly outside their apartment.[10]

His birthday present that year was a pair of football cleats, a brand named after the French football hero Raymond Kopa: "I remember this pair of Kopas that I got for my twelfth birthday. They cost four hundred and fifty francs. To give them to me, my father saved up for a year. His wallet took a hit! But when I got them it was like a dream. Those shoes really marked me." Two years later, when France defeated Brazil in the semifinal round of the 1986 World Cup, Zidane and his brothers went out into the street to celebrate with friends in front of their apartment. "Tomorrow," he remembers thinking, "it will be my turn."[11]

Even among the very strong players in Castellane, Zidane stood out. "It was impossible to take the ball from him," recalls his brother Farid. "He was the youngest, but he always made us win." He practiced hard. Starting at eight in the morning he was outside with his ball, kicking it against a wall. "Then a friend arrived," recalls a neighbor, "then another, and they started a game. It could last hours." "We played constantly," recalls Zidane. "It was pure joy, because in the street there was no obligation, you could do what you wanted with the ball."[12]

Zidane wasn't particularly interested in school. "It's not that he can't [do the work]," his teachers told his parents. "It's that he doesn't want to." He was always waiting anxiously for the bell to ring so he could get together with his friends to play football. Teachers invited him to play in their own lunchtime games, and one teacher remembers that Zidane always showed "tremendous talent." Summer vacation was two and half months of football. Because their parents didn't have many vacation days, the kids at Castellane spent most of their time hanging out at the foot of the towers where they lived. "When we didn't play, we talked, we messed around, we fought." But the game brought them together. If there were just a few of them, they played in a tunnel next to their apartment block. "But when there were a bunch of us on each team," Zidane recalls, "we went to the concrete of the Place Tartane." They used pots to mark the boundaries, rocks and clothes for goals. Unlike Thuram, who had the grass of the Fontainebleau forest to play on, Zidane had only concrete. "We didn't know what grass was," he says. The Place Tartane was Zidane's training ground: "Everything I've learned about playing, I learned there. In the street. With my friends, we always tried to invent a new feint. Anyone who discovered something had to show it to everyone else. We practiced the new move until everyone could do it well. . . . I took the ball, I invented things."[13]

His teammates, writes one biographer, were "white, black, Kabyle," in a way that "prefigured the famous 'black-blanc-beur' French team of the 1998 World Cup." Among them was Malek Kourane, who would remain a lifelong friend and later lived in Italy with Zidane and his family. From the beginning Zidane always wanted to take penalty kicks. Once they played in a tournament where the first prize was a bicycle. Their team was awarded a penalty kick. "I'm taking it," declared Zidane, but Kourane took it instead, and missed. They lost the game. Kourane recalls, "[Zidane] ran after me all afternoon, he was so pissed off. He really wanted that bike!"[14]

In Castellane football was also a way of staying out of trouble. It was played on "neutral terrain," Zidane's biographer writes, "in the midst of tensions it appeases." "When your nose is glued on a ball, no one looks at you the wrong way," Zidane recalls. "No one tries to start trouble with you. In the *quartiers*, sometimes all it takes is the wrong look for something to start. Then it goes really fast. . . . Since I played all day long, I didn't have time to think about anything else. Football helped me avoid doing stupid things." His parents found it reassuring that they could watch their sons play in the Place Tartane from the window of their kitchen and could call to them if they needed to. As long as they were playing football, they were safe.[15]

Zidane remembers that his neighborhood, with six thousand people one of the largest in Marseille, was considered "one of the toughest" and most violent in the area, though its problems were shared by other *banlieues* around Paris and Lyon. At the time tensions between *banlieue* residents and police were beginning to boil over in parts of Marseille. In the summer of 1981 police raided the Cité de la Cayolle, injuring women, children, and older residents in the process. Infuriated young men in the neighborhood rioted, setting shopping centers and police stations on fire. During that period there were similar uprisings in other *cités* in France, notably outside Lyon. Young men sometimes entertained themselves, and taunted police in the process, with what they called "rodeos." They stole a car and led police on a high-speed chase, before jumping out of the car, setting it on fire, and escaping into the labyrinths of their projects.[16]

After he left Zidane remained connected to his *cité*. His closest friends are those he grew up with in Castellane, and he sponsors a sports association there. "I'm very proud of having lived in my neighborhood," he says. What he learned there was that, as the "son of an immigrant," he had to be "twice as strong as a French person."[17]

In a photograph of the youth team of Castellane's AS Foresta, a nine-year-old Zidane stares out with tense shoulders, squinting. The shirts of the team sport the name of a sponsor, a furniture store called Sauvage (Savage). He is team captain, wearing a tricolor band on his arm. At ten, on another local team, Zidane was saddled with greater responsibility. At one all-day tournament he scored the winning goals for his team in the first two games. Having barely slept the night before, he was exhausted by the third game. "I'm taking you home," his father said. "You can't do that," said the coach. "Why not?" asked Smaïl. The coach responded, "[Without him] the team doesn't exist. We'll lose the tournament." "Too bad for the tournament," was Smaïl's final word. They left and Zidane's team lost. Soon the coach of a better local team, Septèmes, came looking for Zidane. His name was Robert Centenero and he drove around Marseille in his tiny car, packing his players in as if it were a bus to take them to games. The first time he went to Castellane to pick up Zidane, Centenero had his tires slashed. But he kept returning; it was worth it.[18]

Playing for Septèmes, Zidane was able to travel outside of Marseille, to other parts of France, to the Alps and Perpignan. When he was thirteen he was invited to play a game with the French national youth team. Soon afterward Jean Varraud, a coach at the youth training academy in Cannes, saw Zidane playing. It was, he remembers, "sublime." "I saw a kid," he announced on his return to Cannes. "He has hands in the place of his feet!" In addition to his obvious skill, what attracted him to Zidane was his attitude, his hunger to succeed. "I immediately knew this boy would become a great player. He had an exceptional speed in his feet, something I'd never seen before and I've never seen since! He also had a side to him, the 'warrior' side of the disadvantaged neighborhoods. He was hungry!"[19]

Varraud brought him to Cannes for a short training period and confirmed that he had an "amazing talent when the ball was at his feet, transforming it into a magic toy" whenever he got hold of it. Jean Fernandez, the coach for the Cannes professional team, was also amazed when he saw Zidane play, wondering why no recruiter had found him yet. Fernandez had been born in 1954 in Algeria. His father, a settler of Spanish descent, was a fisherman. When Algeria became independent in 1962 the family left and settled in a small town in the south of France. Fernandez played professional football at Marseille, Bordeaux, and then Cannes before retiring and becoming a coach. Through his encounter with Zidane, two individuals whose families had been on opposite sides of the Algerian war came to work together in a collaboration with far-reaching implications for French football.

At Cannes the coaches noticed one big problem in Zidane's playing. During one of his first games the ball came toward him in the air, perfectly placed for a header. But Zidane ducked. In Castellane he had never practiced headers. His coaches urged him to work on that and, luckily for France, he did.[20]

⚇

Though Zidane was only fourteen, Varraud invited him to come to the youth football academy at Cannes. Zidane's parents were willing, but only if Varraud found the boy a family to stay with, since it was too far to travel back and forth to Marseille. Varraud found Zidane a home with parents of another player at the academy, who warmly welcomed him. But Zidane was, at first, deeply unhappy. He called his family regularly from a phone booth near the house, but it wasn't much consolation. "All of a sudden," he remembers, "I lost what was most important to me: my parents and my friends. I was really miserable. For a year, every night, I cried silently into my pillow. I wanted to go home. And, at the same time, I told myself I had to hold out."[21]

Zidane made friends among the young players at Cannes, many of whom were of immigrant background—North and West African, Armenian, Italian—and also from Marseille. He also met a young woman, a student at a youth arts academy. Her name was Véronique Fernandez, and she was part of a French family with roots in Spain. They were both far from home, "deracinated" in Cannes, and though Zidane was extremely timid—"Talking to a girl was like going to prison," he recalls—they eventually started dating. Soon after, Zidane was called up for military service, though the army, sensing which battlefield really mattered in 1980s Europe, placed him in a special unit that had long greeted athletes, the Bataillion de Joinville. The unit allowed Zidane the time off he needed to continue playing and training with Cannes. When he was at the barracks, he remembers, he called Véronique ten times a day. Within a few years the two were married, and Véronique gave up her training as a dancer to raise their children. Their traditional marriage is often celebrated in the French media as a contrast to the flashy lives of other professional footballers.[22]

As Zidane played in competitions with Cannes, he earned mixed reviews from coaches and managers. Some criticized his playing style, seeing him as technically brilliant but too nonchalant and not enough of a goal scorer. One team manager declared, "He's playing an outdated football." By the 1980s, in the midst of an increasingly competitive and money-driven world of professional sports, many managers and coaches were obsessed most of all with the effectiveness of the players. The defensive style of play perfected in Italian football was becoming increasingly popular. The result, though, was that the possibilities for offensive plays were reduced, and with them the possibility of the creative and often beautiful runs that set the hearts of fans pounding. What sustains many football fans and players are its remarkable and surprising gestures, the way a player seems literally to be dancing with the ball. Such moves can sometimes seem superfluous, even a distraction, if you are focused entirely on scoring goals. But to many fans they also represent the soul of the game. Zidane was always a technically brilliant player, his swaying, loping run on the field unpredictable, his moves with the ball—tapping it over a player's head, kicking it with the side of his foot behind him, tapping it with the outside of his foot quickly to another player—often breathtaking to watch. The journalist Jean Philippe, an early and avid fan of the player during his years at Cannes, enjoyed this about Zidane: "He plays a football that is eternal, pertinent. Not outdated but avant-garde." He is one of the few who transforms the game into an "awesome spectacle." Years later the owner of Real Madrid, where Zidane played the last years of his professional career, described well how, when Zidane enters a game, he "oxygenates it" and "allows it to breathe." A Spanish journalist writing about a legendary goal scored by Zidane in 2002 for Real Madrid in the final of the European Cup effused about Zidane's "gravity and speed" that allowed him to take a ball "fallen from the sky" and power it into the goal. "At times," he wrote, Zidane too "seems to have fallen from the sky." Early on, some were already predicting Zidane's future. The brother of one of his teammates at Cannes declared to his friends at the university, "In Cannes, there's a guy who lived with my family. He's the future captain of the French team!"[23]

Getting there, of course, meant navigating the world of professional football. And professional football, as Zidane quickly learned, was about money and deals, a world in which players, especially young ones, have little say. He did enjoy his first rewards. In 1989, at seventeen, he played his first game on the Cannes Division 1 team, against Nantes, which fielded his future captain on the French national team, Didier Deschamps, as well as Marcel Desailly. For that game he got a bonus of five thousand francs, which he sent to his parents. In 1991 he scored his first goal for Cannes. At the suggestion of Jean Fernandez, the president of the Cannes club had promised to get him a car when that happened. "I was expecting a used car," Zidane remembers, but he got a brand-new red Renault Clio, presented to him at a party in front of all the Cannes players.[24]

Despite these promising beginnings, Zidane's career soon seemed in danger. After a string of bad seasons, Cannes was being demoted to Division 2, and Olympique de Marseille, which had expressed an interest in the player earlier, decided not to recruit him. Zidane was traded to the Girondins de Bordeaux, a less prestigious team than l'OM, but still in Division 1. The whole process left Zidane unhappy. "They sold me like an animal," he declared to the head of the local fan club in Cannes.[25]

Football players, like other athletes, usually have very little say in their transfers from team to team. They are bought and sold in negotiations between team owners and coaches. Throughout the twentieth century some athletes have complained about this, and a few have even compared their situation to a kind of slavery. As early as the 1930s players who flouted the emerging regulations governing amateur and professional playing were said to be maroons, like slaves who had escaped from plantations. In 1963 Raymond Kopa, angry about the regulations governing professional football contracts, declared, "Players are slaves. . . . The professional footballer is the only man who can still be bought and sold without his consent." Five years later footballers joined the student and worker uprising of May 1968, occupying the offices of the French Football Federation and demanding that players be given more power in negotiating their contracts. The metaphor of slavery has also repeatedly been used to describe the situation of professional athletes in the U.S.[26]

Of course comparing athletes who make millions of dollars a year to slaves strikes some people as absurd. In 2006 the use of the metaphor stirred up a brief controversy. It involved Claude Makelele, the Congo-born French footballer who has been a key player for the country. At the time he was playing for Chelsea in England, and though he had expressed a desire to retire from international play, he was still being called on by the coach of the French team, Raymond Domenech. According to F.I.F.A. rules coaches have the right to tap any player they wish. Exasperated on the player's behalf, Chelsea's coach declared, "Makelele is a slave." The F.I.F.A. rules he went on, told a player, "You are a slave, you have no human rights." Domenech responded sarcastically, "That's right, he is a slave, I am a slave-driver, I whip him and he goes." Lilian Thuram, who has pushed for greater acknowledgment of the true history of slavery in France, sharply criticized the Chelsea coach for his statement: "What shocks me is that people talk about slavery without knowing what it is." The fact that he could compare the situation of Claude Makelele to that of a slave, Thuram declared, made it clear he had no idea what slavery actually was.[27]

Whether or not it can be compared to slavery, a career in professional football is full of possible pitfalls. Despite his initial disgust at the system he was entering, Zinedine Zidane ultimately learned to navigate it with great expertise and to great profit. Much later he described the pressures placed on football players by "financial interests" and the "sometimes savage demands placed on [players] by the biggest of the European clubs." Football is a minefield: "You have to anticipate the crimes of mercenaries on the field, get around crooked contracts, bounce back, impose yourself, score anyway." Zidane has expertly navigated his career, profiting enormously as a player and commercial icon with endorsement deals. But such comments suggest that he saw himself in some ways as trapped by powers he could never fully escape, even if he could sometimes briefly outrun or outdribble them.[28]

⊛

The Girondins made waves in the French professional league during the 1980s and gave Zidane a generous monthly salary of forty thousand francs (the equivalent of about eight thousand U.S. dollars). There he met Bixente Lizarazu, a player from the Basque country who prided himself on this affiliation, draping his region's flag around himself after a victory in 1995. Lizarazu was the captain of the team and impressed Zidane with his intellect and knowledge, though Zidane didn't appreciate it so much when Lizarazu teased him about his balding head, telling him he looked like a monk. He also reconnected with Christophe Dugarry, whom he befriended when they both played on the French national youth team a few years earlier. Dugarry was from Bordeaux and took Zidane under his wing; the two opened up a brasserie in the town. In 1998 Dugarry, Lizarazu, and Zidane all played together, in a fluid and practiced way, on the French national team. In Bordeaux Zidane also got the nickname that was to stick with him, the one that would be chanted countless times by fans, "Zizou," apparently coined by his coach at Bordeaux, Roland Courbis, during a training session.[29]

In 1994 Zidane was selected with the French national team in a World Cup qualifying game against Czechoslovakia. It was a remarkable debut. He was substituted in late in the game, with France down two points. In two minutes he scored two goals, guaranteeing a tie rather than a loss. He also had an excellent season with the Girondins, who defeated the powerhouse AC Milan during a Champions League game. These performances got him noticed by Italy's Juventus, which recruited him in a huge deal that brought the Girondins an infusion of cash and multiplied Zidane's salary exponentially. He was following a well-trodden path from France to Turin. Michel Platini had played there for five years in the 1980s, and Didier Deschamps was playing there when Zidane arrived. Playing for Juventus, Zidane got a chance to play against, and trade jerseys with, his childhood idol, the Uruguayan Enzo Francescoli, after whom he named his son.[30]

But Juventus was an intense and difficult environment. The physical training was brutal. His first three weeks involved an intense boot camp—he was placed in the charge of a trainer nicknamed "the Marine"—and sometimes he worked so hard that he threw up. As he later described it, Juventus was "the club where you work harder than anywhere else," and it improved his game and his physical condition enormously. So too did playing in what was perhaps Europe's most experienced and most intense leagues, alongside some of the most brilliant players of the day. Zidane—like Thuram, Deschamps, David Trezeguet (all of whom played at Juventus at one point), and many other players on the French national team of the 1990s—owes to Italy much of the strength he demonstrated in international competitions. During these competitions, again and again, Zidane would end up playing against the Italian players, many of them close friends, with whom he spent much of his professional career. Italian players pushed him throughout his career. Eventually one of them pushed him too far in the stadium in Berlin where he played his last game.[31]

Football had helped keep Zidane out of fights in Castellane, but at Cannes it started getting him into fights. The stakes were high, and players sometimes cracked. At one early game played with the Cannes team in Marseille, the referee kicked Zidane off the field for a foul, and as he was walking past the other team's bench, a player walked up and punched him. Zidane didn't punch back then, though in another game soon afterward he crossed the field to join a melee that broke out between players. Sometimes he used the style of fighting for which he would ultimately become legendary: the *coup de boule,* or head-butt. During one tournament Zidane gave a *coup de boule* to a defender and was sent off the field with a red card. Not long afterward, during a division championship match, he struck another player and was banned from the field for three weeks as a result. His coach, Jean Varraud, punished him by ordering him to clean the locker room. He also told Zidane that he would always have to deal with aggressive and even violent opponents on the field because he protected the ball so well that defenders didn't know how else to get it from him: "If one day you don't get hit, it'll be because you're not good anymore!" Zidane was also impatient with aggressive fans. In 1991 Cannes fans booed and hissed the nineteen-year-old, angry at him for failing to score in an important game. Zidane responded with a quick *bras d'honneur*—raising a fist in the French version of "Fuck you"—stirring up even more ire among the fans.[32]

Zidane always issued an apology and a self-criticism after he struck other players. But he didn't stop hitting them. In 1993, playing for Bordeaux, he slugged Marcel Desailly and was sent off with a red card. "I was hassled, insulted. I lost it when I hit Desailly and I regret it. . . . I take total responsibility," he declared at the time. Two years later he slapped a German player across the face. During his years with Juventus he was expelled from five games for hard tackles or striking other players, culminating in 2000 when, during a Champions League game against Hamburg, after a foul by a defender, he sent a powerful *coup de boule* into the shoulder of the German player. He seemed at first to be aiming for the player's head, but thought better of that, moving slightly to whack him in the shoulder instead. He was sent off the field with a red card. The sight of Zidane striding off the field, expelled, his face set in anger, would be a constant in his life as a player.[33]

Did Zidane's background as a child of the *banlieue* and of Algerian immigrants shape the kind of provocations he received, the way he experienced them, and the way he responded? These were questions that commentators and fans regularly posed, most insistently at the end of the World Cup of 2006. As Zidane was growing up and then moving into professional football, hate crimes against North Africans were on the rise, notably in Marseille. Among all immigrant groups, North Africans, particularly Algerians, were regularly singled out in the political discourse of far-right parties, in polls, and in the broader language of race as being the most dangerous and problematic of immigrants.

"I never suffered from racism," Zidane claims in one autobiography. Though he did occasionally hear racist comments in the courtyard or at school, he "never worried about it and never suffered from it" because he knew he hadn't "done anything to provoke the animosity." The relatively segregated residential situation in which he grew up, though shaped by larger patterns of racial and social marginalization, also limited his encounters with overt racism: "When I was little, all my friends were from the Maghreb or foreigners." Zidane left his neighborhood at a young age; if he had lived in Marseille as an older and more mobile teenager, his experiences and perspectives might well have changed. Instead he entered the relatively protected world of the football academy and as a result was never, according to his account, in "contexts where people were racist." He does claim to have enough familiarity with racism to immediately sense it in some people: "When someone asks me for an autograph I can tell if [that person] is racist." Usually he senses it in the parent of a child who is a fan, and he signs anyway, since there is no point in punishing children for the attitudes of their parents.[34]

Racist attitudes among fans and other players put the athletes who are its victims in a particular kind of pressure cooker. They are subject to infuriating provocations. If they respond, they can easily get a reputation as temperamental players who can't control their aggression. They are usually advised to ignore the insults and take revenge on the field. That was the strategy taken by John Barnes, the Jamaican-born player who was among the first black players on the English national team in the 1980s and whose time playing for Liverpool in the 1980s inspired a rival team to dub them "Niggerpool." Racist chants and banana throwing by fans, he claimed, just inspired him to play better, since scoring a goal was the best way to shut them up. Zidane said in 1998 that that was his approach too: "When someone really insults me, I tell myself what I always do in that situation: that I'll take my revenge on the field."[35]

Of course what is said on the field and in the stadium is just a small part of what is being said, and being done, outside it. In 1998 Zidane was transformed by fans and commentators into a powerful and inspiring rejection of racism in French society. For a little while it almost seemed that all it might take to conquer racism was something as simple as a goal, or maybe two.

France's first game in the 1998 World Cup (against South Africa) took place in Marseille. "Tonight, I'm going to be proud of being French," Zidane told himself as he prepared to play. Coach Jacquet made sure his players understood the momentousness of the occasion. "Tonight," he declared, "we have a rendezvous with History." But the vindication Zidane achieved that night had less to do with history than with friendship. In the chorus of complaints that accompanied the run-up to the World Cup, commentators singled out Zidane's teammate Christopher Dugarry for regular abuse. Some claimed that he wasn't any good and that he was on the national team only because Zidane insisted on it. The suggestion infuriated Zidane. As they began the game against South Africa, the French fans in the stadium were clearly unsympathetic to Dugarry. When he sent the ball wide off a pass from Zidane early in the game, the crowd booed him loudly, as they did again when the South African goalie picked off the ball from him. Then, in the thirty-fourth minute, Zidane sent a corner kick that sailed toward Dugarry, who pummeled the ball into the South African goal with his head. As he ran toward his teammates, elated, he stuck out his tongue at the crowd. It was the first French goal of the tournament, and the photograph of Dugarry taunting the crowd with his tongue sticking out would become one of several iconic images of the summer.[36]

The next game produced a very different image. In the midst of the French victory against Saudi Arabia, Zidane, after a rough tackle from a defender that left both of them sprawled on the ground, stood up and raked his cleats across the waist of the Saudi player lying beneath him. He was immediately expelled from the game, and from the next two French games as well. At a practice session at Clairefontaine a few days later, he complained with another player about all the red cards being handed out during the tournament, muttering that the referee who had given him the red card was a "bastard." A few months later he admitted that the gesture had been a mistake, a failure on his part in a game in which it is vital to avoid tackles, to "develop the eyes of a butterfly so that you can guess what is coming from behind." But he also tied the incident to the fact that financial interests and the demand for efficiency encouraged an increasingly ugly and cynical style of play. "I don't regret anything today about my expulsion during the game against Saudi Arabia," he said. "I don't have any remorse. I just believe that with experience you make fewer mistakes and that you learn to resist provocation. That's the difference between a player who is 20 years old and one who is almost thirty. . . . In the future, I'll know how to avoid getting tricked."[37]

Back on the field against Italy Zidane shone, sending several near misses against the Italian goal and scoring France's first penalty kick. During the game against Croatia he was once again a central player, helping to assure France's place in the final. Except for his penalty kick against Italy, he didn't score in either of the games. Indeed he hadn't yet scored in the World Cup at all. As the final approached, many French fans, coming down off the victory against Croatia, were worried that their team wouldn't be capable of winning against the brilliant Brazilians.

"Victory is within us," read the Adidas posters and billboards plastered throughout France that summer, sporting a black-and-white portrait of a determined-looking Zidane. He had signed a lucrative endorsement deal with the company. The star Brazilian striker Ronaldo, meanwhile, had signed a competing deal with Nike. He was featured in a commercial that—using humor impossible to imagine in a post–9/11 world—showed him and other Brazilian players wearing blue Nike T-shirts playing an impromptu game in an airport, twisting their way out of the hands of security guards, kicking footballs through security scanners, booting the ball across a runway, dribbling through the baggage claim area. Ronaldo ultimately takes a shot at a goal made of two metal posts, but he hits one of them and turns around with his hands on his head, grinning in frustration.

Some joked at the time that the World Cup was less a France-Brazil match than an Adidas-Nike face-off. In fact many still consider the outcome of the France-Brazil game to be the result of corporate intervention on the field. After suffering a bizarre seizure the morning of the final game, Ronaldo was taken to the hospital, and he was not on Brazil's original roster. Rumors circulated at the time that he had been poisoned by an overzealous French chef. When the Brazilian team took the field that night, however, Ronaldo was there. But he seemed sluggish and weak throughout the game, which clearly affected the Brazilian effort. Rumors have swirled from that day on that it was Nike, which in addition to its deal with Ronaldo also had a contract with the Brazilian coach, Mario Zagallo, that forced Ronaldo onto the field. According to this version of events, the corporation wanted its figurehead on display that night whether he could play well or not. Nike has vociferously denied this story, calling it "absurd and insulting," and so has Ronaldo. Still, in 2000 the Brazilian Congress carried out an inquiry into the issue of Nike's involvement in Brazilian sport. The inquiry turned up no clear proof of Nike pressure during the 1998 World Cup, but it didn't lay the rumors to rest. Like many great World Cup games, the Brazil-France match of 1998 is still being played out, over and over again.[38]

For Zidane, the game against Brazil was "a night that changed everything." He had played well in the friendly matches leading up to the World Cup and was the first player in history to score in the new Stade de France when it opened a few months before the tournament. But in the previous years he had gone through two disappointing losses in the European Cup finals with Juventus. Having made it into the final game of the World Cup, he decided, "This match against Brazil should be the game of my life.... [It should also be] the final game of an entire people.... And that is exactly what we offered."[39]

Throughout France crowds thronged to bars and cafés to watch the game and gathered in plazas in front of giant screens set up for them. France became a giant stadium. In Marseille families from the *cités* went to the Prado in the center of town to watch the game, even though there were giant screens set up near where they lived. "The inhabitants of these neighborhoods," one activist explained, "announced in their own way that they wanted to be like everyone, with everyone else." Others took advantage of the moment to protest the walls built around French citizenship. In front of the abbey church of Saint-Denis, not far from the Stade de France, a group of *sans-papiers* and their supporters held a demonstration. In their hands they held red cards, which they offered to ruling French politicians, demanding, "Papers for everyone!"[40]

Twenty-seven minutes into the game Thuram ran the ball up the left side of the field and passed it to Christian Karembeu. The Brazilian player Roberto Carlos battled him for the ball as it rolled toward the edge of the field. Carlos tried to nudge it so that it would go off the side of the field, giving the French a throw-in rather than a more dangerous corner kick. But the ball just barely rolled the wrong way. An angry Carlos kicked the corner flag, and the referee cautioned him for the outburst.

Before the game Aimé Jacquet had told his players about a weakness of the Brazilian team: too confident on free kicks and corner kicks, the Brazilians didn't organize coverage of individual players. Emmanuel Petit took the corner kick, sending the ball sailing right in front of the Brazilian goal. Starting a little way back from the goal, unmarked by the Brazilians, Zidane ran forward into the crowd of players, weaving about, trying to find the ball. "The ball arrived in the heart of the Brazilian defense," he recalled, and his "head was drawn to it like a magnet to the iron." He leaped up, pivoted his head, and sent the ball streaking into the goal, stunning the goalie and the crowd. While Brazilians groaned in shock, French fans erupted. Zidane kept running toward the edge of the field, jumping up on the wall that lined it and onto the other side, sending photographers scattering, pounding his fist into the air of the exploding stadium. Back on the field he was mobbed and pummeled by his delighted teammates. As he later described it, he experienced the goal as a powerful, even transcendental sign of possibility.[41]

Nineteen minutes later, as the first half was coming to an end, Thuram once again sent the ball forward, lobbing it fast and far up the field to Stéphane Guivarc'h, who took a shot at the goal that was deflected by the Brazilian goalie but rolled out of bounds. France had another corner. Youri Djorkaeff took it, and Zidane did exactly as he had done twenty minutes earlier, rushing forward into the fray at the last minute to catch the perfectly placed ball with his head, pounding it into the net. In one photograph of the moment, Thuram is leaping back to get out of the way, both hands pointing toward the goal, as if he is pushing the ball in on a wave of air. Zidane ran past the goal, kissing his jersey, looking up at the French fans who were jumping, screaming, disbelieving.[42]

In the locker room at halftime the French team was jittery, well aware that

FIGURE 12. In the 1998 World Cup final, Zidane, center with the number 10 shorts, has just headed the ball, sending it toward the Brazilian goal, outside the picture to the left. Thuram, just in front of him, seems to push the ball toward the net. Zidane succeeded in scoring, sending France ahead of Brazil 2–0. © Dimitri Iundt/TempSport/Corbis.

FIGURE 13. Zidane kisses his jersey after scoring his second goal against Brazil in the 1998 World Cup final. © Dimitri Iundt/TempSport/Corbis.

FIGURE 14. At the 1998 World Cup final, goal-keeper Fabien Barthez, having just punched the ball away from Ronaldo, flies through the air as Thuram looks backward at the ball in relief. Patrick Hertzog/AFP/Getty Images.

Brazil could equalize and win in the second half. The French team suffered a blow in the sixty-seventh minute of the game when Marcel Desailly, having received the second of two yellow cards for a hard tackle against the Brazilian player Cafu, was expelled from the field. The French were down ten players to eleven, and there was enough time for the brilliant Brazilian team to come back. Jacquet replaced Youri Djorkaeff with the young Patrick Vieira, a more defensive player. And the French held on. At one point Ronaldo charged toward the goal with the ball, Thuram in hot pursuit. But the French goalie Fabien Barthez charged forward and grabbed the bouncing ball, and Ronaldo catapulted over him and onto the ground. Zidane continued to play brilliantly, "illuminating the Stade de France."[41]

As the minutes slid by, the players on the French bench grew more and more elated, barely able to contain themselves. Then, as the game drew to a close, Emmanuel Petit dribbled the ball past several Brazilian defenders and streaked it into the goal. French fans and players jumped up and down, waiting for the end. The seconds ticked by. The whistle blew, and they charged out onto the field. Fabien Barthez crouched and sobbed with joy in front

FIGURE 15. Lilian Thuram runs toward the French fans with the tricolor flag in his hand, celebrating France's World Cup victory over Brazil on 12 July 1998. John Sibley © Maxppp, Panoramic, Action Press/ZUMA.

of the goal. Bernard Lama lifted him up, exclaiming, "Champions stand up!" Lilian Thuram ran alone toward the edge of the field, shaking a French flag, holding up his jersey. The French fans roared in jubilation. For the first time in the history of this worldwide competition invented by a Frenchman, France had won the World Cup.[44]

French officials, including President Jacques Chirac and Prime Minister Lionel Jospin, lined up on the field to present the trophy. Michel Platini was also there; like Chirac he wore a French football jersey under a black blazer. Led by their captain, Didier Deschamps, the players climbed onto the platform in front of them, blocking from view the row of state officials. The team was now France's most beloved and prominent representative.

With their trophy the players gathered on the field again, erupting into a spontaneous singing of the "Marseillaise," joined by the thundering crowds in the stadium. As the team lined up for their victory photo, an employee of the stadium who was picking up the bottles strewn around the field sidled up to the team, dancing and smiling, and got himself into the photograph.

Eventually someone noticed and told him to move away. The man was cropped out of the photos, but he left his trace on the television footage of the event. And, in a sense, his gesture was a fitting one for the beginning of the celebrations that would shake France for days. The victory, many would repeat again and again, belonged to everyone in France—every group, every color, every age, every status.[45]

When Zidane grasped the World Cup, he thought about the makeshift trophy he and his friends used to play for in Castellane during the tournaments they organized on the Place Tartane, next to his family's apartment. The matchups were determined by drawing lots "like in the World Cup," Zidane recalled. The jackpot was made up of one or two francs dropped in a cardboard box by each player. The winners of the tournament took the jackpot with them, along with a trophy, a plastic bottle "with aluminum paper wrapped around it."[46]

Running the victory lap with his teammates, Zidane glanced into the bleachers and saw his old friends from Castellane. "We looked at each other. It was a profound look, as vast as the football fields that we ran around on as kids." He ran to embrace them. "We stayed there, locked together, for long minutes, far from the world, far from glory, far from the officials. . . . [I could smell] all those Marseille afternoons, all those summer evenings when we killed time by teasing each other. And they were shouting in my ear, 'you're the kid from the *cité*, our buddy who scored those two goals.'"[47]

Crowds thronged around the bus that brought the French players back to the chateau at Clairefontaine. While other players laughed and joked, Zidane was, as he remembered it, "unable to move": "I couldn't talk, I could only smile." Then he traveled home, in his mind, to a place he had never lived, his father's village in Algeria.

I thought about the murmurs that were rising up from the paths of the village where my father was born, over there in the region of Little Kabylie, in Boukhèlifa. Traveling those sinuous and dusty paths, under the stars, I thought of all those children who would soon be imitating me. This both scared me and filled me with joy. I thought of all those elders who still live in Little Kabylie, and considered the intensity of their happiness. And I promised to go visit them one day. The night of the 12th of July, then, didn't just belong to the players on the French team.[48]

For Zidane, the moment of victory was a rare chance to sew together seamlessly the two flags that had always shadowed him.

SEVEN

La France Métissée

THROUGHOUT FRANCE PEOPLE RUSHED OUT into the streets in mass celebration. "It's a victory for all of France!" one television commentator joyously announced. A journalist reporting from the Champs-Elysées—where 1.2 million gathered that night—tried to describe the scene. She was surrounded by wild cheering, and beer and champagne flew through the air. Marcel Desailly, watching the scene from the studio, jokingly complained that his after-game plan—"[to] go have a drink at my favorite bar on the Champs-Elysées"—had been ruined. The television commentators tried to find a historical comparison for what was unfolding. Some said it looked like the rallies after electoral victories, like those that swept France in 1981, when the socialist François Mitterand won, except that the euphoria was unanimous: "All French people are happy," one commentator declared. "There is only one political party tonight." Others concluded that there had not been celebrations in France of this kind since the 1944 liberation of Paris from the Germans: "This may be the largest celebration in the history of France."[1]

Annick Cojean of *Le Monde* described an effervescent chaos, a seemingly infinite joy, and a world in which all barriers and rules disappeared: "There was no more hierarchy, or convention. No more disdain, no more bad mood. No more social classes, no more provincials or *banlieusards*. Nothing but the extraordinary, like a world upside down. No more landmarks! It was mad-Paris, uncontrollable-laughter-Paris, delirium-Paris. Chaos-Paris, joy-Paris, love-Paris. Paris the center of the world, colored and multi-colored, fraternal." People jumped into fountains, danced the cancan in the middle of the street, and chanted over and over again, "Zidane!" They wrapped French flags around strangers, who became instant friends. Everyone used the informal *tu*, "took each by the neck and said, 'It's awesome, no?,' and looked up into the sky as if they were looking at stars." "The days before the World Cup

FIGURE 16. Fans throng the Champs-Elysées on the night of the 1998 French World Cup victory, watched by Zidane's face projected onto the Arc de Triomphe. Jack Guez/ AFP/Getty Images.

were flat, they were gray," explained two young men. "But tonight: aïe, aïe, aïe! For tonight, for nothing but tonight, it was worth being born!"

The victory, Cojean wrote, gave people the "right to exaggerate." "The World Cup, it's the melting-pot. And the melting-pot is progress, and deliverance," announced a worker in a Citroën factory. It liberated others to do something they never otherwise would have done: parade with a French flag. "Seriously," wrote Cojean, "when was the last time Paris saw its youth parade around in the tricolor with such joy, pride, and invention?" A young Moroccan student studying in France saw the celebrations as a "symbol" of a "new France" that recognized the beauty of its diversity "in the image of its football team": "Don't you think they complement each other? Thuram the defender, Deschamps in the centerfield, Zidane the striker. Why not a Parliament inspired by the formula?" "Sunday night, in Paris," concluded Cojean, "there were no red lights, nothing outlawed, no more taboos."[3]

"From every street, from every metro station," another journalist wrote, "flooded the same joyous and mixed-up multitude: couples and their incredulous children, young girls painted blue, kids from the *banlieue* celebrating Zidane and Thuram. . . . The crowd looks like its team: it's a resolutely plural France, celebrating its victory with the combined rhythm of the trumpet and the drum." Like a throng of pilgrims, millions tried to get to the Champs-Elysées, particularly to the Arc de Triomphe, the epicenter of the celebration. Soon, though, the crowd made it impossible to get there, so the celebration spilled out along the avenues leading to the Arc. Celebrants gently transgressed boundaries, observing wealthy diners in the luxury restaurant Fouquets, watching them through its windows "like fish in an aquarium." Crowds around the presidential palace demanded, "Chirac with us!"[4]

A few days later, on 14 July, Chirac responded during the traditional Bastille Day garden party held in the Elysée. The event is usually a fairly sleepy, official affair, but this time the invitees grew into a large and boisterous crowd. They greeted the jeans-wearing members of the team ecstatically, and Chirac adventurously waded through the throng, shaking hands. The president had reason to be pleased, having reaped an increase in his popularity rating of 15 percent as a result of the victory, while Prime Minister Jospin's rating increased 10 points. One celebrating woman, though, declared that politicians must "feel jealous" about what was happening, knowing that no matter how much they tried, they could never match the fervor let loose by the victory over Brazil.[5]

At one point the celebrations turned terrifying and deadly: a confused and frightened woman drove her car into the crowd around the Arc de Triomphe, killing one man and wounding at least eighty people, eleven of them seriously. In the midst of unbridled joy the scene was bloody and shocking. The driver leaped out of her car and fled the scene in fear of retribution, though she was later found. As the police rushed into the area, there were some scuffles with celebrants, a few of whom threw bottles at them. Rapidly the area was taken over by emergency personnel and Red Cross volunteers, who rushed the wounded to nearby hospitals.[6]

The incident didn't stall the celebrations, which broke out in every city and town in the nation. In the port of Le Havre a concert of ships' horns celebrated the victory, and in every city in France parades of honking cars draped with flags filled the avenues. In Corsica, where the French state is often viewed with hostility, celebrants fired guns into the sky while drivers of cars sporting the symbol of the clandestine Corsican nationalist movement unfurled French flags as they cruised in celebration. In Martinique, despite the fact that some restaurants harbored as many supporters of Brazil as of France, celebrants paraded through towns in their cars and danced on beaches. French fans in New York, Tokyo, Santiago de Chile, and Montréal went into the streets, cheering and waving tricolor flags.[7]

If the effusion surrounding the victory was in itself not surprising—the same kind of celebrations take place in any country whose team has won the World Cup—what was remarkable about the 1998 celebrations in France was the way they were immediately tied to a powerful, even utopian sense that the victory represented and promised a profound social and political transformation, one that would release France from inequality and racism and allow a new society to flourish. Looking in from outside France, and looking back in hindsight, the extent, intensity, and deeply political nature of the enthusiasm set off by the World Cup victory can seem naïve, superficial, even absurd. Perhaps it was all those things, but in fact many millions of people did experience the victory as a powerful moment of communion, one that allowed them to imagine both the past and the future in a new way. The victory, writes one historian, was "a moment of collective grace" based on "an anti-racist message": "Victorious and multi-colored, the French team defeated both the enemies of football and the enemies of immigration." Of course the celebrations didn't resolve the issues of racism and the hauntings of empire, which continued to lurk at the heart of the celebrations themselves. But they did provide a space for people to cross and even trample on the borders and suspicions that shaped their daily lives, to enact, at least for a few days, a concrete utopia of harmony and to experience, if in a fleeting way, what it might mean to live in a very different world—one in which France was at ease with itself in all its diversity, accepting of its global past and multicolored future.[8]

"When France discriminates," a twenty-five-year-old named Ibrahim declared on the Champs-Elysées, "it loses. . . . In this case, we had to win, we had to." A pharmacist named Zora cried as she watched the crowd. "Look,

FIGURE 17. Spanish artist Ana Juan crafted this portrait of the power of football, suggesting that it could have been a potent secret weapon for a leader like Napoleon Bonaparte. Drawn during the 1998 World Cup, it was published on the cover of the *New Yorker* on 13 July, the day after the French victory. Courtesy of Ana Juan.

there are no fences, nothing between us. We want a World Cup every year, every day!" "It's too beautiful, too beautiful, France is waking up," her friend Nathalie exclaimed. At the Hôtel de Ville a young woman named Estelle, belting out the "Marseillaise," said, "It's a communion, a kind of utopia." During the days of celebration people constantly broke spontaneously into choruses of the "Marseillaise," and one scholar remembers how it became a personal soundtrack for many individuals, who whistled it to themselves while they walked down the street.[9]

Others gave a slightly different meaning to the victory. "Blacks and Arabs, it's your victory tonight," one young man shouted. "Give them papers!" responded another. In Saint-Denis a Malian family teased a line of police they passed on the street. "Tomorrow is a day off! No parking tickets!" they declared. "A few policemen smiled," the journalist reported. "Not all. . . . Then the demand got stronger. Tomorrow, no parking tickets, and the right to asylum!" While many celebrated the communion of victory as if it represented an already existing society, others used the occasion to celebrate a specific victory—that of "blacks and Arabs"—in order to demand acceptance and change.[10]

The experience in the streets provided a concrete example of the kind of future that might be possible. "People, for once, weren't racist any more," declared one fifteen-year-old living in a *cité* in a provincial town. "We went into the center of town to celebrate, they smiled at you, they talked Usually, here, when you're black or *reubeu* [i.e., *beur*] people are hostile." But that night, when some of the kids from the *cité* jumped on top of a brand-new Peugeot, the driver "honked and laughed." Others interviewed in the town concurred that the celebrations were a rare moment of unanimity. Still, there were clear limits to how far the celebrations had changed attitudes. Asked if the expressions of unity might help engender better understanding in the town, one shopkeeper responded by placing the onus on the residents of the *cités*: "It depends if they want to integrate themselves. But it's true that, the other night, they had the French flag." "It's sad to say it," another person added, "but for once they didn't come into town to smash things up." Indeed some people celebrated the victory and emitted racist statements almost in the same breath; they complimented Zidane and then made racist anti-Maghrebin remarks, "without it appearing to anyone to be a contradiction." "If those Arabs are good," commented one man in a town in the Alps, "it's because they're tightly controlled."[11]

The day after the victory a bus carrying the players drove up the Champs-Elysées. The throng of fans packing the avenue forced the bus to move at

FIGURE 18. Algerian and French flags mingle as fans surround a bus carrying the French team up the Champs-Elysées on 13 July 1998. Coach Aimé Jacquet stands with his arm raised above the players. © Philippe Caron/Sygma/Corbis.

a snail's pace; eventually it stopped, surrounded by a crowd that the five companies of France's tough riot-control police, the C.R.S., couldn't part. Mixed in with the many French tricolor flags were the green, red, and white of Algerian flags. The crowds were especially desperate to see Zidane, "the prophet." At first Zidane sat on the top deck of the bus with his young son, Enzo, sleeping on his lap, his face protected from the sun by a T-shirt printed for the occasion that said "France, champion of the World," but police brought him down into the bottom of the bus in order to hide him from the crowd. From afar, people in the crowd strained to see the team. Who was that player carrying the flag? "He's black, anyway," determined one bystander. "That doesn't narrow it down much," retorted a young black man proudly. "They say footballers are stupid," said one smiling father, his four-year-old daughter sporting sunglasses painted red, white, and blue. "But who else could create such a spirit of communion? Look: we're all different, but we all share the same passion."[12]

The reigning idols of the 1998 celebration were Thuram and Zidane. Their actions on the field deeply, and dramatically, marked the spirits of French spectators. The two players secured the final two victories for the team, each of them by scoring two goals in totally unexpected ways. For Michel Platini, living vicariously a World Cup victory that he had never achieved, it seemed as though the victory was almost divinely ordained. "When a kid like Thuram suddenly starts scoring goals even when he admits himself that he has 'two left feet' in front of the goal," beamed Platini, "and when Zidane scores two victorious headers when that isn't his strong point, and when the final takes place in beautiful weather when people feared it would be terrible, you tell yourself that, yes, the French team had to win." The turf on which they had played was treated as the site of a miracle, producing relics to be distributed among the faithful: five thousand pieces of turf were cut up and sold for 120 francs (about twenty-five dollars) each.[13]

Thuram and Zidane had surpassed themselves, working wonders on the field that rebounded throughout French society. But they also symbolized most forcefully the idea that this team represented the arrival of a new kind of French nation. "Zidane and Thuram," wrote Dominique Sanchez in *Le Monde*, "gave *beurs* and blacks a new vision of themselves by generating not just consensual recognition but quasi-general adulation.... Suddenly, the youth of the *cités* saw something they had every reason to doubt, given the stigmatization of all kinds that they experienced—that one's ethnic origins wouldn't necessarily block a rise to the top, that it is possible to be the child or grandchild of Africans, to have Guadeloupean or Kanak roots, and to incarnate the nation to the point of becoming a national hero." Of course, Sanchez warned, the World Cup wouldn't bring about change unless it was followed by investment in the *banlieue* of the kind that Saint-Denis itself had seen in the construction of its stadium. But the victory inspired many young people in France, particularly in the *banlieues* and in the neighborhoods around Saint-Denis itself, to use sports as a path to success. Football clubs in the *banlieue* saw a large increase in the number of players, with ninety thousand joining to play in the 1998–99 season. The new generation of players were dubbed the "baby-boomers of the World Cup."[14]

Journalists, intellectuals, and politicians seeking to interpret the victory expressed varied and often conflicting ideas about what it meant about France and its future. In its front-page report on the celebrations of the World Cup, *Le Monde* sounded a note of mixed hope and caution. "Of course, everything is still the same," the newspaper declared. France's troubles could not be erased by a football game. Still, "the idea that something has changed, or can change, in the collective consciousness" was itself a victory. Other commentators emphasized that the real lesson of the World Cup was that patriotism was still alive and still essential. "White France," another journalist wrote, found itself "moved" when it discovered that the "dark idol" Thuram sang the "Marseillaise," "off tune maybe, but with all his heart.... Young and old, small and big, those with roots in the *hexagone* [metropolitan France] and those who were 'imported,' all now hum in unison with the eleven gods of the stadium and their round ball, around a single slogan: 'France.'"[15]

Just as they had after the victory against Croatia, some conservative commentators and politicians emphasized the fact that young people of immigrant backgrounds had rallied to the French flag. Thierry Mariani, the mayor of a small French town known for his hard-line stance on immigration, took tentative pleasure in the fact that the "majority of those who marched like madmen around the town hall with French flags were *beurs* and blacks." He added, with more than a hint of paternalism, "It was both surprising and agreeable." A deputy from another conservative party found the enthusiasm of the children of immigrants "extremely positive," but he added that it was just part of a larger change they needed to make in their attitude toward France.[16]

"Even the Algerians flew French flags," Marcel Desailly commented in a similar vein. "These are people who normally live in Algeria in their minds," he claimed, "but that day in July they were hanging out of windows, waving the French flag. Unbelievable." The victory, he argued, allowed them to perceive France in a different way, and to "let out emotions that were buried. . . . Even if it was only for two hours, it's enough." Though less supercilious in tone than conservative politicians, Desailly similarly emphasized that immigrants and their children found an opportunity to embrace their Frenchness.[17]

For many others, however, the real import of 1998 was that it decisively challenged French racism. The minister of youth and sports, Marie-George Buffet, celebrated the lesson that diversity "is what makes France strong." A city official in Paris hoped that "this black, blanc, *beur*" team would inspire people to jettison their "racist ideas." Intellectuals involved in debates about immigration and citizenship and activists involved in antiracist campaigns similarly rejoiced at the victory. The well-known Moroccan-born writer Tahar Ben Jelloun, who in 1984 had published a harsh critique of French racism ironically titled *L'Hospitalité française,* wrote that he had 'surprised himself" and been taken up in the "passing euphoria" of the World Cup. He and his friends in Morocco had joyously supported France during the final. The World Cup had shown the globe that "France is a country made up of several colors"; its lesson was "precisely that the victorious France is the France *métissée.*" The term *métissée* means "mixed" and traditionally has been used in France and its empire to describe a person whose ancestry brought together Europeans and Africans, Native Americans, or Asians. In recent decades it has also increasingly been taken up as a way of celebrating the encounter and merging of cultures taking place in contemporary France. The World Cup, Ben Jelloun's statement suggested, had exposed and valorized what France truly was: a multicultural and multiracial society. And it showed that rather than being a cause for concern or condemnation, this reality was a source of strength, a foundation for victory.[18]

Many declared enthusiastically that the victory of the French team represented a decisive defeat of the Front National. "Where's Le Pen tonight?" wondered Brahim, holding an Algerian flag, as he celebrated the victory in Paris. "I'd like to talk to him!" "He's at the Bois de Boulogne"—a park on the edge of Paris frequented by prostitutes—"with the Brazilians!" came the response from the group around him. "People have said that *les Bleus* have contributed to the combat against Le Pen: I'm very happy and very proud of that," said Aimé Jacquet. Fodé Sylla, the president of France's leading antiracist organization, S.O.S. Racisme, saw the victory as the symbolic culmination of decades of activism and organizing: "Everything we have fought for over the years has finally found its translation." A priest who had worked in a *banlieue* area went further, arguing that football was more powerful than political organizing: "The World Cup is better than ten years of antiracist campaigning." Several other commentators made similar claims. Sami Naïr, an Algerian-born scholar of immigration and consultant to the French government, declared of Zidane, "He does more with the motion of his hips than ten or fifteen years of policies of integration."[19]

In the days after the World Cup such claims were boosted by a surprising volte-face on the part of the conservative politician Charles Pasqua. He was the interior minister of France from 1986 to 1988 and again from 1993 to 1995. Pasqua was intensely disliked by many on the left in France because of accusations of corrupt business dealings and the reforms in immigration law he had put in place, which were considered draconian. The "Pasqua laws" made it harder for the children of immigrants to get French citizenship and harder for *sans-papiers* to get legal documentation. In 1993 Pasqua declared that the government should resist the creation of a "pluri-cultural" society in which immigrants retained their own distinctiveness. "If France does not suit them," he declared, they should "get the hell out": "Those who want to live on the national territory must become French and assimilate our culture. We don't have to put up with the others."[20]

And so it came as a surprise when, a few days after the World Cup, Pasqua suddenly sided with the activist groups who had battled him for years, calling for the regularization of all the *sans-papiers* in France. In an interview he explained that the World Cup victory had shown the French that "integration has been 90% successful. . . . At such moments, when France is strong, it can be generous, and it should make a gesture." His political organization published a statement explaining that the French victory had "united the national community," bringing together people "of all origins," and it represented the "victory of Republican integration." Many French people were rediscovering a lost feeling of national pride, Pasqua's organization argued, while "all the youth born out of immigration" were "finally discovering" it. The statement was both celebratory and patronizing, suggesting that individuals whose parents or grandparents were immigrants had never before felt pride in being French. The position was largely a cynical way of striking out against Jacques Chirac, a longtime political ally turned enemy in the previous years. Still, the volte-face of Pasqua seemed to suggest that what happened on the football field could have concrete and far-reaching political consequences.[21]

After becoming prime minister in 1997, Lionel Jospin created a commission to study French immigration laws and propose reforms. Headed by the historian Patrick Weil, the commission presented a range of suggestions for rolling back the Pasqua laws, especially to open up more opportunities for students and professionals. Jospin might have taken advantage of the euphoria surrounding the World Cup victory to push through far-reaching and significant reforms in immigration policy, but even many of the provisions proposed by the Weil commission, which were relatively moderate, were not fully put into effect. Ultimately Jospin and others in the government perhaps failed to take advantage of the momentary opening in the political debate generated by football in the summer of 1998. Their lack of initiative cost them politically in the coming years as the right took control of the rhetoric and policies regarding immigration.[22]

Political activists, however, continued to try to mobilize the World Cup victory in support of more open and humane immigration policies. In September 1998 S.O.S. Racisme plastered Paris with large posters that showed a black player from the French team with his back to the camera walking off the field. "That night," the poster announced, recalling the moment in the World Cup final when Marcel Desailly was expelled by the referee, "all French people were scandalized by the expulsion of a black person." The message was clear: the French should extend their interracial sympathies beyond the football field and stand up against the expulsion of African immigrants from France.[23]

A comical short film aired on French television a few months after the World Cup crystallized the idea that football could defeat the Front National. Introducing the film, the announcer stated, "The victorious tricolor team did more to advance the ideas of integration than fifteen years of dithering about how to respond to the Front National." The film, called *Godzidane,* takes place in a bar during the World Cup, where a group of white Frenchmen are gathered to watch a game. As the team sings the "Marseillaise" on screen the barman declares, "Shit! What a gang of foreigners. There aren't many real Frenchmen among them." A customer concurs: "They don't even know how to sing the Marseillaise right!" Then, across the screen, comes an ominous message: "France was shadowed, more and more, by racism." The door of the bar opens, and a young man who looks North African enters. He asks cheerfully for a coffee, and the barman says, "There's no coffee." "A Coke?" "No Coke." "Tonight," the barman adds, "we want to stay among ourselves." "Among real French people, if you see what we mean," adds his wife. "After all, it's *our* final!" a customer says. "We're still in our homeland, right?" the wife shouts, as the young man is grabbed roughly and pushed out the door.

Suddenly the café starts to shake, and out the window a huge foot, wearing a football cleat and sock inscribed with the name of the French Football Federation, smashes a car on the street. As the terrified racists from the café run outside, the camera pans to a giant with the face of Zidane, destroying everything in his path. In an exaggerated Marseille accent, Godzidane concludes the film by announcing, "France, 3; Le Pen, o."[24]

Yet the hope that Zidane and his teammates could smash racism and create a world without prejudice rapidly came to seem fantastical. One October 1998 editorial lamented that the "surprising euphoria" of the summer hadn't succeeded in "reducing the social crisis produced by the combined effects of unemployment and immigration. . . . Zidane wasn't able to produce the hoped-for miracle." The president of one antiracist organization complained that, while in July he had "a lot of hope" that the idea of a "plural France" had been cemented, the victory "turned out to be nothing more than a fireworks display." A community activist in Saint-Denis recalled that "the youth mobilized around a team that, for once, represented them," but were soon disillusioned once they realized that despite the high hopes of the summer, very little had actually changed. Another man took the long view: "I saw the World Cup as a great step forward towards the disappearance of racial discrimination, but I think it's my children who will profit from it."[25]

Marcel Desailly looked back on the celebrations of 1998 as a second "liberation" of France but was cautiously optimistic about its influence on French society. "I don't know about long-term change. Perhaps 90 percent of people may not change their ideas. But maybe another 10 percent of people might have started to think differently." Desailly was the only player from the team who, in the years immediately following the World Cup win, publicly promoted a political cause, arguing in favor of implementing policies modeled on those in the United Kingdom and the United States that require media companies to include a certain quota of minorities in their programming.[26]

Polls taken a year after the World Cup victory suggested that many French people remained confident that the victory could help transform their society. Seventy percent agreed that the World Cup brought together people of different origins in France, and 55 percent thought that it contributed to the improvement of relations between immigrants and nonimmigrants. One journalist remained confident of the importance of the previous year's events. He wrote that the victory was indeed a kind of second liberation because it was a defeat for Jean-Marie Le Pen, "who had almost succeeded in his coup by pretending to incarnate the subterranean voice of the French people."[27]

Whether as a resounding defeat of Le Pen, as a promise of something better, or as a momentary euphoria that soon ceded to the ongoing ugliness of social reality, the World Cup victory continued to resonate in France. For several years, even as the government failed to enact significant reforms, activists sought to capitalize on the victory as they pursued social transformation. In 2002 Mohand Ouahrani, with the support of an organization dedicated to aiding "integration and the struggle against discrimination," published a book aimed at drawing on the victory of 1998 to carry out a broader social transformation in France. He hoped that those who had celebrated the 1998 victory would help to "spread ideas of tolerance and solidarity" and "continue to fight racism." His goal was to "contribute to integration throughout the Republic," without requiring people to "deny or reject their roots." As Ouahrani admitted, despite the euphoria of the 1998 victory and the "communion" that took place on the Champs-Elysées in its wake, several years later people's "mentality" still hadn't evolved, and discrimination persisted: "A football game, even a mythic one, didn't have—it's true—the power to fix all of the problems of French society with the touch of a magic wand." Still, the ideal of a "multicolored France" was more than the "dream of a summer night on the Champs-Elysées"; it could be built "day by day in the *cités*" and ultimately triumph.[28]

Looking back on the celebrations of 1998 several years later, Lilian Thuram presented a rich reading of both the possibilities and the dangers embedded in the events of that summer. Like many others, he rejoiced in the expression of an inclusive joy on the part of the French population. He recalled being overwhelmed by the sight of the crowds on the Champs-Elysées during the victory parade:

> There was an extraordinary atmosphere, and I would never have thought that football could create so much happiness. In this crowd, you could see the real France, not the banal idea that people have about French people, but the true France, heterogenous. I think those people were proud of their team because they saw themselves in every one of its players. It was the image of the nation, the image of France.
>
> It was like a message: Look carefully at this country which shows itself as it is, as it has been and as it will be, a site of intermingling of communities. The victory ... was, at that precise moment, the mirror of the history of France. That was what was beautiful and moving. Maybe many of the people on the Champs-Elysées felt that as they saw Zidane, Thuram, Desailly, Barthez,

Lizarazu, Deschamps, Djorkaeff, Karembeu . . . France was represented. There was no ambiguity, no hypocrisy, no lie. The crowd expressed a spontaneous, heartfelt joy.[29]

At the same time, however, Thuram was wary of the ways the victory was co-opted and used for particular, and limited, political ends. He was clearly disappointed at the way the significance of what had happened on the football field had been channeled into a traditional interpretation of "integration" in France, in which immigrants were expected to fit into rather than add to and expand the culture. "A few days after that celebration," he said, "I heard an argument I didn't like: 'Look at the French team, it's the example of what *integration* can produce.' . . . I didn't understand how you could talk about integration after this victory. What was the link between that word and the celebration of generosity we had experienced? . . . The celebration had been recuperated, twisted, emptied of its meaning."[30]

The team's victory was "appropriated and abused," used to pass on a vision that Thuram found offensive: "Become a football player if you want to integrate yourself" or "Look, integrate yourselves, France is strong." But for Thuram, the reason for the outpouring of joy around the team was precisely because people felt liberated from the "shackle" of a certain idea of integration. France united around its team *because* it was "Armenian, Algerian, African, Antillean, Kanak, Basque, Breton. . . . The country could look at itself: each of the components of its population was visible and present in its national football team." The promise put forth by the team, Thuram suggested, was precisely that it was possible, indeed valuable to be a French person with a particular history and a particular background, and that there was no conflict between these two things: "France should take advantage of the energy of all these people who are united, just as its football team took advantage of the energy that came out of the cultural differences of its players. That's how I see my country." It was precisely because players were different and worked together harmoniously—rather than being "integrated" into one unit—that made it possible for them to win. The celebrations illuminated an alternative political possibility, a world in which the multiplicity of histories that have shaped France were accepted on equal terms, in which the experiences and histories of the children of the French Empire would be understood as something that was *already* an essential part of France.[31]

Thuram was uncomfortable with the way the victory was turned into a self-congratulatory celebration of *integration* in France. And he feared that many commentators who were using the term were really envisioning a form of *assimilation* in which immigrants were asked to abandon their cultures and their pasts in order to gain acceptance in French society. Just as individuals would "lose themselves" if they renounced a part of what made them who they were, Thuram warned, a "nation that rejects some of the elements that compose it" would end up losing itself. The victory of 1998 was not a confirmation that the reigning models of citizenship and immigration were working in France. It was a crucial opportunity to question and critique these models and to build on celebrations that provided a promising alternative. The mass communion that took place in the streets in 1998, liberating many from the shackles of their own uncertainty about their place in French society, should serve as a charter for a different way of being French. It could be, Thuram argued, a foundation for an alternative model for the nation, a plural France based on communion and the acceptance of multiple pasts.[32]

By propelling him into an unexpected stardom, the World Cup had provided Thuram with a unique opportunity to speak out. In the following years he took advantage of this in a way that very few athletes have, seeking to mobilize and channel the hope he had produced on the football field into social and political change off it. Through writings, appearances on radio and television, and cultural and political activism he established himself as a well-known and widely respected public figure and thinker.

While the 1998 World Cup produced a new political voice in Lilian Thuram, it also represented the arrival of a global brand: Zidane. Already well known as a football player, he was swamped with requests for endorsements and accepted many, receiving millions of dollars for appearing in advertisements for products from Adidas to Dannon yogurt (He had his standards, though, and refused one endorsement offer that would have involved having his picture on plastic shopping bags, with the argument that people end up dropping the bags and walking all over them.) According to a July 2000 survey, he was the most beloved personality in France, outranking even Abbé Pierre, famous for his work among the poor in France.[33]

But beyond success and fame, what did Zidane symbolize? He could be, of course, proof that a person with humble roots can achieve both financial success and public recognition. According to one journalist, among the kids in the north of Marseille who all knew his name, "he's not a model: he's further away than that, inaccessible. But he remains a hope, a dream." Unlike Thuram, Zidane has rarely intervened in politics. His friend, the comic

Jamel Debbouze, has one interpretation of why this is the case: "Zidane is too important to be co-opted. He is huge compared to politicians. You put Sarkozy next to him, it's like the Green Giant next to the grumpy Smurf!"[34]

In a 1998 book Zidane did present the victory as both a political symbol and a personal vindication for his family and for Algerian immigrants more broadly. He described his return to Marseille that summer, when he paraded with some of the other Marseillais on the winning team: "I saw all those faces on the Canebière, all those kids, those men, those women, Black, Arab, African, maybe Armenian or simply Provençal, and suddenly I told myself that the arrival of my father in France in the 1960s was a stroke of luck for my generation." It was hard for his father to leave his village, to "abandon his roots, his parents, everything he had loved before. . . . But . . . [he left] so that he could discover another culture, another reality." His father, along with millions of other Algerians, had "worked hard in France to find a place in the sun." The World Cup victory was also his father's victory "and that of all those Algerians who are proud of their flag, who made sacrifices to feed their families but never abandoned their culture." Zidane added, "There was something very moving about seeing all those Algerian flags mixed in with the French ones in the streets on the night of our victory. This alchemy of victory proved suddenly that my father and my mother had not made the journey for nothing: it was the son of a Kabyle that offered up the victory, but it was France that became champion of the world. In one goal by one person, two cultures became one."[35]

Zidane presented his action on the football field as a moment of crystallization and redemption, in which a single action on a massive stage could bring fragments and oppositions together, casting the history of upheaval and exile into something meaningful. This powerfully optimistic reading of what had happened claimed that Zidane's goals signaled and sealed the merging of two cultures. His first goal against Brazil was perhaps the best "single image" he could imagine "to illustrate the power of integration." He recalls, "Without thinking, without calculation—I promise you—I kissed the blue jersey of the French team. . . . Me, the son of a Kabyle, whose friends' names ring like Mediterranean pebbles, the Yazid of the northern neighborhoods of Marseille, an Algerian born in France, I kissed the jersey of this land that saw me grow up, kissed it for a long time. That's integration, isn't it?" In Zidane's reckoning, it seemed as though this fleeting moment on the football field could make sense, and hope, out of the chaos and tragedy of history. The victory, he wrote, was "like a great earthquake of joy." It was "as though there was justice, as though the struggles and suffering couldn't last for ever." But he made these points as lightly and playfully as he handled the football, always maintaining the conditional "as though" and concluding his optimistic evocation of the sacrifices of parents with a wink: "It's wonderful, isn't it?" In retrospect it seems Zidane thought better of some of his more optimistic claims, for when his book was republished in 1999 some of these passages, including his evocation of the "alchemy of victory," were deleted without explanation and without a trace.[36]

Zidane also declared forthrightly that the French team's 1998 victory was "the most beautiful response to intolerance." He recalled that Jean-Marie Le Pen had complained that players weren't singing the "Marseillaise" passionately enough and remained "skeptical about the French reality that was offered up by [the] team." Zidane lamented that even if such comments had pained the players, they were too busy demonstrating their competence on the field to respond. But he saw the victory of 1998 as a scathing response: "Frankly, what does it matter if you belt out the Marseillaise or if you live it inside yourself?" Adding a dose of his own skepticism about the content of the anthem, he added, "Do we have to shout this warriors' song to be patriotic? . . . Who won the world championship? The France of a single region, of a single culture, or a single village? Certainly not." Then, using the roster of players as a map of France and of the world, he wrote:

> The France that won starts in the Basque country of Lizarazu, extends to the Cathar country of Lavelanet where Fabien Barthez first played, strings out to the beaches of Bernard Lama's Guiana, treats itself to a change of scenery on the paths of Accra, in Marcel Desailly's Ghana, rests in bourgeois Bordeaux with Christophe Dugarry, continues in Brittany with Stéphane Guivarc'h, sings amidst the crickets in the Gard with Laurent Blanc. . . . It's the map of our heart, the proof that integration is possible, and especially solidarity, a kind of cement that can in fact give some confidence back to the French. . . . Our team is the sum of individuals. We all have our stories, more or less difficult. But we all had to believe we had a chance. We had to persuade ourselves we were as strong as other nations. And we won.[37]

In the wake of the World Cup victory in 1998 Jean-Marie Le Pen responded not by ignoring the victory but by trying to shape its meaning in a particular way. A Front National communiqué issued on 13 July "rejoiced" at the fact that the victory had helped the French population "rediscover its patriotic reflexes, its national anthem, and its tricolor flag." The party congratulated the team for its "magnificent victory," singling out its coach and "the principal artisan of the final victory, Zinedine Zidane." But the party also described Zidane not as an immigrant or an Algerian, but as "a child of French Algeria." The player, in other words, was embraced as a product of the French Empire.[38]

Soon afterward a leading member of the National Front, Bruno Gollnisch, declared that if Zidane was "acceptable to the French," it was because his father, Smaïl, had been an *harki*. The *harkis* were Algerians who fought on the French side during the war of independence, and many of them fled to France at the end of the war to escape reprisals. The claim was difficult to sustain—Smaïl was in metropolitan France throughout the war, whereas the *harkis* fought in Algeria itself—but nevertheless it circulated for a few years. During a France-Algeria match in October 2001 some fans of Algeria apparently flew a banner declaring "Zidane-Harki." In April 2002, asked about the presidential campaign during which Le Pen had made it into the run-off election against Chirac, Zidane finally spoke up in order to crush the rumor: "I want to be precise about this, once and for all: my father is not an *harki*. . . . I don't have anything against *harkis*," he added, sensitive to the fact that this group has long felt stigmatized within both French and Algerian society, "and I don't want to get involved in what is going on. I simply want to say that my father was not an *harki*, he was an Algerian, and I am proud that my father is Algerian. . . . My father never fought against his country."[39]

This rumor, though, continues to circulate, even making its way into scholarly work. Indeed, in a study of race and football in England published in 2001, before Zidane's public statement on the matter, three scholars present the rumor as a significant and illustrative fact. "Zidane's father," they write, "had been a soldier—a 'harkis' *[sic]*—who came to France after fighting alongside the colonialists in *opposition* to Algerian independence." They use Smaïl Zidane's supposed affiliation with French colonialism to argue that the idea of "multi-cultural France" celebrated around the 1998 victory was in fact the expression of a form of "neo-colonial accommodation." There was a continuity, they suggest, between the service of Zidane's father to the French Empire and the service of Zidane to a new "myth" of multiculturalism.[40]

Another scholar, Elizabeth Ezra, similarly argues that the vision of a "black-blanc-beur" France was just old colonial wine in a new bottle. In the early twentieth century French officials had celebrated the existence of a "Greater France," epitomized in the 1931 Colonial Exhibition, a global empire united in one project even as it embraced its cultural diversity. In both the 1930s and in 1998, Ezra argues, French elites celebrated diversity in a way that excused and even protected the continuing exclusion of the descendants of empire. One contemporary journalist, she notes, described residents of Marseille transforming their port city into "the universe for a night, as in the colonial period." "African matrons," he went on, beat drums, though it was difficult to see what color most people were "beneath the red, white and blue face paint." Another commentator wrote, "The French victory is the victory of what we once called, without shame, 'Greater France.' . . . What would we be without those of foreign origin who sing the Marseillaise?" He thanked the Antilles and Africa, and twice—for Zidane's two goals—thanked Algeria's Kabyle region. "The 'black-blanc-beur' image of national unity," argues Ezra, "is not an old model of integration but, rather, a new model of empire." For her, the French "colonial unconscious" was at work in *both* the exclusionary discourses of the far right and the "multi-cultural" rhetoric used to counter it in 1998.[41]

France's postcolonial present is clearly shaped by the history of empire, and so is its football team. The commentator Alain Finkielkraut put it bluntly: "If we have Zidanes on our team and the Poles don't it's not because we're less racist. It's because we have a colonial past. That's nothing to be proud about." But the relationship between past and present is complex, not a story of easy correlation or descendants, but of echoes, in which the highly charged terrain of belonging, nationalism, race, and memory comes together in and around the particular form of football. When both commentators and critics evoked the links between the ideology of Greater France developed during the early twentieth century and the celebrations surrounding the 1998 World Cup, they focused primarily on the ways empire envisioned and instituted a racial order in the colonies. In this scenario the emphasis was always on how the imperial center had carried out and justified its control. But this is only part of the story of colonialism, for already in the early twentieth century ideas of Greater France were loudly contested and mobilized to varied ends by colonial administrators, reformers, and young activists from the colonies who sought to expand citizenship and rights within the colonial context. Such figures, notably Aimé Césaire and Leopold Senghor, saw possibilities for transformation during this period as well. The link between colonial past and postcolonial present is certainly there, but both that past and the present are too complex to sustain the argument that multicultural rhetoric simply provides a cover for colonial or neocolonial exploitation.[42]

Many of those who rejoiced in 1998 did so because they sensed that the colonial past was present in but ultimately superseded by what happened on the football field. *L'Equipe,* a newspaper that generally resists linking sport and politics, trumpeted the fact that "Zidane the Beur, Deschamps and Lizarazu the Basques, Desailly and Vieira the Africans, Thuram the Antillean," and "Karembeu the Kanak," among other players, all "unified their destiny for the grandeur of the country: They are all its children, of enormous will, the delicious fruits of a history that is bloody, painful, that teases us at times, ancient and recent, but in the end unifying, pacifying, 'integrating.'" Football, *L'Equipe* hoped, promised not a repetition of the past or an erasure of it, but the possibility of reconciliation, the idea that out of a history of conflict and confrontation had come something beautiful, something that embodied the best of French values. Though with more caution than *L'Equipe,* Thuram and Zidane had suggested something similar in their responses to their victory. Precisely because it had emerged from and showcased the history of empire, football could inspire the construction of a future that was based on this past, in all its complexity. Football, like France itself, was the product of empire. And that represented not just a shackle, but also the possibility of emancipation.[43]

By 2000 the optimism of 1998 had faded substantially. That summer, however, it was briefly, if intensely, revived when Zidane, Thuram, and most of their teammates from 1998 competed for France in the European Cup of Nations. In the semifinal France played Portugal, leaving many Portuguese immigrants in France and their children with split loyalties. "Tonight, it's my homeland against the country that welcomed me," one twenty-year-old said. France won, thanks to a goal by Thierry Henry that tied the game 1–1 and then a successful penalty kick by Zidane in overtime. Then, in the final, a squad featuring most of the players from the previous World Cup confronted Italy in a tense and remarkable game. Italy scored a brilliantly played goal early on and held their 1–0 lead through most of the game. In the ninety-fourth minute, with seconds to go until the end of the game, French player Sylvain Wiltord—another of the players on the team with Caribbean roots, whose family is from Martinique—scored a miraculous goal from the left side of the Italian penalty area, sending French fans jumping and the game into overtime. At the time, the "Golden Goal" rule was still in effect, and during the first overtime session David Trezeguet volleyed a pass into the Italian net, winning the game and the championship for France. With this victory the team became the first in history to successively win the World Cup and the European Cup.[44]

Paris again erupted in celebration in a replay of 1998. Four hundred thousand people gathered on the Champs-Elysées, and celebrants flooded into the streets and plazas of Paris and other French cities. Some again chanted, "Zidane Président." A retired professor on the Champs-Elysées rejoiced about the "mixed crowd, as diverse as the French team," which "makes us forget Le Pen." This time, however, the party didn't end so well. Late in the evening a few people broke windows along the Champs-Elysées, and the police fired tear gas into the crowd, some of whom fought back. In Marseille police faced off against celebrants who shattered windows. More than two hundred people were hurt in Paris and Marseille, and the police arrested many others.[45]

In the end, the victory of 2000 felt more like an aftershock of 1998 than the beginning of a new era. Still, some commentators once again described the victory as a sign of a new political reality. The prominent writer and political figure Françoise Giroud celebrated the "mixed" and "international" team, most of whom "live in foreign countries." Making a virtue out of what Le Pen had once criticized about the team, she rejoiced that these players "live globalization like it's their second nature," while expressing a "natural patriotism" that was also a "cosmopolitan patriotism." They were a vanguard whose openness to the world, she argued, was slowly seeping into political life in France as well. In Le Monde a journalist described the football team as "prophets in their own land" and "scouts" who illuminated the direction the country needed to take.[46]

Politicians eager to improve the situation of immigrants in France sought to capitalize on the 2000 victory in an ongoing effort to grant long-term residents in France the right to vote in local elections. They pointed out that Zidane's parents, having lived in France for nearly half a century but who have never sought French naturalization and remain Algerian citizens, didn't have the right to vote, even in municipal elections whose results profoundly impacted their daily life. One deputy in the National Assembly asked Zidane himself to speak up on the issue. Having fought for France on the football field, he should make a similar effort so that his parents could gain the right to vote. Zidane, however, didn't intervene publicly. And despite the fact that a small majority of French people supported the change, the reform still hasn't come, and in today's political climate in France it seems unlikely it will come any time soon. Smaïl and Malika, who are regularly celebrated in the French media as the good parents of the nation's favorite son, still can't vote in France.[47]

What remains of those July 1998 days? One novelist attempting to answer that question, as well as to ride the wave of euphoria surrounding the victory, turned it into an opportunity for romance. François Parent, businessman, occasional writer, great fan of exclamation points, and partisan of often awkward attempts to replicate the slang of *banlieue* youth, quickly wrote a novel entitled *Black, Blanc, Beur* in the wake of the World Cup victory. In it a teenager of North African descent named Fatima (who prefers to be called Shannon) falls in love with a white boy named Jean-Baptiste. The two have to confront the displeasure of their families and friends, which the novelist suggests might have been insurmountable before 1998. But the events of that summer bring the couple together (Fatima, at first uninterested in football, becomes impassioned with the team, something she shares with Jean-Baptiste) and create the context for their love to find acceptance in French society.[48]

If Parent found the idea of transforming the celebrations of 1998 into at least one lasting relationship, it was perhaps because, already by 1999, the gains of that moment seemed so fleeting. Ultimately, though, there's no way to measure the impact of the victory on people's spirits. July 1998 remains a touchstone, a golden memory of a moment of intense, unbridled joy. It was a sporting season that echoed the remarkable 1966 World Cup when England, playing on their home turf, won the trophy. Writing in the *New Yorker* at the time, Alastair Reid described how the event became "a kind of national fairy tale" that "had about it that incredible sporting perfection that always might, but seldom does, happen." It was a perfection that was "gradual and intricately devised, a perfection that a goodly part of those who saw it felt they would nod over happily in their old age, smiling a secret, faraway smile." That itself was no small thing. And, given what has happened since, the memory of that moment also serves as a refuge for hope.[49]

EIGHT

An Unfinished War

SEVENTY-NINE MINUTES INTO THE GAME, with France leading Algeria 4–1, Sofia Benlemmane decided it was up to her to prevent defeat. A football player on a Division 1 women's team and an employee at a telecommunications company, she was a citizen of both countries on the field. But the flag in her hand was Algerian, and she held it tightly as she jumped over the barrier between the stands and the turf. She landed behind the Algerian goal and ran into the middle of the field. The surprised players stopped and watched, while security guards on the sidelines hesitated for a moment to go onto the field, allowing her to run unhindered. Two men jumped onto the field to follow her. Both they and Benlemmane were soon wrestled to the ground by onrushing security guards, but by then it was too late. Dozens more people ran onto the turf, many carrying their Algerian flags, others in the jersey of the Algerian team. Exhilarated, they ran, danced, twirled, and shouted on the field. A chubby boy of no more than fourteen danced goofily, looking up to the sky, caught in a moment of sheer joy.[1]

Since football's beginnings as a spectator sport, fans have invaded the turf to celebrate goals, protest referees' decisions, and sometimes stop a game. The move is radical but in some ways a logical extension of passionate fandom. Many fans truly experience themselves as part of the team, believing that their chants and banners are essential to victory, which is why some people refer to fans as the "the twelfth man." There are times when your team simply *cannot* lose, when the outcome can't be left to the crazy roulette of football. There are fences in many stadiums to make it impossible for fans to jump onto the field, but these can be dangerous. Most of those killed at Heysel in 1983 suffocated as they were pushed against such a fence. The Stade de France was built without such fences, and it was an easy jump onto the field from the stands and, for a fast runner or a determined crowd, not that hard to sweep past the security guards.

FIGURE 19. Sofia Benlemmane charges onto the field in the seventy-ninth minute of the France-Algeria game, Stade de France, 6 October 2001. Olivier Morin/AFP/Getty Images.

The French team had been greeted with hostility from the start of the match, when some of the fans of the Algerian team hissed and booed during the playing of the "Marseillaise," as well as booing the names of the French players—except for that of Zidane. Some also threw batteries at them. Sitting on the bench, Thierry Henry muttered, "It's sad," while Emmanuel Petit joked ruefully, "I should have brought my Walkman. I picked up four batteries." As the pitch invasion started, people threw bottles at French officials who were watching the game, hitting the sports minister Marie-George Buffet. The security guards surrounding Prime Minister Lionel Jospin pushed him toward the exit, but then he decided to go back to his seat, where he sat alone, watching the chaos on the field.[2]

The pitch invasion at the Stade de France was viewed as something much more serious than a game being broken up by some unruly kids. Eleven million T.V. viewers had tuned in for the game, but many more tuned in once news about the disruption of the game spread; ultimately fourteen million watched on television, making it a national spectacle almost on par with World Cup matches. "Integration is dead," declared the journalist Max Clos in an editorial in *Le Figaro,* sounding a note of alarm echoed by many other commentators. Clos had frequently complained about the unwillingness of North Africans in France to integrate, writing in 1990 that as a group they "refused assimilation into French society whose values they don't recognize and whose rules they refuse to follow." The events at the France-Algeria game confirmed his suspicions, and he was infuriated by the way the communist Buffet responded. When she heard the "Marseillaise" being booed, Buffet explained, she thought about "integration" and asked herself why those in the stadium "felt the need to boo." Clos thought the answer was obvious: those who booed might be French citizens, but they "hate France, are French only on paper and not in their hearts, claim their belonging to the Algerian nation and often to the Muslim religion." Bin Laden, he claimed, was "considered a hero" in the *banlieue,* where many were turning to *communautarisme,* emphasizing the needs of their community over those of the nation. This approach, often seen as the result of the baneful influence of the so-called Anglo-Saxon model of multiculturalism practiced in the United States and the United Kingdom, is considered by many French intellectuals to be dangerous and antirepublican. Echoing the sentiments of other prominent thinkers, Clos worried that France would soon end up populated by a fragmented set of groups "with no link between them, condemned to permanent conflicts" and even "civil war." The only solution was to reassert "order" in the *banlieue* through tough policing and an attack against the soft approach of social workers trained in Marxist and Freudian approaches to handling delinquency. Declared Clos, "We are at war."[3]

A deputy in the national assembly made a similar plea, earning applause when he demanded that all people on French soil be made to respect the values and laws of France, and warning that the lack of order in the *banlieues* created a fertile terrain for terrorism. The involvement of the French-born Zacarias Moussaoui in the 9/11 attacks was by then well known and served as an example of the dangers of militant Islam in the *banlieue.* To conservative commentators, the invasion of the pitch at the Stade de France was part of a larger and decisive conflict.[4] While other commentators took a less dramatic view, many concluded that the events at the Stade de France signified the defeat of hopes for the integration of immigrants and the ultimate proof that the hopes incited by the World Cup in 1998 were nothing more than a mirage.

In fact October 2001 was a repeat of the summer of 1998 in one important way: once again football became a powerful symbol that seemed to diagnose French social reality. In many ways what happened in the Stade de

France was relatively minor, especially in comparison to the violence that has sometimes surrounded football games in Europe. No one was wounded or killed. But people responded to it as a major political event, even a tragedy, as a setback and a threat. Even before it happened the France-Algeria match was burdened with tremendous symbolism, given the task of resolving the irresolvable, of somehow confronting and surpassing an unfinished war that still haunts French society. As one Algerian newspaper put it, what happened after the game was simply a new page in a seemingly unending conflict. Though it went mostly unremarked, October 2001 also was the fortieth anniversary of the day the Paris police chief put into effect a curfew aimed at Algerians, prompting the demonstration that ended in police killings in the streets of Paris.[5]

Decades before, in 1958, football was drafted as a weapon in the Algerian war of independence, and in 2001 it seemed as though the war still wasn't over. The situation, of course, was completely different. In 1958 the Algerian revolutionaries were proposing a very specific and realizable solution to the conflict between France and Algeria: the creation of a new, independent, postcolonial state. In 2001 those who rooted for Algeria and stormed onto the field were mostly French citizens of Algerian background. By supporting the Algerian team *against* the French team they were also responding to their sense that France still refused to see them as fully French. But ultimately they had nowhere else to go. This was a problem that had to be resolved within French society.

Still, Benlemmane's charge onto the field with the Algerian flag eerily echoed one of the most famous images that has sought to capture the meaning of the Algerian Revolution: the final, rousing scene of the classic film *The Battle of Algiers,* where two women carrying the Algerian flag confront a line of French policemen; they charge forward, dancing, are pushed back and then push forward again, symbols of an unstoppable revolution.

It was no accident that the football field became the theater for a confrontation over the relationship between France and Algeria and the place within French society of people of Algerian descent. For the entire twentieth century football had been a central vehicle for politics in Algeria, a site of conflict and negotiation over colonialism and postcolonial relations. In 1913, two decades after the arrival of the sport in Algeria, a football club called FC Musulman de Mascara was founded. During the next decades self-styled "Muslim" football clubs proliferated in the French colony. The term *Muslim* was used by the colonial administration in Algeria as a *legal* (rather than specifically religious) category to differentiate the local population from Europeans, settlers from France, Italy, Malta, and elsewhere on the continent. When football teams began using the term to describe themselves, it was an "expression of a desire to differentiate [themselves] from the colonizers," a way of asserting social and cultural difference.[5]

By the 1920s nearly one-fifth of the Algerian football clubs were Muslim, and the teams became a symbol for the colonized community. They often chose names that foregrounded and celebrated Islamic religious heritage. The important Mouloudia Club Algérois, founded in 1921, for instance, took its name from the celebration of the birth of Mohamed. The team's uniforms were red and green, and indeed almost all of the Muslim teams in Algeria used red, green, and white, especially green on their jerseys and banners. These colors all had some link to Islam. Green, of course, is symbolic in the religion, and both white and red are believed to have been prized by Mohamed. Many uniforms and flags also were decorated with crescents or five-pointed stars, both used as symbols of Islamic states. By wearing such uniforms, players and fans carried out a powerful "transgression of the colonial social order," emphasizing their connection to a particular and oppressed community. But starting in the 1920s these colors and symbols were also increasingly used by different political organizations resisting colonial rule, and they eventually were taken up by the National Liberation Front and the independent nation of Algeria itself. In a world in which political organizing was dangerous and political organizations often subject to colonial repression, it was at football matches more than any other space that the colors and symbols associated with anticolonial activism were worn and flown, week after week, symbols both of support for a specific team and of pride and allegiance in a larger stance of resistance.[7]

By the 1920s and 1930s, with anticolonial organizations such as the Etoile nord-africaine, founded in 1926, and later the Parti du peuple algérien (P.P.A.) on the rise, football games increasingly channeled broader political conflicts. Teams with mostly native Algerian players became "active symbols of the community," and games between Muslim and European teams often involved violent confrontations, both on the turf and in the stadium.[8] Each match presented a potential political problem. Local officials requested authorization from the police chief of their region before allowing games to be played, and the police watched and reported on what took place in the stadium, often describing "ethnic confrontations." Police worried about the activities of one football club in the town of Djidjelli in Algeria's Constantine region, which was founded in 1936 and had direct links with local political groups and unions. "Football matches in Djidjelli are nothing more than noisy meetings," one official complained, where those who supported nationalist causes sought to attack Europeans, as well as Algerians they considered to be pro-colonial. Before one game the team asked for a moment of silence to mourn six people killed by the French police a few weeks earlier. Riding their bus to another game, the players sang the communist anthem, the "Internationale," in Arabic.[9]

When a Muslim team won, it seemed to promise that other, larger victories might be possible as well. By the mid-1930s Algerian nationalists such as Messali Hadj, who had emerged as a leader of Algerian workers in Paris in the late 1920s and was the founder of the P.P.A., held packed political meetings in football stadiums. In 1936, at the stadium in Algiers, Hadj, who had just returned to Algeria after thirteen years in France, electrified a meeting of twenty thousand with a dramatic speech that ended with his calling for the end of racist laws and shouting "Long live the Algerian people!" "This blessed land that is ours cannot be sold, traded, or given to anyone," he added, picking up a handful of dirt from the football field and raising it in the air.[10]

Activists well understood the potential for political organization through football. However, mobilizing the sport was often complicated, for if it unified communities it could just as easily create spaces in which different communities came into comradely contact as they played together on the field. Although this would become less and less common as time went on, there were always football teams that fielded a mix of players, both European and Muslim. Belgacem Hamrouchi, born in Souk-Ahras in Algeria, was recruited to a majority European team in Bône in the late 1920s. He brought some of his former teammates from Souk-Ahras to join him, including a Maltese man named Faïs, "who loved Arabs and called himself an Arab." Hamrouchi also became a referee, and during one game when the conflicts between players and between fans were particularly strong, he decided to empty the stadium and have the game played with only seven supporters for each team looking on. His playing and his forceful refereeing earned him "a lot of deference" in the football world, which "facilitated many things, even much later when [he] was first arrested by the colonial authorities." By the 1930s Souk-Ahras had several clubs, including one Muslim club, though its longtime goalkeeper was the Maltese man who had played with Hamrouchi in Bône. In the 1940s he created a new football club and refused to include the word *Muslim* in its name, as he was urged to by local activists from the P.P.A. "Sport is not

Muslim, Christian, or Jewish," he told them. "Anyone who wants to come play football in my club will be welcome." In fact, though, his team was made up mostly of Arab players, and its games against the main European club in the town were highly charged contests. As Hamrouchi himself admitted, he partly refused to call his team a Muslim club to avoid problems with the administration, but on the field he promised to "show them what [the team was] capable of." By the early 1950s there was frequent violence between fans of the two teams. There were, recalls one man, "two or three Arabs" who played on the European team, one of them a local policeman, who were "considered sell-outs" and were insulted during the games, some of which were moved to "neutral" territory in other towns to avoid violence.[1]

Members of the P.P.A. were prominent in many football clubs. They were a majority, for instance, in the Mouloudia Club Algérois and seem to have directly controlled several other clubs. At one point the P.P.A. created its own football team, and police suspected that the profits made from ticket sales by at least one club were donated directly to what they considered to be subversive political groups. Political groups organized fans of Muslim clubs, urging them to cheer against European teams, strengthening their institutional presence by organizing security details to prevent these conflicts from turning into physical violence. Generally, though, even when there were many activists within a club, most clubs remained officially autonomous. They could lose their subsidies from the colonial state if they didn't, and the seemingly apolitical nature of football associations actually accentuated their political value, for they provided a somewhat protected space for political discussion and recruitment. The political work of football went on even when there was no explicit organizing involved. Large sectors of the Algerian population, notably its youth, saw sport as a crucial mode of expression. Although some critics complained that football was a distraction from politics, football clubs ultimately played a crucial role in developing the symbolic terrain of nationalism and sustaining and encouraging its public expression. The colors increasingly associated with the aspiration for an independent Algeria were flown regularly, and fearlessly, at weekly football matches.[12]

Football matches also allowed communities in Algeria to make links with a larger Arab world. In 1938, when a team from Tunis played a club in Philippeville, Algeria, many locals joined together to root against their local team, made up of people from the European settler community. "Even though the team composed of Muslims was from Tunis," a French official complained, all of the *indigènes* (native Algerians) supported them "against their local team": "It was clear that only one thing mattered to the Arabs: the victory of their coreligionists." Sports, he lamented, had become for them the expression of a "struggle between the races."[13]

The French colonial regime tried hard to undermine the potential for nationalist mobilization through football. In 1928 they banned matches between teams composed either of Europeans or *indigènes* and urged the merging of Muslim and European clubs. But football organizations basically ignored these orders. In the 1930s French officials tried a different approach, requiring teams to field a quota of European players during games as a way of undermining the symbolism of conflict between communities. Though they canceled a few games when teams violated the order, they ran up against strong resistance from the football clubs of all communities in Algeria. The policy also highlighted some of the contradictions of their broader colonial policy; when one Muslim team sought to comply with the quota requirement by taking on several Jewish players, officials declared that these players weren't considered Europeans. (Many Jews in Algeria were from communities that had been in the region long before French colonization, but the French government had granted all Jews French citizenship in 1870.) Clubs resented such interference in their choice of players; they certainly knew that sports rivalries, though they might be dangerous, packed the stadiums. Although the rule requiring a quota of European players was never fully enforced, it did contribute to the anger of many Algerians, who saw the attempt by the colonial state to force European players onto their teams as one more discriminatory measure. By the 1930s it was clear that football, far from serving to assuage the colonized or assist the colonizers, as Pierre de Coubertin had hoped decades earlier, was one of the most significant public vehicles for protest in Algeria.[14]

On 8 May 1945 two young teenage boys, Hamid Kermali and Amar Rouaï, were playing football near a market in Sétif, Algeria, when they heard the sound of an approaching crowd. It was Armistice Day, and the French government had declared that in celebration of the end of the war, tricolor flags as well as the flags of French allies should be flown throughout Algeria. But they prohibited the flying of any other emblems. They clearly had in mind the Algerian flag, which nationalists were increasingly deploying during demonstrations. Coming on the heels of the Popular Front reforms in colonial administration, the years of war had created a political opening in Algeria. Activists made increasingly radical demands. Among them was Ferhat Abbas, a native of Sétif who in the 1930s agitated for political assimilation

but by the 1940s was calling for independence. Abbas and other organizers saw the celebration of the armistice of May 1945 as an ideal moment for voicing their demands and organized a demonstration. The response of the local police and army was stunningly brutal. The day World War II ended, another war began in Algeria.[15]

Sétif, like most towns throughout France and its empire, had a monument to the dead of World War I. At the head of the march Kermali and Rouaï saw a group of young Muslim Scouts carrying flowers to place at the foot of that monument in honor of the many local soldiers who had died in the recent war. (Scouting organizations had proliferated in the previous years, and many activists saw the organizations as an ideal place to prepare boys for possible military conflict and to inculcate cultural pride, as well as introducing them to the songs and symbols of Algerian nationalism.) Both Kermali and Rouaï had lost their fathers to French wars. Rouaï's, a veteran of World War I, had returned home with his lungs scarred from a gas attack and ultimately died as a result. Kermali's was an officer in the French army who was killed early in World War II. Perhaps the boys thought of their fathers as they joined the march. Or maybe they were just curious.[16]

Behind the Muslim Scouts were militants from the nationalist P.P.A. Along with French and allied flags, they carried protest signs—"Down with colonialism," "We want to be equal"—and banners demanding the release of the imprisoned activist Messali Hadj. Such slogans were a common sight in Algeria, where militants had long demanded increased political rights and legal inclusion in the French nation. But one of the marchers also carried a more provocative symbol, an Algerian flag. Another had a banner that read "Long live free and independent Algeria." There was little organized security surrounding the march, but a group of policemen, seeing the banner and the flag, ran into the crowd to grab them, and a fight broke out. Then, suddenly, one of the policemen pulled out his gun and shot the man carrying the Algerian flag. Kermali and Rouaï watched him fall. Several other marchers were killed by shots fired from nearby windows. Much of the crowd scattered, but the Muslim Scouts kept on marching and placed the flowers at the foot of the monument, though a group of bystanders promptly trampled them. Behind them, some of the demonstrators decided to take revenge. Although the leaders of the demonstration had urged participants to leave weapons at the mosque where it began, many had kept knives and other weapons, and now they coursed through the town, randomly attacking people and killing twenty-nine.[17]

As news about the events in Sétif spread throughout the surrounding area, people on both sides of the suddenly widened colonial divide began attacking each other. There were chaotic conflicts in the town of Guelma, and in several villages in the area groups attacked and killed members of the European settler community. French army units and local militias launched a rapid and ultimately much more deadly response. The police announced a curfew in Sétif, and soldiers—some of them Algerians or Senegalese—fired rifles and sometimes machine guns at people who broke the curfew. On the edge of the town a nine-year-old named Rachid Mekloufi watched from the window of his apartment as people running from the French police tried to hide in a field of wheat beside the road. The French set up a machine gun near the field and began firing at the fleeing people, gunning them down one by one. Mekloufi recalls hearing laughter coming from the machine-gunners. In the countryside soldiers and armed civilians, some of them organized into militia units, rounded up and executed people, seemingly at random. Though officers and officials presented the massacres as a response to the sporadic attacks against Europeans, in fact a majority of victims were unarmed and uninvolved, and many were children, women, and elderly people. Corpses lined many roads; others were burned or thrown into mass graves in gullies and ravines. The French sent planes to bomb villages, using bombs developed by the British to drive out soldiers entrenched in bunkers. When they were dropped on villagers out in the open, the effect was so horrifying that the British refused to supply the French with any more bombs, fearing that they would face serious problems in the Arab world if they were seen as supporting the massacres.[18]

Throughout May 1945 the army carried out massive roundups and summary executions. They set up tribunals that rapidly condemned many suspected rebels to death by firing squad. The chaos and fragmentation of the massacres, as well as the immediate attempts to cover them up, have made it notoriously difficult for historians to establish how many people were killed. The French government admitted 1,500 deaths; the Front de Libération Nationale of Algeria, basing its claim on a report made by the U.S. embassy at the time, later claimed that 45,000 were killed. A recent history asserts that in May and June 1945 alone a staggering 20,000 to 30,000 people died, most of them in massacres and executions.[19]

In the wake of the massacres a football team in Guelma took the field dressed entirely in black as an act of protest and mourning for the victims. The gesture was clearly a political message aimed at the French; white, rather than black, is the traditional color of mourning in Algeria. But the team clearly wanted the French to understand. They did, and in response banned the formation of any new Muslim football club.[20] A few months later, however, a policeman noticed that another Muslim football team took the field singing "In Our Mountains." This was very likely the anthem of the P.P.A., composed in 1932, which announces that "the voices of free men have risen" to call the nation "to independence."[21] In 1947, after a game between a European and a Muslim team, a policeman reported that several dozen vehicles carrying fans of the latter paraded through town making "obscene gestures" and shouting "nasty puns" at "the European population." Given the "ever-increasing number of Muslim supporters and especially their state of mind," the policeman urged that matches between Europeans and Muslims be banned, warning that they would very likely, "in the near future, degenerate into extremely serious fights."[22]

Of course the French had already tried banning matches. Soon they would have much more to worry about than fights at football games, even serious ones. Sétif was a foundational moment for the Algerian Revolution, a moment of repression that seemed to signal the end of hopes for a peaceful solution in the colony. Although Albert Camus wrote about the events, urging the French government to begin a dialogue with activists like Abbas, his was an isolated voice. By the early 1950s many activists in Algeria were convinced that an open war against the French was the only way to win independence. Ahmed Ben Bella, an accomplished football player who had played briefly with Olympique de Marseille in 1941 and was a decorated World War II veteran, joined Messali Hadj's P.P.A. in the wake of the Sétif massacres. A decade later he was one of nine activists who launched the first armed campaign of the F.L.N. He later became president of Algeria. The events also marked the lives of the young footballers Kermali, Rouaï, and Mekloufi, who thirteen years later, playing as professional footballers in France, would be called on to serve the Algerian Revolution.[23]

Football, having helped lay the foundation for the independence movement, became a central part of it. In Algiers organizers debated and planned in cafés "decorated with cups, banners, and sometimes yellowing photographs" recalling sports victories. Political activists, artists, and athletes gathered together, "passionately discussing the same ideal, like members of a family." "Politics teamed up with football," recalled one activist, as "the chants of the stadium rang out like chants of war."[24]

In September 1954 an earthquake struck the region of Orléansville (today Chlef) in Algeria, killing a thousand people and leaving many more homeless. A football match was rapidly organized in Paris to raise money for the victims. The game was to pit a "North African selection" against a team of leading players in France. Looking for strong players, the coach of the French side asked an Algerian professional footballer, Hamid Bouchouk, whether he would join. But Bouchouk, sympathetic to the nationalist movement in Algeria, refused. "For me, playing for the French team is not a great honor," he said. "Playing on the football team of my own country would be one." Although Bouchouk wasn't recruited to the North African selection, which included Larbi Ben Barek and several other leading Algerian footballers, he must have been happy when they defeated the French team 3–2.[25]

Several months earlier, during the 1954 World Cup, a group of men from the newly formed F.L.N. met in Switzerland. Planning an uprising, they used the World Cup as a cover to travel unnoticed. In November they launched a series of attacks that began what became known as the Battle of Algiers. In 1955 the French declared martial law in Algeria and sent the army to crush the uprising, using mass imprisonment and widespread torture. In that year a game in Algiers between the Mouloudia Club Algérois and a European club team ended in a violent riot. Soon afterward the F.L.N. ordered all Muslim teams to pull out of the leagues in which they had played for decades.[26]

In the legendary 1966 film *The Battle of Algiers,* directed by Gillo Pontecorvo, the F.L.N. leader Yacef Saâdi, who wrote the original script for the movie and also helped produce it, played himself under the name El-Hadi Jaffar. Saâdi was a footballer before the war, playing in games that sometimes created opportunities for friendly and comradely exchanges with members of the European settler communities. Such exchanges became more and more difficult as the war in Algeria went on. When Saâdi went to survey the damage from a bombing of a beachfront casino he ordered in 1957, he saw in the rubble the corpse of a friend he had played football with, along with his fiancée. Such experiences probably shaped the way such bombings are portrayed in the film, which dwells on and unflinchingly portrays the loss of life among European settlers the bombings caused.[27]

For decades *The Battle of Algiers* has framed the way many people outside Algeria have thought about the war of independence. Though the film is a startling and forthright portrayal of the brutality of the conflict, it is also ultimately a rousing story that celebrates the triumph of the revolution as part of a broader triumph of colonized peoples over their colonial oppressors. But the Algerian Revolution was also a terrifying and brutal event that involved bloody internecine conflicts between different factions within the national-ist movement and produced a victory only at a terrible human cost. In some ways, as we look back at the revolution we find ourselves facing sometimes incommensurable versions of the same event, some heroic and some tragic, unable to fully take stock of the fact that it's all part of the same story.

Though the killing began in Algiers, it was not long before it spread to metropolitan France, where the F.L.N. launched a series of operations, sometimes using football as a cover. In 1957, during the final game of the French Cup between Angers and Toulouse—a team with two Algerian-born strikers, Hamid Bouchouk and Said Brahimi, both of whom scored for their team in that day's victory—the F.L.N. operative Ben Sadok assassinated Ali Chekkal, the president of the Algerian assembly who opposed independence, as he was watching the game. The Algerian novelist Rachid Boudjedra later wrote a searing novel about the incident.[28]

As F.L.N. recruiters looked for operatives in France, one of them turned to a football player named Abdelaziz Ben Tifour. He grew up poor on the outskirts of Algiers and played football in the streets with a balled-up piece of paper. At twelve he was noticed by the coach of a local team, and at seventeen left for Tunis, where he was noticed by recruiters from the French professional team in Nice. By the late 1940s he was a rising star in the French football world. In 1952 he was selected to play for the French national team, and in 1954 he played for France in the World Cup before playing for the North African selection a few months later. In 1957 Ben Tifour, who had just opened a café in Nice, was approached by a man working for the F.L.N. who asked him to collect the "revolutionary tax" for the party among Algerians in Nice. At first Ben Tifour kept his activities secret from his French wife, but eventually he told her about them.[29]

Other football players also signed up with the F.L.N., including Abderrahmane Ibrir, who fought in World War II, joined the Girondins de Bordeaux in 1946, and subsequently played for Toulouse and Marseille. Considered one of the best goalkeepers of his generation, he played on the French national team six times in 1949 and 1950. He stopped playing in 1956, returned to Algeria, and joined the F.L.N. His status as a veteran of both the army and the French national team didn't protect him. The French army arrested him in 1957, and he was imprisoned for three years in isolated prison camps, where, like many others, he was tortured.[30]

One of the goals of the F.L.N. was to convince the French population that their war was a just one and deserved support. In Algeria the F.L.N. repeatedly bombed public places, targeting the civilian population. But in metropolitan France they primarily carried out targeted assassinations of police and political figures, as well as organizing demonstrations. In addition to seeking support among the French, the F.L.N. also sought international legitimacy, reaching out to the United Nations, hoping that countries that had recently gained their independence would support them.

But how does an insurrectionary movement present itself as the representative of a nation? In 1958 an F.L.N. operative named Mohamed Boumezrag proposed an answer to that question. The F.L.N., he argued, needed a football team. And it had everything it needed to form one. Algeria, after all, already had a large number of extremely successful footballers, many of them famous and beloved in France. If they were to choose Algeria over France, the result would be stunning. The F.L.N., one scholar writes, could show both France and "the entire world" that their revolution was not "a series of bloody and disorganized revolts" in Algeria, but a "true war of national independence." The goal of the operation, as Boumezrag explained in 1958, was to create a well-publicized "shock" that would force the French population to realize what was happening in Algeria.[31] As a journalist writing in *Le Figaro* would describe it in 2001, the F.L.N. decided to paraphrase Clausewitz: "Football is the continuation of war by other means." Football players were to become "ambassadors of the birth of a nation."[32]

It was a promising idea, but its success depended on whether football players were willing to sign on. They had a lot to lose. Many found their life in France much better than the life they had left in Algeria. They were well paid and, as successful athletes representing various French cities, accepted and even beloved by residents of the towns where they lived. Many had married French women and had children with them. Furthermore most of the players the F.L.N. hoped to recruit were under contract with their football clubs, and many were at the peak of their careers. Some were doing military service at the Bataillion de Joinville, the unit specially created for athletes, where Zinedine Zidane served decades later. If those footballers doing military service left France, they would be considered deserters. Finally, if the plan was to work it had to be a complete surprise, so contacting the players was a delicate operation.

The F.L.N. could count on some football players. Ben Tifour already worked for them. Another player, Hamid Kermali, remembering the scenes he had witnessed in Sétif as a young teenager, also supported the F.L.N. But he had struggled for his success in France. At nineteen, after years of playing football in Algiers, he stole enough money from his mother to travel to France, where he knocked on the door of a recruiter for a small French team that a friend had told him about. Kermali's start in professional football was slow, but with the help of a well-established older player from Sétif, Mokhtar

Arribi, the first from the town to succeed as a professional footballer in France, Kermali made his way to a contract with the prominent Cannes team. He married a French woman and they had a daughter. By 1958, playing for Olympique de Lyonnais (alongside the Martinican Camille Ninel), he was widely touted as a player with a future on the French national team. But when the war in Algeria began he supported the F.L.N. financially and helped operatives in Lyon avoid capture by the police. In early April, at the end of a game in Paris during which he scored two brilliant goals for Lyon, the F.L.N. operative Mohamed Boumezrag approached him confidently. "My name is Boumezrag," he told Kermali. "I am part of the French federation of the F.L.N. We need you. Algeria needs you. Be ready."[33]

Boumezrag, the mastermind of the F.L.N. operation, secretly contacted players, using those he had already convinced to urge others to join the mission. Amar Rouaï, Kermali's friend from Sétif, was playing professional football at Angers. He had very mixed feelings; for him France was both a country "he had learned to hate in Algeria" and a country he "loved" for the way it had "greeted him with open arms, offering him rights and respect." In France he was a "citizen like anyone else," with political rights he had been denied in Algeria. Still, when Boumezrag contacted him, he agreed to join the F.L.N. team.[34]

In some cases Boumezrag recruited several teammates from the same professional team. By 1958 Abdelaziz Ben Tifour had been recruited to play at Monaco, where he had three Algerian teammates. One of them, Abderrahmane Boubekeur—part of the 1954 North African selection—was committed to the nationalist cause, and Boumezrag had little difficulty getting him to join the project, especially since he was no longer a starting player at Monaco. But another, Kaddour Bekhloufi, was a young player whose career was just taking off, and Mustapha Zitouni, twenty-nine years old, another veteran of the 1954 North African selection, had been selected to play on the French national team in the 1958 World Cup. In fact the French coach was using Zitouni as a cornerstone of the team. In March 1958, after a brilliant game played for France against Spain, he was offered an attractive transfer deal by Real Madrid. With his French wife he had two young daughters.[35]

"Couldn't we leave *after* the World Cup?" Zitouni asked when Boumezrag invited him to join the F.L.N. team. He was ready to give up his life in France, but it was tough to give up an opportunity that represented the ultimate dream for any football player. But Boumezrag explained that it was precisely by disappearing *before* the World Cup that Zitouni could make the most powerful statement. France had chosen him. France needed him. If he refused to play, he would be striking hard against France and assuring the attention of the French population. Zitouni understood the argument, and realizing that "history had caught up with him" accepted the invitation. He would become the "flag-bearer for a new kind of soldier" who fought on the football field. To prepare for his escape, Zitouni began spreading the rumor that he and his wife were getting divorced, which helped to explain why they were packing up their apartment. Their friends were surprised, for the couple had always seemed blissfully happy. When a few weeks later they found out what happened, they were relieved. Zitouni and his wife were not getting divorced; they were just in an indeterminate exile, and in open war with the French government.[36]

Aside from Zitouni's, Rachid Mekloufi's recruitment was perhaps the most significant of the group. Since his childhood in Sétif, Mekloufi had become one of the most brilliant and famous footballers in France. He was a pillar at Saint-Etienne, which in the 1950s and 1960s reigned as the nation's greatest team. He had played on the French national team starting in 1956, helping to guarantee its qualification for the 1958 World Cup, and was on the roster for the competition in Sweden. Mekloufi was doing his military service, and indeed had led the French military football team to a world championship in 1957. This meant that his departure from France would be an act of desertion. But, perhaps remembering what he had seen in Sétif as a boy, he quickly made his decision. His participation meant that the operation was much more likely to succeed.[37]

Individually or in groups, the players disappeared from their homes in France in mid-April 1958, making their way across the Italian border to Rome. Conveniently, Zitouni and Rouaï were playing against each other in a game at Saint-Etienne. During the game Rouaï tackled Zitouni at one point, and Zitouni whispered to him, "Hey, don't hurt me at the last minute!" The two left together that night. Luckily for them, news of their disappearance was overshadowed in the press by the resignation of a high-ranking French government official. Passing into Italy, Mustapha Zitouni joked with a border patrol agent, who was used to seeing him on the train and asked him, "Hey Mustapha—wandering again?" When news finally spread about the departure of the players, border agents became more attentive, and two players recruited by the F.L.N. were caught as they tried to escape from France. One of them was imprisoned for a year. All of the other players, however, arrived successfully in Rome. The F.L.N. wanted to wait until the players were all in Tunis to announce the formation of their team, so the players avoided journalists and soon left for Tunis.[38]

When they arrived there, they had a bit of a shock. They had expected that they would be greeted by representatives of the F.L.N., but no one was at the airport to meet them. They made their way to a downtown hotel, and when they contacted the local F.L.N. leaders it turned out that no one was aware of the operation. The movement already had a football team, they were told, composed of players in the F.L.N army. Soon, however, the F.L.N. leaders in Tunis opened up the newspaper and learned that the departure of the Algerian football stars was front-page news throughout France. "Nine Algerian footballers have disappeared," announced the French sports daily *L'Equipe*. Lamenting the political symbolism of the desertion of the Algerians, the newspaper proclaimed, "The French team still exists, even if the word 'France' has taken on a narrower meaning." The magazine *Paris-Match* ran a special section on the defections, declaring, "These stars of French football have become *fellaghas*," that is, members of the armed Algerian resistance. Recalling the relatively muted response among the French public to the assassination of Ali Chekkal during the French Cup game the year before, an editorialist at *Le Monde* griped, "The French public is more sensitive to the disappearance of Algerian footballers than Algerian politicians." He was right, and the F.L.N. leadership in Tunis realized they had a media coup on their hands. They quickly issued a press release, declaring that the players had left France to join in the struggle for Algerian independence. "[At a time when] France is fighting a merciless war against their people and their country," the statement announced, "[the players] refused to give French sport their support, whose importance is universally recognized." The statement also insisted that, "like all Algerians," the footballers had "suffered from the climate of anti–North African and anti-Muslim racism" in France.[39]

Several of the players were unhappy with this characterization. Many, after all, were married to French women and had close relationships with French players and coaches. As Ben Tifour put it, the players were not "anti-French," and in their statements several players recalled the friendship they shared with people in France. Though they opted to make a dramatic political statement in joining the Algerian independence movement, they also refused to break with the cosmopolitan world of football in which they had lived. Indeed they passionately followed the French team during the 1958 World Cup, several of them rooting for France. They cheered when, thanks to goals by Raymond Kopa and Just Fontaine, the French advanced to the quarter-finals in mid-June. The players on the French team, meanwhile, stayed in contact with their former teammate Mustapha Zitouni, sending him a postcard from Sweden signed by the entire team. Of course the players who left in 1958 were also spared the steadily worsening situation in France itself. Footballers who joined the F.L.N. team just a few months later described how Algerians were increasingly stopped by the police and insulted in the streets or at school. And as they played, their opponents often shouted "Dirty *fellagha*!" and "Go home!" Still, the players would repeatedly find themselves out of sync with the revolutionary leaders of the F.L.N. During one early match they were told at halftime by an F.L.N. leader that they were playing "for a million." They assumed they were being promised a financial reward if they won, as was often the case in professional and international football matches. Afterward, however, the official told them, "You played and won for a million Algerians."[40]

Having clearly understood the political power of the defection of the Algerian footballers, the F.L.N. quickly mobilized to create an Algerian team. They gave all of the players who defected salaried positions as part of the F.L.N., paying them significantly more than other organizers in the movement, and gave each an apartment in Tunis. The F.L.N. requested that F.I.F.A. recognize the team as the national team of Algeria and allow them to play in international competition. Not surprisingly, F.I.F.A. refused since Algeria was still a colony of France, but they went further than that. When, in late April 1958, a tournament was organized in which the F.L.N. team was to play against the Moroccan, Tunisian, and Libyan national teams, F.I.F.A. threatened to sanction any nation that played against Algeria. Libya wasn't worried—they were already suspended by F.I.F.A.—but both Tunisia and Morocco, having recently gained their independence from France, had applied for membership in the organization and were awaiting a response. In an act of political solidarity the Tunisian and Moroccan leadership decided to participate in the tournament anyway; the tournament itself was named after Djamila Bouhired, an F.L.N. militant who had been tortured by the French. Several months later, when F.I.F.A. once again demanded that no Moroccan teams play the F.L.N. team, the king of Morocco ordered the tournament to go forward.[41]

On 9 May 1958 the Algerian team took to the field for the first time to play against Tunisia. The stands were packed with soldiers from the Algerian Armée de Libération Nationale. Many of them were wounded, recovering in Tunis, bandaged or standing on crutches, and most carried their gun over their shoulder. When the speakers blared out the Algerian national anthem, the "Kassaman," the crowd sang it passionately. "For the first time" the Algerian flag, "green and white, decorated with a crescent and a red star, flew in the blue sky." For years the flag had been the symbol of the underground resistance movement in Algeria, and its colors were flown at local football matches in the colony for decades. But in Tunis it took its place as the flag of a country that came into official existence through its football players. Months later, during another game played in Morocco, a fierce wind roared through the stadium and ripped several national flags from their posts; the Algerian flag was untouched. Some in the stands saw this as a sign that Algeria too would ultimately be left standing.[42]

If the team effectively represented Algeria, of course, it was because it played well. Although most of its members had never played together, they quickly clicked, playing spectacular football, "intelligent, twirling," with a "flamboyant and inspired attack." Not everyone was pleased, however. After their defeat of a Moroccan team in November 1958, the recently retired Larbi Ben Barek, now a Moroccan citizen, spoke to the press lamenting the loss. But as the team traveled, even in places where they were essentially unknown they quickly drew large crowds. In addition to playing in Tunisia, Morocco, and Libya, in early 1959 they toured Jordan and Iraq, where they impressed crowds and the Iraqi government, which made a large financial donation to the F.L.N.[43]

From May through July 1959 the team toured Bulgaria, Romania, Hungary, Poland, Czechoslovakia, and the U.S.S.R. The football federations of these countries were relatively protected from possible reprisals by F.I.F.A., thanks to their centrality and influence in the organization, whose vice president at the time was from the Soviet Union. For leaders in these countries, hosting the team was a useful way to claim a link with this growing anticolonial movement directed at one of the key nations in Western Europe. For the F.L.N. the tour meant that the Algerian flag would be raised in towns throughout Eastern Europe and the Algerian anthem sung before thousands of spectators.[44]

In Romania the Algerian team played their first game in a largely empty stadium but earned high praise in the media: "A wave of enthusiasm submerged the country. Romanians wanted to see the Algerians, who they nicknamed the 'brown diamonds,' play again." Additional games were arranged in the capital of Bucharest. This time the stadium was packed, and the media compared the team to the star Brazilians. It was both an athletic and a diplomatic victory: "From then on, the entire Romanian population knew that a war of independence was taking place in Algeria." What the players spread, though, was not just the knowledge of this far-off conflict, but also a sense of connection to it gained by watching, and coming to love, a memorable team of players from the aspiring nation. In Poland the team was greeted much less warmly. The Polish government had good relations with France and feared reprisals from F.I.F.A. They refused to raise the Algerian colors or have the anthem sung at the scheduled game. But when the F.L.N. players responded that they would not play in such a situation, the Polish officials relented. Once again the flag was raised and the revolutionary anthem sung in another country. Later, in Moscow, the F.L.N. team had a little time to be tourists and even got a chance to watch the Harlem Globetrotters, who were visiting at the time.[45]

At the end of their trip they could pride themselves on having spread their message, putting Algeria and its independence struggle on the map for many residents of Eastern Europe and the Soviet Union. At a time when the F.L.N. was pushing for support and recognition in the United Nations, this was a significant contribution.

In late 1959 the F.L.N. team traveled to North Vietnam, where they were feted by leaders who, just a few years before, had won their own independence from France. They visited a town populated by Algerians, Moroccans, and Tunisians who had deserted from the French army in Vietnam and fought for the country's independence; the Vietnamese government had given them an agricultural cooperative in return for their service. The community had a football team, of course, and they played a game against the F.L.N. team. The Algerian players also met with Ho Chi Minh in Hanoi, who recalled how he had stopped in Algiers on his way back to Vietnam after a period of incarceration in France. It was a "beautiful country," he recalled: "I understand [why] you would fight for it." The F.L.N. team trounced all of the Vietnamese teams they played during their visit, including the national selection. General Võ Nguyên Giáp, the commander at the 1954 battle of Dien Bien Phu, where the French suffered a decisive defeat, good-naturedly predicted, "We defeated France, and you defeated us, so you will defeat France!" The team was then hosted in China. On the way back home they stopped in Germany, where the football federation considered organizing a game but backed off due to threats from F.I.F.A. For the next two years the team continued to tour, returning to several countries visited in 1959.[46]

In 1958 Ferhat Abbas, who had just become the president of the provisional government of Algeria set up in Morocco, declared that the creation of the F.L.N. team had "advanced the cause of Algerian independence by ten years." Their presence throughout the world attracted crowds in a way that no other political representative could. In France the departure of well-loved and well-known footballers left a mark on the population and helped transform the image of Algerian nationalists. "People who had a father or son serving in Algeria knew a war was going on there," recalled Rachid Mekloufi in 2008. "But a large majority of French people didn't know anything about the situation there. It was when they learned that we had joined the struggle alongside the F.L.N. that they became conscious of the situation." Football crystallized the aspirations of Algerian nationalism, and the F.L.N. team produced the trappings of official recognition—the flag, the anthem—wherever it went. And, though it took some time, eventually state institutions caught up with football.[47]

NINE

Reconciliation

AT THE END OF THE WAR most of the F.L.N. players stayed in Algeria, some of them in government positions, others as coaches or team managers. Seven of them joined the Algerian national football team, which F.I.F.A. officially recognized in 1963. In their first years in international competition they did well, defeating Czechoslovakia and West Germany in early games, and in 1965 played the Brazilian team in Algiers. In the next few years, however, the team did poorly, and most of the F.L.N. veterans went on to other things.

After a short stint in Switzerland, Rachid Mekloufi returned to France to play with his former team, Saint-Etienne. How would Mekloufi, the man who deserted France in 1958 to join an anti-French revolutionary movement, be greeted when he walked onto the field? Unsure, the managers of Saint-Etienne kept his return a secret. But when he entered the field for the first time in a game at Cannes, fans greeted him with smiles and applause. He didn't disappoint them, scoring a goal in his first game and helping to secure a victory. The next game, however, was in Saint-Etienne itself, and his presence on the team was no longer a secret. The club received a letter from a fan who threatened to kill the "deserter" Mekloufi. When he entered the field for the match, a crucial one for the team, there was silence. If he played badly the fans could easily have turned on him. But a few minutes into the game Mekloufi, coursing down the field, received a perfect pass, dribbled around one defender, then another, and passed it on to a teammate. The fans jumped out of their seats to cheer him on. Over the course of the game he made the decisive passes on the three goals that allowed his team to win, and fans were ecstatic: "Rachid—their Rachid—was back." It was the beginning of a brilliant continuation of his career, which culminated in 1968, when Saint-Etienne won the French Cup thanks to two goals scored by Mekloufi. When President de Gaulle handed over the Cup he announced to the team, "You are France!" That night in Saint-Etienne seventy thousand fans celebrated in the streets, chanting "Mekloufi, Mekloufi!"[1]

When he retired from professional football soon afterward, Mekloufi returned to Algeria and became the coach of the Algerian military team. In 1975 he led the team to the Jeux méditerranéens, a regional tournament held in Algiers that year. In the final of the tournament they faced the amateur selection of the French national team. The game garnered little attention in France, but in Algeria it became a national event, rich with symbolism. "An Algerian military team, coached by a former French international player who was considered a deserter during the Algerian war," would be "playing against the former colonial power." The game, furthermore, took place just a few days before French president Valéry Giscard d'Estaing visited Algeria, the first visit from a French president since independence. The stadium in Algiers was packed with 100,000 spectators, including the Algerian president Houari Boumedienne, a former F.L.N. fighter. It was a tight match, and when the French took the lead the Algerian president left his seat. He was unable, observers assumed, to bear the thought of watching the French flag raised and hearing the "Marseillaise" sung in victory on Algerian soil, though he later claimed he was just going to the bathroom. With three minutes left in the game an Algerian player scored, and in overtime the team scored again and secured a victory. Algiers rose up in a massive celebration, larger than anything seen since the moment of independence.[2]

The accords that established Algerian independence in 1962 stipulated that children born in France to Algerian citizens, who would automatically be given French citizenship at the age of majority, would also be considered citizens of Algeria, thus holding dual citizenship. But Algerian citizenship came with a cost: two years of military service in Algeria. However, for footballers playing in European professional leagues who were born in France to Algerian parents it created an opportunity. In the early 1980s the Algerian government began offering these athletes a spot on the national team. If they hadn't played for the French national team (which according to F.I.F.A. rules disqualified them from playing for another team), they could play for Algeria. Some in the Algerian government viewed Algerians living abroad with some suspicion, but turning to these players seemed to be the best way to assure qualification for the World Cup. There was some tension between the Algerian- and French-born players. Still, the team clicked, and for some of those born in France, playing for Algeria was a kind of homecoming. "Here, in Algeria," said French-born Nourredine Kourichi, "I really feel as if I am at home." The strategy was a success. In 1982 Algeria made it into the World Cup.[3]

In France Algerians and their children also supported the team, among them Zinedine Zidane, who pinned up a poster in his room of Djamel Zidane, one of the star players of the Algerian team. The young Zidane saw his namesake as a model and an inspiration. In the first game in the group stage of the World Cup, the Algerian team carried out a stunning upset, defeating the powerhouse West German team, 2–1. "We have proven, once again, that football is not an exact science," the Algerian coach announced modestly. The victory sent Algerians into a massive celebration, with singing, dancing, and parades in the street, in a kind of repetition of the independence celebrations of 1962 and those of 1975. The victory was seen as a larger symbol: the victory of a small former colony over one of the richest countries in Europe in a match that could only have happened thanks to the World Cup. One Algerian journalist described a "shock wave" that "shook the entire country" at the moment of victory. While Algeria celebrated, he went on, thousands of miles away in Germany kids were reaching for an atlas and asking, "Hey dad, where's Algeria?"[4]

Soon afterward, however, Algerian hopes were dashed. The German and Austrian teams, who could both qualify for the next round of the competition with the right score during their final match, colluded to end Algeria's hopes for the Cup. Germany had to win their final game, but because of earlier victories Austria would go on as long as they didn't lose by too many points. The Germans scored early in the game and then passed the ball around between them, while the Austrians played lazily, assuring the 1–0 score that would send both of them on. Although it was clear that the teams had agreed to this plan, F.I.F.A. could not nullify the results. The Germans went on to defeat France in the famous Seville semifinal. The bitterness against both teams would last among fans of Algeria for several decades. Though Algeria made a strong showing again at the 1986 World Cup, the team's fortunes declined after that as the country spiraled into an increasingly bloody civil war. And so when, in 2001, Algeria got the opportunity to play against France, the reigning world champion, fans were thrilled. Some, like Sofia Benlemmane, were also willing to do anything to make sure their team didn't lose.[5]

Football had been drafted, to powerful effect, as a weapon of war during the Algerian Revolution. Could it be mobilized as powerfully in the service of reconciliation? That was the question posed in 2001, when for the first time in history the two lead football teams of Algeria and France finally faced off, in the stadium where France had won its World Cup three years earlier. The game was a long time coming; in fact it had initially been scheduled to take place in Algiers in 1999 but was called off because of security considerations. At the request of the Algerian government it was rescheduled to take place at the Stade de France in 2001. Both the French and the Algerian governments considered it an important diplomatic gesture. In the pages of the leftist newspaper *L'Humanité* two anthropologists studying the culture of football, Christian Bromberger and Alain Hayot, emphasized the powerful significance of the match. "A football game," Bromberger noted, "chosen voluntarily, requires a kind of pacification in the relationship. You don't play a football game against a country you are at war with." Forty years after the Evian accords, which had ended the Algerian war, Hayot noted, the people of France and Algeria were finally accepting peace "on the human level" through this friendly football match. The event represented "the beginning of a Franco-Algerian reconciliation, and the true beginning of the work of mourning for the French."[6] History, one journalist noted, would be dramatically present on the field on the night of the game, to the point that it might overshadow the game itself.[7]

As the game approached, Djamel Belmadi—one of the stars of the Algerian team, who had been born in France in Saint-Denis and played professionally for Olympique de Marseille—suggested that the events of 9/11 made the encounter even more important. He relished the chance to play against Zidane, whom he described as a "model for all of us." And he announced, "In the present situation, soccer should send a message of peace and brotherhood."[8] Algerian immigrants in France, as well as their children and grandchildren, passionately discussed the long-awaited match. "Between two cultures, between two countries, between two national teams," which one should they choose? In July perplexed children asked the French minister of sports, Marie-George Buffet, for her advice on the question. She told them to "applaud both teams," as she would do. "But I didn't convince them," she admitted. The game forced "the ultimate choice." The fact that the star of the French team was Zidane made the choice even more complicated. As one anthropologist noted, the game might crystallize "antagonistic feelings within the same person." Many would find a way to balance their divided loyalties, Bromberger predicted accurately, but others would come to the game eager to demonstrate a "desire to be recognized in a society that still does not recognize them."[9]

Many football fans in France had faced similar choices over the years. Portuguese immigrants often supported the Portuguese team, and in 2006, when the team faced France in a quarterfinal match, there were many Portuguese flags and jerseys in the streets. The same went for those of Italian background. Such choices, however, were never imbued with ponderous political significance, because the question of whether Portuguese or Italian immigrants could be truly French was, at least by the late twentieth century, rarely raised. Algerians and their descendants, however, were regularly suspected of not being truly French. The war between the two nations still lurked in the politics surrounding the Algerian presence in France. The rise of Islamic terrorist organizations in France in the late 1990s, a development intertwined with the brutal civil war ripping Algeria apart during the decade, hardened perceptions of North African immigrants. After 9/11 the sense of menace and distrust only deepened. Prominent French intellectuals criticized Islam, among them the writer Michael Houellebecq, who declared, "The most idiotic religion is definitely Islam," inciting a controversy in the weeks before the France-Algeria game.[10]

For one journalist writing in *Le Figaro* the game would be nothing less than a "test" of the "solidity of national cohesion" in France. When Zidane "evokes Algeria," the journalist noted, he says "my country": "The Algerian, Tunisian, and Moroccan flags are happily flown by young French people from the *cités* when they celebrate a victory" of the French team. "The 'black, blanc, beur' France follows several flags." Could France be like the United States in the wake of 9/11, when a "mosaic of peoples" were united by the fact that they were "first and foremost proud to be American"?[11]

Some politicians weren't willing to find out and demanded that the match be canceled because of concerns about the possibility of a terrorist attack. The right-wing politician Bruno Mégret derisively described Saint-Denis, where the match would take place, as a zone that had suffered "foreign Afro-Muslim colonization." He called the game a "menace to public order" and said it would be "an insult to the French people" to let it happen. He was, he pronounced after the game, proven right by the pitch invasion by Algerian fans: "It's proof that immigration is a major danger because it brings Islam and Islamism. The danger is not at a doorstep. It is inside our house."[12]

In the days before the game police arrested three people suspected of planning a terrorist attack during the game, and someone sent them an anonymous letter threatening Zidane with assassination. On the day of the match several people telephoned the head of the French Football Federation to make bomb threats; he decided to ignore them, though he ordered bomb-sniffing dogs deployed throughout the stadium for the entirety of the game. There were also reports that some might use the occasion to demonstrate support for Osama Bin Laden, though the leftist mayor of Saint-Denis denounced such reports as baseless. The fears of incidents in the stadium cost at least one man a ticket. Named Mourad, he got in touch over the phone with a local administrator who had access to tickets. But when, as part of his request, Mourad spelled his name, the man responded, "Are you kidding me? You're an Arab, right? You think we're going to fill the stadium with Arabs after what happened in New York?"[13]

Kabyle activists in France, meanwhile, announced that they would use the game as an opportunity to protest Algerian state policies that suppressed the Kabyle language and culture. One activist said that the game was an opportunity for them to "affirm [their] solidarity with those who are fighting for democracy and liberty in Algeria." The president of Algeria, probably to counter the bad press the country would receive from such demonstrations during the high-profile event, announced shortly before the game that his government was planning to grant the Berber language spoken by the Kabyles status as one of Algeria's national languages, as had long been demanded by activists. Fans of a different political persuasion considered bringing a banner to the stadium that announced their support for the Algerian government in its war with Islamists in the country.[14]

Despite all the threats of disruption, many in the French press looked forward to the game, hoping that the magic of sport could help to bury the past. The magazine *France Football* published a special issue celebrating what it called "a game for history." In an editorial the prominent sports writer Gérard Ernault (borrowing an image from Patrick Demerin's 1986 essay on the French team at the Seville World Cup) hoped for a "reconciliation" stretching from the French port of Dunkirk to the Algerian desert outpost of Tamanrasset. Demerin had written of his hope that reconciliation would come through the fielding of a diverse French team; now Ernault hoped that such reconciliation would be achieved when opponents in an old conflict met in a football game.[15]

As the game approached, fans arrived from Algeria, some of them on special charters that were organized by Algerian airlines. Fans decorated bars in the neighborhood of Belleville with Algerian flags, and conversations in the main mosque in Paris centered on the game. Many fans of Algerian background decided to support the Algerian team. One young engineer declared that he was "100%" behind the Algerian team; born in France of Kabyle parents, he declared that Algeria was his country and that he always spent his vacation there. Selim, a security guard, was also of French nationality, but he would wear a green and white jersey to support the Algerian team when he went to the stadium. Some tried to find a way to support both teams at once. A woman named Sarah went to the game with her Algerian father and French mother, wearing a French jersey and carrying an Algerian flag. "She's from both shores," her mother explained.[16] But the dominant colors in the stadium that day were the green, white, and red of the Algerian flag. One Algerian newspaper reported that fans felt as though they were not in Paris but in the July 5th stadium in Algiers, named after the date of Algerian independence. A journalist noted that Saint-Denis was "the largest Algerian town outside of Algeria," and so in a sense both teams would simultaneously be playing at "home and away."[17]

At the beginning of the game the Algerian national anthem would be performed officially on French soil for the first time, in front of tens of thousands of people in the stadium and millions of television viewers. The anthem was composed in 1956 by an F.L.N. activist imprisoned by the French. It rivals even the "Marseillaise" in its evocation of the glory of bloody war, invoking "the lightning that destroys" and the "generous blood being shed" so that "Algeria will live." "We are soldiers in revolt for truth," the song declares. "When we spoke, none listened to us / So we have taken the noise of gunpowder as our rhythm / And the sound of machine guns as our melody." The fact that the anthem was to be performed highlighted the importance of the event as a long-overdue public "recognition of the Algerian nation." But it also inevitably recalled the conflict the football match was meant to bury.[18]

How did Zinedine Zidane feel about playing against Algeria? The question was discussed heatedly in the weeks before the game. One fan of both Algerian and French nationality told a journalist that he wanted Zidane to wear the Algerian jersey during the second half of the game. There was a precedent for this. In 1977 Pelé, then playing for the New York Cosmos, took the field for the final game of his career against the Brazilian team Santos, where he had started his professional career. He scored a goal for the Cosmos in the first half, but at halftime he put on the jersey of the opposing team and played for them. That game, of course, was an exhibition match and primarily billed as Pelé's last game, a celebration of his sporting career, and the symbolic stakes were much lower. Such an elegant solution wasn't available to Zidane.[19]

"For the past few days," Zidane told a reporter in Madrid, "I've been running into people of Algerian background on the street who have been asking me to go easy. . . . As I've said, even if it won't please Roger Lemerre [the French coach], if there is one game where we end up with a tie, one day, I'd choose this one." He reassured French fans that the team would "do everything to win the game": "But if at the end of it it's a tie, I won't be too disappointed."[20] Facing other journalists before the game he tried to avoid saying much more. "I'm the only one with Algerian origins on the [French] team, and I'm proud of that," he told the newspaper *Le Figaro*. But he would be "quite happy" if he could "just talk about sports" rather than about the larger politics of the game.[21] Speaking soon afterward to *Le Monde* he at first refused to comment on his personal feelings: "We're here to talk about a game, not about my country. The story that exists between me and Algeria belongs to me. I don't want to talk about it now." He turned the conversation to another matter, but in the end he admitted, "I will experience a little tightening of the heart when I walk into this game." Then he added ominously, "If I walk into it. . . . For the first time in my life, I won't be disappointed if France doesn't win. My dream would be a 0–0 game."[22]

Other players shared some of Zidane's sentiments. "I have a lot of Algerian friends," said Thierry Henry, "and it will be difficult for me," though he added that his feelings could not compare with "what Zinedine will be living through." Coach Lemerre, meanwhile, sought to address Zidane's conflict by suggesting that the game itself was a peaceful contest "between brothers": "It's not important whether Zidane's family is Algerian or French. He has the luck to live in France, a peaceful country, but he has Algerian blood. He should be proud of that. For him, it will be a match between friends. Not one nation against another, but brothers against brothers."[23] Asked how he felt about seeing Zidane on the opposing team, the Algerian coach Rabah Madjer, who had been a professional player in France in the 1980s, responded, "Obviously, we would have liked to have him on our side, but he chose his camp. We're nevertheless very proud of him. Zizou is still a model."[24]

The president of the antiracist organization S.O.S. Racisme, however, worried that Zidane's comments would confirm suspicions that Algerians were not truly loyal to France. He would have preferred it "if Zidane proclaimed instead that he was French, that he is a French accomplishment and a French joy." He added, "I don't care about the tightening in his heart when he plays against Algeria—it does us no good!" In *Le Figaro* a commentator ordered Zidane to make a choice: "Yes, we'd like Zinedine Zidane, who doesn't hide his tenderness for the Algeria where he has his roots, to describe himself clearly—by which I mean only—as French." *L'Equipe* magazine dreamed of a Zidane turned eloquent peacemaker:

And what if tonight, on the turf of a packed Stade de France, Zinedine Zidane picked up the microphone in front of the 80,000 spectators watching this historic game and spoke to this "black, blanc, beur" crowd, which will bring together without commentary French from here, French from over there, *harkis, pieds-noirs,* Algerians and so many other supporters from other horizons. And if in front of this multicultural France that we are also so proud of, the son of Malika and Smaïl, who left their Kabyle village for the *banlieue* of Paris and then the northern *quartiers* of Marseille, pronounced a few words on this long-awaited night. . . . Zinedine constantly repeats that he expresses himself with the ball at his feet and that he reserves his eloquence for the turf, and only for the turf. But if there was one exception in his career, it should be for tonight. Just a few words to say that, nearly forty years after Algerian independence, this match that we thought for so long would be impossible carries with it immense hope, and that he is one of the sons who will make it possible to heal the wounds. Algeria and France, the common history of these two countries is made up of light and shadow, love and hate, passion and craziness too.[25]

It was a compelling vision: Zidane, the global icon, the child of Algerian immigrants, speaking to the crowd and to the world, using the opportunity to end decades of hostility and anger, putting the demons of history to rest. But what precisely could Zidane have said to accomplish that?

When Benlemmane ran onto the field late in the game, Zidane, who had scored early, was already in the locker room. Most of the players on the field at the time of the pitch invasion jogged off when urged to do so by security personnel. Marcel Desailly even admitted after the game that he had been frightened. Lilian Thuram, however, refused at first to leave the field. "I stayed on the field," he later wrote, "because I think there are certain circumstances where you have to confront people and speak to them directly. I just wanted to catch one of the kids and make him understand his behavior was catastrophic." A "black teenager" ran past, and Thuram grabbed him. A security agent, "persuaded [Thuram] wanted to fight him," held the player back. But he wanted to give the kid a lecture, not a thrashing. Thuram wanted to say, "Do you realize what you are doing? Do you realize the message you are sending? Do you realize that television is filming you, that you are throwing yourself into shit, and pushing all your friends there too? Do you realize that you are reinforcing all of the prejudices people have about you? And later on you'll cry and say that no one understands you."[26]

The kid, "stunned," looked back at him, "as if to say 'I didn't do anything.'" "In fact," writes Thuram, "for him it was a game. He had gone onto the field with his friends, without aggressiveness, simply to perform a little and say to his friends 'Did you see me on TV?'" Even if their intention was benign and apolitical, Thuram asserted, it was a mistake on their part not to understand the political impact of their actions: "I knew, after all the discussions I had had on the events of September 11th, how heavy the impact of these images would be, how deeply prejudices would be reinforced." Indeed soon after the game he accepted an invitation to join the French government's Haut Conseil sur l'Intégration, a commission devoted to dealing with the problems of racism and marginalization in France. Thuram's teammate Mikaël Silvestre, also of Guadeloupean background, similarly feared that the incident would propel a return of racism and a rise of the Front National.[27]

Eventually escorted off the field, Thuram shouted out as he walked, "They are justifying everything! They're justifying everything people think about them. . . . And they wonder why there is still prejudice!"[28] As he later recalled, a security agent of Algerian background said to him, "These little idiots ruined everything again." But calling them "little idiots," Thuram wrote, was too convenient: "Most of these kids were French children of Algerian origin, whose parents and grandparents had a tragic history with France. They only knew snippets of it, usually the most bloody. It is even harder for them to feel French because, often, they are not recognized as such. . . . Let's stop the hypocrisy that affirms that they are 'Algerians,' or 'Arabs,' or 'little idiots' who hissed at the national anthem. We have to accept the truth: on the night of the 6th of October 2001, it was truly French people who hissed at the 'Marseillaise.'"[29]

Many commentators had a much more negative, and much less sympathetic, view of the actions of those who invaded the field in the Stade de France. "They betrayed the players of the Algerian team, and they betrayed the hope of all the people of Algeria," declared an apoplectic French commentator, Francis Maroto, on the France 2 television station. "Singing the anthem of the country of your birth is totally normal. But you never boo the anthem of the country that has extended you asylum." It was, continued Maroto, a "question of respect." The *voyous* (thugs) were "going to need to learn a little respect." Christophe Josse, another commentator, sought to calm Maroto's fury by presenting what was meant to be a reassuring counterpoint. He watched the game with a young football player named Jacques Fati, the captain of the French under-seventeen team. For Josse, Fati represented a case of successful integration into French society. Fati's mother was from Cape Verde, and his father was the result of a "Senegalo-Vietnamese *métissage*," as Josse put it, and Fati was "born in a *cité*" in France. "He showed that it's possible to be a good boy" and both "show respect" and "gain respect," as well as "showing your identity while still being a good boy." According to Josse, Fati had "a strange look in his eyes" when the pitch invasion took place. Though Maroto and Josse responded differently to the events at the France-Algeria game, both did so by unselfconsciously placing themselves in the position of parents evaluating the behavior of children. Maroto chided the "voyous" who had invaded the pitch, while Josse complimented Fati for being a "good boy." Just as many commentators had in 1998, they interpreted events on the football field as a portent of the larger social issues.[30]

Politicians, meanwhile, demanded the formation of a commission to investigate the events on the field. Some suggested that the security guards, many of them recruited at the last minute from the *banlieue* regions, had been complicit with those who invaded the pitch. *Le Figaro* magazine claimed that some of the guards had chased after fans on the field while "having as much fun as they were."[31] Although none of the security personnel was ever charged, several of those arrested on the field that night were, including Sofia Benlemmane. In court in late November she was "combative," according to one journalist. Defending her decision to rush onto the field, she said, "[There are] emotions that you just can't control . . . [because it] isn't every day that you see Algeria play." The prosecutor, who admitted never having been to a football game, admonished Benlemmane harshly for running onto the field bearing "a certain flag." The accused responded, "It's not 'a certain flag.' It's the Algerian flag!" "It wasn't a French flag, and you were in a French stadium," responded the prosecutor. "I am proud to be Algerian," Benlemmane retorted. "I was born and have lived in Algeria. I have double nationality. And the flag I carried is that of the country where I was born." She was found guilty, fined ten thousand francs, and given a suspended jail sentence of seven months.[32]

Just as they were before the match, journalists were intensely interested in Zidane's reaction to the situation. The coach took him out of the match at halftime, and he went back to the locker room and showered before the pitch invasion began. After the game he left the stadium without saying anything and never spoke about the incident. That, however, didn't prevent the French media from speaking for him. The television station France 2, in its report on the incident, showed a short film about Zidane explaining that he had not been to Algeria in fifteen years and that the country was "a distant memory, a sensation." A voice-over declared, "Zizou left yesterday's match profoundly humiliated by a hundred young losers who respect nothing, not their origins, not the country that has welcomed them, not their flag, not the one who has made them dream. Last night, they slapped their idol. Zidane had never been booed. They should be ashamed of themselves."[33]

Fans of the Algerian team expressed similar disappointment. An Algerian-born football coach in France condemned the pitch invasion: "[The] youth who played with our flag . . . have made all the people of Algeria unhappy." Some fans interviewed after the game similarly complained of those who went onto the pitch, "They're not fans, they're thugs." One commentator wrote that those who stormed the field had "no respect" for Algeria, which "they barely knew": "Most of them were born and grew up on the banks of the Seine. They are the proof that France has a problem with a part of itself."[34]

The anthropologist Alain Hayot concurred that, ultimately, the invasion of the field by fans was the reflection of an internal French problem: "It was the expression of a portion of the *beur* youth that wanted to express, with great exaltation, the pride they felt [at] having Algeria on French soil." He urged that people not exaggerate what had happened: "There was no bomb, no riot, no violence. Everyone went home quietly." There is nothing wrong, he argued, with "affirming" both one's origins and one's belonging to the French nation: "That is one of the great lessons of the French team. Its players have the capacity to be citizens of the world, recognizing difference, and at the same time represent France."[35]

To the philosopher Robert Redeker, however, the incidents at the France-Algeria game were the actions of a "crowd of *banlieusards* who are anti-republican and hostile to the ideals of the French Revolution." Those who ran onto the field were "declared enemies of institutions" and, as their wearing of sportswear with corporate logos proved, "fanatics of the most extreme capitalism, that of Nike and Adidas." The night, he insisted, represented the "definitive defeat" of the "sappy" declarations of those who argued that sports could help "integrate" the youth into republican institutions. While many commentators lamented that the events of October 2001 represented the negation of the celebrations of 1998, for Redeker they were their "revealing complement," showing that sports are nothing more than a fetishistic practice driven by unfettered capitalism. "Sport is not civic education," he insisted, but instead simply encourages "fetishism" and consumption.[36]

What is striking about such responses is that, like the flood of enthusiasm that greeted the World Cup victory in 1998, they seem completely out of proportion. A football game, like many other football games throughout history, had been interrupted by a pitch invasion. Why was that such a big deal? The disproportionate reactions point to the fact that football in France had become a terrain of incredible political investment and symbolic meaning. As the president of S.O.S. Racisme understood, the France-Algeria game would be a powerful tool for those who wished to portray the dream of a multicultural France as nothing more than a silly, indeed a dangerous utopia: "When we want to remember the 1998 World Cup, its images of fraternity, they'll respond with France-Algeria."[37]

On 14 November Jean-Marie Le Pen gathered his supporters in front of the Stade de France and announced that, once again, he would run for president during the upcoming election. He chose the site, he explained, because it was where "a few weeks ago, our national anthem was booed." In the campaign that followed, Le Pen went further than he ever had before in his various bids for president. In April 2002, in an election shaped by record abstentions among voters and a deeply fragmented pool of candidates on the left, as well as the clear decline in popularity of the Socialist Party, Le Pen got nearly 17 percent of the vote, nearly as much as President Chirac, who got just under 20 percent. This put him in second place, ahead of all the other contenders, and got him into the second round of the election. To prevent the National Front from winning the presidency, voters had only one choice: Chirac.[38]

The threat of Le Pen as president incited a group of French athletes to issue a petition calling on the French people to vote for Chirac. None of the members of the French football team signed it. But Marcel Desailly announced on his website that he hoped people would vote against Le Pen. "Democracy is on the line," he wrote, describing Le Pen as "aggressive" and "intolerant." He gained the support of other players on the team, including Thuram, Karembeu, Lama, and Willy Sagnol, who proposed signing a joint declaration against Le Pen. Claude Makelele made the statement that "solidarity between colors" had always existed in France and that it was crucial to preserve this. In a press conference Zidane urged people to vote, and he made it clear which side he was on. It was "very important," he said, for people to "think about the consequences of voting for a party that doesn't correspond at all to French values." Other players, however, remained aloof, including Thierry Henry and Christophe Dugarry, who announced that he wasn't going to vote. Finally, ten days before the second round of the election, the players agreed to support a collective statement, issued by the team captain Desailly, criticizing "the resurgence of attitudes that are dangerous for democracy and liberty, particularly in a France that is multiethnic and multicultural and rich in its diversity." Le Pen shot back that the voice of the football players had "no more importance" than that of other voters. But demonstrators taking part in a massive anti–Le Pen mobilization on 1 May made use of the symbolism of the team, wearing French football jerseys as a way to "reappropriate the French flag" and express a kind of "nostalgia for the joy" of the 1998 celebrations.[39]

In the second round Chirac won a decisive victory, receiving over 80 percent of the vote, with Le Pen getting only slightly more votes than in the first round. But the episode left many people in France demoralized. For those who looked forward to the 2002 World Cup in the hopes that France and its multiethnic team would do well, the nightmare had only begun. As the world champions, France qualified automatically for the competition. Their first game pitted them against a remarkable team from Senegal. As had been the case with the France-Algeria game in 2001, the matchup was rich with symbolism, pitting a former colony against a former colonizer. It also highlighted some of the ironies of such international competitions, since nearly all of the players on the Senegalese team played professionally in France, while almost none of the players on the French team did. For one of the French players, the Senegal-born Patrick Vieira, the game took on a more personal meaning, just as the France-Algeria game had taken on for Zidane the year before. Interviewed the day before the game, he described the matchup joyfully as something "extraordinary," a "gift from God": "It will be a celebration for me and for my entire family, part of which lives in Senegal." But, he assured French readers, it was "above all a competition," and he would give everything to win: "I love Senegal, I'm proud that I was born there, but I grew up in the *hexagone* [i.e., in metropolitan France] from the age of eight, and I defend the colors of France." Of his childhood in Senegal, he said, he remembered only "flashes": "I remember when I played football in the street with my friends." Since then, he had returned to Senegal only once, when he was twelve: "It's a country that I don't know anymore." Comparing himself to Desailly returning to his Ghanaian roots, he explained that he wanted to "learn everything" about Senegal and to "make up lost time" in his relationship with the country of his "origins." Asked if he felt "more European or African," Vieira responded that he had never posed that question to himself, because "African culture" had always been transmitted to him by his family, among whom he had grown up speaking Wolof. During the game, he said, he wouldn't worry over the fact that he could have been playing for Senegal if things had been different. But, he admitted, his family would be torn, "even if in the end they will choose France." For the French team the game would be vital, and as always there was "a risk of defeat."[40]

Playing Senegal in Seoul, France got close to scoring on two occasions, with shots by David Trezeguet and later Thierry Henry bouncing off the post. But the Senegalese team outplayed the French, with Papa Bouba Diop (then playing professionally in Switzerland) scoring a brilliant, scrappy goal, pushing the ball in after he fell on the ground. He ripped off his Senegalese jersey and threw it onto the ground on the edge of the field, then led several players in a dance around it. In Paris Senegalese supporters paraded joyfully in the streets, while French fans returned glumly home. In the next game France managed only an uninspiring scoreless tie against Uruguay, and after that they were eliminated from the competition by Denmark. The 1998 World Champions left the 2002 World Cup without scoring a single goal. Meanwhile, on the night of France's elimination, Senegal moved onto the next round of the competition. (They went on to defeat Sweden, becoming the second African team to make it to the World Cup quarterfinals, before being defeated by Turkey.) While supporters of the Senegalese team celebrated at the Hôtel de Ville, a few infuriated French fans hurled insults at them, some of them racist. The understanding and communion of 1998 seemed long gone. One reader writing to the newspaper *Libération* wondered whether the poor showing of the French team was not, in a sense, a reflection of the mood of the country. For whom, and for what, would they be winning in 2002? For a country in which a far-right politician who was hostile to everything the team stood for was popular enough to make it into the second round of an election? Maybe the loss was a kind of payback, a way for the team to tell the French that they didn't deserve their team and the victory they offered the nation in 1998.[41]

Although Zidane shone during an early game against England in the 2004 European Cup, the team again was eliminated early on, and afterward both Zidane and Thuram decided it was time to quit. Though both continued playing professional football, they announced that they would no longer be playing on the French national team. In principle, the French coaches had the right to call them up anyway, but they respected the wishes of the two players. It seemed the end of an era.

⚽

Since 2001 there has not been another pitch invasion in the Stade de France. But there has been plenty of booing. The France-Algeria match helped produce a durable football tradition in which fans boo the "Marseillaise" before games between French and North African national teams, inciting outraged commentary and condemnation by French politicians and journalists. In the fall of 2007, for instance, at the beginning of a Morocco-France friendly match, fans enthusiastically booed the "Marseillaise." Bloggers discussing the incident afterward downplayed the event, saying that only a small number of fans had hissed, mostly to get attention, and that it signified nothing more than the rivalry between two teams. But one man who attended the game defended his decision to boo the French national anthem: "I hissed at the Marseillaise and I'm not hiding. . . . I'm Moroccan, I live in France, but you should remember that it is under that Marseillaise that France colonized and exploited [its colonies]." As long as France did not apologize for this exploitation, and for the colonial atrocities committed in the "name of liberty," he would continue to "boo everything French." A video briefly posted on (and then removed from) YouTube in the fall of 2008 made a similar point, juxtaposing the boos aimed at the "Marseillaise" with footage of massacres carried out by French troops in colonial Algeria.[42]

A year later, in October 2008, a friendly match took place between Tunisia and France in the Stade de France. Tunisian fans came out in force. The organizers of the match did everything possible to diffuse the charged symbolism of the confrontation between the two teams. Rather than walking out in separate ranks, as teams usually do, the teams entered the field mixed together. They stood, intermingled rather than separate, during the two national anthems, while little kids stood in front of them wearing Tunisian and French jerseys. On the field was one of the new stars of the French team, Karim Benzema, whose parents are from Tunisia. The singers chosen to sing the French and Tunisian anthems were women of Tunisian background. During the Tunisian anthem, fans in the stadium were exhilarated, some turning their faces to the sky with their eyes closed, savoring the fact that they were hearing the song in the heart of France. But when the next singer took up the "Marseillaise," despite everything that had been done to suggest that France and Tunisia were reconciled, boos and hisses rained down from the stands.

TEN

Burn

IT'S TOUGH TO BE A CAR IN FRANCE. For starters, you are probably small; you have to be in order to fit into those tiny parking spaces. It's reasonably likely that, at some point, your rearview mirrors will be ripped off by a passing motorist when you park in a narrow street. And, to top it off, the most common form of protest in France involves burning you to a crisp. If you are alone at night, or your driver fled at the sight of a group of young men surrounding you, your last minutes will go like this: First, they will rock you back and forth until they can lift you up on one side, tipping you up and over, onto your side or back. When the gas starts leaking from your engine, invitingly trickling down the pavement, your tormentors will dare each other to light the stream on fire. The police might be on their way, but they will arrive too late for you. When one of the gang finally does throw a match on the gas, or else expedites the process with a Molotov cocktail brought for the purpose, you will burst into brilliant flames, lighting up the surrounding apartment blocks, your last moments captured on cell-phone cameras as you turn to ash and twisted metal to the sound of cheers.

The French penchant for car burning, displayed most powerfully in October and November 2005 during three weeks of *banlieue* insurrection, shocks most Americans. Here owning a car is considered a sacred right, a basic necessity for nearly everyone except those who live in New York and a few other major cities. In France a car is something different. Since public transportation works, for the most part, quite well (when there isn't a strike, that is), and since insurance premiums, the courses required to get a license, and gas and parking are all expensive, owning a car is a sign of a modicum of economic stability. To poor *banlieue* residents who buy a car, it often represents a major investment. But having one in and around the *banlieue* is risky. Between January and November 2005, before the worst of the *banlieue* riots took place, twenty-eight thousand cars were burned in France, sometimes

FIGURE 20. A car burns in Clichy-scus-Bois, 31 October 2005. Philippe de Poulpiquet © Maxppp, Panoramic, Action Press/ZUMA.

during confrontations with the police, sometimes in isolated acts of vandalism. Over the course of three weeks in November rioters torched nine thousand cars, fourteen hundred of them on one particularly fiery night. When the French police declared on 17 November that the situation in the *banlieue* had returned to "normal," it was because "only 98 cars had been torched the previous night—the routine daily average."[1]

Cars are a perfect medium for arson: they are everywhere, and they conveniently carry with them the seeds of their own combustion. The rioters of 2005 also targeted buildings, particularly state buildings such as police stations, schools, libraries, and gymnasiums. But, though a few stores in and around the *banlieue* (notably some automobile dealerships) were burned, rioters rarely looted stores. Their most sustained and visible tactic over the course of three weeks of revolt was car burning, which by 2005 was already a well-established and popular form of urban violence, a highly theatrical, visible, and dramatic method of getting attention. One of the remarkable characteristics of the tactic is that it is almost never deadly. During three weeks of insurrection, when night after night and week after week hundreds of thousands of youths clashed openly with the police, only one person died—a man who, while standing outside hoping to protect his car from being vandalized, was struck in the head by someone running past. The confrontations left hundreds injured, most of them police and rioters. One handicapped woman was horribly burned when the bus she was on was attacked and she was unable to get off. Still, especially given the length of the riots in October and November, the death toll was remarkably low compared to similar riots in Los Angeles in 1992, when more than fifty people died. This was a point several government representatives, including Nicolas Sarkozy, regularly repeated after the events with some satisfaction, presenting it as a mark of the professionalism and effectiveness of police tactics, ignoring the fact that it had as much to do with the strategic choices of the rioters themselves. In fact, although the number of guns in the *banlieue* has increased, there were only a few isolated incidents when they were used against the police, though at one point two policemen were wounded by shotgun pellets. This seems to have been the result of a conscious choice on the part of rioters. Whatever its cause, the low death toll is indeed quite striking. More people died in one night of celebrations during the World Cup of 2006 than during the entire *banlieue* insurrection of October and November 2005.[2]

The riots represented a striking challenge to the French government, and to French society as a whole. Night after night, in the communities ringing Paris and France's other cities, confrontations churned on between the police and groups of young men. They burned, looted, and hurled bottles and rocks at police. The riots never spread outside the *banlieue* neighborhoods to the city centers, so many in France continued to live their lives uninterrupted. But the *banlieues* became war zones, with street battles going on every day in many areas. After weeks of the burning the French government declared a state of emergency, resuscitating a law used to repress anticolonial revolt in Algeria and France in the 1950s and 1960s and applied in New Caledonia in the 1980s. The state of emergency established a curfew in *banlieue* neighborhoods and gave extended powers of search and seizure to the police. Whether because of the new measures or just the exhaustion of the rioters, the insurrection petered out by mid-November.

Many of the journalists, scholars, intellectuals, and pundits who responded to the November 2005 crisis described the riots as little more than a pointless, nihilistic burst of directionless rage. In fact there was a concerted and largely successful effort on the part of many intellectuals and politicians to disqualify the participants as political actors and to render any political interpretation of their actions suspect. But even many sympathetic observers lamented that the *banlieue* youth didn't create an organization, present a list of demands, or even offer up leaders who could speak on their behalf.

Some settled on the term *proto-political* to describe the riots. Indeed the very question of what to call the events was itself highly political, with the police opting for *urban violence*, activists often using the term *revolt* or *insurrection*, and many others settling on the less value-laden term *riots*.[3]

But one has to hold a particularly anemic vision of what constitutes politics to think of the *banlieue* riots as apolitical. "There are certainly times," writes one scholar, "when burning cars is a political act." Indeed it seems reasonable to describe the three-week-long series of events, composed of many series of smaller confrontations and riots, as an insurrection. Early on Nicolas Sarkozy claimed that many of the rioters were immigrants. In fact, however, the vast majority of those involved in the riots were French citizens; only 7 percent of those arrested were born outside of France, most of those longtime residents of the country. When they were asked what drove their actions, many of the rioters spoke as French citizens. They explained, as one sociologist has written, that "they didn't need to integrate themselves because they are French, and proud of it." They felt, however, that their rights *as* French citizens were being violated. They were fed up with the situation in their grim and poor neighborhoods, their lack of opportunities, and most of all a daily life peppered with harassment by the police. They were angry at the way they were treated by the French state, particularly by the police, and specifically by Interior Minister Sarkozy. Most of all, participants who were interviewed, as well as the organizations that sprang up in the *banlieues* during and after the insurrection, constantly demanded one thing from public authorities: "the recognition and minimal *respect* they deem themselves entitled to." In pursuing this respect they followed a well-established and venerable French tradition: they rose up in revolt.[4]

Subject of so much fear, fascination, dogmatism, and condemnation, the youth of the *banlieue* have struggled to create political organizations capable of speaking and lobbying on their behalf. There exists a patchwork of activist groups and local organizations that have sought to do so over the years. And, as such political outbursts often do, the November 2005 insurrection led to the creation of several such groups, including AClefeu (Stop the Fire) and Banlieue Respect, which have sought to mobilize voters, present candidates for local office, and lobby government leaders in the years since. Such groups provide a forum for crucial debates about how residents of the *banlieue* can best push for change, and many activists within them, while they express sympathy and understanding about the anger that drove the riots, also deplore and criticize the use of violence as a political strategy. They sometimes do so on moral grounds, but many also insist, with strong evidence to support them, that the use of violence is ultimately counterproductive, providing the government with new opportunities to put in place harsh, punitive approaches with the support of much of the electorate. One rap artist, Diam, included a pamphlet in a 2006 CD explaining how to register to vote. "One vote = Ten Molotov cocktails," it announced.[5]

But when activists urge residents to pursue traditional avenues of political mobilization they often confront a deep skepticism. During a meeting organized by a group called Devoir de mémoire (Duty of Remembrance), which mobilized celebrities with *banlieue* roots (including Lilian Thuram, the actor Jamel Debbouze, and several hip-hop musicians) to encourage *banlieue* residents to vote, one resident of Clichy-sous-Bois demanded, "You want us to register to vote. To vote for who? Who represents us?" Indeed it is a fact of French political life that until very recently there have been almost no French officials or representatives of North African or African immigrant background. There are some exceptions. In June 2005, for instance, Azouz Begag, an Algerian-born scholar who grew up in the shantytowns outside Lyon during the 1950s, took up the newly formed position of minister of equal opportunity. He was the first cabinet minister of Algerian background appointed since Algerian independence and one among a significant group of politicians, *banlieue* mayors, activists, and intellectuals who have long agitated for better schools, employment, and housing in the *banlieue,* as well as for more effective monitoring and suppression of racial discrimination. Still, as Begag himself noted a decade earlier, many in the *banlieue* have become deeply cynical about the established forms of politics available to them, which they feel inevitably simply co-opt any leaders they offer up, without anything concrete changing in the process.[6]

The most widely publicized and televised voices speaking on behalf of the *banlieue* in the media are hip-hop musicians, who through music and interviews seek to describe and channel the disenchantment and rage felt by many of its residents. They rose to prominence, ironically enough, in part thanks to a law that requires radio stations to play a certain quota of French-produced music. Because French hip-hop is more popular (and, let's admit it, a lot better) than most French pop and rock, radio stations often obeyed the law in part by playing hip-hop. Starting in the 1990s a series of prominent hip-hop musicians warned about the danger of an uprising in the *banlieue,* and some singers openly called for one. In the wake of the riots in 2005 several artists sought to tell the story of what happened from their perspective. One collective of artists released a CD called *Insurrection* whose cover announces, "Any regime born in oppression can only perish through insurrection." The artwork on the case presents the uprising as a new French Revolution, showing a black man with a turban holding a tricolor flag alongside an image from the French Revolution of a woman wearing the red Phrygian cap worn by the famed *sans-culottes,* the urban revolutionaries who supported the radical Jacobins during the revolution. Above them is written "La France aux humains" (France for all humans) and, underneath, "Sans-Culottes 2006." The CD itself sports a historical engraving of the taking of the Bastille in 1789. With this imagery the artists lay claim to a right sacralized in the French Declaration of the Rights of Man, the right to insurrection.[7]

Though such groups have a significant following in France, they have a limited capacity to reach and influence older generations of French people. Several hip-hop artists, most famously Suprême N.T.M., have been brought to court by the French state, which has accused them of encouraging violence against the police, though the major effect of these trials has been to increase the popularity of the accused bands. In the midst of the 2005 insurrection, 153 senators and deputies declared that music was to blame and asked the Ministry of Justice to charge seven hip-hop groups they accused of "hatred of France and anti-white racism." The politicians were a bit behind the times, though, for several of those they accused of having incited the riots had in fact been disbanded for several years by 2005.[8]

There is, however, one well-established national institution that *is* dominated by young men who grew up in the *banlieue* and is difficult to accuse of "hatred of France": the French national football team. The famed French comedy show *Les Guignols de l'Info* (imagine the *Daily Show* performed with puppets) pointed this out in a scene aired at the time of the 2005 uprising. One image showed the lineup of the French team "before curfew [was] put in place for people in the *banlieue*": the Caribbean players Thuram, Wiltord, Abidal, Gallas, Malouda, Henry, and Anelka; the African-born Alou Diarra; Vikash Dhorasoo, born in the Maurice Islands in the Indian Ocean; and two white players, Fabien Barthez and Gael Givet. The next screen showed the team "after the curfew put in place by Sarkozy." On the field were the two white players, Barthez and Givet.[9]

Among these disappeared players, there was one who chose to speak out forcefully on behalf of and as one of the *banlieue* youth: Lilian Thuram. Though Thuram had long been politically active, the events of November 2005 inspired him to take a series of high-profile and confrontational political positions. Only occasionally joined by his teammates, Thuram is unique for the extent, the consistency, and especially the quality of his political involvement. Although it is difficult to say exactly how *banlieue* residents themselves evaluate the content and significance of his interventions on their behalf, his activism has earned him hostility in some government circles and admiration among many politicians and intellectuals. In 2006 the historian Pap Ndiaye argued that for racial diversity in sports to have a broader social impact it was necessary for players to "invest themselves" in "civic life"; he singled out Thuram as the best model of how this could be done, calling him a man of "enormous courage."[10]

In 2001 Lilian Thuram was recruited from the Italian team Parma to play with Juventus. The team had just sold Zidane to Real Madrid and used the windfall profits they made from the deal to offer Thuram and his team Parma the largest transfer fee ever paid for a defensive player. Having reached the stratospheric heights of professional football, however, Thuram couldn't escape the racism of football fans. Early in his career in Italy, in 1996, he played with Parma against AC Milan, which featured the legendary player George Weah (later a candidate for president in Liberia) and a French player of Senegalese background, Ibrahim Ba. For the entire game, Thuram remembers, Parma fans chanted, "Ibrahim Ba eats bananas under Weah's house." Afterward Thuram wanted to make a statement condemning the fans, but the publicity director for the team argued that the chants were "nothing serious," an opinion shared by his teammates. "I was infuriated: how could you think that what had happened for ninety minutes was just a minor incident?" Thuram spoke about the incident to the press, asking fans whether they really thought it was right to say that "blacks are monkeys." Fans responded at the next game with a banner demanding "Thuram, Respect Us." "The world," he recalls, "was upside down." It was not the last time he would confront such hypocrisy. In 2001 fans of rival team Fiorentina hurled racist insults at Thuram when he was on the field with Juventus. It happened again in 2003, when Juventus played the Greek team Olympiakos. Even as they hurled racist taunts against Thuram, though, the Greek fans cheered their star player, Thuram's friend and teammate on the French team Christian Karembeu.[11]

Such incidents have been depressingly common throughout Europe. In one famous incident in Treviso in 2000 fans of the team booed Nigerian player Akeem Omolade and held up a banner announcing, "We don't want black players on our team." Some left the stadium when Omolade entered the field. The players rallied around him, and at the next game they came onto the field with their faces painted black to express their displeasure with racist fans. Blackface was used again the next year in a series of newspaper advertisements meant to attack racism in Italian football. Star Italian players appeared in two photographs; in one they appeared with the "white skin they were given at birth," in the other with "a black one created by makeup." Photographs of Lilian Thuram completed the spread. Some players, meanwhile, needed their own antiracist education. In 2000 a Champions League game pitted Arsenal, a team with a number of black players, including the French star Patrick Vieira, against the Roman team Lazio, a club infamous for its racist and anti-Semitic fans. Lazio's star player was the Serbian Sinisa Mihajlovic, who taunted Vieira with racist comments on the field while fans booed him and other black players on the Arsenal team. Vieira complained publicly, and Lazio forced Mihajlovic to read an apology before the team's next home game.[12]

Players also sometimes run into some of the more bizarre articulations of racism that crop up in everyday life. In 2008 the footballer William Gallas, a star of the 2006 World Cup team, stopped by a store in Paris to pick up some Dom Perignon champagne. Gallas went into the store and asked for eight bottles, but the store owner told him he could sell only two bottles of Dom Perignon at a time. Gallas said nothing, bought two bottles of the Perignon and two of another champagne, and left. Then he asked his chauffeur (who is white) to go in and ask for four bottles of Dom Perignon, which the store owner sold to him without comment. When Gallas went back into the store to demand an explanation, the owner said, "You should have told me you were William Gallas." Gallas issued a formal complaint against the store, and a report on the incident was posted on a website devoted to French Antillean affairs, Montray Krévol. "Apparently, being black and a member of the French football team doesn't make you fully French, but rather French with a difference," the site lamented.[13]

One of the most famous racial incidents in recent years involved the coach of the Spanish national team, Luis Aragonés. In 2004, during a training session, Aragonés chose a curious way to motivate one of his players, José Antonio Reyes. At the time Reyes was playing at Arsenal, where one of his teammates was Thierry Henry. "Locking horns with Reyes," a British journalist reported, "heads touching and staring into his eyes, Aragonés launched an aggressive if jokey tirade in which he tried to persuade the 21-year-old that he should believe more in his ability and that he is a better player than Henry." Aragonés told Reyes, "Tell that black shit that you are much better than him. Don't hold back, tell him. Tell him from me. You have to believe in yourself, you're better than that black shit." Spanish journalists recorded the scene on video. Aragonés attempted to stave off the controversy that exploded in response to his comments by declaring, "I am a citizen of the world. Some of my best friends are black, including those I have known since childhood. The fact that I make a joke in order to motivate a player does not mean I am racist in the slightest."[14]

Thierry Henry complained to F.I.F.A., and the organization punished Aragonés with a fine of three thousand euros, which, given his salary, amounted to a light tap on the hand. A disappointed Henry launched a campaign called "Stand Up, Speak Up." Backed by Nike, the campaign created television advertisements featuring Henry and other footballers, including the Brazilian Ronaldinho and the Dutch Ruud Van Nistelrooy, urging viewers to stand up against racism. The organization sold five million bracelets made of intertwined black and white thread and raised millions of euros for antiracist education. Henry hoped to make "hard-core" racists feel "less comfortable spouting their racism" in the stadium by creating a countercurrent among fans. "In five, six, seven years I'll be retired," he said, "and I want to be able to watch football on TV or attend a match and not hear a single racist insult."[15]

Campaigns against racism in sports have garnered powerful institutional and corporate support in the past decade, and antiracist slogans and statements are now a staple of international football competitions as well as many professional games. Football authorities and police have also clamped down on fan racism, expelling spectators who sing racist chants and sometimes downgrading teams to a lower division when they have failed to control their own fans. Lilian Thuram has participated consistently in these institutional efforts, speaking frequently at conferences and meetings about racism in sports and working with associations such as the French Foot Citoyen, which organized a series of football games against racism in March 2007. In 2006 he testified before F.I.F.A, describing racism in football as "a plague," and helped convince the organization to institute stiffer penalties against teams who fail to suppress racism among their fans.[16]

Thuram, though, has also expressed a remarkable level of sympathy toward stadium racists. "When there are monkey shrieks, people ask me if I feel hurt. I say no, because I'm not a monkey. . . . Those people are caught up in what is, unfortunately, a totally understandable logic," he explained in May 2006. "When people are racist it comes from somewhere. It's linked to a whole history, and unfortunately they are still stuck in that history." Fighting racism requires "education" rather than "rebellion." "You have to put yourself in a position in which you won't suffer from racism," he said. "Because it's the racists who are suffering. They haven't understood that society is in perpetual motion, that throughout time there has been a mixing of peoples, and that it's not going to stop." In 2005, however, Thuram had an experience in which he felt personally insulted. The man who insulted him wasn't on the football field with him or haranguing him from a seat in a stadium. He was the French minister of state, Nicolas Sarkozy.[17]

"You've had enough, right?" Nicolas Sarkozy asked an elderly woman peeking out of her window. "You've had enough of this gang of *racaille*. Well, we're going to get rid of them for you." It was 25 October 2005, and Sarkozy was taking an evening stroll through the *banlieue* of Argenteuil. Hostile crowds welcomed him to the neighborhood with shouts of "Sarko, on t'encule!" (Sarko, up your ass!). Some threw projectiles, sending him and his police entourage scurrying for cover, while a few of them opened umbrellas to use as shields. Elsewhere in the neighborhood Sarkozy had calmer interactions with residents, some of whom had come out of their apartments in bathrobes and pajamas to talk about the problems of crime in the neighborhood. What stuck with Sarkozy from that night, however, was the promise he made to the elderly woman to rid her neighborhood of its *racaille*. The term is a harsh one, which can be translated as "rabble" or "scum," and many were shocked to hear a French official use it, as Sarkozy did.[18]

It was the second time in a few months that Sarkozy had made headlines by visiting a *banlieue*. In the summer of 2005 an eleven-year-old boy in the Cité de la Courneuve, outside Paris, was killed by a stray bullet. Sarkozy went to the neighborhood after the killing; speaking to reporters, he announced passionately and aggressively, "We are going to clean up this place, we are going to clean it out with a Kärcher." The metaphor was vivid but poorly chosen. A Kärcher is a high-pressure hose used to clean the dirty façades of buildings, sending out abrasive chemicals to rip the dirt off the surface, leaving the stone underneath nice and white, the spray taking away everything in its path. For many in the *banlieue* horrified by the killing Sarkozy's words sounded particularly threatening, suggesting that the neighborhoods as a whole needed to be cleaned out with a hose, their residents like the dirt encrusted on an old building. Azouz Begag criticized Sarkozy's choice of words: "I use the term 'to clean' when I talk about cleaning my shoes, or my car. You don't 'clean' a neighborhood."[19]

Sarkozy's summer declaration crystallized the sentiment among many *banlieue* residents, especially the young men who often found themselves in conflict with the police, that Sarkozy, who promised to establish stricter policing in the *banlieue*, was in fact an enemy of the *banlieue* itself. That was one reason he was greeted with such rancor in Argenteuil several months later. The town mayor, who had grown up in Argenteuil and stated that he had "never had any problems with anyone," paid a price for having greeted the minister. Two days later his car was burned. Youths told him "with a smile, that there was probably a relationship between" the arson and the visit. A member of Sarkozy's own party told a journalist, anonymously, that other elected officials in the *banlieue* were "shivering" with worry, saying, "Let's hope he doesn't come to our neighborhood next time."[20]

The term Sarkozy used in Argenteuil, *racaille,* was often used in other contexts, notably as a badge of honor in some hip-hop music, where it is sometimes rendered through the syllabic inversion commonly used in *verlan* (slang) as *caillera*. It also showed up in the writings of political commentators on *banlieue* life. Azouz Begag, for instance, as Sarkozy quickly pointed out when Begag criticized him for his use of the term, had written in *Le Monde* in 2002 about "those who are called 'racaille' or 'caillera' . . . who everyone is afraid of." These guys, however, sounded substantially less menacing than the ones Sarkozy was promising to get rid of in 2005. According to Begag, the *racaille* frightened people by "riding scooters without helmets, riding on the sidewalk, endangering pedestrians, going through red lights, and rejecting all the codes of social conduct." Begag's goal was to describe how residents in the *banlieue* found their lives disrupted by unruly and disrespectful youths, whose conduct he deplored. But these teenage boys weren't particularly menacing, just obnoxious in a way that is familiar to people the world over. Although Begag criticized the behavior of some youths, he never suggested that it was necessary to "get rid" of anyone.[21]

Within two days of Sarkozy's visit to Argenteuil, his use of the word *racaille* had taken on a new meaning because of the tragic death of two young teenage boys in the *banlieue* of Clichy-sous-Bois. The town is particularly isolated, with no metro or train service; it was originally built in anticipation of the construction of a highway that never materialized and has a very high unemployment rate—over 30 percent among young people—and a concentration of people of North African and African background of about 80 percent. On 27 October, during a school holiday and in the midst of Ramadan, a group of boys from Clichy decided to pass the time by organizing a football tournament. "Half of Clichy is good at football," one of the boys later explained, "because there's nothing else to do." One of them, fifteen-year-old Bouna Traoré, one of eleven children of Mauritanian parents, whose father worked nights as a street cleaner in Paris, was known as an excellent player with good technique. He had a younger brother who was even better and was at a football academy in Le

Havre that was considering recruiting him. But the football stadium at Clichy was, as one young man from the neighborhood put it, "totally rotten and full of rocks." So the group decided to walk to the next town over to use the stadium there. In the group was also seventeen-year-old Zyed Benna, a champion runner and strong football player, who had arrived with his family from Tunisia three years earlier and whose father also worked as a street cleaner in Paris. The kids left in their athletic clothes, but without identification papers. "Our parents had so much trouble getting them," Bouna Traoré's brother later explained, "that they are very careful with them. Kids lose everything."[22]

Heading home around 5 P.M. to make it in time for the breaking of the daily Ramadan fast, the group took a detour and entered a construction site where low-income housing was being built. What were they doing there? The police insisted at the time, and continue to insist, that they were planning on stealing something, but it's as likely that they were just curious or messing around. From a nearby window, however, a man saw them and called the police. When the police arrived soon afterward the panicked kids began running. "We don't have to run—we didn't do anything," shouted one of them, but the rest were not convinced. They knew how things tended to go with the police and were scared. Without their identification papers they would certainly be brought into custody and their parents would have to come get them, which would likely earn them punishment at home. Zyed, in particular, was clearly worried about his father's reaction. "If the cops catch me," he shouted as he ran, "my dad's sending me back to the *bled*"—that is, to Tunisia. The group ran into a vacant lot nearby, and there a few of the slower ones were caught by the police. But Zyed, Bouna, and a third boy, a Kurd named Muhittin Altun, who had recently arrived with his family, were faster and stayed ahead of the police, running toward a nearby cemetery. By then, however, the police had been warned of the boys' whereabouts, and several cars began to cut off their escape routes. There was one place for the three to go: over a wall into an electrical station. They hid there for half an hour, and at some point, trying to find a dark place to hide, Zyed and Bouna touched a live part of the transformer. They were instantly killed by twenty thousand volts of electricity. The burst that killed them also knocked out the power in nearby buildings, including at the police station.[23]

Muhittin, badly burned, climbed his way out of the station and found some of his friends, telling them what had happened. The group of friends, along with Traoré's parents, gathered outside the electrical transformer, calling the names of the two boys. "We waited, we waited so long," recalls Traoré's brother. "Longer than at the A.N.P.E." (the national employment

Zyed et Bouna

FIGURE 21. A memorial portrait of Zyed Benna (left) and Bouna Traoré displayed on a banner as part of a photographic exhibit in Clichy-sous-Bois, 13 October 2006. Joel Saget/AFP/Getty Images.

office, famous for its eternal and usually fruitless waits). "We even waited longer than at the consulate," he added. Traoré's father struck his head against the wall that surrounds the station, while his mother cried. The police had left the scene once they lost track of the boys, without calling employees of the electrical company, who, if they had gone into the area when the boys first entered it, might have prevented the deaths. It was the friends of the two boys who had called an ambulance. Days later Bouna Traoré's family sent his body to be buried back home, in Mauritania.[24]

Many residents in the neighborhood, familiar with the rough tactics of the police, immediately blamed them for the deaths. As news of what had happened spread, young people stormed out into the streets in Clichy-sous-Bois, burning cars and trash cans. Many of them had known Zyed and Bouna personally; others there and in *banlieue* regions elsewhere that soon rose up as well felt that what had happened could have easily happened to them. When the police arrived the youth stood their ground, throwing rocks and bottles and hurling insults. The confrontations continued through the next day and night.[25]

On Saturday morning a group led by a twenty-four-year-old resident held a

FIGURE 22. The silent march mourning the death of Traoré and Benna. The T-shirts read, "Dead for nothing." © Jean-Michel Turpin/Corbis.

silent march mourning the death of Bouna and Zyed, parading with T-shirts and banners announcing that the two were "Dead for Nothing." Other peaceful memorials were organized in the coming year, including a football tournament held in the youths' honor in June 2006.[26] But confrontations with the police continued that night and on Sunday, when in the midst of one confrontation police threw a tear gas canister into a mosque full of older men and women, who rushed out in panic. Though the police claimed the action was a mistake, it further enraged many residents, particularly since local Muslim leaders had spent several days in the streets trying to calm the situation, often placing themselves between police and rioters. One resident lamented the way the police overreacted, reigniting conflicts when they seemed to be dying down. In one *cité* near Saint-Denis a group of kids ten to twelve years old gathered around the football field they played on, which they cherished because it had recently been upgraded to synthetic turf. They were afraid that police vans and trucks would park there, destroying it. But even as a local community activist was convincing the kids to go home, a police helicopter began flying overhead, and soon troops of police rushed into the area, firing rubber bullets, sending everyone running for cover.[27]

FIGURE 23. Players at the June 2006 football match honoring Benna and Traoré at the stadium in Clichy-sous-Bois. Muhittin Altun, who was with the boys in the electrical station and survived, is third from the right. Jean Ayissi/AFP/Getty Images.

Sarkozy's response to the deaths of Bouna and Zyed infuriated many in the *banlieue*. The day after their deaths he declared that the boys had been trying to steal something at the construction site (though there was no proof of this) and that the police weren't pursuing them when they went into the electrical station. "It seems," he added, strangely nonchalant, "that two among them electrocuted themselves." A few days later he explained that the boys could not have been running from the police since the police had returned to the police station twenty minutes earlier with the boys they had caught. But the fact that the police had simply left without calling the electrical company to warn them that the boys had gone into the transformer station struck many as an act of serious, if not criminal, neglect. An internal investigation into what happened that night ultimately cleared the police of serious wrongdoing, though they were criticized for not doing more to help the boys, especially since recorded messages make clear that the police knew the boys had entered the electrical station and that they were in serious danger. Sarkozy, however, portrayed the boys as being guilty of a crime and the police as innocent of any wrongdoing. And, unlike the intelligence services of the French police, which provided a relatively nuanced reading of the insurrection that highlighted its roots in the experience of social exclusion and economic marginalization, Sarkozy insisted throughout the events that the participants were nothing more than delinquents who needed to be treated as such.[28]

Initially confined to Clichy-sous-Bois, the insurrection began to spread, first to nearby *cités* to the northwest of Paris, and then to other *banlieues*. The turning point came on 2 November, when the French football team from Lille was playing Manchester United at the Stade de France in Saint-Denis, close to some of the neighborhoods that had seen violent confrontations since 27 October. Experience had shown that before, during, and after such matches there could easily be fights between fans, and eight hundred policemen were assigned to keep order at the stadium. The police were drawn from the same units that were being called on to stop the riots; *banlieue* rioters realized that as long as the police were at the stadium they would not be patrolling their neighborhoods. The riots spread and gained force that night. A large Renault dealership was attacked and destroyed, and there were bold attacks against outnumbered police units. That night, recalled a group of policemen, "everything fell apart." It was a "nightmare" during which they had to defend themselves against very rare "frontal attacks." One officer stated, "They came at us from all directions and we had trouble responding." Spectacular photographs and footage of that evening's riots, including some taken by a film crew who were forced out of their van and then filmed it being set on fire, flashed around the world. The Internet lit up with discussions about the events, and throughout the riots blogs and cell phones were used to share news and photographs and videos of burning buildings and cars.[29]

Now the insurrection was not restricted to just a few neighborhoods, or even a region outside Paris. It became a national event, with uprisings spreading throughout *banlieue* neighborhoods surrounding most major cities in France. "There is a clear syndrome of mimesis," one police official lamented. As the riots spread, the tactics of the uprising evolved. At first groups of youth engaged in long confrontations with lines of riot police, throwing rocks and bottles, burning cars and trash cans, retreating and then returning. In the end this amounted to a losing battle. As the insurrection wore on, the actions became more "sporadic and disseminated" and were "organized by little groups that were impossible to stop." "They move fast and are very mobile, they destroy everything systematically, and it is almost impossible to arrest them at the time," the director of one police unit explained.[30]

The results, *Le Monde* reported, were "spectacular": "Cars burn in the middle of the street, and you can just barely see shadows that seem to dance around the flames, the towering smoke, and the carcass; nearby, a fire truck is trying to put out a vehicle parked next to a building; further on, trash cans are burning; and even further, the carcass of a truck; a container full of glass bottles is spilled on the road; stones and broken bottles cover the ground. The smell of burned rubber invades the air, while a little further off you can hear motors exploding." When they entered the *cités* the police had to drive or walk along streets between high towers. Rioters gathered on the rooftops and rained rocks and bottles down on them, using their apartment blocks as fortifications to defend themselves against the unwelcome invaders.[31]

Throughout the 1990s there were sporadic but regular riots in different French *banlieues*. They usually began with the death of a young resident either fleeing or in the hands of the police. Outside Lyon in 1990, after a young man died in a motorcycle crash while trying to escape the police, youths fought against C.R.S. riot police. The next year a security guard at a supermarket in a *banlieue* outside Paris shot and killed a young man, and again youths rioted. A few months later an eighteen-year-old, Aïssa Ihich, died in custody after the police refused to give him his asthma medication, and enraged youths burned cars and fought the police once again. The insurrection of 2005 started in the same way. But unlike previous riots, it metastasized, spreading throughout the country and becoming a sustained, national uprising.[32]

In 1995 the in-your-face hip-hop group Suprême N.T.M.—the initials stand for "Nique ta mère" (Fuck your mother)—released a song with a menacing, prophetic refrain: "Why are we waiting to start burning? ... Everything should have already exploded.... [It is] all going to end up badly.... World war, you wanted it, here it is.... The bourgeoisie should tremble, the *cailleras* are in town. Not to party, but to burn the place down."[33] In the same year the film director Mathieu Kassovitz released *La Haine* (Hate). Kassovitz came up with the idea for the film when he and the actor Vincent Cassel, who stars in the movie, attended a demonstration protesting the death of a young black teenager in police custody. He shot the film in a Paris *banlieue* with a few professional actors. The character played by Cassel finds a gun in his *cité*, dropped by a policeman during a riot the night before, and considers using it to kill a policeman. An ominous parable frames the film. "It's a story about a guy who falls off a fifty-story building," another main character, Hubert, announces at the beginning of the film. "As he passes each floor, he says to himself, 'So, far, so good!'" As Hubert talks the screen shows the planet

Earth, and as he finishes the story a Molotov cocktail enters the edge of the frame, falling. "But it's not the fall that counts, it's the landing," Hubert tells us as the Molotov cocktail hits Earth, filling the screen with flames, opening the way for documentary footage of the protests and riots in France.[34]

Ten years later the toxic situation portrayed in the film seemed unstoppable. *Banlieue* residents endured regular harassment and frequent abuse at the hands of the police. Meanwhile the police had the dangerous job of patrolling the *banlieues,* playing cat and mouse with bands of youths who sometimes lured them into ambushes so they could attack them in force and burn their cars. Even before his famous *racaille* comment, many people in France blamed Sarkozy for making the situation worse. He took up the position of minister of the interior in 2002 and quickly cut back programs of neighborhood policing set up during the 1980s in an attempt to respond to rioting. In early 2003, speaking to a group of policemen in Toulouse, he attacked one of them who was talking about a football tournament they had organized with local youth as part of a project to make connections between police and the community. "You're not social workers," Sarkozy declared. "Citizens expect you to concentrate on stopping delinquents." In a speech several months later in the same town he reiterated his complaint more forcefully: "You're here to stop hoodlums, not organize football matches." (During the 2005 riots in Toulouse a group of young men would satirize the statement and critique Sarkozy's policies when they offered to play football with a group of policemen rather than fight with them.) Under Sarkozy community policing programs were not completely eliminated, but they were certainly "drained of blood," according to one journalist. His administration also substantially decreased state subsidies to organizations and associations in the *banlieue* that provided recreation, community centers, and other forms of local assistance. Activists and *banlieue* mayors criticized the cutbacks, but there was little effective political opposition to the new tactics, which appealed to many French people worried about criminality. Some municipalities managed to maintain a strong presence of local associations, including Marseille, which police intelligence services and others argued was probably one reason why the city saw relatively little violence during November 2005.[35]

The cutbacks in neighborhood policing worsened the already tense relationship between police and residents in many *banlieues.* Young men who lived there frequently found themselves stopped by fast-moving squads of police who swept through their *cités* and whom residents experienced as an unpredictable, even invasive force. While many in the *banlieue* resent the petty crime in their neighborhoods and are eager for more effective policing,

FIGURE 24. Young men in a Toulouse *banlieue* offer to play football with the police in the midst of the riots, 10 November 2005. © Jean-Philippe Arles/Reuters/Corbis.

they also feel solidarity with the young men who receive the brunt of often aggressive police attention. During riots, writes one scholar, though they are "the first victims of the violence (the cars that are burning are theirs)," they also "resent the uneven-handedness of the police towards their kids, the merry-go-round of officials making immediately forgotten promises and the demonization of their living environment by the media."[36]

More experienced policemen who know residents better are often able to evaluate situations more effectively and sometimes diffuse them. In Clichy-sous-Bois during the early days of the riots, one policeman explained to a journalist that although they caught two young men with scarves and gloves that smelled of gasoline—they had clearly been making Molotov cocktails and were ready to cover their faces in order to fight the police—the police were not going to arrest them. "It's not the time to add insult to injury," he said. "A kid in prison equals a martyr. The neighborhood doesn't need that." But the broader situation militates against such understanding. Since postings to *banlieue* neighborhoods are unattractive to many in the police force, those who can get transferred elsewhere opt to do so, which means that much of the force in such areas is very young, often inexperienced, and unfamiliar with the territory in which they operate. Conflicts in the *banlieue* thus are often between two groups of young French men, both locked into situations they are seeking to escape. Many police recruits come from smaller towns or rural areas in France, and the police force is largely white. Lacking leverage and control over often hostile youth, some turn to using excessive force, inciting more hostility and encouraging residents' perspective that they are the enemy.[37]

Some police see the situation as akin to war and act accordingly. In the middle of the riots one French television crew secretly filmed a remarkable and telling interaction between a young black man and a group of policemen who stopped him and a friend. The young man protested that he wasn't doing anything, to which a policeman responded, "Ta gueule" (Shut up). "Do you want us to bring you to the electrical transformer?" another of the policemen asked. Someone nearby started shouting insults at the police, to which one responded, "Do you want to grill with your friends? Do you want to go into a transformer? Come here and we'll put you there." Given that he was being threatened with death, the tenor and content of the young man's response were striking. He turned to one of the policemen to make a point of French grammar. "I'm using the *vous* form with you," he said, emphasizing that he was speaking to them in the polite form used to denote respect, "and your colleague is responding to me in the *tu* form. I'm trying to be respectful." They were "in France," the young man went on, adding, "Liberté, fraternité. . . . If this is the way it is, do you think the neighborhood is going to calm down?" "We don't give a shit if the neighborhood is calm," responded one policeman. "In fact, the worse it gets, the happier we are."[38]

When they were interviewed by journalists during the riots, *banlieue* residents spoke of their feeling of permanent marginalization. "We've had papers for generations but we're not French like other people," a forty-year-old resident of Clichy-sous-Bois complained.[39] Young rioters suggested that they had no choice but open revolt. "It's just a beginning," one announced. "We're going to keep going until Sarkozy resigns."[40] "We're not *racaille*," said an eighteen-year-old named Tedji. "We're human beings. We exist. The proof? The cars are burning."[41]

Nearly every French pundit and intellectual seemed to have a theory to explain the events, some more bizarre than others. At a conference at New

York University the literary critic Tzvetan Todorov explained, according to another scholar attending the conference, that "the riots were caused by the dysfunctional sexuality of Muslim youths obsessed with behaving in a 'macho' way." When "skeptical members of the audience observed that non-Muslim police officers" along with Sarkozy "seemed equally macho in their behavior," Todorov "simply smiled and refused to elaborate further." Carrère d'Encausse, a scholar of Russian history and secretary of the Académie Française, similarly veered into amateur ethnography, announcing that the problems were the result of the practice of polygamy among West African Muslims in France. Two French politicians, including Gérard Larcher, the minister of employment, concurred with this theory. The mayor of one *banlieue* and a representative in Sarkozy's party similarly argued that delinquents were "often from polygamous families." Polygamy was, of course, long used as a marker of the supposed "barbarism" of West Africans by colonial administrators and has frequently popped up in politicians' speeches on immigration. In a 1991 speech Jacques Chirac imagined the horror felt by a "French worker" living next door to a West African man with "several wives" who was forced to deal with the "noise and odor" of the family.[42]

Politicians on the far right responded to the 2005 insurrection by lobbying for harsh repression. Philippe de Villiers demanded that the government send the army into the *banlieues* and cut off all social security payments to families who let their children go out at night. Marine Le Pen, the daughter of Jean-Marie, asked that a state of emergency be put into effect to require "certain people"—she didn't say who, but the implication was clear enough—to stay home. Members of Sarkozy's party, Union pour un Mouvement Populaire, broadly concurred, and several of them also urged the government to declare a state of emergency.[43]

This was quite easy to do thanks to the legacy of the Algerian war. The 1955 law to crush the anticolonial rebellion in Algiers, used again in Paris in 1961, was still on the books. It was used only once since then, during the 1984–85 uprising of the Kanak in New Caledonia. But the government considered it an ideal tool and invoked it to call a state of emergency in November 2005. The law allowed for "the closure of public spaces, search-and-seizures, house arrests, and the censorship of the press," giving the police broad leeway in suppressing the insurrection. The government extended police and officials everywhere in France the right to set up curfews and to search houses and apartments at any time of day or night. In addition officials in the departments that included *banlieue* areas had the right to outlaw meetings and close cafés and theaters. A majority of representatives in the national assembly, including many on the left, approved the curfew, seeing it as the only way to restore order in France.[44]

To the journalist Philippe Bernard, however, the use of this law was chillingly provocative. The "rage" that drove the insurrection, he wrote in *Le Monde,* may not have been expressed "in the rhetoric of the union or the university," but it was not "a declaration of war." It was instead an action by "French citizens" who were furious about their exclusion and were "destroying so that they will be heard," knowing that "for the past twenty-five years, politicians and the media have only taken them seriously when they take violent action." In two weeks, he added, the insurrection had "transformed the landscape of French society" more profoundly than any political or union activity had for a long time.[45]

In his response to the events, President Chirac insisted that "children of the difficult neighborhoods" were "daughters and sons of the Republic." But, Bernard complained, the actions and words of the government largely contradicted this "nice proclamation." He found it impossible to imagine a French minister insulting French farmers or truckers the way Sarkozy had insulted residents of the *banlieue.* No other social group in France would ever be singled out in this way: "Which other French people are regularly referred to in the 'tu' form by the police? And against which other citizens would the government exhume a law conceived to repress colonial rebellion?" The use of this law called up the "painful memories of the police repression of the 1950s and 1960s," especially against Algerians, and suggested that the same tactics were appropriate for containing "the *cités* where their children and grandchildren live."[46]

Early in 2005 a group calling themselves the Indigènes de la République (Natives of the Republic) declared that colonialism had never really ended in France. "France was a colonial state," they said. "France is still a colonial state!" The same strategies used to police and suppress colonial subjects, they argued, were being used in French territory against residents of the *banlieue:* "The children of the colonies are, in France, relegated to the status of immigrants, of second-class French citizens." The group organized a series of conferences to discuss the links between the colonial past and the present. They gained a new platform when, in February 2005, the French National Assembly passed a law requiring schools to teach the "positive role" of colonialism, particularly in North Africa, setting off a firestorm of debate that eventually led to the abrogation of the law by Chirac. Many French intellectuals and scholars disputed the claim by the Indigènes de la République that social relations in contemporary France were a continuation of the colonial order, calling such comparisons simplistic. But, as Bernard noted, the actions of Sarkozy and the French government justified such claims when they used a law created to enable colonial repression to carry out the "pacification" of the *banlieue*. Indeed one of those who authored the declaration of the Indigènes de la République wrote in 2006 that the government had effectively assented to the arguments of the text when it enacted a state of emergency based on colonial precedent.[47]

The French police made 2,900 arrests during the course of the insurrection, and a week after the state of emergency was put into effect the conflagration was over. The government soon passed a series of measures that were meant to address the problem of unemployment in the *banlieue*. One measure, the introduction of a contract allowing employers to fire workers under twenty-five without explanation, immediately incited the ire of many university and high school students. They took to the streets, and for several weeks in February and March 2006 France was once again shaken by youth protests, until the government withdrew the provision. In the end the *banlieue* uprisings as well as the student protests that followed may have been a political boon for Sarkozy, elected president two years later with strong support from voters who saw him as a tough-minded proponent of law and order unafraid to stand up to the youth of the *banlieue*. Sarkozy never apologized for his use of the terms *Kärcher* and *racaille*. At a political rally in mid-November 2005 he declared, "The central cause of unemployment, despair, and violence in the suburbs," he declared, "is not discrimination or the failure of schools . . . it is drug traffic, the law of the *bandes* [gangs], the dictatorship of fear and the resignation of the Republic." "Clearly, if the criminals and thugs don't like our security policy," Sarkozy wrote in an op-ed piece in *Le Monde* at the beginning of the riots, "French people support it." It was a telling declaration, for it suggested that he considered those who were rioting were *not* French. If state forces did not restore order, he warned, France would be overtaken by the "order of the mafia, or of fundamentalists."[48]

While the French government put its state of emergency into effect, Lilian Thuram and the rest of the French national football team flew across the Atlantic to Martinique. For the first time in history the French team would play a game in the Antilles, a friendly match against Costa Rica. Although the population of the Antilles had given the French team many of its important players over the years, not once had they been able to see the team play in the islands. Starting in 1998 Thuram and other Antillean players urged the French Football Federation to organize a game in the Caribbean, but without success. Then, in August 2005, a charter plane carrying more than two hundred Martinican postal workers going on vacation crashed in Venezuela. Thuram and Thierry Henry successfully pushed the F.F.F. to send the team to Martinique in order to play a benefit match for the families of the victims. "I hope we can give a little comfort to those who have suffered," declared Thuram.[49]

The French team defeated Costa Rica 3–2 in an exciting game played before eighteen thousand supporters. Thuram brought his teammates to meet Aimé Césaire, the poet and political figure widely venerated in the French Antilles. Thuram gave Césaire a signed Juventus jersey, which Césaire hung on the wall in his office. The journey brought together the members of the team as they prepared for the 2006 World Cup. "Something happened over there," Thuram later recalled. "Playing over there really touched me.' As they were arriving at the stadium to train for their game, his teammate and old friend Claude Makelele told him, "We're in Africa here!" "What did you think the Antilles looked like?" Thuram responded. Another player, Willy Sagnol, remembered that in Martinique the team "forged a common spirit."[50]

The visit to Martinique also turned out to be a crucial turning point in the political life of Lilian Thuram. Local journalists covering the visit knew that most of the players they welcomed had grown up in the *banlieue,* and they asked them what they thought about the insurrection. Thierry Henry demurred, but his teammate Eric Abidal said, "The rope was pulled tight and it broke. Not everyone is lucky enough to have a job. It's been going on for a while, and people are sick of having to stay where they are. There's a collective sense of exasperation." Florent Malouda described the events as "inevitable." Thuram gave the longest statement: "It's a delicate situation. [The government has] emphasized the lack of security [i.e., crime in the *banlieue*]. That's something that unites people: who doesn't want to live with security? The problem is that then you have to find guilty people. And what's behind such statements is the idea that the people who live in the *banlieue* are the problem. But violence is never meaningless. You have to understand where the malaise comes from. Before talking about insecurity, we should talk about social justice." Thuram admitted that he was "irritated" and felt personally attacked by the language Sarkozy had used: "I also grew up in the *banlieue*. When someone says we have to clean it out with a Kärcher ... Maybe Sarkozy doesn't know what he is saying. But I take it personally. I say to myself: Wait—what has to be cleaned? I'm from a *banlieue*. What are they going to clean? . . . I was also told: 'You are a *racaille.*' But I am not a *racaille.* What I wanted was to work. Maybe he hasn't understood the subtle difference."[51] Thuram doubted the riots would help bring about change: "I'm mostly sad for [the rioters], because in a way they are in a circle, and it's going to play itself out against them again. Because people are going to say: look, you saw it, what are we going to do with these people?" But for Thuram, the real question was: "Why does one become aggressive?"[52]

Thuram's comments circulated quickly and widely. He was famous and well liked, a representative of France, a lover of the "Marseillaise," an irreproachable patriot. His statements had power both as an attack against Sarkozy and as a high-profile attempt to provide a sympathetic and alternative explanation for the fires burning throughout France. At least one young man from the *banlieue* was glad to have Thuram on his side. Participating in a heated televised debate with Nicolas Sarkozy, he argued that it was the tactics of the police that had caused the riots. "I don't accept your argument," Sarkozy said. "I don't accept yours," the young man shot back. "Let me tell you something," a stern Sarkozy responded. "We're not in the street here, we're in polite company." He went on to criticize the way the young man spoke. "If that's the way you speak here, it gives us a good idea of what it's like in your neighborhood," Sarkozy admonished. The young man responded by calling up the example of Lilian Thuram, complimenting him for the way he "spoke up, and represented the *cités*": "Respect to Lilian Thuram," he said to a glaring Sarkozy. He wished more celebrities would speak up as he had: "Because, frankly, we don't get much of a hearing."[53]

Sarkozy tried to diminish the significance and legitimacy of Thuram's response by suggesting that the footballer had no reason to feel attacked by the use of the word *racaille.* He said, "[Thuram is someone] who I know and who I also like very much," but he added, "It's been a very long time since he has lived in a *banlieue. . . .* So I don't see why he is shocked." Given his wealth and success, Sarkozy suggested, Thuram did not have the authority to speak on behalf of the *banlieue.*[54]

Sarkozy's dismissive response to Thuram's comments made them seem even more significant. On his return from Martinique Thuram was invited to speak on the television channel Canal+ and was given time to lay out in detail his thoughts on Sarkozy and the *banlieue.* Thuram was conciliatory toward Sarkozy but insisted that because the political leader represented the state he ought to be "very careful about the terms he uses." "All the people of the *banlieue,*" Thuram reiterated, took it personally when he used the term *racaille.* Though the youths of the *banlieue* were French, they had "a hard time considering themselves French." Already frustrated at their lack of opportunity, they experienced Sarkozy's use of the term *racaille* to be a particularly disturbing attack because it came from a high-ranking politician. Thuram also defended his right to speak for the *banlieue,* since he remembered what he had lived through growing up there: "Thank God, I haven't forgotten. . . . I have a memory, and I know where I come from and what I lived through. And I know it's hard." He insisted that "those who are burning cars" were a minority, and that their actions would just compound the "bad image" of the *banlieue.* "But I also understand," he added.[55] "I haven't forgotten who I am, or where I come from," he repeated in January. "My friends still live in the *banlieue.*"[56]

For Thuram the essential problem was the lack of recognition between the youths of the *banlieue* and the French state, and French society more broadly. The youths were part of the problem, because "in general they refuse to think of themselves as French." But the issue was to understand "why they refuse": "You have French papers, but you need to feel that you are considered to be French. If you think that the French state doesn't recognize you as such, then the response is a kind of rejection. But that rejection is just a way of saying: ok, you don't recognize me, well I'm not French." If they had trouble integrating themselves into society, it was also true that "people don't integrate them well either." But the problem was so difficult to confront, even intractable, Thuram remarked, because racist attitudes and suspicions were deeply rooted in the longer history of French colonialism. There was, therefore, "in-depth work" to be done: "The ideal is for us to live together, and to live together we have to respect one another, and to respect one another we have to know one another, and to know one another we have to learn to know one another. . . . I think we have a common history. But you," he said, pointing to two white participants on the show, "don't have the same history as me. You became French through one history, and I became French through another."[57]

Thuram and Sarkozy had a private meeting to discuss the matter, though afterward neither of them publicly shared the content of the conversation. Throughout the first half of 2006, during which there were a few riots in the *banlieues* outside Paris, Thuram continued to speak out. On a French television program in May 2006, for instance, he reiterated his argument that rejection breeds rejection. The major cause of the *banlieue* insurrection of 2005, he insisted, was the fact that "young people feel like they are being attacked by the police. . . . People ask the question: Do the people who live in the *banlieue* love France? Of course they love France." The question, he suggested, was whether France loved them.[58]

As the conversation continued, another guest on the program suddenly asked Thuram, "Why don't you sing the Marseillaise?" It was a strange question to pose to Thuram, reflecting not a little ignorance, since anyone who has ever seen him before a game knows that he sings the "Marseillaise" with remarkable verve. Indeed Zidane joked in 1998, "Thuthu and the Marseillaise—that's an amazing spectacle!" But the question was a sign of the times. In the wake of the 2005 insurrection Le Pen's lingering complaint about French football teams not being patriotic enough had returned.[59]

Thuram was clearly taken aback. He smiled and searched for an answer, but the questioner insisted, "I mean why you, football players, don't sing the Marseillaise." Thuram's response, interestingly, was not to say what he could easily have said: But I do sing the "Marseillaise"! Instead he said that it was a strange question, and that whether you sang or not didn't mean anything. The host soon interrupted and moved the discussion on to other questions. But a few months later Thuram had the opportunity to respond to similar accusations leveled at the team from a position of strength, when he and his teammates were coasting on the wings of victory.

ELEVEN

Coup de Boule

"GOD IS BACK!"

Thus announced an ebullient Thierry Henry when he learned that Zinedine Zidane was returning to the French team. Zidane had long resisted the entreaties of the French coach, Raymond Domenech. But something happened one night at 3 A.M.: "I suddenly woke up, and I spoke to someone." Who? Zidane at first wouldn't say. No one, not even his wife, knew who it was. "It's an enigma," he later said, but "don't look for the answer, because you won't find it." Zidane spent several hours "alone" with the voice he heard, and during that time he made the "decision to come back." Journalists and fans, of course, couldn't help but ask him the obvious question: Had God spoken to him? Zidane has rarely talked about his own religious beliefs, and many seemed thrilled at the prospect of discovering his spiritual side. But a slightly exasperated Zidane later explained that there was nothing 'religious" about his experience. The voice was that of one of his older brothers, giving him advice. Even if the trigger for his return wasn't a mystical experience, though, many in France treated this hoped-for second coming as the return of the messiah. What made it even better was that with Zidane back on the roster, two other veteran players who had retired from the team, Lilian Thuram and Claude Makelele came back as well.[1]

Led by Zidane and Thuram, the 2006 team reminded people of the multi-ethnic 1998 team. But whereas black players had been a significant presence in 1998, in 2006 they were the majority on the team. Seventeen of twenty-three players had family histories that connected them to the colonies in the Caribbean, Africa, and the Indian Ocean. The largest group of promi-nent players—including Thuram, William Gallas, Thierry Henry, Florent Malouda, Sylvain Wiltord, and Eric Abidal—came from French Caribbean families, while Makelele and Patrick Vieira were born in Africa. Among the three white players prominent on the team was Franck Ribéry, a Muslim. He converted to Islam at the time of his marriage to his wife, Wahiba Belmadi, a French woman of Algerian background. His marriage, as well as his conversion, had been celebrated in Algeria, and after the World Cup he traveled there. He was delighted to be welcomed by several members of the Algerian F.L.N. team from the 1950s, saying that his parents-in-law had frequently spoken to him about the team. Ribéry prays to Allah when he enters the field, and in 2006 he explained that his religion gives him "his strength on the field and off it."[2]

The previous year the French commentator Alain Finkielkraut had stirred up a major controversy with a series of comments about the French football team that he made in an interview with the Israeli newspaper *Ha'aretz*. The comments came in the midst of his discussion about the 2005 insurrection, which he described as an expression of "hatred of the West" among Muslims in France. Discussing the pitch invasion at the 2001 France-Algeria match, he declared, "People say the French national team is admired by all because it is *black-blanc-beur*. Actually, the national team today is black-black-black, which arouses ridicule throughout Europe. If you point this out in France, they'll put you in jail, but it's interesting nevertheless that the French national soccer team is composed almost exclusively of black players." These and other comments from the interview were reproduced in French newspapers, notably *Le Monde*, and drew a firestorm of criticism. A few days later, in a television interview on Europe 1, Finkielkraut apologized. He explained that he was merely trying to point out that the makeup of the French team was a "French peculiarity," "a consequence of colonialism," and "a post-colonial privilege." He sought to link his statement to the "laughter" of his father, who used to point out that there were no "French" on the football team of his day, which was dominated by Polish, Italian, and Portuguese players.[3]

As France emerged from a lackluster showing in the first phase of the World Cup, Jean-Marie Le Pen picked up where Finkielkraut left off. A decade after making his comments about the French team during the 1996 European Cup, perhaps thinking he smelled defeat, Le Pen again went on the offensive against the French team. He complained that the players, particularly Zidane and Barthez, weren't singing the "Marseillaise" before the match. He also declared that the coach had "perhaps exaggerated the proportion of players of color" on the team, and that as a result the French population didn't feel itself "represented" and felt less "warmth" than they had in 1998. The far-right newspaper *Minute* published a headline the day after Le Pen's comments that asked, "Are there too many blacks on the French team?"[4]

Le Pen made his comments just before France's game against Spain. As the game began, the youthful Spanish team seemed poised to win, hopping like gazelles as they warmed up on the field, ready to outrun the aging Zidane and Thuram. Early in the game the referee awarded them a penalty kick and they scored. Then, in the fortieth minute, Patrick Vieira managed to tap a ball out in front of Franck Ribéry, who in a thrilling burst of speed powered down the field, outrunning two defenders and slipping the ball past the Spanish goalie. In that instant it seemed as though France was being carried along by Ribéry's short, fast, unstoppable legs. Then, however, the tied game dragged on. The French defense held through most of the second half, but so did the Spanish. Ten minutes before the end of regulation time, Thierry Henry ran into the Spanish defender Carles Puyol and fell dramatically to the ground, holding his head. As Puyol looked to the stands with his hands in the air in outrage, the referee awarded a free kick to the French. The ball was far outside the penalty box, but the always dangerous Zidane stepped up to take it. He lobbed the ball toward the goal, and it bounced off one French player's head, floating toward Patrick Vieira, who slammed it into the goal with his head. Ten minutes later Zidane went streaming forward, outwitted Puyol, and sent the ball streaking into the Spanish goal again. As the elated players hugged when the game ended a few minutes later, Thuram gestured to them that they should thank the fans in the stadium. Zidane, Thuram, and several other players put their hands out as if flying, running, jumping, and shouting at the cheering fans. Celebrants flooded the streets of Paris in the wake of the striking victory.

The Spanish coach on the sidelines that night was Luis Aragonès, who had famously called Thierry Henry a "black shit" a few years earlier, and the French players well remembered the insult. During the game Aragonès at one point shouted from the sidelines after Vieira struck a Spanish defender in the face with his hand while dribbling the ball away. He wanted a penalty called, but the referee seemed not to have noticed the transgression. Vieira looked straight at Aragonès and put a finger to his lips, then waved his hand to tell him to sit down. The gesture was about the foul, but it was also about more than that. It was a complement to Henry's campaign. "Stand Up, Speak Up." Where Henry had urged people to speak up against racism, Vieira was telling a Spanish coach famous for a racist comment, "Shut up and sit down."

The victory on the field also gave the team the opportunity to speak back to Jean-Marie Le Pen. As usual, it was Thuram who took up the challenge. Asked about Le Pen's comments, he responded, "He says there are too many black players. I don't know what to say since, personally, I'm not black." There was laughter after this comment, but Thuram was quite serious. In an interview with Achille Mbembe after the World Cup, he explained what he meant by declaring "I'm not black":

> I wanted to say this: "It is not because of my color that I am on the French team. I was not chosen because I am black. They didn't choose Barthez because he is white. They chose Barthez and Thuram because it's the French team, and they're French." That was the meaning of my response to Le Pen. It wasn't about the fact that I am not black. Because, precisely, I am black and everyone knows it. Do you see? What is important is to have a certain political and intellectual sensibility that allows me to say: "I am not black. I am French." Or: "I am not white. I am French." It's a sensibility that makes it possible to detach nationality from the tragedy of a certain history of color, a certain history of racial classification.[5]

Thuram publicly questioned Le Pen's right to define what it meant to be black and what it meant to be French. "You can feel French without singing the Marseillaise," he declared. (Anyone watching the game could see proof of this, since President Jacques Chirac, presumably a relatively patriotic man, stood silently, like Zidane, during the anthem.) But Thuram did more, seizing the occasion of France's victory to question Le Pen's understanding of the history of France. "Mr. Le Pen seems not to know that there are black French, blond and brown-haired French. What surprises me is that he has been a candidate for president several times and that he doesn't understand French history. It's as if an American looked at a basketball team and said 'Whoa, there are only blacks!'" He invited Le Pen to come celebrate the team's next victory with them, suggesting that doing so would "change his mind." He ended with these words: "We are very, very proud of being French. He might have a problem. But we don't have a problem. Long live France! Not the one he wants. The true France!"[6]

For French fans the euphoria that followed the victory against Spain was tempered with a certain anxiety. In the next game France was to play Brazil, the team that won the Cup in 2002. What's more, Brazil had actually gone undefeated in World Cup games since it lost against France in 1998. French fans mobilized as if the quarterfinal game were the final. And they were treated to a remarkable game. The two teams held each other off successfully until the beginning of the second half. The Brazilian player known as Kaká (easier to remember than his full name, Ricardo Izecson dos Santos Leite) ran up toward the French goal on the left side of the field, closely covered by Thuram, who battled him successfully for the ball and then sent it forward. Though the Brazilians almost got possession in the midfield, a brilliant move by Zidane, who kicked the ball lightly over Ronaldo and then headed it to Eric Abidal, moved the ball forward to the French striker Florent Malouda. Then a whistle blew. The Brazilian defender had tugged at Malouda's shirt. The French had a free kick.

The ball was at some distance from the Brazilian goal, but Zidane would take the kick. The Brazilians left one French player dangerously unmarked: Thierry Henry. Zidane sent a beautiful curving ball through the air toward the right side of the goal, and Henry powered in from the side and kicked the ball over the goalie's head and into the net. It was just before the fifty-seventh minute in the game, still time for Brazil to strike back. But thanks to the solid defending of Thuram and Gallas, they never did. Brazil, seemingly unstoppable against so many teams, was once again defeated by France and was knocked out of the competition. While crowds thronged the streets, commentators effused about Zidane's beautiful playing. Pelé declared that Zidane was "the magician of the game," and many wrote that he showcased the brilliance usually associated with the great Brazilian players. *Le Figaro* dubbed Zidane "the Brazilian."[7]

Throughout the spring of 2006 French filmgoers had the opportunity to watch Zidane play an entire game with his professional team, Real Madrid, in the documentary *Zidane: A 21st Century Portrait*. The filmmakers had set up seventeen cameras in the stadium, and rather than following the ball, followed Zidane himself. The film, interestingly, ends with a red card for Zidane. Now, in the World Cup, it sometimes seemed as if Zidane was making his own film. The player, *Le Monde* wrote, had used the France-Brazil game to exhibit his skills: "The parade of his technical exploits made this quarterfinal look a bit like a documentary, as if the captain of les Bleus wanted to summarize in an hour and a half all that he knew how to do."[8]

One more team stood between France and a place in the World Cup final: Portugal, with its young star Christiano Ronaldo. The French team secured an early lead through a penalty kick. Then, throughout a grueling game, they held on. Thuram seemed to be everywhere, diving horizontally to head the ball away from his goal, stopping the runs of Portuguese strikers. As in 1998 he played a decisive role in getting the French team to the final. At the end of the game, elated, he declared, "Football is amazing. . . . If you ask yourself: 'What is happiness?,' try putting together a ball and a little kid. And watch what happens between them. . . . Today I'm 34, but I feel like a ten-year-old kid who's watching the World Cup and thinks it is wonderful. I hope the party is going to continue, because it's too beautiful. Like any dream, it has to end well. Otherwise, it will be a nightmare for us."[9]

The victories over Spain, Brazil, and Portugal set off huge celebrations throughout France that seemed to rival those of 1998. But the *banlieue* insurrection of the previous year haunted the street celebrations. After the win over Portugal that secured the French a place in the final, at least half a million celebrants crowded onto the Champs Elysées, flying Algerian and French flags, shouting "Zzzizzzzou!" Walking down the avenue, two young men carried a sign that was also a response to Sarkozy: "The *racaille* are going to bring us back the World Cup! Isn't it wonderful?" An article in *Le Monde* reported on the sign, explaining that the evocation of the *racaille* was a "wink" directed at the "important number" of players on the team "born of immigration." On the newspaper's web forum, one man wondered how *Le Monde* could use this phrase, when in fact the largest group of players came from the overseas territories of the Caribbean and therefore had no history of immigration in their background. "Can the author cite the names of the players who are 'born of immigration'? How many?" A woman wrote that after the riots of the previous year she had no desire to participate in the celebrations and wished the team itself would change its name to "The team of children born of immigration and of the descendants of slaves": "I would raise that flag without hesitation," she noted. "No need to point out that I am myself a *racaille* of the same kind as Zidane."[10]

The group Les Indigènes de la République celebrated the victory as an opportunity to attack Alain Finkielkraut and, once again, respond to his comments from the previous year. They posted a tongue-in-cheek "communiqué" issued by an invented organization called F.I.F.A., the Fédération Indigène de Football Anticolonial (Indigenous Federation of Anticolonial Football), announcing, "The *racaille* are in the final!" It addressed its "sincere condolences to Alain Finkielkraut" and those like him who suffered the "anti-secular provocations" of the "Muslim Ribéry" and the "anti-white pogrom that the Black-Black-Black team, led by Zidane the Saracen, has just perpetrated in the semi-final of the World Cup." For the Indigènes, the centrality of Zidane and Ribéry in bringing victory to France highlighted the absurdity of Finkielkraut's claims that Islam threatened the French Republic.[11]

In the streets, meanwhile, the celebrations of victory sometimes shaded into something else. On the night of the victory over Brazil, while crowds in Paris chanted, as they had in 1998, "Zizou Président!," police clashed with celebrants in the Vieux-Port of Marseille.[12] On the Champs-Elysées after the victory against Portugal, a few people threw bottles at the police, and some chanted "Sarko, on t'encule!" (Sarko, up your ass!), a favorite expression of the November 2005 riots. Five people died in the celebrations that night, including a man who in a fit of euphoria got on top of a subway train and then fell off. The police arrested 350 people, 190 of them in Paris, and 45 police officers were injured. Vandals attacked a police station in Paris, and, of course, they burned cars—a total of 345 after the games against Brazil and Portugal. The churning battles with police that had peaked in November 2005 were, in a sense, invading the celebrations, a reminder that the vision of the republic being played out on the football field was far from being realized off it.[13]

In the midst of the World Cup games, in a judicial court in Paris, five French citizens released from the U.S.-operated Guantanamo Bay detention camp—one of whom was described in *Le Figaro* snidely as a *petit banlieusard* (little kid from the *banlieue*) and who had been recruited by Islamists in his neighborhood—were condemned for "associating" with others in preparation for acts of terrorism. But the trial judge underlined her "repugnance" for the Guantanamo detention camp and refused to sentence them to further time in jail. Politicians and activists had another debate about whether "visible" minorities should be counted in the census in order to enable policies of "positive discrimination." In Rabat a conference between representatives of African and European nations aimed at finding ways to cooperate on the problem of immigration started the day after the World Cup final. Protests and debates continued in France over a controversial decision by Minister of State Sarkozy to expel school-age *sans-papiers*. Activists organized to resist the arrests of students. One Moroccan high-schooler was deported to Casablanca on 7 July. A French survivor of Auschwitz wrote to *Libération* that the deportations reminded him of his own arrest as a schoolboy in 1944. "My republic hurts me," he wrote.[14]

For the night of the final World Cup game on 9 July 2006, Sarkozy ordered the mobilization of eighteen thousand police in the Paris region, including several thousand C.R.S., giving orders for "firmness against *casseurs* [vandals] and troublemakers." While giant screens were set up in some towns in France, in Paris those that had decorated several sites in 1998 were absent in 2006. Instead the games were projected in stadiums on the edge of the city. Many who gathered on the Champs-Elysées were unable to follow the game, except through the shouts from packed cafés nearby. The mobilization of police helped spread rumors that the evening could turn violent, especially in the case of a defeat. As it turned out, such predictions were wrong. Whatever violence might have lingered in Paris that night was channeled straight into the chest of an Italian player by Zinedine Zidane.[15]

In Paris on the day of the World Cup final, it seemed as though Zidane was inexorably heading for a place in the Panthéon, the temple of French heroes. "Enter here, Zinedine Zidane," invited Gilles Dhers and Christian Losson in *Libération*, quoting a line from a famous and rousing 1964 speech by the French writer André Malraux welcoming the ashes of resistance hero Jean Moulin into the Panthéon. "Panthéonization by the planet assured. Presidentialization demanded by the French crowd. Purification of the souls of sinning journalists (who doubted) implored. . . . The man will dance his final ballet Sunday night against Italy. . . . The scene: the Final of the World Cup. The audience: three billion television spectators. Passport to eternity in case of victory, a ticket to canonization even in case of defeat. . . . For everyone today, Zidane is the talent of Maradona and the charisma of Pelé. A mix of the Abbé Pierre and Gandhi. Of Martin Luther King and the Dalai Lama." And not only the French were enthusiastic: one British newspaper effused, "Allez Les Bleus!," noted Dhers and Losson, which was "a bit as if the Michelin Guide started celebrating English cuisine." At the same time they sounded a note of caution. Calling him a "hyphen between generations, religions, communities," they pointed out that Zidane had also been burdened, perhaps too heavily, with the hopes and fantasies of his fans: "Let us never forget what we made him carry and what he had to deal with, that he carried grace and was carried by it. And that like a Houdini wrapped in leather, he always escaped those who thought they captured him, buried him, or magnified him."[16]

The journalist Antoine de Gaudemar, meanwhile, announced that if France won that night, Zidane's story would end up with "all the dimensions of a model Hollywood screenplay": "A child of a Kabyle immigrant who grew up in the northern neighborhoods of Marseille, a child of the street who turned international star, ... [who also experienced a] descent into hell with a premature retirement, ... [and] finally an aging player carrying out an incredible comeback, to give the *Bleus* the Cup for a second time.... Glory, downfall, resurrection and apotheosis: what perfect dramaturgy!" The comic Jamel Debbouze, he noted, had termed this "galloping adoration" *Zidanite*. But, warned Gaudemar after noting that the *New York Times* had called Zidane "the coolest guy on the planet," it all seemed "almost too much": "On the pitch, he can also be mean, resentful, violent, and in life, jealous, stingy, and bitter, no? Zidane is a hero, certainly, but he remains a man, just a man." Maybe, he seemed prophetically to suggest, the movie we were all about to see would end less like a comfortable Hollywood romance than like a somber, philosophical French film.[17]

In the first half of the game Zidane played beautifully once again, performing his skills as he had against Brazil. When the French team won a penalty kick after Italian defender Marco Materazzi tangled with Florent Malouda in the penalty box, Zidane launched his *panenka*, bouncing the ball against the top rim and into the goal. "He's mad!" a joyful but disbelieving Fabien Barthez shouted to the sky. "I decided to do it as I was running up," he later said, "because I wanted it to stay." Pressed by another journalist, he provided an explanation of what football should be: "I told the other players, we should score spirits as we score goals. People have to remember this final."[18] In *Libération* the Israeli writer Etgar Keret effused about the *panenka,* in which Zidane "shot the ball with the sophistication and breezy nonchalance of a kid playing in the courtyard of his house." Tying Zidane's playing to his background in the *cité* of Castellane, he added, "With the most *banlieuesard* penalty of the history of the World Cup, he confirmed for us for the hundredth time that the pleasure of the game is more powerful than all ambitions, aspirations, and money linked to status."[19]

Italy equalized the score when Materazzi headed the ball into the French goal off a corner kick. The game churned into overtime at 1–1. Zidane powered a remarkable header—an echo of his goals in the 1998 World Cup—toward the Italian goal, but goalkeeper Gianluigi Buffon made a brilliant save. Minutes later Materazzi and Zidane jockeyed for the ball. The Italian tugged at the Frenchman's shirt. According to Materazzi's later descriptions of the incident, Zidane turned to him and said, "If you want my jersey so badly you can have it at the end of the game." Zidane began to jog away, but Materazzi let fly a string of insults. Zidane kept going, then stopped

FIGURE 25. Zidane and Marco Materazzi the instant after the *coup de boule*. John MacDougall/AFP/Getty Images.

and turned around. He jogged back toward Materazzi. Then, powerfully, he head-butted Materazzi in the chest. The Italian collapsed.

"Nobody—neither spectators nor referees—saw anything," the writer Jean-Philippe Toussaint recalled, because everyone was watching the ball, which was elsewhere. In a way, Zidane's "invisible and incomprehensible" attack almost seems to have "never happened." Except for a tiny number of observers in the stadium, all that the other billions of spectators ever saw was a replay. After a few confused minutes the referee conferred with a lineman who apparently saw the incident, and then pulled a red card out of his pocket. Zidane walked off the field, head hanging down, past the World Cup. As he sat alone in the locker room, out on the field the French team lost to the Italians in penalty kicks when David Trezeguet sent his shot against the top bar of the goal. It was a stunningly quick, unexpected, and dramatic end to Zidane's lifelong performance on the football field. The delighted Italian team got the Cup, its fourth, and Italy erupted into a mass celebration.[20]

After the game the crowds on the Champs Elysées, under the towering image of Zidane projected on the Arc de Triomphe, walked about aimlessly. The defeat took on a particularly pensive tone. Everyone had claimed that, win or lose, there would be partying in the streets to celebrate the wonderful run of the French team. Zidane's *coup de boule* derailed that. People were in the streets but unable, for the most part, to raise their spirits enough for even a little flag waving or shouted renditions of the "Marseillaise." They spoke to each other and to passing strangers. And everywhere people asked, What was Zidane thinking? Should they blame Zidane? Chalk the whole thing up to the madness of football, and move on? Or try to find some meaning in it all? Already it was becoming clear that Zidane's exit was much more than just a depressing end to a brilliant career. Like his victory in 1998, it was an incitement to think, to talk, to rehearse, to predict, and to imagine.

The following is a nonexhaustive list of the effects generated by Zidane's *coup de boule*:

1 red card
2 F.I.F.A. hearings
1 condemnatory editorial in *L'Equipe* that lamented the poor example
    provided by Zidane to children
1 comparison between Zidane and *Billy Budd*[21]
1 comparison between Zidane and the hero of Albert Camus's *The Stranger*[22]
1 article by a professor of classics in the intellectually prestigious French
    magazine *Esprit* proposing a "mythological" reading of Zidane's *coup
    de boule,* describing Materazzi as "the principal instrument of the divine
    Nemesis" sent by the gods to respond to Zidane's hubris in taking his
    panenka in an overly arrogant way[23]
Understanding and forgiveness on the part of Jacques Chirac
1 supportive comment from Fidel Castro
1 video composition in which Zidane head-butts Fidel Castro[24]
1 online video game allowing players to *be* Zidane and deliver not just one
    but many *coups de boule* against Materazzi, though the game *always* ends
    (no rewriting of history here) in a red card from the referee
1 hit song
A seemingly inexhaustible flow of conversations and exchanges between
    friends and strangers, turning and twisting around the interpretation
    of the *coup de boule* and its meaning

FIGURE 26. Another of the effects of the *coupe de boule:* graffiti in Zanzibar celebrates Zidane's head-butt, calling him a hero, summer 2006. Courtesy of Niels Hooper.

Zidane's *coup de boule* was instantly iconic. The image spread virally on the Web, watched over and over again millions of times. A song called "Coup de Boule," written by dispirited but inspired French musicians within twenty-four hours of the final game, was posted online in order to help France deal with what had happened. In a self-satirizing Afro-pop style, punctuated by the shout "Coup de Boule, Coup de Boule!," it provided an early and hilarious draft of the story of Zidane's exit and became an immediate hit in France. All summer long dancers in clubs repeated Zidane's gesture, over and over again, by the thousands, reliving the *coup de boule* and making it their own.[25]

"People in France have been thinking hard about why Zidane did it," wrote Adam Gopnik in the *New Yorker* a few days later, "and what it means, and have thereby been honoring the national belief that it is really not possible to think too hard about things." The first published step in the conversation was an editorial in *L'Equipe* the day after the final. Addressed to Zidane in the distancing *vous* form, it began, "Zinedine, do you know that the hardest thing this morning is not to understand why the *Bleus,* your *Bleus,* lost a World Cup that was within their reach yesterday. It is explaining to tens of millions of children throughout the world how you allowed yourself to deliver that *coup de tête* [i.e., *coup de boule*] against Marco Materazzi, ten minutes before the end of overtime." The game, the writer noted, seemed to "belong" to the French team, and to Zidane: "[At times] in the Berlin Olympic Stadium where the history of the world has also been written, you were even Ali, the ultimate genius of the ring . . . But neither Ali, nor Pelé, nor Owens, or any other sacred monster of their greatness, of that which you were on the point of joining, so violated the most elementary rules of sport." Whatever the "horrible" things that Materazzi had surely said just before, it was a "stupid gesture" that "ended [Zidane's] fabulous career with a sad red card": "What, this morning, are we to pass on to our children, to all of those for whom you had become a living example, for posterity?" And how could he leave his "companions" alone on the field? "I imagine you are very miserable this morning," the editorial concluded, wondering how Zidane would explain his actions to his four sons and how this could have happened to "the man that you are." It was a crushing condemnation that suggested that the "last image" of Zidane's career would always remain an act that expelled him from the paradise he was about to enter.[26]

Some on the far right in France gloated at the defeat and what they saw as the characteristic action of Zidane. "Ciao voyou!" (Bye-bye, hoodlum!), announced the headline of *Minute.* A leader of the Front National told a journalist, "The Romans have beaten Gauls who don't really look like Gauls." Another announced that the victory would be celebrated in Italy like those of the "best periods" of the Roman Empire; the only thing lacking would be "Zidane the African, chained up as Vercingétorix the Gaul once was." Bruno Gollnisch, the second-highest-ranking leader of the Front National, said that although the team might represent "the France of tomorrow" it did not "correspond to the France of today." "I would have supported a little positive discrimination," he stated, sarcastically using the term for affirmative-action-style policies common in France, which would have put "a few more French people of European origin" on the team. A Catholic far-right leader said he felt little regret for the loss of a team made up largely of "mercenaries." In Italy, meanwhile, Robert Calderoli, leader of the right-wing Lega Nord and vice president of the Senate, celebrated the victory of Italy over a France "that has sacrificed its own identity in lining up Blacks, Islamists, and Communists." He added the next day, "It's not my fault if Barthez sings the *Internationale* instead of the *Marseillaise* and if some prefer Mecca to Bethlehem."[27]

Such claims ultimately did a service for Zidane, for their gleeful resentment repelled many who did not want to be aligned with the far right in maligning the player. The somber accusatory tone of *L'Equipe,* with its appeals to the morality of children, seemed a little absurd, as if Zidane's action had trampled on a world of sport otherwise pristine and free from moral flaws. Aided by this onslaught against Zidane, his *coup de boule* rather quickly moved out of the terrain of condemnation and into another realm: that of philosophy.

Three billion people had watched Zidane answer a universal question: How should one respond to an insult? If the worldwide reaction to what he did was so intense it was because all of us can relate to the problem. Of course unlike most people's responses, this one had dramatic collective consequences. It shaped the destiny of the French team in the final of the World Cup, which for many French fans also meant that it shaped the destiny of the French nation itself. Thus French people felt that it was their right, indeed their responsibility, to judge Zidane. And though there are many who still haven't forgiven him, there quickly developed a powerful, widely shared movement that focused on understanding, forgiving, and even celebrating what he had done.

Out on the street, as I picked up a newspaper with Zidane on the cover, a young man beside me said, to no one in particular, "Why did Zidane do it?" We all had an answer. An elderly woman announced that Zidane was perfectly right to do what he did. "He was insulted and he was defending his dignity, which everyone has the right to do," she declared passionately. "And that is why we love Zidane, because he is a man, not a god." With his attack on Materazzi, Zidane had transformed himself from a god into a hero, into a man who did something decisive, courageous, perhaps misguided but profoundly human. To the theater director Anne Delbée, Zidane had done something oddly generous, even Christ-like: "He committed a foul, but at the same time he took on all those humiliations, all those provocations that we don't dare free ourselves from."[28]

"Incapable of scoring goals," Jean-Philippe Toussaint later wrote, paraphrasing and altering the statement Zidane made before the game, the player had decided that he "would score spirits." He chose to end his career by refusing to end his story: "To hold up the World Cup is to accept one's death, while messing up one's exit is a way of leaving things open, unknown, alive." Had Zidane won, the story would have been perfect, Toussaint was suggesting, and it would have been over. Instead Zidane had shattered the image of a happy ending so many had come to the game with, proposing something bewildering, provocative, and unsettling in its place. Anne Delbée wrote that if his gesture had "lost the World Cup," it had also "reinvented theater." It was almost as if, for his final act, Zidane had chosen to deconstruct the sport he had devoted his life to, and the stories woven around it. This—the team, the World Cup—this is just football, he seemed to say. It's just a game. An insult, though, is real, and more important than a World Cup.[29]

The details of the hit seemed to confirm that something rather complicated and indeed highly theatrical had taken place. Zidane made a conscious choice to turn and confront Materazzi. He ignored the first set of insults, and for a time ignored the second. Then he turned around, with a calm and determined look on his face, and began walking back to Materazzi. In the few steps that he took to reach his "adversary," writes an admiring Anne Delbée, she felt she could perceive "the light around him": "He walks as if in a dream, awake among us," with "total lucidity" and concentration. "No one, at that moment, could counsel him, or stop him. . . . He has never been so calm, at peace with his heart, free. . . . He has been waiting for a long time: there have always been too many misunderstandings surrounding him."[30]

If his first choice was to turn around, his second—perhaps even more important—was about how to strike at Materazzi. In France as in many other places, the *coup de boule* is associated with rough street-fighting. Many observers quickly saw it as a link to his childhood in Castellane. As one young man watching the game in Castellane put it, the *coup de boule* proved that Zidane, despite his vertiginous ascent over the years, still carried Castellane within him: "He may have forgotten us, but his *coup de tête,* it's an old remnant of Castellane." A newspaper in Algeria similarly linked the *coup de boule* to Zidane's origins in Castellane and also to the "sense of honor" that many have claimed is particularly strong among Kabyles of Algeria. Variants of this argument—"You can take the boy out of the *banlieue,* but you can't take the *banlieue* out of the boy"—were presented repeatedly both by detractors and supporters of Zidane in the weeks following the event. Whether consciously or not, in choosing this particular form of attack Zidane immediately raised and placed at the center of the symbolic transfer point of the World Cup the question of origins, the question of the *banlieue* and the identity of those who live there, and the question of violence and the *banlieue.* Interpretations of the *coup de boule* that connected the action to Zidane's childhood or his Algerian roots could go in many different directions, of course. They could take on a deeply racist tone, suggesting that his action was characteristic of the violence and lack of control of North Africans as a group. But they just as easily could become an expression of pride in the way that Zidane had stood up for himself and, by extension, for his community.[31]

Zidane, however, also modified the classic *coup de boule,* which is aimed at the victim's head and is a particularly harsh and dangerous way of knocking someone down and possibly unconscious. Zidane did something different, something comparatively less dangerous physically, but also more theatrical: he butted Materazzi in the chest, in his sternum—at his heart. The strike sent the player flying to the ground, but it was also contained, carefully aimed, and calculated. Whatever you thought about it, you had to admit it was a beautifully executed *coup de boule*.

Condensed in this moment, then, was a wide repertoire of symbolic referents. There was Zidane the master football player and master at heading the ball into the goal, as he had proven in the 1998 final against Brazil, now demonstrating his mastery of another art, that of fighting, also carried out with the head. There was Zidane improvising a set form in a highly theatrical way for a particular moment, and Materazzi joining, in some sense, in the theater. There was Zidane, having been thoroughly de-localized to the point of being a god, suddenly being localized sharply again in Castellane, in the *banlieue,* and perhaps in Algeria. But at the heart of the incident was a secret.[32]

"What could Materazzi have said to Zidane?" asked *Le Monde* on 12 July, repeating a question already asked innumerable times by then. Zidane maintained silence on the issue. Materazzi conceded that he insulted the "super-arrogant" player with "an insult like those that we hear exchanged frequently and that are often released on the playing field." Materazzi has a reputation both as a brilliant defender and as a consistent harasser of his opponents on the field. Among his many tattoos are a scowling Viking on his right shoulder and a scowling Native American on his right pectoral. But his statements implied that what he said to Zidane was banal, expected, a normal part of the game. After the F.I.F.A. hearing on the incident, the president of the French Football Federation similarly defined the incident as "profoundly banal," noting that there were "ten thousand" problems of this kind to resolve every year. There were precedents for Zidane's action in French football, notably during the 1984 European Cup when Manuel Amoros reacted to a harsh tackle by a Danish player by head-butting him—in the head, not the chest—and earned a red card and a three-game suspension from a referee who was standing nearby. Yes, such incidents had happened many times before, but the timing had never been so dramatic.[33]

In a sense Materazzi was right that the insults he offered up were common enough, at least if the authoritative tabloid *Paris-Match* is to be believed. As the magazine recounted, after Materazzi pulled Zidane's jersey during play, Zidane said, "If you want my jersey, I'll give it to you afterwards." Then

Materazzi began: "Oh, fuck you, fag!" And as Zidane began to walk away he added, "With your whore of a sister. Shit." Zidane then turned around, and Materazzi said, "Yeah, your whore of a sister." And as Zidane approached, "What's more, I'm going to fuck you up the ass."[34]

But there was not, and still isn't, a completely definitive version of Materazzi's words. Those words, unrecorded, their traces visible on video but unheard, were quickly suffused with desires and fears, just as the *coup de boule* that responded to it had been. The theories about those words multiplied instantly, sustained by claims about Brazil's famous lip-readers and attempts to deconstruct the video. A popular theory asserted that Materazzi had called Zidane a "terrorist" or a "son of a terrorist whore." The *Guardian* in Britain suggested that, just before Zidane hit him, Materazzi said, "You deserve all of this, you butt-fucked Muslims, dirty terrorists." A few briefly claimed that Materazzi had called Zidane an *harki,* an Algerian who fought for France during the anticolonial war, resurrecting the old discussion of whether Smaïl Zidane had been an *harki* that had dragged on between 1998 and 2001. This theory, however, seemed a bit far-fetched and rapidly lost out to other, more popular ideas.[35]

Much of the discussion centered around a seemingly all-important question: Did Materazzi insult Zidane's sister *and* mother, or just his sister? Zidane's mother, Malika, was in the hospital on the night of the game, and some suspected that Materazzi, knowing this, had indeed insulted her, certain that in doing so he would provoke a response from Zidane. Materazzi denied that he called Zidane a terrorist, adding, "[I don't] even know what that means." He later insisted that he made "no reference to his mother, to politics, to terrorism, or religion." "I lost my mother at the age of fifteen," he added. "I have a great deal of respect for mothers. It would not occur to me to offend anyone's mother. . . . I did not know that Zidane's mother was in the hospital, and I send her my best wishes for recovery." In time Materazzi turned the question into a lucrative commercial deal: he was featured in a Nike advertisement in which he was struck by different objects, starting with a bowling ball, then a police battering ram, and culminating in a truck and a wrecking ball (which he elegantly sidesteps), always standing firm, in what was in part a humorous commentary on how swiftly he had fallen to the ground when Zidane struck him. He also published a comical book entitled *What I Really Said to Zidane* (whose proceeds went to support UNICEF) in which he enumerated many possibilities, among them: "French philosophy has really gone downhill since the death of Michel Foucault."[36]

There were juridical stakes involved in defining what Materazzi said, because if he was found guilty of using racist language he would have faced a stiff penalty from F.I.F.A. Materazzi's defense was to insist that he didn't use racist language, that the words he did use were banal and therefore should not have been offensive. No one spoke up, as Anne Delbée notes, to call him to account for his "verbal provocations that prostitute women." Such insults had "become a habit" and are widely accepted as normal and indeed banal, just as Materazzi suggested. For Delbée, part of Zidane's heroism was that he refused the idea that a sexist insult was banal, and instead treated it with deadly seriousness.[37]

Several of Zidane's teammates also defended him. William Gallas accused the Italians of having "cheated" throughout the game and declared, "I can't stand injustice." Florent Malouda said, "Besieged by provocation, even the greatest players end up cracking." Thuram both lamented his teammate's action—"Zidane knows he allowed himself to be trapped"—and criticized Materazzi: "Materazzi gives a negative image to football and he doesn't need to have that kind of attitude, because he's a good player. In football, you savor a victory that you win within the rules. What's the point of winning when you cheat?"[38]

In the days after the World Cup the obsession in Paris shifted quickly from the effect of the *coup de boule* to its cause, and the change of heart suggested that, in a strange way, Zidane had succeeded in something quite remarkable. France had lost the World Cup, and Italy had won it. Although no one could have predicted how Zidane's presence on the field during penalty kicks might have changed the outcome of the game, there were many people who felt that he had let his team down, maybe even condemned it to defeat, through his action. And yet, at least in Paris, after the initial shock it seemed everyone was much more concerned with his instantly legendary *coup de boule*. The initial claim that Zidane had somehow shattered his image and ruined his exit from the sport quickly began to seem premature. Instead he seemed to have taken control of his story. "Zidane," the Israeli writer Etgar Keret announced, "didn't violate his code. Neither the solemnity of the hour, the expectations of the media, or the happy ending that billions of people had written for him dissuaded him." He chose to end his career "not like a 'professional' or like a 'legend,' but like an individual, warm, sensitive, but not always measured."[39] As Roger Cohen wrote in the *International Herald Tribune,* Zidane "chose to write a coda to his story that would have all the complexity of a great novel." Instead of the heroic tale, leading inexorably to joy and celebration, he offered a gesture that incited a "global, virtual argument."[40]

The Algerian press initially followed the lead taken by *L'Equipe* and *Le Monde,* calling Zidane's final act a "ruined ending," but many Algerians immediately defended Zidane, declaring that what he did was a question of "honor." One newspaper declared that if Materazzi had indeed called Zidane a "son of a terrorist whore," many people, "in Algeria at least, will regret that Zidane aimed his *coup de tête* at Materazzi's chest; he should have adjusted a few centimeters higher, at his mouth." Another newspaper accused the French of "ingratitude" toward a player who had "valiantly" defended "the French colors" throughout his career. The Algerian president, Abdelaziz Bouteflika, declared, a bit like Chirac, that although he was "pained" by the incident, he understood what Zidane had done: "In the face of what could only be a serious act of aggression, you reacted, first, as a man of honor, before submitting, without flinching, to the verdict."[4]

Three days after the final game, on 12 July—eight years to the day from the night France won the World Cup in 1998—Zidane issued his first public statement about the incident. Accompanied by some of his brothers he arrived at the television studio in an SUV with tinted windows. Wearing a green army jacket, greeted with chants of "Zizou," and flanked by television screens replaying his *coup de boule,* he explained what he did:

> It was at the moment where he pulled my jersey. . . . He grabbed me, and I told him to stop pulling my jersey. And then, he said some words that were very cruel and repeated them several times. They were crueler than gestures. It was something that happened very fast. They were words that touched me deep inside. They were very personal. It related to my mother, my sister. . . . When you hear such cruel words, you hear them once, and you try to walk away. That's why I did [it]. I am a man above all else and there are words that, sometimes . . . I would have preferred getting a right hook to the face rather than hearing that.[42]

Zidane didn't repeat the words that he had heard but insisted that linguistic violence could be worse than physical violence. Then, responding to the attacks in *L'Equipe,* he said, "I reacted, and of course it is not a gesture one should make. I want to say that loud and clear. This was seen by billions of television spectators, millions of children. To them, I apologize, and also to educators. I know what it's like to have kids. I will always tell them not to let people step on their feet. But also to avoid this kind of thing." Then, having issued a partial apology, Zidane added:

FIGURE 27. Zidane discusses his head-butt on French television, 12 July 2006. Bertrand Guay/AFP/Getty Images.

But no, I can't regret my gesture. That would mean that he was right to say all that. No, he is not right to say what he said, certainly not. What I want to say most of all is that we always talk about the reaction. Of course it is punishable. But if there is no provocation, there is no reaction. The guilty one is the one who provokes.... Do you think that in the final game of a World Cup, ten minutes from the end of a career, it made me happy to do that? Never. I did it because there was a serious provocation. My gesture is not pardonable. I'm just saying that you have to punish the one who is really guilty. And the one who is really guilty is the one who provokes.

Without identifying the specific content of the provocation, Zidane asserted that it was serious enough to deserve retaliation on the field and punishment by F.I.F.A. And then—though he didn't accuse Materazzi of using racial terms—he brought up the broader question of racism:

I'm not here to say my reaction was worthy. I can't say it was something good. I can't say I am proud of this gesture. But FIFA has launched a major campaign against racism. We were all there to overcome that. And when you read in the paper that the vice-president of the Italian Senate declares: "They (*the Italian players*) beat a team of blacks, Islamists, and communists," don't you think that is serious? These are such serious words, such cruel words. That shocks me. So, my gesture, yes. But this sickness, we are all here to fight it.

Zidane's statement made an implicit connection between the broader "sickness" of racism in football, and in European society, and the particular words he heard on the field. This was a direct contrast to the claims of "banality" made by Materazzi.

The content of Materazzi's insults seems, first and foremost, directed at sexual humiliation of Zidane's family and Zidane himself, a classic litany of taunts that nestle comfortably in many public spaces inhabited by young men, whether in France or elsewhere. They were banal—alarmingly so. That such words—sexually violent, homophobic, threatening rape—could be presented as ordinary and by extension acceptable highlighted how common sexist language is in masculine sports culture. Racist language is usually considered far more serious and actionable. Of course, racist insults are themselves often articulated, or cloaked, in the language of sexual violence or degradation. If Zidane brought up racism in his statement—a gesture some considered cynically calculating—it was perhaps because even if Materazzi didn't use explicitly racist language, Zidane experienced the insults as being linked to broader racist stereotypes. By refusing to repeat the insults directed at him, Zidane carefully deflected attention away from precisely what was said to his experience of what was said. If he ended up punishing Materazzi on the field himself, he suggested, it was in part because those who governed football had failed to control verbal provocation in the sport. He presented his reaction as a defense of his dignity, one that he had to deliver, but one that he should not have had to deliver. He didn't deny that such insults were commonplace. But he suggested that their use on the field was part of a broader "sickness" that, in his own decidedly imperfect way, he had sought to stand against. Being Zidane, he pulled off this argument skillfully enough to carry many along with him.

The day after Zidane's statement the theater director Claire Lasne wrote a powerful defense of the *coup de boule,* describing "those few words released, then repeated by a man in blue, those four steps by a man in white to try to escape them, and the brutal stopping of everything. Everything. Money, glory, fear of others—of the entire world—nothing stopped the man in white. Time had to stop. He had to say no." She remarked on the widespread indignation Zidane had incited and agreed that violence should never be seen as an expression of justice or dignity: "Violence is ugly. Scoring a goal is beautiful. A red card is shit. And the Cup, it shines." But it shone, she went on, in the hands of a man who had found the words that were necessary to send the "child of immigrants" off the field in an "ugly, ugly gesture." Like Zidane, without directly referring to the words themselves she connected them to racism, to "this new worldwide tactic in sports: the insult held up as a legitimate weapon, as an instrument of victory. Racist insult, of course. What are all these Blacks and Arabs doing on the football field? Let them run, let them score, and then shut up." Zidane's gesture, she argued, broke with this silence: "The man had often shut up. But not that day. No. To his glory, he stopped for a word. Vive toi, Zinedine Zidane, who put the dignity of a people, or even of a single man, higher than a Cup given by the white world to those who keep quiet."[43]

When F.I.F.A. judged the case on 20 July Zidane was fined 7,500 Swiss francs (about the same in U.S. dollars) and suspended from three games, and Materazzi was fined 5,000 francs and suspended from two games. Materazzi would miss the next France-Italy game, scheduled for 6 September. The suspensions had no effect on Zidane: he had already retired. His replacement punishment was likely only to increase his stature and credibility: he was to work on fund-raising for charitable causes for F.I.F.A., where he would be in the limelight once again. Despite the incident, he was still anointed as the best player of the World Cup.[44]

The question Zidane had posed in his last gesture on the field took on a particular meaning in France in 2006, one directly tied to broader questions of race, exclusion, and history. The *coup de boule* generated such intense debate in France at least in part because it exemplified the larger question of how people in French society, and more particularly the youth of the *banlieue*, should react to the broader set of insults they experience on a daily basis. As *Le Monde* made clear, those who worried about what lesson the children might take from Zidane's head-butt were often worried particularly about what the youth of the *banlieue* might take from it. They lamented that Zidane had become "with one gesture a counterexample for the thousands of kids of the *cités* who dreamed of themselves as a future Zizou."[45] Some readers of *Le Monde* reacted to the F.I.F.A. verdict by once again suggesting that Zidane's action and the justification for it would help to justify violence in the *banlieue:* "Zidane was angry. He can give a *coup de boule* to Materazzi. The lesson: we have to think that the inhabitants of the *banlieue* and the immigrants who are angry can riot in the towns." Others feared that given the favorable response to Zidane in the French media, the *coup de boule* would end up being a kind of juridical precedent in France that would undermine all kinds of authority. One reader responded, "Watch out for the reaction of young people to a reprimand they receive, a scolding look, or an insult."[46]

A very different claim about the link between Zidane and the *banlieue* came from the novelist Serge Quadruppani, in a letter published in *Libération* on 14 July. "Cher ZZ," the letter began, "a few minutes after the *coup de boule* that you placed in the history of our planet, we saw and heard the president of the French Republic absolve you implicitly for this gesture." President Chirac had indeed gone to the locker room after the defeat and spoke with Zidane alone for fifteen minutes. The next day, as Quadruppani put it in his letter, Chirac offered his support and that of "the entire nation" to Zidane, while "all kinds of media VIPs deployed treasures of understanding" based on the idea that "the Italian player disrespected you."

Watching this spectacle, we can't avoid thinking of the thousands of young people born like you in the *cités* who have been in prison or are rotting there today for having rebelled against representatives of order who provoked them and insulted them with the same hypocritical confidence of an Italian player who knows his words will not be recorded. We think of all those young people accused of "outrage and rebellion," of all those who burned cars or were accused of doing so because they felt that the entire society, through its representatives in uniform, disrespected them. And you certainly have not, dear Zizou, forgotten that the scorn and humiliation that is inflicted daily against your little brothers from the *quartiers* and against their parents go much further than insulting their mothers and sisters, all the way to the permanent insults of discrimination, spatial marginalization, and social apartheid.[47]

Quadruppani then asked Zidane to accept this link between his action and those of young people in the *cités*. The footballer, he argued, should ask President Chirac to extend the "same comprehension" he granted Zidane to the many in prison and to lead a movement for a "general amnesty" for the rioters of November 2005, as well as for those arrested during student demonstrations in early 2006. "This would be," continued Quadruppani, "a civic gesture on your part much greater than useless apologies to educators and young people who are confronted, every day, as you were briefly, with the difficulty of expressing their revolt except through transgression. And who, in their gesture of revolt, could say as you did: 'I do not regret it.'" Amnesty for Zidane, Quadruppani argued, logically justified amnesty for others who were forced to resist serious structural insults through mechanisms that were outside the law, condemned by society, and yet their only route for protest. By asking Zidane to take a political stand in defense of the young men of the *banlieue* who had paid a steep price for their rebellious actions this editorial was one of the strongest attempts at transferring the meaning of the *coup de boule* directly into the realm of politics. For the Montréal-based Haitian writer Dany Lafferière, meanwhile, Zidane's action was itself essentially a gesture of affiliation and solidarity, in which he "embraced all those who do not know how to behave in public," particularly "his brothers from the street, whose blood is still boiling."[48]

Thus Zidane's action was connected directly to the daily experience of confrontation, distrust, and insults traded between the police and *banlieue* youth in contemporary France. This conflict, and the meaning it takes on in contemporary France, is tied to a historically much deeper set of questions about the lingering insults of colonial violence and exploitation; about their long-term impact and how they are recalled, revived, and mobilized in the present; about how they were confronted; and about the ways the violence and counterviolence of colonial history is both buried within and haunting contemporary France. Because of who Zidane is, because of what the French football team has come to represent, and because of the particularly rich and

FIGURE 28. Zidane takes his final bow on the balcony of the Elysée Palace, 2006. Philippe de Poulpiquet © Maxppp, Panoramic, Action Press/ZUMA.

potent symbolic site on which he carried out his *coup de boule*, all of this history came bearing down on that remarkable moment on the field, shaping its explosive meaning, rendering it intelligible, even inspirational for many of those who watched it in France, Algeria, and beyond.

If Zidane's action was, on one level, simply that of an individual making a decision based on personal honor, or simply rage, its setting and its composition seem to have assured it permanence as a symbolic question about the meaning of violence, the violence of language, and the meaning of rules and their limits. Although common sense might suggest that insults are everyday provocations that should be ignored, Zidane's comments about the incident suggested something else, something quite utopian: that there should be no insults, that the dialogue of football, and perhaps the dialogue of politics and even daily life should be purged of insult and provocation altogether.

The image of Zidane that most sticks with me is not the one from the field in Berlin, but an image from a balcony in Paris. Whether they won or lost, there was supposed to be a parade on the Champs-Elysées to welcome back the French players from Berlin after the final. But after the defeat, and perhaps more important, after the *coup de boule,* the parade was canceled. The players had lunch with Chirac at the Elysée Palace, as planned, and afterward went out onto a balcony overlooking the Place de la Concorde, where a crowd had gathered to greet them. One by one they stepped forward and waved. David Trezeguet, whose missed penalty kick had sealed the loss to Italy, burst into tears and was consoled by Thierry Henry, and the crowd applauded forgivingly. Zidane, however, remained inside, until Thuram began asking, "Where is Zidane?" "We're making an *haie d'honneur* [an honor guard]," he announced, and then Zidane emerged with a mysterious smile on his lips. He walked to the edge of the balcony and leaned forward. Was it a final bow, after his last performance, to the standing ovation below? Or was it a replay—one among a seemingly infinite number now tumbling through our symbolic universe—of his now canonical exit?

Epilogue
Returns

"I intend to go to Algeria, to find my roots, the land of my parents." That, Zidane explained a few days after the World Cup final, was what he would do with his newfound freedom. Now that he would no longer be under surveillance, "watched and observed" by the public, he was going back to "real life." He wanted to plunge himself into Algeria: "I want to live it," he said. In September 2006 Zidane returned to Algeria for the first time since he was a boy. The Algerian government and people greeted him with as much pomp and attention as and much more affection than a visiting head of state. He traveled to the village Smaïl Zidane left fifty years earlier. Having spent much of his professional life as a symbol of the possibility of reconciliation in France, he was acclaimed as an Algerian hero.[1]

During his visit Zidane met with several members of the F.L.N team in a ceremony at which he received a decoration from the Algerian president. Amar Rouaï, one of the players, expressed some unease at the fact that he and his football comrades had never been celebrated in quite the same way. "Me, personally, I like this guy," he said of Zidane. "But maybe we did too much for him." Referring to one of the F.L.N. players who had given up his chance to play on the French World Cup team in 1958 to join the Algerian team, he added, "I would have liked it if the president had also honored Zitouni." But Rachid Mekloufi, who had also given up his one chance to play in the World Cup, believed that Zidane deserved the honor Algeria bestowed upon him: "Zidane is a great man. His roots call to him. He knew about the F.L.N. team through his father. He's always stayed a child of the *barlieue*. And he understands that he has to give back what football has given him." The comments suggested that, in a way, Zidane was also, as he had been through much of his career, a kind of peace envoy, sent on a mission he never asked for, of finally ending the Algerian war.[2]

⊕

The last French player to leave the field after the defeat against Italy was
Lilian Thuram. With tears streaming down his face, he took a lap to wave in
thanks to French fans, lingering for a time on the field, perhaps remembering
the feeling of victory he had savored eight years earlier. A few weeks later,
after a short stop in Guadeloupe, he was back in the spotlight, though not yet
back on the football field. He traveled to Africa as the goodwill ambassador
for an international organization working to fight sickle-cell anemia, visiting
Senegal, Cameroon, and South Africa. The journey gave him the opportunity to visit Gorée Island, once a French slave-trading port. At the famous
Maison des Esclaves, whose image had decorated the shirts he and Bernard
Lama wore during the 1998 World Cup, he visited holding cells for slaves and
stood in the surf outside a doorway looking out to the ocean known as the
"Doorway of No Return." In Cameroon he kicked off a football match and
then watched from the stands. When a boy sitting on his lap whispered in
his ear that he thought Zidane had been right to strike Materazzi, a shocked
Thuram scolded him.[3]

After his journey to Africa Thuram returned home to Guadeloupe, where
his mother, Mariana, now lives in a palatial house he built for her in Anse-
Bertrand, complete with an infinity pool overlooking the ocean. Holding
a press conference in Anse-Bertrand on his return, he spoke not about the
World Cup but about his journey to Africa. "We must be very strong people,"
he told the audience, "to still be standing here after all that we have been
through." As he finished talking, Thuram had tears in his eyes. His mother
comforted him by rubbing his head and wrapping her arms around him.[4]

Soon afterward Thuram sponsored a local *lewoz,* an evening of dancing
and singing, as he had for several years. It was led by a prominent musical
group and cultural organization called Akiyo. The group's anthem is a retell-
ing of the history of the French Caribbean. "It's not Schoelcher who liberated
us," they call out, referring to the French abolitionist Victor Schoelcher, who
is generally credited with having convinced the new republican government
to abolish slavery in 1848. "It's the maroons who liberated us," they declare,
referring to the enslaved people who escaped from the plantations and lived
in the mountains of the island, often raiding plantations and always pursued
by their former masters and colonial troops. The song calls out the names of
different maroons, placing these otherwise forgotten individuals into the
history of the island, creating a new genealogy for struggle, redemption, and
victory. Thuram sang along that night, and when Akiyo introduced him,

they gave him the highest compliment they could. They called him a maroon, incorporating him into the pantheon of Guadeloupe's heroes, as one of those who has said no.[5]

⊛

In 2007 a model of Lilian Thuram's cranium, "reproduced using a magnetic resonance imaging scanner," was put on display at the famed Musée de l Homme, a museum founded in 1937 and devoted to the history and culture of humanity. Thuram took up a place next to those of "two other Frenchmen: 17th century Philosopher René Descartes, and a well-preserved 30,000-year-old male Cro-Magnon fossil on display for the first time." The exhibit recounted the history of humanity, and the curators had picked Thuram to represent the modern human race because, they said, he is "a campaigner against racism and social injustice" and therefore "a symbol of the unity of humankind." But Thuram's role was also that of an exorcist: the same museum had long housed the remains of a South African Khosa woman named Saarthjie Baartman, the famous "Hottentot Venus," who had been displayed in Europe in the early nineteenth century (as Christian Karembeu's great-grandfathers were a century later). According to one French archaeologist, the display of Thuram's skull was meant to highlight a break with the "racist, colonial context" in which Baartman was presented as a "passive object on display." "Thuram is a modern Frenchman," he explained, "who happens to be black and who affirms himself as equal." With his inclusion in the trilogy presented by the Musée de l'Homme—three French craniums, from a Cro-Magnon man to Descartes and culminating in Thuram—the football player was enlisted to demonstrate that the new France was not the same as the old one.[6]

Thuram continued playing for the French team, serving occasionally as its captain, during the next two years. In the fall of 2006 he left Juventus to play with Barcelona. But he found time to keep up a high-profile barrage of criticisms aimed at Jean-Marie Le Pen and especially Nicolas Sarkozy. In an interview a few weeks after the World Cup Thuram commented that in addition to the *lepénization* of people's spirits, which were damaged by Le Pen's racist ideas, there was a dangerous *sarkoization* going on as well. He attacked the expulsions of immigrants, including schoolchildren, ordered by Sarkozy. "It's incomprehensible: we are in France, a country that calls itself civilized and we accept that people are expelled. . . . I don't understand how we can accept that. What country are we living in? What world do we want to live in?" People were slowly getting used to the idea, he declared, that "those who

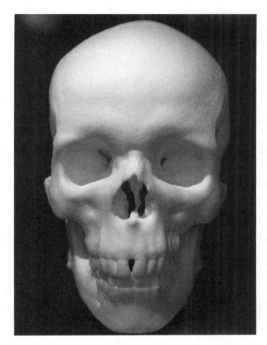

FIGURE 29. The model of Lilian Thuram's cranium put on display at the Musée de l'Homme. François Guillot/AFP/Getty Images.

don't have papers should go die elsewhere" and that "a foreigner has less of a right to live than others."[7]

A few months later, in September 2006, Thuram and Patrick Vieira invited seventy people from a recently dismantled squatter camp at Cachan, a *banlieue* south of Paris that included immigrants seeking access to local housing as well as some *sans-papiers,* to watch their game against Italy, part of the qualifications for the European Cup. The French won the game 3–1, and the match was widely celebrated as a kind of revenge for the loss of the summer, as well as proof that even without Zidane the team could still shine. But Sarkozy and his supporters complained about Thuram and Vieira's action. They saw their expression of solidarity with the *sans-papiers* as a dangerous development that signified a deepening rift between the governing party and the "black-beur" communities in France, especially because Vieira had joined Thuram. One French deputy "close to Sarkozy" worried that this was the beginning of a "contagion" among other French sports stars, and indeed the retired French tennis star Yannick Noah, who in the 1980s had frequently spoken out on political matters, joined in the criticism of Sarkozy, calling him a "little Zorro." One conservative French deputy, Yves Jégo, deplored what he saw as the message of Thuram and Vieira's misplaced empathy: that those who squatted and broke the law would be invited to the Stade de France. The right-wing politician Philippe de Villiers declared that he was "shocked" to see "millionaires presuming to lecture us": "Football players are made to play football."[8]

Soon afterward another politician made headlines by criticizing the makeup of the French team. This time, however, the criticism came from a Socialist politician, George Frêche, a historian and law professor serving as the president of the Languedoc-Roussillon region. At a meeting in Montpelier, where he was once mayor, Frêche declared, "On this team, there are nine blacks out of eleven. What would be normal would be for there to be three or four. That would reflect the society. But if there are so many, it's because the whites are so bad. I'm ashamed of this country. Soon, there will be eleven blacks. When I see this particular team, it hurts me." The comments, unsurprisingly, incited an immediate storm of controversy, but the next day Frêche refused to apologize for them. "I wanted to say that there are not enough whites," he explained. He argued that France needed "a team that represents the sociological composition of France." The provocative statements, one of a series on various topics that ultimately led to Frêche's exclusion from the Socialist Party the next year, echoed both those of Finkielkraut and those of Le Pen and also highlighted the fact that the discomfort about the makeup of the team could cross party lines. Frêche's lament, which suggested that the lack of white players was the sign of a broader decline in French society, highlighted the divergent ways the composition of the French team could be interpreted as a portent of larger social and political transformations.[9]

These statements came in the midst of the presidential campaign, during which Lilian Thuram continued to speak out against Nicolas Sarkozy. He decided to make public some things Sarkozy had said when they met in late 2005. According to Thuram, Sarkozy declared then that the problems in the *banlieue* were caused by "blacks and Arabs." Sarkozy, Thuram consistently warned, really did see France, and its problems, in racial terms. Sarkozy recruited another soccer player, Basile Boli, who was born in the Ivory Coast and had played on the French national team in the 1980s, to join his campaign in an apparent attempt to counter Thuram's criticisms. In April Sarkozy won the election. During his campaign he had criticized the habit of "repentance" for historical injustices such as slavery and Vichy, yet one of his first public appearances as president was at the official consecration of a new national holiday, 10 May, commemorating the abolition of slavery in France. At the ceremony Thuram and Sarkozy exchanged a few unrecorded words. Sarkozy, it later became clear, was keeping an eye on Thuram.

After his election Sarkozy made two appointments that brought children of immigrants into the highest level of French political life. Before Azouz Begag's appointment in 2005, there had been only one government minister in France since World War II who was black or of North African background: Roger Bambuck, the star Guadeloupean runner who represented France during the 1960s, who was minister of youth and sports from 1988 to 1991. His pioneering role in politics highlights how sports can serve as a platform for political representation, since it was his status as a successful athlete that gave him access to the position. But Bambuck's appointment was not the beginning of a larger trend. After his election in 2007, however, Sarkozy chose Rachida Dati, the child of a Moroccan father and an Algerian mother who immigrated to France in the 1960s, to be the new minister of justice, and as secretary of state the Senegal-born Rama Yade. Just thirty years old at the time, Yade grew up in France and lived for a time in a *cité,* with her own share of experiences with racism. (A professor of German literature once told her that, because of her skin color, she wasn't "fit to understand the German soul.") The Sarkozy administration has also been more open than previous administrations to affirmative action–style policies that some groups are increasingly lobbying for. Tellingly and with some distaste the French call such policies "positive discrimination," and many on all sides of the political spectrum see them as a violation of the code of color-blindness that they argue should govern French state policies. Critics of Sarkozy see his pursuit of such policies and his appointments of Yade and Dati as nothing more than cynical tokenism. They also raise broader, difficult questions: Does having an African or North African background in such positions actually do anything to confront the real roots of exclusion in France? Or does it just provide an alibi for larger policies that maintain and even deepen the marginalization of certain groups? The appointments certainly do highlight the fact that parties on the left have long failed to do what Sarkozy has done: diversify the ranks of the highest levels of the French government.[10]

Late in 2008 Sarkozy was looking for someone to name to the new position of minister of diversity, and he approached Thuram. "We had a long talk," Thuram explained in a February 2009 interview. "But, for obvious reasons, I had to refuse." Though he didn't expand on these comments, the suggestion was clear: he had spent a great deal of time criticizing Sarkozy and was not willing to join his government. "Politics is something very noble in which you can't do things half-way. You have to learn things. That's what I'm doing now." Still, he didn't rule out the possibility of going into politics: "One day, maybe." He spoke passionately about events at the time in Guadeloupe, where antigovernment strikes and protests had shut down the island for over a month, suggesting that it might be the vanguard of a protest movement that would shake all of France: "Guadeloupe is often ahead of France in terms of social conflict."[11]

Thuram's final retirement from football had come several months earlier, in the summer of 2008, after a difficult season in Barcelona and a devastating one with the French team at the European Cup. The team was much the same as it had been in 2006, but without Zidane. They were smashed 4–1 by a brilliant Dutch team, during a game in which Thuram made several decisive mistakes. The French then faced Italy in a game they had to win to stay in the competition. Thuram wasn't in the starting lineup, and when his teammate Eric Abidal was expelled early on for a harsh tackle, he stood up, thinking the coach would put him in to hold the defense together. But Coach Raymond Domenech told him to sit down. The French lost, and Thuram sat out his last game with the French team. It was a heartbreaking ending to his career. Soon afterward a potential recruitment to the Paris Saint-Germain team fell through after a doctor reported a previously undetected problem with Thuram's heart. Although it isn't clear how serious the problem is, Thuram's brother had died from a similar condition, and at the urging of his family the footballer decided it was time to step off the stage.

As the newspaper *L'Equipe* announced in an issue honoring Thuram with a front-page "Merci, Monsieur!," he left a remarkable legacy. In 1998 Thuram joked that the point of getting selected for the national team was to get the fancy uniform and duffel bag; once you had that, there wasn't any reason to stay. Ten years later he left, having far surpassed the record for appearances with the French team set by his Guadeloupean predecessor Marius Trésor. Thuram had played, and played well, in 142 games, more than any other player in the history of the team. He played a crucial role in winning the World Cup and the European Cup. Along the way he established himself as a prominent public intellectual and activist in France. Since his retirement he has continued this work by creating the Fondation Lilian Thuram, devoted to studying and attacking contemporary racism, and he travels widely promoting this mission. Whatever new victories Thuram achieves in the next decades, hopefully he will find himself where, in 1998, he imagined he would be at seventy: living in the Antilles: "A straw hat on my head . . . I'm playing dominoes. I've got a view of the ocean. I'm with friends.[12]

Through their remarkable careers on the French national team, Thuram and Zidane delivered several answers to the question of how racism and exclusion should be confronted. Above all, they responded by *being* France, undeniably and victoriously, branding the national consciousness with their presence in an irrefutable and profound way. They proved themselves indispensable, and in so doing challenged those who would have discarded them when they were growing up in the *banlieue* or when their families were seeking entry into France. They did so on the largest stage available to them in 1998. In more recent years Thuram has made himself a spokesman for victims of racial exclusion in France through his eloquent political statements. Zidane left as his final act on stage another kind of response to this question, one that goes something like this: If you insult me with words I experience as a kind of physical violence, I will, no matter the moment or the cost, strike back. I will knock you down, and I will walk away and refuse to regret what I did, because I should be able to live and play free from insults. Whatever one concludes about this response, it will remain a model, a cipher, a symbol, and an endlessly recurring event.

On 10 July 2006, the night after the World Cup final, I sat in the plaza of the Hôtel de Ville in Paris, reeling and exhilarated. Packed with celebrating Italian fans the night before, it was now mostly empty. Near the edge of the plaza, though, stood a young man with a ball at his feet. As people entered the plaza, he kicked the ball to them, and I watched as people stepped around it or kicked it back gingerly before walking on. He was, I realized, trying to start a conversation with the ball. Eventually a few young men walked into the plaza, and they kicked it back when he kicked it to them. They started talking, softly, then sat down, huddled, and talked for a long time. It was a reminder that if sport can be a metaphor it is always a metaphor for dialogue and exchange, for passing to and passing back, making something out of the motion and response. And that within it is both conflict and reconciliation and an eternal return to the next round, when things might turn out differently.

NOTES

PREFACE

1. *The Great Match,* directed by Gerardo Olivares (Film Movement 2006).

2. Uroš Zupan, "Beauty Is Nothing but the Beginning of a Terror We Can Hardly Bear," in *The Global Game: Writers on Soccer,* ed. John Turnbull, Thom Satterlee, and Alon Raab (Lincoln: University of Nebraska Press, 2008), 172–81, quote p. 181.

3. Ian Frazier, "Personal History: Snook, the Fish of Dreams," *New Yorker,* 30 October 2006, 54–61, quote p. 54. Frazier was writing about an unrelated issue—fishing, not football—but his phrase is apt.

4. Michel Denisot, "Une sorte de code d'honneur," *L'Equipe,* 13 July 2006, 3.

INTRODUCTION

1. Frédéric Lohézic, *Zinedine Zidane: Respect!* (Paris: Michel Lafon, 2006), 29; Mohand Ouahrani, *La France tout un monde: Portraits multicolores* (Paris: Le Cherche Midi, 2002), 11.

2. For a detailed description of the events, see Jim House and Neil MacMaster, *Paris 1961: Algerians, State Terror, and Memory* (Oxford: Oxford University Press, 2006), chap. 4; on the memory of the event, see chaps. 9–12.

3. Jean Eskenazi, "Eloge et universalité du football," in *Le Football,* ed. Jules Rimet, vol. 2 (Monte Carlo, Monaco: Union Européenne d'Editions, 1954), 263–69, quote p. 263. Unless otherwise noted, all translations from the French are my own.

4. I draw here on the parallel reflections of C. L. R. James on cricket: "The dramatist ... may or may not succeed." But the cricket player, James writes, literally becomes his side for a moment in the game, so capturing "the fundamental relation of the One and the Many, Individual and Social, Individual and Universal, leader and followers, representative and ranks, the part and the whole." C. L. R. James, *Beyond a Boundary* (1963; reprint, Durham, NC: Duke University Press, 1993), 196.

5. Alastair Reid, "The World Cup," *New Yorker*, 10 September 1966, 152–97, quote p. 170.

6. I draw here on the brilliant work of Christian Bromberger, "Football as World-View and as Ritual," *French Cultural Studies* 6 (1995): 293–311, and Christian Bromberger, Alain Hayot, and Mario Mariotini, *Le match de football: Ethnologie d'une passion partisane à Marseille, Naples, et Turin* (Paris: Maison des Sciences de l'Homme, 1995), quote p. 96.

7. Bromberger, "Football as World-View," 297.

8. Pierre Clanché, "Football, instabilité, et passion," in *Le spectacle du sport*, ed. Bernard Leconte and Georges Vigarello (Paris: Seuil, 1998), 9–23, quote p. 10.

9. Anne Delbée, *La 107e minute* (Paris: Quatre Chemins, 2006), 8–9; Lilian Thuram, *Le 9 Juillet 1998* (Paris: Anne-Carrière, 2004), 71.

10. Joan Tumblety, "The Soccer World Cup of 1938: Politics, Spectacles and la Culture Physique in Interwar France," *French Historical Studies* 31, no. 1 (Winter 2008), 77–116, quote p. 99. On Rimet's vision in broader context, see Bill Murray, *The World's Game: A History of Soccer* (Urbana: University of Illinois Press, 1998), and John Sugden and Alan Tomlinson, *FIFA and the Contest for World Football: Who Rules the Peoples' Game?* (Cambridge, U.K.: Polity Press, 1998).

11. Simon Kuper, *Soccer against the Enemy: How the World's Most Popular Sport Starts and Fuels Revolutions and Keeps Dictators in Power* (1994; reprint, New York: Nation Books, 2006), 1; Franklin Foer, *How Soccer Explains the World: An (Unlikely) Theory of Globalization* (New York: Harper Collins, 2004).

12. James, *Beyond a Boundary*, 65–66, 115, 196; Youcef Fatès, *Sport et tiers-monde* (Paris: Presses Universitaires de France, 1994), 15; Anthony Lane, "The Only Game in Town: Week One at the Olympics," *New Yorker*, 25 August 2008, 26–30, quote p. 30.

13. Writing about the legacies of empire in contemporary France and its "soul-trying ambivalence about its cultural identity," the historian Herman Lebovics argues that an analysis of football matches can "tell us more about the state of the national soul at the end of the century than a whole year" of the leading magazines and newspapers can; see Herman Lebovics, *Bringing the Empire Back Home: France in the Global Age* (Durham, NC: Duke University Press, 2004), 136.

14. Didier Braun, "L'équipe de France de football, c'est l'histoire en raccourci d'un siècle d'immigration," *Hommes et Migrations* 1226 (July–August 2000): 50–56; Xavier Béal, "Football et immigration: Les figures de Kopa, Platini, Zidane dans les médias," http://www.wearefootball.org (accessed 15 July 2008). On immigration, see the classic work of Gérard Noiriel, originally published in 1988 and translated as *The French Melting Pot: Immigration, Citizenship, and National Identity*, trans. Geoffroy de Laforcade (Minneapolis: University of Minnesota Press, 1996), and the work of Patrick Weil, *La France et ses étrangers: L'aventure d'une politique d'immigration, 1938–1991* (Paris: Calmann-Lévy, 1991). The best

study of Algerian immigration is Abdelmalek Sayad, *La Double absence: Des illusions de l'émigré aux souffrances de l'immigré* (Paris: Seuil, 1999).

15. Gary Wilder, *The French Imperial Nation-State: Negritude and Colonial Humanism between the Two World Wars* (Chicago: University of Chicago Press, 2005).

16. I present this argument in detail in my book *A Colony of Citizens: Revolution and Slave Emancipation in the French Caribbean, 1787–1804* (Chapel Hill: University of North Carolina Press, 2004). For a recent work emphasizing the impact of Algerian decolonization on France, see Todd Shepard, *The Invention of Decolonization: The Algerian War and the Remaking of France* (Ithaca, NY: Cornell University Press, 2006); on the early-twentieth-century activism of Caribbean and African students, see Wilder, *French Imperial Nation-State;* on the impact of colonialism and decolonization in France, see Kristen Ross, *Fast Cars, Clean Bodies: Decolonization and the Reordering of French Culture* (Cambridge, MA: M.I.T. Press, 1996), and Lebovics, *Bringing the Empire.*

17. Nacira Guénif-Souilamas, "Zidane: Portrait of the Artist as a Political Avatar," in *Frenchness in the African Diaspora: Postcolonial Strategies of Containment in Contemporary France,* ed. P. Bloom. D. Gondola, and C. Kassama-Tshimanga (Bloomington: Indiana University Press, forthcoming); Franck Baetens, "Le coup de tête de Zidane: Pour une lecture mythologique," *Esprit,* November 2007, 127–47, quote p. 129.

18. David Goldblatt, *The Ball Is Round: A Global History of Soccer* (New York: Riverhead Books, 2006), 5–12.

19. James Walvin, *The People's Game: The History of Football Revisited* (1975; reprint, London: Mainstream Publishing, 1994), 14, 27.

20. Murray, *World's Game,* 1–7; Walvin, *People's Game,* 41–44.

21. On the spread of football through empire, see the classic work of Allen Guttman, *Games and Empires: Modern Sports and Cultural Imperialism* (New York: Columbia University Press, 1994), especially chapter 2.

22. David Sharp, "Jules Rimet's Bananas," *The Lancet* 367 (13 May 2006): 1561–62; Herbert Lottman, *Albert Camus: A Biography* (New York: Doubleday, 1979), 39.

23. Lottman, *Camus,* 40.

24. Roger Chartier, preface to Norbert Elias and Eric Dunning, *Sport et civilization: La violence maitrisée* (Paris: Fayard, 1936), 15.

25. For an analysis of such exclusions in the case of Brazil, see Derek Pardue, "Jogada Linguistica: Discursive Play and the Hegemonic Force of Soccer in Brazil," *Journal of Sport and Social Issues* 26, no. 2 (November 2002): 360–80. On football and the construction of masculinity, see Edouardo Archetti, *Masculinities: Football, Polo and Tango in Argentina* (London: Berg Press, 1999) and Roger Magazine, *Golden and Blue Like My Heart: Masculinity, Youth and Power among Soccer Fans in Mexico City* (Phoenix: University of Arizona Press, 2007).

26. Robert Redeker, *Le sport contre les peuples* (Paris: Berg International, 2002), 54, 68, 86, 117.

27. James, *Beyond a Boundary*, 153, 249–50.

28. Edouardo Galeano, *Soccer in Sun and Shadow*, trans. Mark Fried (1998; reprint, London: Verso, 2003), 209; James, *Beyond a Boundary*, 250.

29. Grant Farred, *Long-Distance Love: A Passion for Football* (Philadelphia: Temple University Press, 2008), 8, 15. For an excellent analysis of the intersection of sport and politics in one context, see Peter Alegi, *Ladluma! Soccer, Politics and Society in South Africa* (Pietermaritzburg: University of KwaZulu-Natal Press, 2004).

30. Nick Hornby, *Fever Pitch* (New York: Riverhead Books, 1992), 192; B.S. Johnson, *The Unfortunates* (1969; reprint, New York: New Directions, 2008). The quote is from Johnson and comes at the beginning of one of his chapters, which are unnumbered and unordered in the book, which is composed of independently bound segments.

31. Farred, *Long-Distance Love*, 150.

32. James, *Beyond a Boundary*, 153, 249–50; Zupan, "Beauty Is Nothing but the Beginning of a Terror We Can Hardly Bear," 181; "Défendre et interroger," interview with Lilian Thuram by Achille Mbembe, 26 July 2006, at http://www.africultures .com/index.asp?menu=affiche_article&no=454226 (accessed 8 August 2006); an English translation of the interview was published in *Chimurenga* 10 (2006): 235–37.

ONE. A BEAUTIFUL HARVEST

1. Jamie Treckler, *Love and Blood: At the World Cup with the Footballers, Fans, and Freaks* (New York: Harcourt, 2007), 6.

2. On the early history of F.I.F.A., see John Sugden and Alan Tomlinson, *FIFA and the Contest for World Football: Who Rules the Peoples' Game?* (Cambridge, U.K.: Polity Press, 1998), 60–61.

3. The photograph is reproduced in Jean-Yves Guillain, *Le Coupe du Monde de Football: L'ouevre de Jules Rimet* (Paris: Amphora, 1998), 35. It is in the collection of Yves Rimet, and the soldiers are described as being part of the 201st Brigade of the 223rd Regiment territorial d'infanterie.

4. Richard S. Fogarty, *Race and War in France: Colonial Subjects in the French Army, 1914–1918* (Baltimore: Johns Hopkins University Press, 2008), 7, 15, 27; Gregory Mann, *Native Sons: West African Veterans and France in the Twentieth Century* (Durham, NC: Duke University Press, 2006), 16–17, 63.

5. Fogarty, *Race and War*, 1.

6. Ibid., 29, 34.

7. I thank Richard Fogarty, Jean Hébrard, Gregory Mann, and Adriane Lentz-Smith for their suggestions about the possible origins of the soldiers in the photo-

graph with Rimet. See Arthur Barbeau and Florette Henri, *The Unknown Soldiers: Black American Troops in World War I* (Philadelphia: Temple University Press, 1974), 113–15.

8. Guillain, *Jules Rimet*, 13–34; James Walvin, *The People's Game. The History of Football Revisited* (London: Mainstream Publishing, 1994), 98; Bill Murray, *The World's Game: A History of Soccer* (Urbana: University of Illinois Press, 1998), 24.

9. Raid Hamrouchi, "L'Intelligentsia du certificat d'etude: Emergence d'une class moyenne musulmane dans l'Algérie coloniale? Le cas d'une famille du nord-est consantinois" (Master's thesis, Ecole des Hautes Etudes en Sciences Sociales, 2008), 39. On the spread of football in Africa, see Nicolas Bancel and Jean-Marc Gayman, *Du guerrier à l'athlète: Eléments d'histoire des pratiques corporelles* (Paris: Presses Universitaires de France, 2002); Bernadette Deville-Danthu, *Le sport en noire et blanc: Du sport colonial au sport africain dans les anciens territories français d'Afrique occidentale (1920–1965)* (Paris: Harmattan, 1997); Bernadette Deville-Danthu, "Note sur l'histoire du sport dans l'empire français" and "Les Jeux d'Outre-Mer," in *L'Empire du Sport*, ed. Pierre Arnaud et al. (Aix-en-Provence: Amaron, 1992), 11–13, 61–68. The parallel process of the spread of sport in the British Empire has been the subject of excellent studies. See, for example, the introduction and essays in J. A. Mangan, ed., *The Cultural Bond: Sport, Empire, Society* (London: Frank Cass, 1992).

10. Pierre de Coubertin, "Les sports et la colonisation," in *Essais de psychologie sportive* (Paris: Payot, 1913), 233–41, 234–37.

11. Murray, *World's Game*, 8, 43–44; Alfred Wahl, "Football et Jeux de Ballon," in *L'Empire du Sport*, ed. Arnaud et al., 44–45, 44.

12. Joan Tumblety, "The Soccer World Cup of 1938: Politics, Spectacles, and la Culture Physique in Interwar France," *French Historical Studies* 31, no. 1 (Winter 2008): 77–116, especially 86–94; Guillain, *Jules Rimet*, 33; Nicholas Ksss, "Football et société en région parisienne: Une histoire sociale du football ouvrier," http://www.wearefootball.org/dossier/80/lire/le-football-ouvrier-en-region-parisienne (accessed 2 February 2009).

13. Guillain, *Jules Rimet*, 28, 112; Murray, *World's Game*, 38; Sugden and Tomlinson, *FIFA*, 60–61.

14. Guillain, *Jules Rimet*, 45–46; Edouardo Galeano, *Soccer in Sun and Shadow* (1998; reprint, New York: Verso Press, 2003), 44–47; Franklin Morales, *Andrade: El rey negro de Paris* (Montevideo, Uruguay: Editorial Fin de Siglo, 2002).

15. See Tony Mason, *Passion of the People? Football in South America* (London: Verso, 1995), chaps. 1–3, quote p. 27; Murray, *World's Game*, 32–36; Sugden and Tomlinson, *FIFA*, 22.

16. Guillain, *Jules Rimet*, 47–61.

17. Murray, *World's Game*, 68–69; Tumblety, "Soccer World Cup of 1938," 78, 99, 111–12; Sugden and Tomlinson, *FIFA*, 102.

18. Yvan Gastaut, "Le football français à l'épreuve de la diversité culturelle," in *Le football dans nos sociétés: Une culture populaire, 1914–1998,* ed. Yvan Gastaut and Stéphane Mourlane (Paris: Editions Autrement, 2006), 218–36, 219–20.

19. Didier Braun, "L'équipe de France de football, c'est l'histoire en raccourci d'un siècle d'immigration," *Hommes et Migrations,* 1226 (July-August 2000): 50–56, quote pp. 51–52; Lucien Jasseron and Bernard Dubreuil, "Le Football en Afrique du Nord," in *Le Football,* vol. 2, ed. Jules Rimet (Monaco: Union Européenne d'Editions, 1954), 63; on Ignace Kowalczyk, see http://fr.wikipedia.org/wiki/Ignace_Kowalczyk (accessed 10 October 2008) and his F.F.F. fact sheet at http://www.fff.fr (accessed 22 September 2009); Jacques Chauvenet, *Larbi Ben Barek: La légende de 'La Perle Noire'* (Toulon: Les Presses du Midi, 1994), 23; http://fr.wikipedia.org/wiki/Mario_Zatelli (accessed 10 October 2008); Pierre Lanfranchi and Matthew Taylor, *Moving with the Ball: The Migration of Professional Footballers* (Oxford: Berg, 2001), 172–73; "Abdelkader Ben Bouali," http://fr.wikipedia.org/wiki/Abdelkader_Ben_Bouali, and "Ali Benouna," http://fr.wikipedia.org/wiki/Ali_Benouna (both accessed 8 June 2008). See also Ben Bouali's and Benouna's fact sheets at http://www.fff.fr. On the players of this period, see also Dominique Grimault, *Les Bleus: La grande histoire de l'Equipe de France* (Paris: Solar, 1998), 141–144.

20. G. Wesley Johnson, "The Ascendancy of Blaise Diagne and the Beginning of African Politics in Senegal," *Africa: Journal of the International African Institute* 36, no. 3 (July 1966): 235–53.

21. Ibid., 247–48. For an overview of voting rights in the French Empire, see Rudolph A. Winnaker, "Elections in Algeria and the French Colonies under the Third Republic," *American Political Science Review* 32, no. 2 (April 1938): 261–77, especially 263–65. On the political rights of residents of the *quatres communes* and Senegal more broadly, see Catherine Coquery-Vidrovitch, "Nationalité et citoyenneté en Afrique occidentale français: Originaires et Citoyens dans le Sénégal Colonial," *Journal of African History* 42 (2001): 285–305, and Alice Conklin, *A Mission to Civilize: The Republican Idea of Empire in France and West Africa, 1895–1930* (Stanford: Stanford University Press, 1997). For an overview of voting rights in Algeria, which were partially extended in 1919, see Todd Shephard, *The Invention of Decolonization: The Algerian War and the Remaking of France* (Ithaca, NY: Cornell University Press, 2006), chap 1.

22. Conklin, *Mission to Civilize,* 155–58; Fogarty, *Race and War,* 4, 51; Mann, *Native Sons,* 68–69; Coquery-Vidrovitch, "Nationalité," 290; W. E. B. DuBois, "The Negro Mind Reaches Out," *Foreign Affairs* 3, no. 3 (April 1925), reprinted in Alain Locke, ed., *The New Negro* (1925; reprint, New York: Atheneum, 1969), 385–414, quote pp. 396–97.

23. Julien Sorez, "Raoul Diagne," in P. Clastres and P. Dietschy, *Dictionnaire historique du sport français* (Paris: Nouveau Monde éditions, forthcoming). My

thanks to Sorez for sharing his unpublished manuscript with me. See also Murray, *World's Game*, 79.

24. Sorez, "Raoul Diagne"; Shephard, *Invention*, 14.

25. Jacques Chauvenet, "La fabuleuse carrière de 'La perle noire,'" and Mario Zatelli, "Larbi avait du talent et du génie," in Chauvenet, *Larbi Ben Barek*, 2–4, 23; Lanfranchi and Taylor, *Moving*, 173.

26. Bancel and Gayman, *Guerrier*, 332; Deville-Danthu, "Note sur l'histoire," 12.

27. Paul Darby, "Football, Colonial Doctrine and Indigenous Resistance: Mapping the Political Persona of FIFA's African Constituency," *Culture, Sport and Society* 3, no. 1 (Spring 2000): 61–87, quote pp. 64–65; Paul Darby, *Africa, Football and FIFA: Politics, Colonialism and Resistance* (London: Frank Cass, 2002), chap. 1, especially 10–15; Lanfranchi and Taylor, *Moving*, 170.

28. Arnaud et al., *Empire du Sport*, 54–55, documents 96 and 100.

29. For the numbers of players, see Deville-Danthu, "Note sur l'histoire," 12; Arnaud et al., *Empire du Sport*, 47, document 76.

30. Wahl, "Football et Jeux de Ballon," 44–45, quote p. 44; Bancel and Gayman, *Guerrier*, 338–41.

31. Didier Rey, "Le temps des circulaires ou les contradictions du football colonial en Algérie (1928–1945)," http://www.wearefootball.org/dossiers/53/lire/le-football-colonial/ (accessed 20 July 2008), 1; Lanfranchi and Taylor, *Moving*, 172; Paul Dietschy, Yvan Gastaut, and Stéphane Mourlane, *Histoire politique des coupes du monde de football* (Paris: Vuibert, 2006), 300–301. For excellent studies of the link between sport, social life, and politics, see Phyllis Martin, *Leisure and Society in Colonial Brazzaville* (Cambridge, U.K.: Cambridge University Press, 1995), chap. 4, and Laura Fair, "Kickin' It: Leisure, Politics and Football in Colonial Zanzibar, 1900s-1950s," *Africa* 67, no. 2 (1997): 224–51.

32. Rey, "Le temps des circulaires," 2; Mahmoud Amara and Ian Henry, "Between Globalization and Local 'Modernity' The Diffusion and Modernization of Football in Algeria," *Soccer and Society* 5, no. 1 (Spring 2004): 1–26, quote p. 6; Fatès, *Sport et tiers-monde*, 32.

33. Lanfranchi and Taylor, *Moving*, 172; Jasseron and Dubreuil, "Le Football en Afrique du Nord," 63.

34. Arnaud et al., *L'Empire du sport*, 41, documents 62 and 63; Félix Eboué, "Le sport en Afrique équatoriale," *Le Monde colonial illustré* 103 (March 1932): 60–61; see also Jacques Dumont, *Sport et assimilation à la Guadeloupe: Les enjeux du corps performant de la colonie au département (1914–1965)* (Paris: L'Harmattan, 2002), 145–46.

35. Arnaud et al., *L'Empire du sport*, 40; Dumont, *Sport et assimilation*, 175.

36. These numbers are calculated from Marc Barreaud, *Dictionnaire des footballeurs étrangers du championnat professionnel français (1932–1997)* (Paris: L'Harmattan, 1998). For the *France Football* statistic, see Dumont, *Sport et assimilation*, 370; for the 1960 numbers, see Lanfranchi and Taylor, *Moving* 174.

37. Lanfranchi and Taylor, *Moving,* 173, 176; Tumblety, "Soccer World Cup of 1938," 104; Chauvenet, *Larbi Ben Barek,* 4. See also Ben Barek's page at http://www.fff.fr and http://fr.wikipedia.org/wiki/Larbi_Benbarek (accessed 30 May 2008).

38. Guillain, *Rimet,* 103.

39. Ibid., 111–13.

40. Tumblety, "Soccer World Cup of 1938," 106.

41. Lanfranchi and Taylor, *Moving,* 173; Braun, "L'Equipe de France," 54.

42. Pierre Lanfranchi and Alfred Wahl, "The Immigrant as Hero: Kopa, Mekloufi, and French Football," in *European Heroes: Myth, Identity, and Sport,* ed. Richard Holt, J. A. Mangan, and Pierre Lanfranchi (London: Frank Cass, 1996), 114–28, quotes pp. 117–18.

43. See Youcef Fatès, *Sport et tiers-monde* (Paris: Presses Universitaires de France, 1994), 34; Grimault, *Les Bleus,* 37, 48; Just Fontaine, interview by Roger Dries, in Chauvenet, *Larbi Ben Barek,* 20. See also http://fr.wikipedia.org/wiki/Just_Fontaine (accessed 13 October 2008). On Lamia, see http://www.amicaledes callois.com/persogeorges.htm (accessed 30 May 2008). On Mahjoub, see http://www.fff.fr/servfff/historique/historique.php?id=MAHJOUB%20Abderrahman; http://en.wikipedia.org/wiki/Abderrahmane_Mahjoub (both accessed 4 August 2008).

44. For studies of how football is used to discuss national characteristics, see David Winner, *Brilliant Orange: The Neurotic Genius of Dutch Soccer* (2001; reprint, New York: Overlook Press, 2008); Edouardo Archetti, *Masculinities: Football, Polo and Tango in Argentina* (London: Berg Press, 1999); Alex Belos, *Futebol: Soccer, the Brazilian Way* (London: Bloomsbury, 2003); Edison Luis Gastaldo and Simoni Lahud Guedes, eds., *Nações em Campo: Copa do Mundo y identidade nacional* (Niteról, Brazil: Intertexto, 2006).

45. Darby, "Colonial Doctrine," 61, 70.

46. Raffaele Poli and Paul Dietschy, "Le football africain entre immobilisme et extraversion," *Politique Africaine* 102 (June 2006): 173–87, quotes pp. 176–79.

47. Darby, "Colonial Doctrine," 73; Alan Tomlinson, "FIFA and the Men Who Made It," *Soccer and Society* 1, no. 1 (Spring 2000): 55–71, quote p. 58; Poli and Dietschy, "Football africain," 177.

48. Murray, *World's Game,* 129–31; Sugden and Tomlinson, *FIFA,* chaps. 2–4, especially p. 133; Tomlinson, "FIFA," 61–66.

49. Geoff Hare, *Football in France: A Cultural History* (Oxford: Berg Press, 2003), 179; Poli and Dietschy, "Football africain," 180.

50. Poli and Dietschy, "Football africain," 179, 182. See also Raffaele Poli, "Conflit de couleurs: Enjeux géopolitiques autour de la naturalization de sportifs africains," *Autrepart* 37 (2006): 149–61.

51. Raffaele Poli, "Football Players' Migration in Europe: A Geo-Economic Approach to Africans' Mobility" in *The Bountiful Game? Football Identities and*

Finances, ed. Jonathan Magee, Alain Bairner, and Alan Tomlinson (Aachen, Germany: Meyer and Meyer Sport, 2005), 217–32, quote p. 231; Poli and Dietschy, "Football africain," 181; Evariste Tshimanga Bakadiababu, *Le commerce et la traite des footballeurs africains et sud-américains en Europe* (Paris: L'Harmattan, 2001); Paul Darby, "The New Scramble for Africa: African Football Labour Migration to Europe," in *Europe, Sport, World: Shaping Global Societies,* ed. Joseph Mangan (London: Frank Cass, 2001), 217–44.

52. Poli, "Migration," 128; Raffaele Poli, "Les professionnels africains dans les clubs suisses de football," in *Suisse–Afrique (18e–20e siècles): De la traite des Noirs à la fin du régime de l'apartheid,* ed. S. Bott, T. David, C. Lutze schwab, and J. M. Schaufelbuehl (Munster, Germany: LIT, 2005), 283–96, quote p. 294; Raffaele Poli, "Des migrants a qualifier: Les footballeurs africains dans quatre pays europeens," in *La mobilité internationale des compétences: Situations récentes, approches nouvelles,* ed. M. Nedelcu (Paris: L'Harmattan 2004), 143–64. For publicized cases, see Gastaut, "Football français," 228–29. Poli, "Football africain," 187 n. 37; "Un footballeur de FC Bourgoin expulsé," *Le Progrès,* 26 September 2007, http://www.footsolidaire.org (accessed 6 November 2008). This website provides information about the mission and activities of M'voumin's organization.

53. *Bamako,* directed by Abderrahmane Sissako (New Yorker Video, 2008); *The Great Match,* directed by Gerardo Olivares (Film Movement, 2006); *Paradise—Three Journeys in This World,* directed by Elina Hirvonen (2008).

54. *Le Ballon d'Or,* directed by Cheik Doukoure (Studio Canal, 1994); http://en.wikipedia.org/wiki/Salif_Keita_(footballer) (accessed 14 September 2008).

TWO. CARIBBEAN FRANCE

1. Marius Trésor, "Sacré Marius" (Carrère Records, 1978); "Représentant les Antilles-Guyane: La Juventus de Sainte-Anne (Guadeloupe) disputera le 6e tour de la Coupe de France," *L'Equipe,* 12 September 1964, clipping in Ministère des Jeunesse et des Sports (hereafter MJS), 790358, folder 5, Centre des Archives Contemporaines (hereafter CAC); Marc Beaugé, "Trésor: L'apport des Antilles est immense," *France-Antilles,* Fort-de-France edition, no. 11644, 9 November 2005, 13; Fernand Pentier, *Ligues et champions de foot-ball, basket-ball, volley-ball, hand-ball* (1983), 10, in Archives Départementales de la Guadeloupe (hereafter ADG), 7J90, Archives de Roger Fortuné (hereafter ARF).

2. Beaugé, "Trésor," 13; http://fr.wikipedia.org/wiki/Marius_Tresor (accessed 8 August 2008); Claude Duneton and Jean-Pierre Fagliano, *Anti-Manuel de Français: A l'usage de classes du second degré, et de quelques autres* (Paris: Seuil, 1978), 224–27; Trésor, "Sacré Marius."

3. Beaugé, "Trésor," 13; "Ave Marius," *France Football,* 9 November 1982, 2–4; http://fr.wikipedia.org/wiki/Marius_Tresor (accessed 8 August 2008).

4. Jean-Yves Guérin and Laurent Jaoui, *Noirs en bleu: Le football est-il raciste?* (Paris: Anne Carrière, 2008), 59; Marianne Mako, *Ces hommes en bleu: 30 vies en confidences* (Paris: Hachette, 1998), 187; Beaugé, "Trésor," 13.

5. Beaugé, "Trésor," 13; Marc Beaugé, Yohann Hautbois, and Alexis Menuge, "Quatre Bleus refont l'histoire," interview with Steve Marlet, Luc Sonor, Gérard Janvion, and Jocelyn Angloma, *France-Antilles,* Fort-de-France edition, no. 11644, 9 November 2005, 14. See also the Wikipedia articles on Marius Trésor, Gérard Janvion, Luc Sonor, and Jocelyn Angloma (accessed 8 August 2008); and more generally http://www.antilles-foot.com for news and interviews with Antillean footballers.

6. Institut National de l'Audiovisuel (hereafter INA), France 2, Journal de 20 heures, 5 July 2006; C. L. R. James, *Beyond a Boundary* (1963; reprint, Durham, NC: Duke University Press, 1993), 233, 238.

7. *Entre les murs,* directed by Laurent Cantet (Canal+, 2008).

8. Jacques Dumont, *Sport et assimilation à la Guadeloupe: Les enjeux du corps performant de la colonie au département (1914–1965)* (Paris: L'Harmattan, 2002), chap. 1; Léopold Camicas, "Nécrologie M. Guy Saint-Clément," *France-Antilles,* Pointe-à-Pitre edition, no. 4879, 15 May 1986, and letter from Suzette Fortuné to Camicas, 16 May 1986, both in ADG, ARF.

9. Dumont, *Sport et assimilation,* chap 1.

10. Ibid., 26, 32–33; Fred Constant, preface to Jacques Dumont, *Sport et formation de la jeunesse à la Martinique: Le temps des pionniers (fin XIXè siècle–années 1960)* (Paris: L'Harmattan, 2006), 8; James Ferguson, *World Class: An Illustrated History of Caribbean Football* (Oxford: Macmillan Caribbean, 2006), ix.

11. Dumont, *Sport et formation,* 36–39, 46, 50.

12. Ibid., 43, 66, 110.

13. Dumont, *Sport et assimilation,* 65, 109, 112, 117, 121, 145; Philippe Gastaud, "Histoire antillaises," *Outre-Terre* 3, no. 8 (2004): 225–34, quote p. 226; Ferguson, *World Class,* 33. On Chartol, see his statement in Pentier, *Ligues,* 8. For a chronology of sports federations in Guadeloupe, see Fernand Pentier, *La vie du Cygne noir de sa fondation à ce jour* (1963), ADG, ARF, 5–7.

14. Brian Weinstein, *Eboué* (New York: Oxford University Press, 1972), 10–11.

15. Ibid., 17–19.

16. Ibid., 17–19, 24–28, 49–50.

17. Ibid., 86, 92, 99; Phyllis Martin, *Leisure and Society in Colonial Brazzaville* (Cambridge, U.K.: Cambridge University Press, 1995), chap. 4; André Gide, *Voyage au Congo, suivi de Le retour du Tchad: Carnets de route* (1927–28; Paris: Gallimard, 1994), 76–77.

18. See René Maran, *Batouala* (New York: Thomas Seltzer, 1922), 9–10; Weinstein, *Eboué,* 69. On Maran and on "colonial humanism" more broadly, see Gary Wilder, *The French Imperial Nation-State: Negritude and Colonial Humanism*

between the Two Wars (Chicago: University of Chicago Press, 2005), especially 163–65.

19. Weinstein, *Eboué*, 134, 150, 308; Dumont, *Sport et assimilation*, 145, 170; Dumont, *Sport et formation*, 104–5.

20. Dumont, *Sport et formation*, 162. Despite the similarity in name, the French colony of Soudan is not the same as present-day Sudan, corresponding instead to contemporary Mali.

21. Weinstein, *Eboué*, 163; Gastaud, "Histoire antillaises," 227; Dumont, *Sport et assimilation*, 159–60, 165, 166, 170, 172. On Popular Front approaches to sport, see Pascal Ory, *La belle illusion: Culture et Politique sous le signe du Front Populaire, 1935–1938* (Paris: Plon, 1994), chap. 12.

22. Pentier, *Cygne Noir*, 5–6, 13.

23. Dumont, *Sport et assimilation*, 159–60, 166.

24. Marc Bloch, *Strange Defeat: A Statement of Evidence Written in 1940*, trans. Gerard Hopkins (London: Oxford University Press, 1949), 37.

25. Weinstein, *Eboué*, 233; Eric Jennings, *Vichy in the Tropics: Petain's National Revolution in Madagascar, Guadeloupe and Indochina, 1940–1944* (Stanford: Stanford University Press, 2001), 9.

26. Jennings, *Vichy*, 11–12.

27. Gregory Mann, *Native Sons: West African Veterans and France in the Twentieth Century* (Durham, NC: Duke University Press, 2006), 18; Weinstein, *Eboué*, 248–51, 299.

28. Weinstein, *Eboué*, 299, 302. For a critique of the reforms, see Frederick Cooper, *Decolonization and African Societies: The Labor Question in French and British Africa* (Cambridge, U.K.: Cambridge University Press, 1996), 157–58. On the stadium, see Martin, *Leisure*, chap. 4.

29. Jennings, *Vichy*, 84–124; Dumont, *Sport et formation*, 157.

30. Jennings, *Vichy*, 119, 122, 123, 126–27.

31. Weinstein, *Eboué*, 290–91; Jennings, *Vichy*, 124–25.

32. Jennings, *Vichy*, 125–27; Dumont, *Sport et assimilation*, 205.

33. Weinstein, *Eboué*, 310–17; *L'U.S.B.T. fête le 14 Juillet 1945, date anniversaire de la Prise de la Bastille et de la Libération des Antilles françaises* (1945), ADG, ARF. A commemoration of Eboué's death was organized two years later, in 1947, at the Eboué stadium; see Fernard Pentier and Bettino Lara, *Cinquentenaire de l'Union sportive Basse-Terrienne, 1933–1983* (1983), ADG, ARF.

34. Dumont, *Sport et assimilation*, 292–94, 304; Fernand Pentier, *La Trophée Caraïbe* (1984), ADG, ARF.

35. Dumont, *Sport et assimilation*, 305.

36. Ibid., 316–17.

37. Ibid., 318–19.

38. Pierre Lanfranchi and Matthew Taylor, *Moving with the Ball: The Migra-*

tion of *Professional Footballers* (Oxford: Berg, 2001), 176; Vikash Dhorasoo and Stéphane Régy, "Gattuso," *So Foot* 56 (June–July 2008): 30–36, 34.

39. Dumont, *Sport et assimilation,* 318–319. On Ninel, see http://fr.wikipedia .org/wiki/Camille_Ninel (accessed 1 October 2008), and Michel Nait-Challal, *Dribbleurs de l'indépendance: L'incroyable histoire de l'équipe de football du FLN Algérien* (Paris: Editions Prolongations, 2008), photo 1 in insert; Fédération Française de Football to Maurice Herzog, Haut Commissaire à la Jeunesse et aux Sports, 15 December 1961, MJS, 790358, folder 2, CAC; R. G. Nicolo to F.F.F. President, 27 August 1964, MJS, 790358, folder 3, CAC. On Nicolo's biography, see http://www.africamaat.com/Georges-Nicolo-un-grand-savant (accessed 8 August 2008); Beaugé, "Trésor."

40. Alfred Wahl, "Football et Jeux de Ballon," in *L'Empire du Sport,* ed. Pierre Arnaud et al. (Aix-en-Provence: Amarom, 1992), 44–45; Gastaud, "Histoire antillaises," 229; Pentier, *Cygne Noir,* 5–7.

41. Dumont, *Sport et assimilation,* 368–69; Chronology of departments and territories in the French Cup, September 1972, "Coupe de France de Football: Department et territories d'Outre-mer," MJS 790358, folder 1, CAC. On the Ministry of Youth and Sports, see Lindsay Krasnoff, "Goals and Dreams: The Quest to Create Elite Youth Athletes in France, 1958–1992" (Ph.D. diss., CUNY Graduate Center, 2009), chap. 4.

42. "Annexe III, Coupe de France de Football," unsigned note received 13 June 1963, MJS, 790358, folder 1, CAC; "L'Outre-Mer en Coupe," *France Football,* 7 September 1970, clipping in MJS, 790358, folder 9, CAC.

43. Ligue de Football de la Martinique to Minister of Youth and Sports, 31 July 1967, CAC 790358, folder 6; Prefect of Guadeloupe to Minister of Youth and Sports, 13 September 1967, MJS, 790358, folder 6, CAC.

44. On the events of 1967, see Raymond Gama and Jean-Pierre Sainton, *"Mé 67": Mémoire d'un événement* (Pointe-à-Pitre, Guadeloupe: Soged, 1985).

45. Dumont, *Sport et assimilation,* 371–72.

46. Gastaud, "Histoires antillaises," 4.

47. Pentier and Lara, *Cinquentenaire,* ADG, ARF; Dunières Talis, *Les problèmes du développement du sport à la Guadeloupe* (1973), ADG, ARG. The Talis pamphlet presents extracts from *l'Etincelle,* the newspaper of the Communist Party in Guadeloupe.

48. Dumont, *Sport et assimilation,* 370.

49. Fred Reno, "Equipe de France ou équipe des Antilles? Le sport de haut niveau comme espace d'identification multiple," *Outre-Terre* 3, no. 8 (2004): 235–47, quote pp. 237–38; Dumont, *Sport et assimilation,* 384.

50. Wahl, "Football et Jeux de Ballon," 45; Dumont, *Sport et formation,* 15; Dumont, *Sport et assimilation,* 390.

51. Pentier, *Trophée,* 15–16, ADG, ARF. See also http://www.concacaf.com; http://en.wikipedia.org/wiki/Martinique_national_football_team, and http://

en.wikipedia.org/wiki/Guadeloupe_regional_football_team (both accessed 23 September 2008).

52. Beaugé, "Trésor," 13; Beaugé, Hautbois, and Menuge, "Quatre Bleus refont l'histoire."

53. Patrick Dessault, "Thierry Henry: La France au cœur des Antilles," *France-Antilles*, Fort-de-France edition, no. 11644, 9 November 2005, 12.

THREE. CROSSINGS

1. Patrick Demerin, "Seville," *Autrement* 8c (May 1986): 120–25, quote p. 124.

2. Dominique Grimault, *Les Bleus: Le livre officiel de l'équipe de France* (Paris: Solar, 1998), 51; Jean Tigana and Rodolph Hassold, *Jean Tigana: L'enfant de la balle* (Paris: Calmann-Lévy, 1982), 104.

3. Didier Braun, "L'équipe de France de football, c'est l'histoire en raccourci d'un siècle d'immigration," *Hommes et Migrations* 1226 (July–August 2000): 50–56, quote p. 55.

4. Grimault, *Bleus*, 63, 72, 88–89; Tigana and Hassold, *Jean Tigana*, 12, 15, 20.

5. Tigana and Hassold, *Jean Tigana*, 116–17, 124.

6. Geoff Hare, *Football in France: A Cultural History* (Oxford: Berg, 2003), 143; Institut National de l'Audiovisuel (hereafter INA), "Le Club du mondial: Au cœur de la Coupe," FR 3 (France 3 television station), 9 July 1998.

7. Hare, *Football in France*, 143. My thanks to the historian Jean-Pierre Sainton, who recalled the worries of Antillean fans regarding Trésor.

8. Michel Platini and Patrick Mahé, *Ma vie comme un match* (Paris: Editions Robert Laffont, 1987), 199–203.

9. Annie Collovald, "Des désordres sociaux à la violence urbaine," *Actes de la recherche en sciences sociales* 136–37 (March 2001): 104–13, quote p. 104 n. 6; Mustafa Dikeç, *Badlands of the Republic: Space, Politics and Urban Policy* (London: Blackwell, 2007), 40–48.

10. Hare, *Football in France*, 133; Demerin, "Séville."

11. Braun, "L'Equipe de France," 55–56.

12. "Les nouveaux-nés de l'année," *France-Antilles*, Pointe-à-Pitre edition, no. 987, 3 January 1972, p. 8; Lilian Thuram, *Le 8 Juillet 1998* (Paris: Anne-Carrière, 2004), 16.

13. Thuram, *8 Juillet*, 18.

14. Joseph Ghosn and Pierre Siankowski, "La France, le Mondial, Zidane et Moi," *Inrockuptibles* 555 (18–24 July 2006): 29–35, quote p. 31; Mohand Ouahrani, *La France tout un monde: Portraits multicolores* (Paris: Le Cherche Midi, 2002), 17; Thuram, *8 Juillet*, 15, 19.

15. Ghosn and Siankowski, "La France," 31.

16. Thuram, *8 Juillet*, 21.

17. Ibid., 20.

18. Ibid., 22–24.

19. Association Générale des Etudiants Guadeloupéens, *L'Emigration travailleuse Guadeloupéenne en France* (Paris: L'Harmattan, 1978), 5–6. On Antilleans in France, see also Michel Giraud, "Le malheur d'être partis," *Esprit,* February 2007, 49–61.

20. Thuram, *8 Juillet,* 26–30.

21. INA, "Frequenstar: Lilian Thuram," M6, 11 July 1998; "A.N.P.E. (Travailler, c'est trop dur)," Nèg' Marrons, *Rue Case Nègres* (Sony Music, 1997).

22. Paul A. Silverstein and Chantal Tetreault, "Postcolonial Urban Apartheid," 11 June 2006, http://riotsfrance.ssrc.org, 3 (accessed 11 June 2006), 3–4, 9; Dikeç, *Badlands,* chap. 3.

23. Silverstein and Tetreault, "Postcolonial Urban Apartheid," 3–4; Dikeç, *Badlands,* chap. 3; François Maspero, *Roissy-Express: A Journey through the Paris Suburbs* (New York: Norton, 1994); Thuram, *8 Juillet,* 37.

24. Thuram, *8 Juillet,* 33.

25. INA, "Frequenstar: Lilian Thuram," M6, 11 July 1998; Thuram, *8 Juillet,* 36–37.

26. Loïc Wacquant, *Urban Outcasts: A Comparative Sociology of Advanced Marginality* (Cambridge, U.K.: Polity Press, 2008), chaps. 5–7, quote p. 209.

27. Ibid., 206–7. On homicide statistics, see E. G. Krug, K. E. Powell, and L. L. Dahlberg, "Firearm-Related Deaths in the United States and 35 Other High- and Upper-Middle-Income Countries," *International Journal of Epidemiology,* no. 27 (1998): 214–21.

28. Silverstein and Tetreault, "Postcolonial Urban Apartheid," 3; Wacquant, *Urban Outcasts,* chaps. 5–7.

29. Ghosn and Siankowski, "La France," 32.

30. Ouahrani, *Monde,* 17; Marianne Mako on INA, "Le Club du mondial: Au coeur de la Coupe," FR 3, 9 July 1998.

31. Thuram, *8 Juillet,* 33–35.

32. Wacquant, *Urban Outcasts,* 29, 169–74; Thuram, *8 Juillet,* 37, 39–41.

33. Thuram, *8 Juillet,* 31; Ghosn and Siankowski, "La France," 31–32.

34. Thuram, *8 Juillet,* 103–4.

35. INA, "Frequenstar: Lilian Thuram," M6, 11 July 1998; Thuram, *8 Juillet,* 35, 41–43.

36. INA, "Frequenstar: Lilian Thuram," M6, 11 July 1998; Thuram, *8 Juillet,* 43–45.

37. Thuram, *8 Juillet,* 44; Ouahrani, *Monde,* 18. On the *sport-études* sections, which exist at both *collège* and *lycée* (i.e., middle school and high school) levels in France (including one in Martinique), see Hare, *Football in France,* 100.

38. Thuram, *8 Juillet,* 47–50. On the development of specialized sports tracks in French schools during the 1970s, see Lindsay Krasnoff, "Goals and Dreams:

The Quest to Create Elite Youth Athletes in France, 1958–1992" (Ph.D diss., City University of New York Graduate Center, 2009), chap. 6.

39. INA, "Frequenstar: Lilian Thuram," M6, 11 July 1998; Lilian Thuram, preface to Thomté Ryam, *Banlieue noire* (Paris: Présence Africaine, 2006), 7–9.

40. Jean-Philippe Rethacker, "Les Jeunes" in *Le Football*, vol. 1, ed. Jules Rimet (Monaco: Union Européenne d'Editions, 1954), 79–92, quote p 79.

41. Hare, *Football in France*, 25–32.

42. Ibid., 166–71.

43. On the construction of the Stade de France, see Alain Hayot and Manuel Delluc, *Le Stade de France: Théâtre du Football* (Paris: Editions Cercle d'Art, 1998). David Beriss, commenting on H-Net Network on Caribbean Studies, 13 July 2006, described football clubs as "one of the most widespread types of organization among people of Caribbean origin in France." Although it does not focus in detail on football (though its cover is adorned with a photo of Lilian Thuram), Beriss's book *Black Skins, French Voices: Caribbean Ethnicity and Activism in Urban France* (New York: Westview, 2004) provides a detailed analysis of the work of cultural and community groups among French Caribbean populations in metropolitan France. See also Paul Silverstein, "Sporting Faith: Islam, Soccer and the French Nation-State," *Social Text* 65, 18, no. 4 (Winter 2000): 25–53; *La Haine*, directed by Mathieu Kassovitz (Les Productions Lazennec, 1995).

44. Rethacker, "Les Jeunes," 79; Hare, *Football in France*, 101–2, 117. On the creation and functioning of the Centres de formation, see Krasnoff, *Goals*, chap. 6. For a detailed study of state policies surrounding sport in France during the post–World War II period, see Jean-Paul Callède, *Les politiques sportives en France: Elements de sociologie historique* (Paris: Economica, 2000), chap. 5.

45. See "Arrêté du 14 Novembre 2002 approuvant la convertion type de formation de la Fédération française de football," *Journal Officiel de la République*, 23 November 2002, 19385–88, http://www.legifrance.gouv.fr. This law seems to be an updating of standard contracts that had been in place at least since 1984, when a set of new laws regarding the regulation of athletics was put into place. My thanks to Lindsay Krasnoff for sharing this document with me; see her *Goals*, chap. 6, for more details. See also Hare, *Football in France*, 101.

46. Hare, *Football in France*, 104; *Une équipe de rêve*, directed by René Letzgus (Star Production, 2006).

47. Jean-Philippe Rethaker, "Auxerre: The Ultimate Youth Academy," in *Le Foot: Legends of French Football*, ed. Christov Rühn (London: Abacus, 2000), 18–23; P. Tournier and Jean-Philippe Rethaker, *La formation au footballeur: Comment devenir un professionel* (Paris: Amphora, 1999); Hare, *Football in France*, 102.

48. Hare, *Football in France*, 104–5; Rethacker, "Auxerre," 22.

49. Thuram, *8 Juillet*, 48–50, 52, 124.

50. Ouahrani, *Monde*, 17; Thuram, *8 Juillet*, 52–53.

51. Thuram, *8 Juillet*, 53.

52. Ibid., 54–56, 68–69; INA, "Frequenstar: Lilian Thuram," M6, 11 July 1998; INA, TF1 *20 Heures*, 9 July 1998.

53. Anthony King, *The European Ritual: Football in the New Europe* (London: Ashgate, 2003), chap. 5; Marcel Desailly, *Capitaine* (Paris: Stock, 2002), 70.

54. King, *European Ritual*, chap. 6; Hare, *Football in France*, 142, 144–46; Georges Vigarello, *Passion sport: Histoire d'une culture* (Paris: Textuel, 2000), 178.

55. Hare, *Football in France*, 105, 190.

56. Vincent Duluc, "Un défenseur monumental," *L'Equipe*, 2 August 2008, 2; John Foot, *Winning at All Costs: A Scandalous History of Italian Football* (New York: Nation Books, 2006), xxiii; INA, "Frequenstar: Lilian Thuram," M6, 11 July 1998.

FOUR. ROOTS

1. Marcel Desailly, *Capitaine* (Paris: Stock, 2002), 196; Lilian Thuram, *Le 8 Juillet 1998* (Paris: Anne-Carrière, 2004), 127.

2. Desailly, *Capitaine*, 16–19, 346–47.

3. Ibid., 21–27, quote p. 27.

4. Ibid., 194–96.

5. Ian Thomsen, "French Take Their Revenge on Bulgaria," *International Herald Tribune*, 16 June 1996; Desailly, *Capitaine*, 196–97.

6. Desailly, *Capitaine*, 196–98; Yvan Gastaut, *Le métissage par le foot: L'intégration, mais jusqu'où?* (Paris: Autrement, 2008), 24–25; Thomsen, "French Take Their Revenge."

7. Christian Lanier, "Thuram-Desailly fils de Trésor-Adams," *Le Progrès*, 1 July 1998.

8. Thuram, *8 Juillet*, 129, 183, 200; Institut National de l'Audiovisuel (hereafter INA), "Frequenstar: Lilian Thuram," M6, 11 July 1999; Stéphane Meunier, *Les Yeux dans les Bleus* (Paris: Canal +, 1998).

9. Thuram, *8 Juillet*, 195.

10. Jean-Yves Guérin and Laurent Jaoui, *Noirs en bleu: Le football est-il raciste?* (Paris: Anne Carrière, 2008), 241; Gastaut, *Le métissage*, 22–23.

11. Louis Porcher, "Enjeux interculturels," in *Le spectacle du sport*, ed. Bernard Leconte and Georges Vigarello (Paris: Seuil, 1998), 105–17, quote p. 110.

12. Simon Kuper, *Soccer against the Enemy: How the World's Most Popular Sport Starts and Fuels Revolutions and Keeps Dictators in Power* (1994; reprint, New York: Nation Books, 2006), 10.

13. Onyekachi Wambu, "Marcel Desailly and the Second Liberation of Paris, 1998," in *Le Foot: Legends of French Football*, ed. Christov Rühn (London: Abacus, 2000), 268–84, quote p. 274.

14. Dave Hill, *Out of His Skin: The John Barnes Phenomenon* (1989; reprint,

London: When Saturday Comes Books, 2001), 89, 90, 233–39; Grant Farred, *Long Distance Love: A Passion for Football* (Philadelphia: Temple University Press, 2008), 1–2.

15. Les Back, Tim Crabbe, and John Solomos, *The Changing Face of Football: Racism, Identity and Multiculture in the English Game* (London: Berg, 2001), 253–54.

16. Desailly, *Capitaine*, 227; Guérin and Jaoui, *Noirs en bleu*, 18.

17. Dan Franck, *Zidane: Le roman d'une victoire* (Paris: Pocket 1999), 62; Emmanuel Petit, *A Fleur de Peau* (Paris: Editions Prolongations, 2008), 94; Desailly, *Capitaine*, 234.

18. Desailly, *Capitaine*, 226–27; Gastaut, *Le métissage*, 26.

19. Gastaut, *Le métissage*, 26–27.

20. Ibid., 26.

21. Ibid., 27.

22. Ibid., 24, 27; Raffaele Poli, "Conflit de couleurs: Enjeux géopolitiques autour de la naturalisation des sportifs africains," *Autrepart* 37 (2006): 149–61, quote p. 157.

23. Gastaut, *Le métissage* 28–29; Porcher, "Enjeux interculturels," 10.

24. Kuper, *Soccer against the Enemy*, 294–95; Adam Robinson, *Terror on the Pitch: How Bin Laden Targeted Beckham and the England Football Team* (Edinburgh: Mainstream Publishing, 2002).

25. On football hooliganism in England, see Gary Armstrong, *Football Hooligans: Knowing the Score* (London: Berg, 2003), and Back, Crabbe, and Solomos, *Changing Face*, who argue that it involves only a minority of fans whose actions sustain unfortunate and overgeneralizing images of football fandom that overlook its complicated and contradictory meanings and the relative rarity of serious violence. An excellent study of one group of fans in England is Garry Robson, *"No One Likes Us, We Don't Care": The Myth and Reality of Millwall Fandom* (London: Berg, 2000); see also Bill Buford, *Among the Thugs* (New York: Vintage, 1993).

26. Back, Crabbe, and Solomos, *Changing Face*, 227; Adam Gopnik, "Endgame: A Soccer Skeptic Learns to Stop Worrying and Love the Game," *New Yorker*, 13 July 1998, 28–33; Gastaut, *Le métissage*, 33–34.

27. Vézaine de Vezins, "Le parcours du onze tricolore donne naissance à une nouvelle fibre co-cardière française: La patriotisme jovial du Mondial," *Le Figaro*, 11 July 1998; Gastaut, *Le métissage*, 33; INA, TF1 20 Heures, 9 July 1998.

28. Geoff Hare, *Football in France: A Cultural History* (Oxford: Berg, 2003), 82–83; Patrick Mignon, "Supporters ultras et hooligans dans les stades de football," in *Le spectacle du sport*, ed. Leconte and Vigarello, 45–57, quote p. 47. On Liverpool, see Farred, *Long Distance Love*, 35; Paul Silverstein, "Sporting Faith: Islam, Soccer and the French Nation-State," *Social Text* 65, 18, no. 4 (Winter 2000): 25–53, quote p. 36; Hare, *Football in France*, 85–86; "Un supporteur du PSG tué par

balle par un policier," *Le Monde,* 24 November 2006; "Nicolas Sarkozy annonce des mesures contre les hooligans parisiens," *Le Monde,* 25 November 2006. On the most recent controversy surrounding P.S.G., see "Les Boulogne Boys, association de supporteurs parisiens, 'condamne' la banderole contre le FC Lens," *Le Monde,* 31 March 2008; "La banderole de la honte," *Le Monde,* 1 April 2008.

29. Back, Crabbe, and Solomos, *Changing Face,* 269.

30. Gastaut, *Le métissage,* 31; Gopnik, "Endgame," 28.

31. Didier Daeninckx, "La marque de l'histoire," 10 March 2005, amnistia.net, http://www.amnistia.net/biblio/recits/kanaky_401.htm (accessed 17 July 2008); Alice Bullard and Joël Dauphiné, "Les Canaques au miroir de l'Occident," in *Zoos humains: Au temps des exhibitions humaines,* ed. Nicolas Bancel et al. (Paris: Editions la Découverte, 2002), 118–26. The other essays in this collection provide a panorama of the phenomenon of "human zoos" during this period. Eboué and Diagne were both involved in the exhibition; see Brian Weinstein, *Eboué* (New York: Oxford University Press, 1972), 126. On the Guadeloupe exhibit, see Jacques Dumont, *Sport et assimilation à la Guadeloupe: Les enjeux du corps performant de la colonie au département (1914–1965)* (Paris: L'Harmattan, 2002), 134. On the Colonial Exhibition generally, see Herman Lebovics, *True France: The Wars over Cultural Identity* (Ithaca, NY: Cornell University Press, 1992), chap. 2.

32. Didier Daeninckx, *Meurtres pour mémoire* (Paris: Gallimard, 1984); Daeninckx, "La marque de l'histoire."

33. Mohand Ouahrani, *La France tout un monde: Portraits multicolores* (Paris: Le Cherche Midi, 2002), 29; Marianne Mako, *Ces hommes en bleu: 30 vies en confidences* (Paris: Hachette, 1998), 33, 50.

34. Robert Aldrich and John Connell, *The Last Colonies* (Cambridge, U.K.: Cambridge University Press, 1998), 131–37.

35. Alfred Wahl, "Football et Jeux de Ballon," in *L'Empire du Sport,* ed. Pierre Arnaud et al. (Aix-en-Provence: Amarom, 1992), 44–45, quote p. 44. On the incorporation of New Caledonia into the French Cup, see the correspondence in Centre des Archives Contemporaines (hereafter CAC) 790358, Ministère de la Jeunesse et des Sports (hereafter MJS), Article 1, Folders 4, 7, 14; Didier Braun, "L'équipe de France de football, c'est l'histoire en raccourci d'un siècle d'immigration," *Hommes et Migrations* 1226 (July–August 2000): 50–56, quote p. 55; http://fr.wikipedia.org/wiki/Jacques_Zimako (accessed 7 November 2008); Ouahrani, *La France,* 30.

36. Mako, *Ces hommes,* 49; Guérin and Jaoui, *Noirs en bleu,* 45, 241.

37. Gastaut, *Le métissage,* 26; Guérin and Jaoui, *Noirs en bleu,* 241; Ouahrani, *La France,* 30.

38. The song and the scene are captured in Stéphane Meunier's documentary *Les yeux dans les Bleus 2: Dans les coulisses des Bleus 2002* (Canal +, 2002).

39. Didier Daeninckx, *Cannibale* (Paris: Gallimard, 2000), 13, 93.

40. Daeninckx, "La marque de l'histoire."

41. For an overview of this process, see Géraldine Faes and Stephen Smith, *Noir et Français!* (Paris: Panama, 2006), part 2.

42. "Frequenstar: Lilian Thuram," M6, 11 July 1999.

43. Desailly, *Capitaine*, 250.

44. Thuram, *8 Juillet*, 136.

45. Desailly, *Capitaine*, 239; Franck, *Zidane*, 61–62.

46. Desailly, *Capitaine*, 240.

FIVE. TWO GOALS

1. Marcel Desailly, *Capitaine* (Paris: Stock, 2002), 246–47.

2. These scenes are captured in the documentary film by Stéphane Meunier, *Les Yeux dans les Bleus* (Canal +, 1998).

3. Desailly, *Capitaine*, 249.

4. Yvan Gastaut, *Le métissage par le foot: L'intégration, mais jusqu'où?* (Paris: Autrement, 2008), 51.

5. Dan Franck, *Zidane: Le roman d'une victoire* (Paris: Pocket, 1999), 42–45; Lilian Thuram, *Le 8 Juillet 1998* (Paris: Anne-Carrière, 2004), 155; Desailly, *Capitaine*, 244.

6. Institut National de l'Audiovisuel (hereafter INA), TF1 20 Heures, 9 July 1998; Christiane Lecomte, "Le 'musulman' Zidane sifflé par les Croates de Mostar," *Le Monde*, 10 July 1998, 5.

7. José Carlin, "Brothers in Arms: Les Bleus Win the World Cup, 1998," in *Le Foot: Legends of French Football*, ed. Christov Rühn (London: Abacus, 2000), 59–70, quotes p. 67.

8. INA, TF1 20 Heures, 9 July 1998.

9. Meunier, *Les Yeux dans les Bleus*; INA, "Les six minutes," M6, 9 July 1998.

10. Meunier, *Les Yeux dans les Bleus*; INA, "Le Club du mondial: Au cœur de la Coupe," FR 3, 9 July 1998; Martin T. Laventure and Michel Gamyr, "Lilian Thuram, né pour être le premier," *France-Antilles*, Pointe-à-Pitre edition, no. 8540, 11–12 July 1998; INA, "Les six minutes," M6, 9 July 1998.

11. "Deux petits Albanais rebaptisés Thuram," *France-Antilles*, Pointe-à-Pitre edition, no. 8539, 10 July 1998, p. 5; INA, TF1 20 Heures, 9 July 1998.

12. Laventure and Gamyr, "Lilian Thuram"; Gastaut, *Le métissage*, 51; INA, TF1 20 Heures, 9 July 1998; INA, "Le Club du mondial," FR 3, 9 July 1998.

13. Dominique Le Guilledoux, "Si le mélange réussit au football, il peut se faire dans la rue," *Le Monde*, 12–13 July 1998, 18.

14. Ibid., 18.

15. INA, "Le Club du mondial," FR 3, 9 July 1998; Florence Couret and Emmanuelle Reju, "'Le mondial vaux dix ans de campagne antiraciste,'" *La Croix*, 15 July 1998, 7.

16. INA, TF1 20 Heures, 9 July 1998; Olivier Bertrand et al., "Drapeau tricolore, foule multicolore: Des Champs-Elysées à Mantes-la-Jolie, tout le monde a crié 'On a gagné.' Même les sans-papiers," *Libération,* 10 July 1998.

17. Le Guilledoux, "Si le mélange," 18; Bertrand et al., "Drapeau tricolore, foule multicolore."

18. INA, TF1 20 Heures, 9 July 1998; Bertrand et al., "Drapeau tricolore, foule multicolore."

19. Le Guilledoux, "Si le mélange," 18; Bertrand et al., "Drapeau tricolore, foule multicolore."

20. Le Guilledoux, "Si le mélange," 18.

21. Frédéric Chambon, "Les Bleus jouent pour ceux qui n'ont pas de billets," *Le Monde,* 11 July 1998, 8; Le Guilledoux, "Si le mélange," 18.

22. Desailly, *Capitaine,* 252; Chambon, "Les Bleus jouent," 8; Gastaut, *Le métissage,* 34.

23. Bertrand et al., "Drapeau tricolore, foule multicolore."

24. Ibid.

25. Ibid.

26. Pascal Villebeuf, "Ce maillot est une relique à Fontainebleau," *Le Parisien,* 10 July 1998, 3.

27. Dominique Le Guilledoux, "Le 12 Juillet, ce sera la deuxième fête nationale," *Le Monde,* 14 July 1998, 16.

28. INA, "Tous en finale," TF1, 12 July 1998.

29. *France-Antilles,* Pointe-à-Pitre edition, no. 8538, 9 July 1998, 1; "Des milliers de Cayennais fêtent bruyamment la qualification de la France," *France-Antilles,* Fort-de-France edition, no. 9456, 10 July 1998, 20; Laventure and Gamyr, "Lilian Thuram," 1, 3.

30. INA, "Frequenstar: Lilian Thuram," M6, 11 July 1999.

31. Christian Jaurena, "Saint-Denis, côté ville et côté stade," *Le Monde,* 14 July 1998, 16.

32. "Réaction: Lother, le père de Thuram: 'Il tient son talent de moi,'" *France-Antilles,* Pointe-à-Pitre edition, no. 8538, 9 July 1998, 20; K. N., "Je n'ai pas de père," *Le Parisien,* 10 July 1998, 6.

SIX. TWO FLAGS

1. Dan Franck, *Zidane: Le roman d'une victoire* (Paris: Pocket, 1999), 15, 88–90.

2. Ibid., 109.

3. Alix Delaporte and Stéphane Meunier, *Zidane* (Studio Canal, 2007); Institut National de l'Audiovisuel (hereafter INA), "20 heures le journal," France 2, 5 July 2006.

4. See Jim House and Neil MacMaster, *Paris 1961: Algerians, State Terror, and*

Memory (Oxford: Oxford University Press, 2006), 265–74, for a discussion of the "strategic silence" of many Algerian immigrants during the 1960s and 1970s. For an excellent study of the different generations of Algerian migrants, see Abelmalek Sayad, *La double absence: Des illusions de l'émigré aux souffrances de l'immigré* (Paris: Seuil, 1999). On the racism experienced by Algerian migrants during the colonial period, see Neil MacMaster, *Colonial Migrants and Racism: Algerians in France, 1900–1962* (New York: St. Martin's Press, 1997).

5. "Vu d'Algérie, un match plus que symbolique," *L'Humanité*, 6 October 2001.

6. Pierre-Louis Basse, *Zidane-Dugarry: Mes Copains d'Abord* (Paris: Mango Sport, 1998), 12. On Zidane and the Kabyle language, see Marianne Mako, *Ces hommes en bleu: 30 vies en confidences* (Paris: Hachette, 1998), 57.

7. See Paul Silverstein, "Stadium Politics: Sport, Islam and Amazigh Consciousness in France and North Africa," in *With God on Their Side: Sport in the Service of Religion,* ed. Tara Magdalinski and Timothy J. L. Chandler (London: Routledge, 2002), 37–55, especially 48–52. For a detailed discussion of the history of the Kabyle and their activism, see also Paul Silverstein, *Algeria in France: Transpolitics, Race and Nation* (Bloomington: Indiana University Press, 2004).

8. Basse, *Zidane-Dugarry,* 12; Yvan Gastaut, *Le métissage par le foot: L'intégration, mais jusqu'où?* (Paris: Autrement, 2008), 43.

9. Franck, *Zidane,* 24.

10. Basse, *Zidane-Dugarry,* 6, 8, 11, 53; Baptiste Blanchet and Thibaut Fraix-Burnet, *Zidane: Le Dieu qui voulait juste être un homme* (Paris: Ramsay, 2006), 39.

11. Franck, *Zidane,* 53, 86.

12. Frédéric Lohézic and Gilles Lhote, *Zinedine Zidane: Respect!* (Paris: Michel Lafont, 2006), 30, 31.

13. Franck, *Zidane,* 82–83; Blanchet and Fraix-Burnet, *Dieu,* 36.

14. Lohézic and Lhote, *Respect,* 30–31.

15. Jean Philippe, *Zidane: Le roi modeste* (Paris: L'Archipel, 2002), 69–70; Franck, *Zidane,* 84.

16. Franck, *Zidane,* 80–82; Paul A. Silverstein and Chantal Tetreault, "Postcolonial Urban Apartheid," 11 June 2006, http://riotsfrance.ssrc.org (accessed 17 October 2008), 5.

17. Franck, *Zidane,* 94–95.

18. The photograph is reprinted in Etienne Labrunie, *Zidane: Maître du jeu* (Paris: Timée-Editions, 2005), 20, and Lohézic and Lhote, *Respect,* 32; Blanchet and Fraix-Burnet, *Dieu,* 40, 43; Franck, *Zidane,* 98–99.

19. Labrunie, *Maître du jeu,* 21; Philippe, *Roi modeste,* 19; Franck, *Zidane,* 11; Lohézic and Lhote, *Respect,* 33.

20. Philippe, *Roi modeste,* 11–12, 21, 55; see also http://fr.wikipedia.org/wiki/Jean_Fernandez (accessed 8 November 2008).

21. Franck, *Zidane,* 102; Philippe, *Roi modeste,* 24.

22. Blanchet and Fraix-Burnet, *Dieu,* 55; Franck, *Zidane,* 61, 106–8.

23. Philippe, *Roi modeste,* 67, 86–87. For the coach of Real, see Stéphane Meunier and Alix Delaporte, *Comme dans un rêve* (Studio Canal, 2002). On the 2002 goal, see Javier Marias, "Fallen from the Sky," in *The Global Game: Writers on Soccer,* ed. John Turnbull, Thom Satterlee, and Alon Raab (Lincoln: University of Nebraska Press, 2008), 72–73; see also Philippe Dubath, "Zidane and Me," in the same volume, 245–50.

24. Franck, *Zidane,* 104–5; Blanchet and Fraix-Burnet, *Dieu,* 68.

25. Philippe, *Roi modeste,* 94.

26. On the use of the term *maroon,* see Geoff Hare, *Football in France: A Cultural History* (Oxford: Berg, 2003), 20. On Kopa and the protests of 1968, see François René Simon, Alain Leiblang, and Faouzi Mahjoub, *Les enragés du football: L'autre Mai 68* (Paris: Calmann-Lévy, 2008), 26–27.

27. "Domenech Rekindles Makelele Row," BBC Sport, http://news.bbc.co.uk, 29 August 2006; "Domenech: 'Je suis esclavagiste,'" Nouvelobs.com, 29 August 2006.

28. Basse, *Zidane-Dugarry,* 56, 76.

29. Blanchet and Fraix-Burnet, *Dieu,* 76–91.

30. Ibid., 83, 97.

31. Ibid., 100; Franck, *Zidane,* 52–53.

32. Philippe, *Roi modeste,* 7–8, 39, 60–61; Andrew Hussey, "ZZ TOP," *Observer,* 4 April 2004.

33. Blanchet and Fraix-Burnet, *Dieu,* 18.

34. Franck, *Zidane,* 81; Mako, *Hommes,* 57.

35. Dave Hill, *Out of His Skin: The John Barnes Phenomenon* (1989; reprint, London: When Saturday Comes Books, 2001), 137; Franck, *Zidane,* 33. The same advice on how to deal with racism was given by a coach to his Latino players on a high school team in North Carolina; see Paul Cuadros, *A Home on the Field: How One Championship Football Team Inspires Hope for the Revival of Small Town America* (New York: Harper, 2006), 86.

36. Franck, *Zidane,* 58, 66–68.

37. *Les Yeux dans les Bleus,* directed by Stéphane Meunier (Canal+, 1998); Basse, *Zidane-Dugarry,* 76.

38. "Football: Nike's Role in Ronaldo Mystery under Microscope," *Independent,* 18 December 2000.

39. Basse, *Zidane-Dugarry,* 86–88. For his earlier goal in the Stade de France, see Philippe, *Roi modeste,* 130.

40. Florence Couret and Emmanuelle Reju, "'Le mondial vaux dix ans de campagne antiraciste,'" *La Croix,* 15 July 1998, 7; Gastaut, *Le métissage,* 34.

41. Basse, *Zidane-Dugarry,* 86.

42. Ibid., 88.

43. Philippe, *Roi modeste,* 152.

44. Meunier, *Les Yeux dans les Bleus.*

45. INA, "Tous en finale," TF1, 12 July 1998.

46. Franck, *Zidane*, 216–17; Philippe, *Roi modeste*, 153.

47. Basse, *Zidane-Dugarry*, 35–36; Philippe, *Roi modeste*, 154.

48. Basse, *Zidane-Dugarry*, 88–89.

SEVEN. LA FRANCE MÉTISSÉE

1. Institut National de l'Audiovisuel (hereafter INA), "Tous en finale," TF1, 12 July 1998.

2. Annick Cojean, "A la Bastille, un 14 juillet 'en plus drôle,'" *Le Monde*, 14 July 1998, 3.

3. Ibid.

4. Philippe Broussard, "Plus d'un million de personnes on fêté la victoire sur les Champs-Elysées," *Le Monde*, 14 July 1998, 3.

5. Etienne Labrunie, *Zidane: Maître du jeu* (Paris: Timée-Editions, 2005), 101; Dominique Le Guilledoux, "Le 12 Juillet, ce sera la deuxième fête nationale," *Le Monde*, 14 July 1998, 16.

6. "Une voiture dans la foule faisant quatre-vingts blessés," *Le Monde*, 14 July 1998, 3.

7. Yvan Gastaut, *Le métissage par le foot: L'intégration, mais jusqu'où?* (Paris: Autrement, 2008), 52; *France-Antilles*, Fort-de-France edition, no. 9459, 15 July 1998, 15.

8. Gastaut, *Le métissage*, 57. For the fullest analysis of the planning and impact of the 1998 World Cup in France, see the the excellent collection edited by Hugh Dauncey and Geoffrey Hare, *France and the 1998 World Cup: The National Impact of a World Sporting Event* (London: Frank Cass, 1999), notably John Marks, "The French National Team and National Identity: 'Cette France d'un "blue métis,"'" pp. 41–57.

9. Le Guilledoux, "Le 12 Juillet," 16; Albrecht Sonntag, *Les Identités du football européen* (Grenoble: Presses Universitaires de Grenoble, 2008), 16 n. 11.

10. Le Guilledoux, "Le 12 Juillet," 16; Christian Jaurena, "Saint-Denis, côté ville et côté stade," *Le Monde*, 14 July 1998, 16.

11. Gastaut, *Le métissage*, 61–62.

12. Labrunie, *Maître*, 101; Pierre-Louis Basse, *Zidane-Dugarry: Mes Copains d'Abord* (Paris: Mango Sport, 1998), 93; Frédéric Potet, "500,000 personnes ont accompagné la parade des Bleus sur les Champs-Elysées," *Le Monde*, 15 July 1998, 12.

13. Interview with Michel Platini, *Le Monde*, 15 July 1998, 12; Gastaut, *Le métissage*, 106.

14. Dominique Sanchez, "La banlieue, l'autre vanqueur du Mondial," *Le Monde*, 24 July 1998, 10; Gastaut, *Le métissage*, 104.

15. "La parabole Jacquet," *Le Monde,* 14 July 1998, 1, 14; Vézaine de Vezins, "Le parcours du onze tricolore donne naissance à une nouvelle fibre cocardière française: La patriotisme jovial du Mondial," *Le Figaro,* 11 July 1998.

16. Gastaut, *Le métissage,* 91–92.

17. Onyekachi Wambu, "Marcel Desailly and the Second Liberation of Paris, 1998," in *Le Foot: Legends of French Football,* ed. Christov Rühn (London: Abacus, 2000), 268–84, quote p. 282.

18. Gastaut, *Le métissage,* 92, 108.

19. Jaurena, "Saint-Denis," 16; interview with Aimé Jacquet, *Le Monde,* 18 July 1998, 18; Florence Couret and Emmanuelle Reju, "'Le mondial vaux dix ans de campagne antiraciste,'" *La Croix,* 15 July 1998, 7; Gastaut, *Le métissage,* 44.

20. *Le Monde,* 21–22 March 1993, 11; Mustafa Dikeç, *Badlands of the Republic: Space, Politics and Urban Policy* (London: Blackwell, 2007), 30.

21. Gastaut, *Le métissage,* 93; Olivier Biffaud, "Charles Pasqua à contre-emploi," *Le Monde,* 20 July 1998.

22. For Weil's report, to which I contributed as a member of the commission, see Patrick Weil, *Pour une politique d'immigration juste et efficace* (Paris: Documentation Française, 1997).

23. Gastaut, *Le métissage,* 102–3, 107.

24. INA, "Le vrai journal," Canal +, 4 October 1998.

25. Gastaut, *Le métissage,* 103–4.

26. Wambu, "Marcel Desailly," 281–83; Gastaut, *Le métissage,* 114.

27. Gastaut, *Le métissage,* 109.

28. Mohand Ouahrani, *La France tout un monde: Portraits multicolores* (Paris: Le Cherche Midi, 2002), 5, 7.

29. Lilian Thuram, *Le 8 Juillet 1998* (Paris: Anne-Carrière, 2004), 156.

30. Ibid., 156–57.

31. Ibid., 157.

32. Ibid., 157–58.

33. Gastaut, *Le métissage,* 123.

34. Dan Franck, *Zidane: Le roman d'une victoire* (Paris: Pocket, 1999), 49; Jamel Debbouze, "'Tout a une fin, même les étoiles filantes,'" *Paris-Match* 2982 (12–19 July 2006): 56–57.

35. Basse, *Zidane-Dugarry,* 11–12, 24.

36. Ibid., 12, 37, 86, 88; Gastaut, *Métissage,* 43.

37. Basse, *Zidane-Dugarry,* 61–62.

38. "Le FN fait de Zidane un 'enfant de l'Algérie française,'" *Le Monde,* 15 July 1998, 12.

39. "L'homme du jour Zinedine Zidane," *L'Humanité,* 30 April 2002. See also Andrew Hussey, "ZZ TOP," *Observer,* 4 April 2004.

40. Les Back, Tim Crabbe, and John Solomos, *The Changing Face of Football: Racism, Identity and Multiculture in the English Game* (London: Berg, 2001),

273. This distortion of Zidane's family story is striking in a book that is otherwise carefully argued and documented.

41. Elizabeth Ezra, *The Colonial Unconscious: Race and Culture in Interwar France* (Ithaca, NY: Cornell University Press. 2000), 148; Gastaut, *Le métissage*, 81. Through a reading of a photograph taken in 1998 that positions a man of North African background as being on the edge of the celebration of the French team, Herman Lebovics makes a parallel but distinct argument about the persistence of exclusion in *Bringing the Empire Back Home: France in the Global Age* (Durham, NC: Duke University Press, 2004), 138.

42. See Gary Wilder, *The French Imperial Nation State: Negritude and Colonial Humanism between the Two World Wars* (Chicago: University of Chicago Press, 2005).

43. Gastaut, *Le métissage,* 38, 43.

44. Ibid., 117.

45. Ibid., 115.

46. Ibid., 121, 123.

47. Ibid., 118.

48. François Parent, *Black-blanc-beur: Roman* (Paris: La Bartavelle Editeur, 1999).

49. Alastair Reid, "The World Cup," *New Yorker,* 10 September 1966, 152–97, quote p. 152.

EIGHT. AN UNFINISHED WAR

1. Yvan Gastaut, *Le métissage par le foot: L'intégration, mais jusou'où?* (Paris: Autrement, 2008), 139; Sébastien Homer, "Verdict severe à Bobigny," *L'Humanité,* 21 November 2001. Footage of the event can be seen at Institut National de l'Audiovisuel (hereafter INA), "Stade 2," France 2, 7 October 2001.

2. *Les Yeux Dans Les Bleus 2,* directed by Stéphane Meunier (Canal+ Video, 2002); Gastaut, *Le métissage,* 137–39.

3. Gastaut, *Le métissage,* 141; Max Clos, "L'intégration est morte," *Le Figaro,* 12 October 2001. On his 1990 statements, see Azouz Begag, "La révolte des lascars contre l'oublie à Vaulx-le-Velin," *Les Annales de la recherché urbaine* 49 (1991): 114–21, quote p. 117.

4. Gastaut, *Le métissage,* 144.

5. Mahfoud Amara, "Soccer, Post-Colonial and Post-Conflictual Discourses in Algeria: Algérie-France, 6 Octobre 2001, 'ce n'était pas un simple match de foot,'" *International Review of Modern Sociology* 32, no. 2 (Autumn 2006): 217–39, quotes pp. 226–27, 230.

6. Didier Rey, "Le temps des circulaires ou les contradictions du football colonial en Algerie (1928–1945)," http://www.wearefootball.org/dossiers/53/lire/

le-football-colonial/ (accessed 20 July 2008), 1. On the use of *Muslim* as a legal term in Algeria, see Todd Shephard, *The Invention of Decolonization: The Algerian War and the Remaking of France* (Ithaca, NY: Cornell University Press, 2006), chap 1, especially p. 12; Youcef Fatès, *Sport et tiers-monde* (Paris: Presses Universitaires de France, 1994), 29, 32.

7. Youssef Fatès, "Les marquers du nationalisme: Les clubs sportifs musulmans dans l'Algérie coloniale," *Quasimodo* 3–4 (Spring 1997): 121–29, http://www.revue-quasimodo.org, quotes pp. 123, 126–27. For a list of some of the major Muslim clubs, see Benjamin Stora, "Algérie, années coloniales: Quand le sport devient un facteur de mobilisation politique," in *Jeu et sports en Méditerranée: Actes du Colloque de Carthage, 7–8–9 November 1989* (Tunis: Alif, 1991), 143–53, quote p. 146–47. On the parallel politicization of football in colonial Brazzaville, see the excellent study by Phyllis Martin, *Leisure and Society in Colonial Brazzaville* (Cambridge, U.K.: Cambridge University Press, 1995), especially chap. 4.

8. Rey, "Le temps des circulaires," 2–3.

9. Fatès, *Sport et tiers-monde,* 29–31.

10. Rey, "Le temps des circulaires," 5. On Hadj, see Benjamin Stora, *Messali Hadj: Pionnier du nationalisme algérien, 1898–1974* (Paris: Editions de l'Harmattan, 1986), especially 147–49; Jean-Louis Planche, *Sétif 1945: Histoire d'un massacre annoncé* (Paris: Perrin, 2006), 40.

11. Raid Hamrouchi, "'L'Intelligentsia du certificat d'etude': Emergence d'une class moyenne musulmane dans l'Algérie coloniale? Le cas d'une famille du nord-est consantinois" (master's thesis, Ecole des Hautes Etudes en Sciences Sociales, 2008), 30, 43, 84.

12. Fatès, *Sport et tiers-monde,* 29–31; Hamrouchi "Intelligentsia," 84–86; Stora, "Algérie, années coloniales," 148–50.

13. Fatès, *Sport et tiers-monde,* 30.

14. Rey, "Le temps des circulaires," 2–4.

15. Michel Nait-Challal, *Dribbleurs de l'indépendance: L'incroyable histoire de l'équipe de football du FLN Algérien* (Paris: Editions Prolongations, 2008), 10–11; Planche, *Sétif 1945,* 10.

16. Nait-Challal, *Dribbleurs,* 11–12. On scouting in Algeria, see Hamrouchi, "Intelligentsia," 87–89; Boucif Mekhaled, *Chroniques d'un massacre: 8 Mai, 1945, Sétif, Guelma, Kerrata* (Paris: Syros, 1995), 53–57.

17. Planche, *Sétif 1945,* 136–43.

18. Ibid., chaps. 9, 13; on the British, see p. 164. On Mekloufi, see Nait-Challal, *Dribbleurs,* 13.

19. See Planche, *Sétif 1945,* especially the introduction and chap. 16; Mekhaled, *Chroniques,* 160–224.

20. Mahfood Amara and Ian Henry, "Between Globalization and Local 'Modernity': The Diffusion and Modernization of Football in Algeria," *Soccer*

and *Society* 15, no. 1 (Spring 2004): 1–26, quote p. 6; Fatès, *Sport et tiers-monde*, 32; Stora, "Algérie, années coloniales," 148.

21. Rey, "Le temps des circulaires," 6; Mekhaled, *Chroniques*, 55.

22. Stora, "Algérie, années coloniales," 147.

23. Jacqueline Lévi-Valensi, *Camus at Combat: Writing 1944–1947* (Princeton, NJ: Princeton University Press, 2006), 203–27; Nait-Challal, *Dribbleurs*, 189; Pierre Lanfranchi and Matthew Taylor, *Moving with the Ball: The Migration of Professional Footballers* (Oxford: Berg, 2001), 172.

24. Stora, "Algérie, années coloniales," 149.

25. Nait-Challal, *Dribbleurs*, 74.

26. Philip Dine, "France, Algeria, and Sport: From Colonisation to Globalisation," *Modern and Contemporary France* 10, no. 4 (2002): 495–505, quote p. 499.

27. Donald Reid, "Re-viewing *The Battle of Algiers* with Germain Tillion," *History Workshop Journal* 60 (Autumn 2005): 93–115, quotes pp. 98, 102.

28. Dine, "France," 499; Amara and Henry "Between Globalization and Local 'Modernity,'" 7–8, n. 36; Lafranchi and Taylor, *Moving*, 173; Rachid Boujedra, *Le Vanqueur de la Coupe* (1981; reprint, Paris: Gallimard, 1989).

29. Nait-Challal, *Dribbleurs*, 59–69.

30. Ibid., 168.

31. Ibid., 16, 46.

32. Thierry Oberle, "Vingt-neuf ans après l'indépendance: Une rencontre chargée de symbols," *Le Figaro*, 6 October 2001

33. Nait-Challal, *Dribbleurs*, 29–38.

34. Ibid., 42–44.

35. Ibid., 48–50.

36. Ibid., 51–52.

37. Ibid., 18–28; Pierre Lanfranchi, "Mekloufi, un footballeur français dans la guerre d'Algérie," *Actes de la recherche en sciences sociales* 103 (June 1994): 70–74; Pierre Lanfranchi and Alfred Wahl, "The Immigrant as Hero: Kopa, Mekloufi and French Football," in *European Heroes: Myth, Identity and Sport,* ed. Richard Holt, J. A. Mangan, and Pierre Lanfranchi (London: Frank Cass, 1996), 114–28.

38. Dominique Le Guilledoux, "Des footballeurs entre Paris et Alger," *Le Monde diplomatique*, August 2005, 25; Nait-Challal, *Dribbleurs*, 54, 80, 84. The most detailed account of the escapes from France is provided in the pioneering study by Rabah Saadallah and Djamel Benfars, *Le football algérien à la conquête des continents avec la glorieuse équipe du FLN* (Algiers: ENAL, 1985).

39. Paul Dietschy, Yvan Gastaut, and Stéphane Mourlane, *Histoire politique des coupes du monde de football* (Paris: Vuibert, 2006), 298; Lanfranchi and Taylor, *Moving*, 174; Nait-Challal, *Dribbleurs*, 86–92, 101, photo insert p. 3.

40. Nait-Challal, *Dribbleurs*, 109, 118, 120.

41. Nait-Challal, *Dribbleurs*, 102–3, 106–7 118, 129.

42. Ibid., 108–9, 127.

43. Ibid., 139. For more details on the team's travels, see Saadallah and Benfars, *Football algérien*, pt. 2.

44. Nait-Challal, *Dribbleurs,* 109, 130, 141.

45. Ibid., 147–48, 150–51, 153.

46. Ibid., 161–63.

47. Simon Roger, "Quand le FLN recrutait les footballeurs," *Le Monde*, 13–14 July 2008, 3; Nait-Challal, *Dribbleurs,* 112.

NINE. RECONCILIATION

1. Michel Nait-Challal, *Dribbleurs de l'indépendance: L'incroyable histoire de l'équipe de football du FLN Algérien* (Paris: Éditions Prolongations, 2008), 191–94; Pierre Lanfranchi, "Mekloufi, un footballeur français dans la guerre d'Algérie," *Actes de la recherche en sciences sociales* 103 (June 1994): 70–74, quote p. 70.

2. Nait-Challal, *Dribbleurs,* 221–22; Paul Dietschy, Yvan Gastaut, and Stéphane Mourlane, *Histoire politique des coupes du monde de football* (Paris: Vuibert, 2006), 300–302; Philip Dine, "France, Algeria, and Sport: From Colonisation to Globalisation," *Modern and Contemporary France* 10, no. 4 (2002): 495–505, quote pp. 500–501.

3. Yvan Gastaut, "Les footballeurs algériens en France à l'épreuve des identités nationales," http://www.wearefootball.org (accessed 15 July 2008), 8. See also Dietschy, Gastaut, and Mourlane, *Histoire politique,* 304. On the juridical and social complexities surrounding the Algerian diaspora, see Azouz Begag, "Les relations France-Algérie vues de la diaspora algérienne," *Modern and Contemporary France* 10, no. 4 (2002): 475–82. On the question of dual nationality among Algerian and other African football players, see Raffaele Poli, "Conflit de couleurs: Enjeux géopolitiques autour de la naturalization de sportifs africains," *Autrepart* 37 (2006): 149–61, especially 155.

4. Dan Franck, *Zidane: Le roman d'une victoire* (Paris: Pocket, 1999), 53; Martine Couturie, "L'ancien international algérien, 44 ans, fut, il y a vingt ans, l'idole du numéro dix des Bleus," *Le Figaro*, 6 October 2001; Dietschy, Gastaut, and Mourlane, *Histoire politique,* 296.

5. Dietschy, Gastaut, and Mourlane, *Histoire politique,* 309–10.

6. Yvan Gastaut, *Le métissage par le foot: L'intégration, mais jusqu'où?* (Paris: Autrement, 2008), 126; "Le foot a toujours eu des fonctions ambiguës et contradictoires," Christian Bromberger, interview by Françoise Escarpit, *L'Humanité*, 6 October 2001; "Assumer sa double appartenance," interview with Alain Hayot, *L'Humanité*, 8 October 2001. Hayot's comments were made after the game, but he insisted that what had happened there ultimately didn't erase the symbolic importance of the match.

7. Ivan Rioufol, "France-Algérie: Le test," *Le Figaro*, 6 October 2001; see also Thierry Oberle, "Vingt-neuf ans après l'indépendance: Une rencontre chargée de symboles," *Le Figaro*, 6 October 2001.

8. "Algeria Welcomes 'Peace' Game," BBC Sport Online, 2 October 2001, http://news.bbc.co.uk/sport2/low/football/africa/1575815.stm (accessed 29 October 2007).

9. Gastaut, *Le métissage*, 126, 130.

10. Ibid., 126–27.

11. Rioufol, "France-Algérie."

12. Gastaut, *Le métissage*, 136, 146–47.

13. Patrick Fort and Jean Philippe, *Zidane: De Yazid à Zizou* (Paris: L'Archipel, 2006), 177–78; Gastaut, *Le métissage*, 135–36, 146.

14. "Vu d'Algérie, un match plus que symbolique," *L'Humanité*, 6 October 2001; Sébastien Homer, "Verdict severe à Bobigny," *L'Humanité*, 21 November 2001.

15. Gastaut, *Le métissage*, 130.

16. Ibid., 130, 137.

17. Mahfoud Amara, "Soccer, Post-Colonial and Post-Conflictual Discourses in Algeria: Algérie-France, 6 Octobre 2001, 'ce n'était pas un simple match de foot,'" *International Review of Modern Sociology* 32, no. 2 (Autumn 2006): 217–39, quote p. 229; Oberle, "Vingt-neuf ans."

18. "Assumer sa double appartenance," interview with Alain Hayot. On the anthem, see http://en.wikipedia.org/wiki/Kassaman; http://david.national-anthems .net/dz.htm; http://www.algeria-un.org/default.asp?doc=-anthem; http://www .nationalanthems.us/forum/YaBB.pl?num=1087950647/16 (all accessed 13 March 2008).

19. Gastaut, *Le métissage*, 130.

20. Institut National de l'Audiovisuel (hereafter INA), "Infos," Canal+, 4 October 2001.

21. Gastaut, *Le métissage*, 132.

22. Yves Borden, "France-Algérie, une rencontre aux multiples enjeux," *Le Monde*, 6 October 2001.

23. Gastaut, *Le métissage*, 132.

24. Rabah Madjer, interview by Dominique Pagnoud, *Le Figaro*, 4 October 2001.

25. Gastaut, *Le métissage*, 133.

26. INA, "Stade 2," France 2, 7 October 2001; Lilian Thuram, *8 Juillet 1998* (Paris: Editions Anne Carrière, 2004), 160–61.

27. Thuram, *8 Juillet*, 162; Jean-Yves Guérin and Laurent Jaoui, *Noirs en bleu: Le football est-il raciste?* (Paris: Anne Carrière, 2008), 26; Gastaut, *Le métissage*, 140.

28. *Les Yeux Dans Les Bleus 2*, directed by Stéphane Meunier (Canal+, 2002).

29. Thuram, *8 Juillet,* 162.

30. INA, "Stade 2," France 2, 7 October 2001.

31. Gastaut, *Le métissage,* 142.

32. Homer, "Verdict."

33. INA, "Stade 2," France 2, 7 October 2001.

34. INA, "20 heures," TF1, 7 October 2001; INA, "Stade 2," France 2, 7 October 2001; Yves Threard, "France-Algérie: Le rendez-vous manqué," *Le Figaro,* 8 October 2001.

35. "Assumer sa double appartenance," interview with Alain Hayot.

36. Robert Redeker, *Le sport contre les peuples* (Paris: Berg International, 2002), 65.

37. Gastaut, *Le métissage,* 146–47.

38. Ibid., 147.

39. Ibid., 158–59.

40. Blaise de Chabalier, interview with Patrick Vieira, *Le Figaro,* 30 May 2002.

41. Gastaud, *Le métissage,* 160–61.

42. *Le Monde,* http://www.lemondedublog.com/2007/11/football-france-maroc-marseillaise-et-joueurs-francais-siffles.php (accessed 2 May 2008).

TEN. BURN

1. Piotr Smolar, "Les RG ont recensé 70,000 cas de violences urbaines depuis janvier," *Le Monde,* 4 November 2005; Alec G. Hargreaves, "An Emperor with No Clothes," 28 November 2005, http://riotsfrance.ssrc.org/, p. 1 (accessed 10 August 2008). For an excellent overview of the insurrection, see Paul A. Silverstein and Chantal Tetreault, "Postcolonial Urban Apartheid," 11 June 2006, http://riotsfrance.ssrc.org. For statistics and maps, see http://commons.wikimedia.org/wiki/Paris_suburb_riots.

2. "Une handicapé gravement brûlée," *Le Monde,* 6–7 November 2005, 6; Jean-Michel Dumay, "Violences et vigilance, le face-à-face des banlieues," *Le Monde,* 8 November 2005, 1; David Dufresne, *Maintien de l'ordre: Enquête* (Paris: Hachette, 2007), 48–49.

3. Gérard Mauger, *L'émeute de novembre 2005: Une révolte protopolitique* (Paris: Editions du Croquant, 2006), provides a detailed analysis of the problems of interpretation raised by the 2005 events. On the politics of naming, see 6–7; on the efforts at "political disqualification," see 85–96; for his argument in favor of describing the event as "proto-political," see 131–51.

4. Daniel Merklen, "Paroles de pierres, images de feu," *Mouvements* 43 (January 2008): 131–37, quote p. 131; Michel Kokoreff, *Sociologie des émeutes* (Paris: Payot, 2008), 94–95, 117, 276–77; Loïc Wacquant, *Urban Outcasts: A Comparative Sociology of Advanced Marginality* (Cambridge, U.K.: Polity Press, 2008), 189. On

arrest statistics, see Olivier Roy, "The Nature of the French Riots," 18 November 2005, http://riotsfrance.ssrc.org, p. 2 (accessed 10 August 2008).

5. Kokoreff, *Sociologie,* 97; Hargreaves, "Emperor with No Clothes," 5–6; Paul Silverstein, "Kabyle Immigrant Politics and Racialized Citizenship in France," in *Citizenship, Political Engagement and Belonging: Immigrants in Europe and the United States,* ed. Deborah Reed-Danahay and Caroline B. Brettell (New Brunswick, NJ: Rutgers University Press, 2008), 23–42, quote p. 39.

6. Didier Arnaud, "'J'en ai pas vu un seul d'entre vous pendant les émeutes!,'" *Libération* 7657 (21 December 2005): 14; Azouz Begag, "La révolte des lascars contre l'oublie à Vaulx-le-Velin," *Les Annales de la recherché urbaine* 49 (1991): 114–21.

7. Mac Kregor and Hematon Concept, *Insurrection* (Hematon Concept, 2006). On the quota law and the popularity of hip-hop, see Paul Silverstein, "'Why Are We Waiting to Start the Fire?' French Gangsta Rap and the Critique of State Capitalism," in *Black, Blanc, Beur. Rap Music and Hip-Hop Culture in the Francophone World,* ed. Alain-Philippe Durand (Lanham, MD: Scarecrow Press, 2005), 45–67, especially 53. On the CD *Insurrection,* see Silverstein, "Kabyle Immigrant Politics," 38.

8. Silverstein, "Fire," 45–48; Kokoreff, *Sociologie,* 86–87.

9. Institut National de l'Audiovisuel (hereafter INA), "Le Grand journal de Canal+," 14 November 2005.

10. Laetitia Van Eeckhout, "Pap Ndiaye: L'Intégration par le sport est un miroir aux alouettes," *Le Monde,* 9 July 2006. See also Pap Ndiaye, *La Condition Noire: Essai sur une minorité française* (Paris: Calmann-Lévy, 2008), 224–37.

11. Lilian Thuram, *8 Juillet 1998* (Paris: Editions Anne Carrière, 2004), 104–5; "Racist update: November 2001–April 2002," http://www.furd.org/resources/ Racist%20update.doc (accessed 20 December 2007); "Champions League Football: Juventus and Real Madrid Show Mettle," *International Herald Tribune,* 2 October 2003.

12. John Foot, *Winning at All Costs: A Scandalous History of Italian Football* (New York: Nation Books, 2006), 313–14. "Can Del Piero Inspire Juventus to Glory? Old Lady Puts Hopes on One Young Star," *International Herald Tribune,* 12 September 2001. A detailed timeline of racist incidents in European football from 2004 on is presented at http://sports.yahoo.com/sow/news;slug=ap-racism insoccer-list &prov=ap &type=lgns (accessed 8 February 2005).

13. "Racisme contre le footballeur William Gallas," 16 April 2008, http:// www.montraykreyol.org/spip.php?article589 (accessed 17 April 2008).

14. Sid Lowe, "Spain Coach in Mire over Henry Jibe," *Guardian,* 7 October 2004, http://www.guardian.co.uk/football/2004/oct/07/newsstory.sports (accessed 24 July 2008).

15. Bruce Crumley, "Hate Buster," *Time,* 2 October 2005, http://www.time .com/time/europe/hero2005/henry.html (accessed 24 July 2008).

16. "Thuram Will Receive UEFA Award on Behalf of FARE," http://mailman

.no-racism.net/pipermail/football/2001-August/000026.html (accessed 20 December 2007). On the organization F.A.R.E., see http://www.farenet.org/. Olivier Villepreux, "Sélection de stars contre le racisme," *Liberation,* 3 October 2006. On Foot Citoyen, see www.footcitoyen.org (accessed 10 November 2008); "FIFA Agrees on Stiffer Penalties to Stamp Out Racism," *China Daily,* 18 March 2006, http://www.chinadaily.com.cn/english/doc/2006–03/18/content_544098 .htm (accessed 20 December 2007).

17. INA, "Le Grand journal de Canal+," 14 November 2005; "On a tout essayé," INA, France 2, 17 May 2006.

18. Dufresne, *Maintien,* 95–101; clip from "Arrêt sur images: Banlieues filmer et raconter," by Daniel Schneidermann, France 5, 6 November 2005, http://www .youtube.com/watch?v=9kod2r8kp9Y (accessed 30 September 2008).

19. Raphaëlle Bacqué and Christophe Jakubyszn, "Azouz Begag, principal opposant à Nicolas Sarkozy," *Le Monde,* 2 November 2005, 5.

20. Jean Baptiste de Montvalon and Sylvia Zappi, "Les maires de banlieue critiquent Nicolas Sarkozy," *Le Monde,* 3 November 2005, 12.

21. "Azouz Begag avait déjà évoqué la 'racaille,'" *Le Monde,* 6–7 November 2005, 6.

22. Ariane Chemin, "Le dernier jour de Bouna Traoré and Zyed Benna," *Le Monde,* 9 December 2005; Kokoreff, *Sociologie,* 43–45, 163–66.

23. Chemin, "Dernier jour"; Kokoreff, *Sociologie,* 44–47.

24. Chemin, "Dernier jour."

25. For detailed accounts of the beginnings of the insurrection, see Kokoreff, *Sociologie,* 47–56; Mauger, *L'émeute,* 22–38; Dufresne, *Maintien,* 50–66.

26. The organizers of the march created an organization called Au-délà des mots (Beyond Words) that has remained active in the years since. A video homage to Zyed and Bouna, showing scenes of the march, is at http://www.youtube.com/ watch?v=Ca06_KKw63g (accessed 3 March 2009).

27. Kokoreff, *Sociologie,* 47–56, 236–37.

28. On the investigation into the deaths, see Gérard Davet, "Rapport de la 'police des polices' sur la mort de deux jeunes," and "Nouvelle plainte pour 'mise en danger de la vie d'autrui,'" *Le Monde,* 8 December 2006, 10. On Sarkozy, see Mauger, *L'émeute,* 29–30. For the full text of the intelligence report, see Dufresne, *Maintien,* 131–33.

29. Dufresne, *Maintien,* 63–66.

30. Kokoreff, *Sociologie,* chap. 2; Mauger, *L'émeute,* 38–48; Luc Bronner and Piotr Smolar, "Les violences s'étendent en Seine-Saint-Denis et changent de forme," *Le Monde,* 3 November 2005, 12; Pascal Ceaux, "Un jeune à Aulnay-sous-Bois: Ce n'est qu'un début, on va continuer jusqu'à ce que Sarkozy démissione," *Le Monde,* 4 November 2005, 9.

31. Bronner and Smolar, "Les violences," 12.

32. Silverstein and Tetreault, "Postcolonial Urban Apartheid," 5–6. A list of

the major riots of the 1990s is provided by Mauger, *L'émeute*, 15. For a detailed examination of the 1990 riots outside Lyon, see Begag, "La révolte."

33. Suprême N.T.M., "Qu'est-ce qu'on attend," *Paris sous les bombes* (Sony Music, 1995); Silverstein and Tetreault, "Postcolonial Urban Apartheid," 1.

34. *La Haine*, directed by Mathieu Kassovitz (Les Productions Lazennec, 1995). The recent Criterion collection DVD includes a documentary about the making of the film. Both Kassovitz and Cassel whose brother is the founder of the hip-hop group Assassin (which has been very critical of the French government's *banlieue* policies), have continued to intervene in debates about the *banlieue* since making the movie. Cassel maintained a blog during the 2005 insurrection.

35. Silverstein and Tetreault, "Postcolonial Urban Apartheid," 8; Mustafa Dikeç, *Badlands of the Republic: Space, Politics and Urban Policy* (London: Blackwell, 2007), chap. 4; Dufresne, *Maintien*, 32–94, 141–43; "Nicolas Sarkozy: 'La police de proximité,'" *Maire-Info*, 4 February 2003, http://www.maire info.com (accessed 2 February 2009); Kokoreff, *Sociologie*, 72, 183, 190–91; Piotr Smolar, "L'orientation répressive de la police est remise en question," *Le Monde*, 5 November 2005, 6.

36. Silverstein and Tetreault, "Postcolonial Urban Apartheid," 5, 8; Begag, "La révolte," 115; Roy, "Nature," 1.

37. Luc Bronner and Catherine Simon, "Clichy-sous-bois cristallise les tensions politiques et socials," *Le Monde*, 2 November 2005, 5; Kokoreff, *Sociologie*, chap. 5.

38. Excerpt from TF1 News report, http://www.youtube.com/watch?v=mcf UhnnocWI &feature=related (accessed 30 September 2008).

39. Bronner and Simon, "Clichy-sous-bois," 5.

40. Ceaux, "Un jeune à Aulnay-sous-Bois," 9.

41. Mustapha Kessous, "'L'imam a raison, il faut respecter ce pays!,'" *Le Monde*, 6–7 November 2005, 7.

42. Hargreaves, "Emperor with No Clothes," 1–2; Bertrand Bissuel and Laetitia Van Eeckhout, "La polygamie et le regroupement familial au centre de la polémique," *Le Monde*, 18 November 2005, 1. For Chirac's speech, see http://www.youtube.com/watch?v=eERFYdiDuDE (accessed 15 March 2009).

43. Patrick Roger, "M. de Villiers, Mme Le Pen et les souverainistes réclament un couvre-feu et l'envoi de l'armée," *Le Monde*, 6–7 November 2005, 6.

44. Silverstein and Tetreault, "Postcolonial Urban Apartheid," 2; Raphaëlle Bacqué, "Les couvre-feux sont approuvés par la majorité, acceptés à gauche," *Le Monde*, 10 November 2005, 1.

45. Philippe Bernard, "Banlieues: La provocation coloniale," *Le Monde*, 19 November 2005, 1–2.

46. Ibid.

47. The declaration, along with information about the group, is available at http://www.indigenes-republique.org/spip.php?article835 (accessed 15 September 2008); Sadri Khairi, *Pour une politique de la racaille* (Paris: Textuel, 2006), 7.

48. "Sarkozy: 'Nous ramènerons l'ordre et la tranquilité,'" *Le Monde,* 6–7 November 2005, 1; Silverstein and Tetreault, "Postcolonial Urban Apartheid," 7.

49. F. Gom, "Les Bleus sont arrivés," *France-Antilles,* Fort-de-France edition, no. 11643, 8 November 2005, 8. Thuram had recently decided to come out of retirement and rejoin the French team.

50. C. T., "Césaire a échangé avec les Bleus," *France-Antilles,* Fort-de-France edition, no. 11645, 10–11 November 2005, 2; Joseph Ghosn and Pierre Siankowski, "La France, le Mondial, Zidane et Moi," *Inrockuptibles,* no. 555 (18–24 July 2006): 29–35, quote p. 31. Thuram told us about Makelele's comment during an interview in Barcelona in 2006, but for reasons of space his account of this was cut from the published version of the interview; see Laurent Dubois, Michel Giraud, Marc-Olivier Padis, and Patrick Weil, "Une histoire à transmettre" *Esprit,* February 2007, 117–23. Willy Sagnol, interview by Flore Olive, *Paris Match,* no. 2983 (20–26 July 2006).

51. "Thuram et les Bleus s'engagent dans le débat sur les banlieues," *France Antilles,* Fort-de-France edition, no. 11644, 9 November 2005, 2; INA, "Le Grand journal de Canal+," 14 November 2005; see also "Thuram 'énervé' répond à Sarkozy," *L'Equipe,* 8 November 2006.

52. INA, "L'Equipe des Bleus en Martinique," RFO (Radio France Outre-Mer), 9 November 2005.

53. *France-Antilles,* Fort-de-France edition, no. 11645, 10–11 November 2005, 2.

54. INA, "Le Grand journal de Canal+," 14 November 2005.

55. Ibid.

56. "Thuram: M. Sarkozy n'a toujours pas compris," *Nouvelobs,* 14 January 2006, posted on http://www.labanlieusexprime.org (accessed 24 July 2006).

57. INA, "Le Grand journal de Canal+," 14 November 2005.

58. INA, "On a tout essayé," France 2, 17 May 2006.

59. Ibid.; Dan Franck, *Zidane: Le roman d'une victoire* (Paris: Pocket, 1999), 62.

ELEVEN. COUP DE BOULE

1. Frédéric Lohézic and Gilles Lhote, *Zinedine Zidane: Respect!* (Paris: Michel Lafont, 2006), 12–14; Renaud Dély, "Politique, religion: Tout à sa transparence," *Libération,* 8–9 July 2006, 4.

2. C. K., "Franck Ribéry en visite privée à Tlemcen: 'Je me sens bien en Algérie,'" *El Watan,* 25 July 2006; Dély, "Politique," 4.

3. Interview with Alain Finkielkraut, *Ha'aretz,* 18 November 2005. An English translation of the Europe 1 interview is presented as "Alain Finkielkraut's Interview on Europe 1," on *View from the Right,* http://www.amnation.com/vfr/archives/004639.html (accessed 7 July 2006).

4. "Thuram: 'Si monsieur Le Pen veut venir, il est le bienvenu,'" *L'Humanité,*

30 June 2006; Christophe Forcari, "L'extrême droite célèbre la défaite de Bleus trop noirs," *Libération,* 12 July 2006, 10.

5. "Défendre et interroger," interview with Lilian Thuram by Achille Mbembe, 26 July 2006, http://www.africultures.com/index.asp?menu=affiche_article &no=4542 (accessed 8 August 2006). An English translation of the interview was published in *Chimurenga* 10 (2006): 235–37.

6. "Thuram," *L'Humanité,* 30 June 2006.

7. Elie Barth, "Zidane est le dernier Galactique," *Le Monde,* 3 July 2006; Philippe Delerm, "Le Brésilien," *Le Figaro,* 3 July 2006, 15.

8. Douglas Gordon and Philippe Parreno, *Zidane: A 21st Century Portrait,* (Artificial Eye, 2006); Barth, "Zidane."

9. Grégory Schneider, "Donc, y arriver ensemble," in "Mondial 2006," special section of *Libération,* 8–9 July 2006, 1–2; Institut National de l'Audiovisuel, TF1 20 Heures, 6 July 2006.

10. Luc Bronner, "Les racailles vont nous ramener la Coupe: Si ce n'est pas magnifique!," *Le Monde,* 6 July 2006; "Réaction," at www.lemonde.fr (accessed 7 July 2006).

11. "La racaille en finale!," http://lmsi.net/spip.php?article565 (accessed 5 November 2007).

12. Thibaut Danancher, "La fièvre du samedi soir," *Le Figaro,* 3 July 2006, 19.

13. Bronner, "Les racailles"; Yves Bordenave, "4,000 CRS et gendarmes supplémentaires pour dimanche," *Le Monde,* 9–10 July 2006, 6; Stéphane Joahny, "Un besoin de violence qui n'existait pas en 1998," *Journal de Dimanche,* 9 July 2006.

14. Yves Bordenave, "Pas de retour en prison demandé pour les Français de Guantanamo," *Le Monde,* 13 July 2006, 8; Jean Chichizola, "Les ex-détenus français de Guantanamo jugés à Paris," *Le Figaro,* 3 July 2006; Jean-Baptiste de Montvalon et Laetitia Van Eeckhout, "La France résiste au comptage ethnique," *Le Monde,* 3 July 2006, 2–3; Jean-Pierre Toquoi, "Les pays africains acceptant de s'impliquer dans le contrôle des flux migratoires illegaux," *Le Monde,* 12 July 2006, 4; Jean-Pierre Perrin, "A Rabat, l'immigration à la Sarkozy fait un flop," *Libération,* 12 July 2006, 4; Patrick Roger, "Abdallah Boujraf, 19 ans, est le premier lycéen expulse depuis la fin des cours," *Le Monde,* 9–10 July 2006, 9; S J., "Sans-Papiers: Sarkozy Temporise," *Journal de Dimanche,* 9 July 2006, 13; Maurice Cling, "Mal à ma République," *Libération,* 8–9 July 2006, 5.

15. Joahny, "Un besoin de violence"; Bordenave, "4,000 CRS."

16. Gilles Dhers and Christian Losson, "Vénération Zidane," *Libération,* 8–9 July 2006, 2–3. For another article in a similar vein, see Eric Collier, "Zidane, la touche finale," in "Le Mondial 2006," special section of *Le Monde,* 9–10 July 2006, 1.

17. Antoine de Gaudemar, "Un homme," *Libération,* 9 July 2006, 3.

18. Michel Denisot, "Une sorte de code d'honneur," *L'Equipe,* 13 July 2006, 3.

19. Etgar Keret, "Le geste ultime de Zizou, homme libre," *Libération,* 13 July 2006, 33.

20. Jean-Philippe Toussaint, *La Mélancholie de Zidane* (Paris: Les Editions de Minuit, 2006), 16–17.

21. Marie-Claire Pasquier, "La colère du 'Beau Marin' innocent," *Libération,* 13 July 2006, 4.

22. Roger Cohen, "Camus and Zidane: Views on How Things End," *International Herald Tribune,* 12 July 2006, 2.

23. Franck Baetens, "Le coup de tête de Zidane: Pour une lecture mythologique," *Esprit,* November 2007, 127–47, quote p. 133.

24. "Zidane Contre Castro," http://video.google.com (accessed 10 October 2006).

25. Ludovic Blécher, "'Zidane il a tapé,' la chanson potache se prepare à devenir le tube de l'été," *Libération,* 12 July 2006, 10.

26. Claude Droussent, "L'Edito," *L'Equipe,* 10 July 2006, 1. Similar interpretations dominated U.S. coverage of the event. In "Rules of the Game: Can We Forgive Him?," *New Yorker,* 24 July 2006, 22–23, Adam Gopnik worried about the bad example Zidane's action would set for children; in "Why Some Athletes Crack, and Others Don't," *New York Times,* 16 July 2006, Henry Fountain compared Zidane unfavorably to Jackie Robinson; and in "Sad Ending to a Great Career," *International Herald Tribune,* 11 July 2006, 20, Rob Hugues declared, "Shame on the hero."

27. Forcari, "L'extrême droit," 10. Such statements were extreme, but Calderoli does have the sympathy of some of the players on the Italian team, including Gennaro Gattuso, who in 2008 declared, "[The Lega Nord, Calderoli's right-wing and anti-immigration party] is raising questions that I think are right." Vikash Dhorasoo and Stéphane Régy, "Gattuso," *So Foot* 56 (June–July 2008), 30–36, quotes pp. 34, 36.

28. Anne Delbée, *La 107e minute* (Paris: Quatre Chemins, 2006), 94.

29. Toussaint, *Mélancholie,* 11; Delbée, *Minute,* 76.

30. Delbée, *Minute,* 30–31.

31. Mustapha Kessous, "Zidane, héros lointain et décevant de la Castellane," *Le Monde,* 11 July 2006, 10; "L'Algérie comprend et défend son champion de coeur," *Le Monde,* 13 July 2006. Many writers have discussed Kabyle "honor," including Pierre Bourdieu, "The Sense of Honor," in *Algeria, 1960* (Cambridge, U.K.: Cambridge University Press, 1979), 95–132.

32. Grant Farred, "Zinedine Zidane and the Event of the Secret," *Chimurenga* 10 (2006): 224–30.

33. Pierre Jaxel-Truer, "Mais qu'a bien pu dire Materazzi à Zidane?," *Le Monde,* 12 July 2006, 10; "Materazzi le provocateur," *Paris-Match,* no. 2983 (20–26 July 2006): 46; "Des sanctions pour Zinedine Zidane et Marco Materazzi," *Le Monde,* 21 July 2006.

34. "Match a fait déchiffrer les vraies injures de Materazzi à Zizou," *Paris-Match,* no. 2983 (20–26 July 2006): 43.

35. Jaxel-Truer, "Mais qu'a bien pu dire Materazzi à Zidane?"; Lionel Froissart, "Qu'est-ce qu'il lui a dit?," *Libération,* 11 July 2006, 4.

36. Froissart, "Qu'est-ce qu'il lui a dit?," 4; "Materazzi: 'Je n'ai pas insulté sa mere,'" *L'Equipe,* 13 July 2006, 3; Marco Materazzi, *Ce que j'ai vraiment dit à Zidane,* trans. Denitza Bantcheva (Paris: Editions du Rocher, 2006).

37. Delbée, *Minute,* 60.

38. Ibid., 60–61.

39. Keret, "Le geste," 33.

40. Cohen, "Camus and Zidane," 2.

41. "L'Algérie comprend et défend son champion de coeur," *Le Monde,* 13 July 2006.

42. "Des mots tellement durs," *L'Equipe,* 13 July 2006, 3.

43. Claire Lasne, "Vive toi, Zidane," *Libération,* 13 July 2006, 33.

44. "Des sanctions pour Zinedine Zidane et Marco Materazzi."

45. "Tous ensemble!," *Le Monde,* 11 July 2006, 2.

46. Reactions to "Des sanctions pour Zinedine Zidane et Marco Materazzi," www.lemonde.fr (accessed 30 July 2006).

47. Serge Quadruppani, "Zidane ne doit pas être le seul amnistié," *Libération,* 14 July 2006.

48. Dany Laferrière, "Le geste (et la geste) de Zinedine Zidane vus par Dany Laferrière," 12 July 2006, http://www.congopage.com/article.php3?id_article= 3791; a translation is at http://www.ranadasgupta.com/notes.asp?note_id=69 (both accessed 25 March 2009).

EPILOGUE

1. "Des mots tellements durs," *L'Equipe,* 13 July 2006, 3.

2. Dominique Le Guilledoux, "Des footballeurs entre Paris et Alger," *Le Monde diplomatique,* August 2005, 25. Rouaï "Moi, personnellement, j'aime bien ce gars-là. Mais on a peut-être trop fait pour lui. J'aurais aimé que le président honore aussi Zitouni." Mekloufi: "Zidane est un grand bonhomme. Ses racines l'appellent. Il connaissait l'équipe du FLN à travers son père. Il est toujours resté l'enfant de la banlieue. Il a compris qu'il fallait rendre ce que le foot lui a donné."

3. The journey was recounted in a television special titled *Thuram le defenseur* that aired on France 2 on 7 September 2006. See http://www.dailymotion.com/ video/xdfya_thuram-le-defenseur (accessed 4 October 2006); François Inizan, "Thuram: L'Afrique au coeur," *L'Equipe Magazine,* no. 1258 (5 August 2006): 24–33.

4. See *Thuram le defenseur.*

5. For a description of Akiyo's work, see http://www.akiyo.org, which includes a video of the 29 July 2006 event with Thuram.

6. "Soccer Man on Display," *Science* 315 (16 February 2007): 917.

7. Joseph Ghosn and Pierre Siankowski, "La France, le Mondial, Zidane et Moi," *Inrockuptibles,* no. 555 (18–24 July 2006): 29–35, quote p. 35. Some of these comments were reprinted in Laetitia Van Eeckhout, "Lilian Thuram s'inquiete de la 'sarkoïzation des esprits,'" *Le Monde,* 18 July 2006.

8. Laeïla Adjovi and Catherine Coroller, "Une 'miracle' pour les Doumbia, une victoire pour Cachan," *Libération,* 7 September 2006; Antoine Guiral, "Sarkozy redoute la contre-attaque des sportifs," *Libération,* 9 September 2006; "La droite monte au créneau contre Lilian Thuram," Nouvelobs.com (accessed 19 October 2006).

9. Jean-Yves Guérin and Laurent Jaoui, *Noirs en bleu: Le football est-il raciste?* (Paris: Anne Carrière, 2008), 29–30.

10. See Rama Yade, *Noirs de france* (Paris: Calmann-Lévy, 2007), and the comments of the French economist Eloi Laurent at http://artgoldhammer.blogspot .com/2007/07/rama-yade-guest-post-eloi-laurent.html (accessed 11 December 2008). On broader debates surrounding responses to racial discrimination in France in comparison with those in the U.K., see Eric Bleich, *Race Politics in Britain and France: Ideas and Policymaking Since the 1960s* (Cambridge, U.K.: Cambridge University Press, 2003).

11. Benoit Hopquin and Frédéric Potet, "Les convictions de Lilian Thuram," *Le Monde,* 4 February 2009. On B-World Connection, see http://bworldconnection .com.

12. *Les Yeux dans les Bleus,* directed by Stéphane Meunier (Canal +, 1998); Vincent Duluc, "Un défenseur monumental," *L'Equipe,* 2 August 2008, 2. See the comments of Jean-Pierre Escalettes, F.F.F. president, in *L'Equipe,* 2 August 2008, 2. On Thuram's retirement dreams, see Institut National de l'Audiovisuel, "Frequenstar: Lilian Thuram," M6, 11 July 1998.

ACKNOWLEDGMENTS

This book began during the feverish conversations I had in Paris in the now distant era of Zidane's *coup de boule*. With my friends and colleagues Michel Giraud and Patrick Weil I watched the act and began to think about what had happened, and I continued the discussion the next day both with many randomly encountered people in Paris and over dinner with Frederick Cooper, Rebecca Scott, and Jean Hébrard. Jean's responses as a steadfast French fan were inspiring from the beginning—he got it!—and he both enabled my delirium and left a deep mark on the book. He encouraged me to write it, for which I punished him by asking him to read the entire manuscript, on which he gave me excellent comments.

I also had many long phone conversations with Grant Farred, who became an essential interlocutor as he and I struggled to interpret what happened. And, as always, conversations with Gary Wilder shaped my thoughts, both at the time of the event and after he generously read the manuscript and commented on it. My colleague at Michigan State University Peter Alegi, an expert on the history of football, generously guided me into an unfamiliar literature and was helpful and encouraging throughout the process.

I wrote this book in the midst of a move from Michigan State to Duke University, and the new surroundings, which included an interdisciplinary appointment in both romance studies and history, inspired me to dive in to the project. My colleagues at Duke created the perfect environment for working on this book. I'm grateful to the various institutions who, having invited me to give talks about the Haitian Revolution, kindly allowed me to talk about football in France instead. These include the Institute of French Studies at New York University, the New School for Social Research, the University of Pittsburgh History Department, the University of Liverpool, and the Alice Kaplan Institute for the Humanities at Northwestern University. Then there were those who actually invited me to talk about football, including the Anthropology Department at the CUNY Graduate Center and the Maison Française at Columbia University. I thank all those who commented on my presentations there, particularly Ed Berenson, Elga Castro, Frederick Cooper, Fernando Coronil, Paul Eiss, Charles Forsdick, Stephane Gerson, David Murphy, Hugh Raffles, Julie Skurski, Ann Stoler, and George R. Trumbull IV. I also thank the members of the Triangle French Studies Seminar, notably William Reddy and Don Reid, for their comments. Along the way Lindsay Krasnoff and Nacira Guénif-Souilamas generously shared their works in progress with me.

I was lucky to have two excellent readers at the University of California Press, who also kindly let their identities be known so that I could pepper them with further questions. Paul Silverstein, whose work was essential to me in writing the book, also provided wonderful suggestions that helped improve the book and save me embarrassment on several counts. Alice Kaplan, whose writing serves as a model here, helped me to improve the structure, pacing, and narrative of the book as well as deepen my understanding of many of the points of recent French history. My editor at the University of California Press, Niels Hooper, was enthusiastic and helpful throughout. Thanks also go to my agent, Wendy Strothman, who was excited about the project from the beginning. As I was finishing the manuscript I had the good fortune to meet Garnette Cadogan, who, though he barely knew me, immediately read and commented on it, making crucial and transformative suggestions that have shaped this final version.

I finished this book during the first few months of a year off from teaching spent at the National Humanities Center, with the support of a Duke Endowment Fellowship and a Guggenheim Fellowship. The library staff at the National Humanities Center was magical in its ability to find obscure articles, and Joel Elliot and Phil Barron helped me up my technology game so that I can now show clips of games at whim in my presentations—an essential skill, for how can one really describe a goal with words? The staffs at the Centre des Archives Contemporaines in Fontainebleau, the Institut National de l'Audiovisuel and the Bibliothèque Nationale in Paris, and the Archives Départementales de la Guadeloupe (particularly Dimitri Garnier) were extremely helpful when I walked in looking for traces of football. My research in France was supported by an Arts and Sciences Research Grant from Duke University.

Perhaps the greatest thanks are due to those who suffered through my obsession with this topic the most: my family. André and Marie-Claude Dubois chuckled when I told them about the book, remembering the many sleepless nights I had before my YMCA soccer games as a kid, which taught me the sufferings of the goalie, and the long decade I spent as a punk rocker convinced that sports were mainly a site for the reproduction of patriarchy and capitalism. But they also listened and even started following the rocky fortunes of the French team. Monique Dubois-Dalcq listened to me effuse about Zidane and learned firsthand the quasi-religious state I enter into during a France game. It was, of course, Katharine Brophy Dubois who was most likely to have to respond to the call of "Come look at this goal!" as I trolled the Internet, but who dove into the story with me, helping me find my voice and enthusiastically editing the entire manuscript—twice! And my son, Anton Dubois, who at first wondered, reasonably enough, what all the fuss was about, and who has already (to my relief, I admit) declared in no uncertain terms that he does not want to play youth soccer, eventually caught on and joined me in cheering when *Les Bleus* scored.

This book is, in its way, an offering to the players who over the years have brought me and so many others tragedy and romance in all colors. I am especially grateful to Lilian Thuram, who allowed me, Patrick Weil, and Michel Giraud to do a fascinating interview with him in Barcelona in 2006 (published in *L'Esprit* the next year), and when we left handed me a signed jersey, which I keep as a talisman. May the future follow him.

INDEX

French Cup, 27, 36; and French Antilles, 47, 64–65
French Revolution, 10, 218–19
Front de Libération Nationale (F.L.N.), Algeria, 1, 41, 134, 181, 187–97; football team of, 190–97, 242, 267
Front de libération nationale kanak et socialiste, 111–12
French Equatorial Africa, 58, 100
French Football Federation. *See* Fédération Française de Football Association
French Guiana, xv, 30, 36, 47, 49, 59, 61, 64, 69, 100, 102, 111, 131; Felix Eboué's origins in, 53–54
Front National, 3, 76–77, 101–2, 109, 125, 129, 163, 165, 171–72, 207, 210, 253. *See also* Le Pen, Jean-Marie

Galeano, Edouardo, 18, 28
Gallas, William, xv, 49, 51, 71, 219, 221, 241, 245, 258
Gandhi, Mohandas, 248
Gangs. See *Bandes*
Gard, 171
Garvey, Marcus, 116
Gattuso, Gennaro, 63
Gaudemar, Antoine de, 248–49
Gauls, 253
Gendarmerie, 66
Georges, Pierre, 105
Germany, 8, 29, 48, 57–58, 102, 108, 111, 114, 196, 198; and 1982 World Cup, 75–77, 136, 200
Ghana, xiii, 42, 44; and Marcel Desailly, xx, 98–100, 117, 171, 211
Giáp, Võ Nguyên, 196
Gide, André, 54–55
Giresse, Alain, 75
Girondins de Bordeaux, 47, 142–43, 189
Giroud, Françoise, 175
Givet, Gael, 219
"God Save the Queen," 103
Godzidane, 165–66
Gold Cup, 69–70
Golden Goal, 174
Gollnisch, Bruno, 172, 253
Gopnik, Adam, 110, 252
Gorée Island, 30, 115, 268

Greater France, 172–73
The Great Match (film), xiii, 44
Greece, 220
Guadeloupe, 110, 112, 115, 162, 268–69, 272–73; football in, 8, 47–71; and French Cup, 64–65; independence movements in, 66–68; and 1998 World Cup, 130–32; players from, xv, 48–51, 62–64, 93, 100, 207; Thuram's childhood in, 2, 78–81, 88, 130–32. *See also* Gallas, William; Henry, Thierry; Sonor, Luc; Thuram, Lilian; Trésor, Marius
Guantanamo Bay, 247
Guardian, 257
Guelma, 186
Guignols de l'Info, 219
Guivarc'h, Stéphane, 149, 171
Gullit, Ruud, 102–3
Gwada (expression), 50–51
Gwo-ka music, 79

Ha'aretz, 242
Hadj, Messali, 182, 185, 187
Haine, La (film), 91, 230, 307n34
Haiti, xv, 10, 61, 66, 264
Hamburg, 145
Hamrouchi, Ali, 26
Hamrouchi, Belgacem, 182–83
Hanoi, 196
Hanot, Gabriel, 30, 39
Happiness, Football as, 22, 246
Harkis, 172, 206, 257
Harlem Globetrotters, 196
Havelange, João, 43
Hayot, Alain, 201, 209
Head-butt, by Zidane, xvii–xix, 144–45 250*fig.*, 252*fig.*
Henry, Thierry, xv–xvi, xix, 48–49, 51, 70–71, 134, 174, 178, 205, 237; anti-racism campaign by, 221–22, 243; and 1998 World Cup, 118, 120, 122, 126, 131; and 2006 World Cup, 210, 212, 241, 243, 245, 266
Herzog, Maurice, 64
Heysel, 107, 177
Hidalgo, Maurice, 72, 75
Hillsborough, 107
Hip-hop, in France, 82, 218–19, 224, 230

Martinique, 106; football in, 8, 49–71; and French Cup, 64–65; French national team in, 236–37; independence movements in, 66–68; players from, xv, 63, 174. *See also* Abidal, Eric; Janvion, Gérard; Wiltord, Sylvain

Maspero, François, 83

Materazzi, Marco, xvi–xviii, 249–63, 250*fig.*

Matoub, Lounès, 135

Maurice Island, 219

Mauritania, 224, 226

May 1968, footballers and, 142

Mbembe, Achille, 244

Mbvoumin, Jean-Claude, 45

Mecca, 253

Mégret, Bruno, 202

Mekloufi, Rachid, 9, 40, 46, 77, 186–87, 192, 197, 198–99, 267

Melun, 89

Mesoamerica, ball games in, 14

Métisse, France as, 105, 163

Meurtres pour mémoire (novel), 111

Mexico, 29, 66, 70

Michelin Guide, 248

Middle Ages, 14

Migration. *See* Immigration

Mihajlovic, Sinisa, 221

Minh, Ho Chi, 196

Minister of Overseas Territories, 105

Minister of Youth and Sports, 64, 68, 90–91, 163, 178–79, 201

Minorities, 85

Minute (newspaper), 242

Mitterand, François, 76, 154

Mohamed, 181

Molotov cocktail, 214, 218, 231–32

Monaco, 93–94, 96, 191

Monde, Le (newspaper), 105, 127, 154, 161–62, 175, 193, 205, 224, 229, 235–36, 242, 245–46, 256, 258, 263

Montray Kréyol (website), 221

Montréal, 157

Moors, 87

Morocco, 24, 33, 35–39, 86, 103, 127, 129, 136, 163, 194–96, 213

Moscow, 196

Moulin, Jean, 248

Mouloudia Club Algérois, 181, 188

Moussaoui, Zacarias, 179

Multiculturalism, 86, 98, 102, 106, 109, 127, 163, 172–73, 179, 206, 210–11

Muntari, Sulley, 44

Musée de l'Homme, 269, 270*fig.*

Muslim football clubs, in Algeria, 180–81, 186–88

Muslim scouts, 185

Mussolini, Benito, 18, 29

Naïr, Sami, 164

Nantes, 92, 94, 99, 112, 117, 121, 141

National Assembly, 30, 235

National Front party. *See* Front National

Nationalism: and football, 22; in France, 6, 40–41, 106, 175; in French Antilles, 67; in Algeria, 182–83, 185, 197

Nazi: regime, 58–59; salute, 29

Ndiaye, Pap, 220

Nèg' Marrons, 82

Negritude, 52

Netherlands, xiv, 23, 32, 102–3

New Caledonia, xx, 8, 64, 69, 101, 105, 110–14, 216, 234

New York, 157

New Yorker (magazine), 8, 58*fig.*, 176, 252

New York Times, 249

New York University, 234–35

Nice, 40, 189

Nicolo, Raoul-Georges, 63

Nike: corporation, 147–49, 209, 222, 257; goddess, 29

Ninel, Camille, 63, 191

Nkrumah, Kwame, 42

Noah, Yannick, 270

Noiraude, 87

Noiriel, Gérard, 8

North Africa, 135; football in, 35–36, 92, 188–89, 191, 235. *See also* Algeria; Morocco; Tunisia

North African: football players, xiv, 4, 9, 11, 30, 40, 73, 78, 98, 101, 106, 108, 127, 188–89, 191; residents in France, 3, 8, 11, 13, 30, 78, 82, 85–86, 98, 136, 145, 159, 165, 176, 179, 193, 202, 213, 218, 224, 255, 272. *See also* Algeria; Algerians; Morocco; Tunisia

Wacquant, Loïc, 84
Wales, 69
Weah, George, 220
Weil, Patrick, 165
Weil Commission, 165
Wenger, Arsène, 93
West Africa, xiii, 30–37, 53; football players from, 37, 67; migration to France from, 85; soldiers from, in World War I, 24, 31
What I Really Said to Zidane (book), 257
Wiltord, Sylvain, xv, 49, 174, 219, 241
Wolof, 212
World Cup, 4, 41–43; creation of, xix; in 1930, 29; in 1938, 9, 29, 32; in 1954, 188; in 1958, 95, 191–94; in 1966, 5, 176; in 1978, 72; in 1982, 72, 73 *fig.*, 75–77, 199–200; in 1986, 137; in 1994, 120; in 1998, 3, 92, 102, 109–10, 114 *fig.*, 115–17, 118–32, 146–53, 150 *figs.*, 151 *fig.*, 152 *fig.*, 154–74; qualifying games for, 69, 108; in 2002, 43, 211–12; in 2006, xiii–xv, xvii *fig.*, xx, 3–4, 12 *fig.*, 13 *fig.*, 16, 43, 216, 241–66, 250 *fig.*, 260 *fig.*
World Cup trophy, 29, 152
World Series, 20
World War I, xix, 23–27, 25 *fig.*, 33, 46, 98, 111
World War II, xix, 1, 8, 31–32, 34, 38, 58, 61, 68, 98; and French empire, 57–61, 185, 187, 189, 272
Wright, Ian, 103

Yade, Rama, 272
Yaoundé, 34
You Tube, 213

Zaire, 44, 86, 89. *See also* Congo
Zanzibar, 252 *fig.*
Zatelli, Mario, 30
Zidane, Djamel, 200
Zidane, Enzo, 140, 161
Zidane, Farid, 137
Zidane, Malika, 2, 134, 175, 206, 257
Zidane, Smaïl, 1–2, 133–34, 159, 172, 175, 206, 257, 267
Zidane, Zinedine, 78, 93; Algerian background of, 8, 13–14, 106, 121–22, 127, 134–36, 172, 267; characteristics of play, 140–41; childhood of, 133–34, 136–40; head-butt by, xvii–xviii, 144–45, 249–61, 250 *fig.*, 252 *fig.*, 260 *fig.*; at Juventus, 143–45, 148; and 1996 European Cup, 97; and 1998 World Cup, 126–27, 129–30, 150 *figs.*, 155 *fig.*, 169–72; and politics, 12; professional career, 142–46; and 2001 France-Algeria game, 204–6, 208–9; and 2006 World Cup, xiv–xv, xvii *fig.*, xx, 12 *fig.*, 13 *fig.*, 241–66, 265 *fig.*
Zidane: A 21st Century Portrait (film), 245
Zidanite, 249
Zimako, Jacques, 112
Zitouni, Mustapha, 40, 191–93
Zouk, 100

Text:	11.25/13.5 Adobe Garamond
Display:	Adobe Garamond, Akzidenz Grotesk
Compositor:	BookMatters, Berkeley
Printer and binder:	Sheridan Books, Inc.